The Social World
of Formative
Christianity and Judaism

———————— ESSAYS ————————

IN TRIBUTE TO HOWARD CLARK KEE

The Social World
of Formative
Christianity and Judaism

Edited by

JACOB NEUSNER   ERNEST S. FRERICHS
PEDER BORGEN   RICHARD HORSLEY

FORTRESS PRESS   PHILADELPHIA

Publication of this book has been made possible, in part,
by Boston University, through the good offices of
President John Silber, and through
The Max Richter Foundation of Rhode Island.

Library of Congress Cataloging-in-Publication Data

The Social world of formative Christianity and Judaism.

Bibliography: p.
Includes index.
1. Bible. N.T.—Criticism, interpretation, etc.
2. Sociology, Biblical. 3. Kee, Howard Clark.
I. Kee, Howard Clark. II. Neusner, Jacob, 1932–
BS2395.S56   1988   225.9'5   87–46085
ISBN 0-8006-0875-5

59,978

3207B88   Printed in the United States of America   1–875

Contents

CONTENTS

CONTENTS

Preface

Howard Clark Kee enjoys a distinguished position among his colleagues in the study of religion in late antiquity because of his acuity in joining archaeological to literary study in search of the social foundations of the religious worlds. He has spent many years in archaeological digs in the State of Israel and in Jordan working on the Hellenistic and Roman periods. He is equally well qualified in philological and textual studies—a rare combination indeed. And the movement of his learning, from music to art and archaeology to languages to texts, carried him finally to the social sciences, which he has mastered so as to study the relationship of religion and society in antiquity—the overall theme of this book. He is a principal voice in the study of the social setting of early Christianity in its relationships to both Judaic and Greco-Roman culture. Less widely known is the fact that he is a trained musician of professional quality. His colleagues join in this tribute to the learning, imagination, and insight that through many and important publications serve as guide for both method and result. His findings therefore form a major oeuvre of scholarly achievement, and the methods that have guided him define a principal paradigm for research. A person of remarkable breadth and sensibility, our honoree has further provided us with a model of the good colleague, interested in scholarship *sine ira et studio,* sustaining friendships far and wide, helping everyone and harming none.

Born in 1920 in Edgewater Park, New Jersey, Howard Clark Kee began not in history and religion but in language, literature and music. He studied as an undergraduate at Temple University and received his B.A. in English and Music at Bryan College. Receiving his degree in 1940, he began his career as a professional accompanist in piano, organ, and vocal arrangements in Dallas. Music made possible his scholarly career, and the art and imagination characteristic of his learning are at one with his musical gifts. He studied at Dallas Theological Seminary and earned his Master of Theology degree, majoring in Semitic languages, in 1944. From 1947 to 1949 he fulfilled the residence requirements for the Ph.D. in New Testament at Yale University, supporting himself as organist and choirmaster at Yale Divinity School. He studied at the American School of Oriental Research in Jerusalem in 1949-50 and then joined the Drew University faculty. He completed his doctoral dissertation and received the Ph.D. from Yale in 1951. In that same year he married Janet Burrell. The Kee children are H. Clark, Christopher, and Sarah.

His professional career has graced important colleges, universities, and divinity schools and made a mark on each: he has served as Instructor in Classics and Religion at the University of Pennsylvania, 1951-53; Assistant Professor, then Associate Professor, and finally Professor of New Testament at Drew University, 1953-68; Rufus Jones Professor of the History of Religion at Bryn Mawr College, 1968-77; and Visiting Professor at Princeton University, Swarthmore College, Franklin and Marshall College, and Andover-Newton Theological School. Finally at the climax of a great career, he was called by President John Silber to serve as William Goodwin Aurelio Professor of Biblical Studies and Professor of New Testament in the School of Theology, as well as Chairman of the Graduate Division of Religious Studies, at Boston University from 1977 to his retirement in 1986.

In addition, as exemplary citizen of the academic world, Howard Clark Kee has served in various positions in the Studiorum Novi Testamenti Societas, the Society of Biblical Literature, the American Academy of Religion, the Columbia University Seminar in New Testament, the Boston Area New Testament Colloquium; the Council on Graduate Studies in Religion, the Philadelphia Chamber Orchestra, the American Bible Society, and the Yale Institute of Sacred Music. He was an editor of *Religious Studies Review,* the SBL Dissertation Series, and Biblical Perspectives on Current Issues (Westminster Press), and was a member of the editorial board of the *Journal of Biblical Literature,* the Cambridge Companion to the Bible, and other important series.

Naturally, scholarship of the excellence and distinction of Howard Clark Kee's has elicited an appropriate response from the academic world. He has held a Guggenheim Fellowship (1966-67), has served as Visiting Scholar at the Graduate Theological Union, Berkeley (1974-75), and as Fellow of the Wellcome Institute of the History of Medicine, London (1984), and has held positions as a member of the Library of Congress Manuscript Project in libraries of monasteries in Jerusalem and at St. Catherine's, Sinai, and as Guest Researcher in Hellenistic-Roman Materials of the Department of

Antiquities of the State of Israel. He received an award as teacher-scholar of the year at Boston University in 1983–84 and a summer fellowship from the National Endowment for the Humanities in 1984. He gave a National Endowment for the Humanities seminar for college teachers in 1986 and has given guest lectures at many universities worldwide, including Marburg, Tübingen, Brown, Colgate, Michigan State, Vermont, Massachusetts, Jerusalem, London (King's College), Dublin, Edinburgh, Durham, Aberdeen, Heidelberg, and on and on. The bibliography of his published writings completes the picture of one of the great careers of our generation, happily still in full progress.

The editors express their hearty thanks to President John Silber, Boston University, who has joined in this celebration of one of Boston University's many distinguished professors and helped to make possible the publication of this book. We take pride in his commitment to our project, which does honor to the editors as well as to Howard Clark Kee.

We note also the support of The Max Richter Foundation of Rhode Island at the instance of its trustees in expression of their respect and esteem for the honoree of this volume.

We further thank Dr. Harold Rast and his colleagues at Fortress Press, who are an ornament to scholarly publishing and the academic study of religion as well as to the church that sustains that press. Finally, we express our gratitude to the many colleagues who have supported this project, some by making important contributions to these pages, the rest by expressing their good will and interest in it. We hope and believe that the manifestly considerable work behind this book and its companion represents the appropriate celebration of one of the generation's truly excellent scholars.

This writer and his colleague Professor Ernest S. Frerichs express their thanks to Brown University, which has covered many costs incidental to this project and has always made possible its faculty's unencumbered participation in scholarly ventures. Further thanks are owing to Mrs. Annette Boulay, Administrator of the Program in Judaic Studies at Brown University, for her efficient help in many aspects of the organization of this book.

The volume constitutes one part of our three-part celebration of Howard Clark Kee. The others have come into being through the efforts of this writer's former doctoral students and close co-workers in the inauguration of a new scholarly series with *New Perspectives on Ancient Judaism*, vols. 1 and 2, *Judaism in Society in Ancient Times*, Studies in Judaism series (Lanham, Md., and London: University Press of America, 1987). Those volumes, dedicated to Howard Clark Kee, contain more than two dozen major papers on a single unfolding theme and pay the sustained tribute of the younger generation of scholars in the field of ancient Judaism in particular. Publication of those volumes is owing to Mr. J. E. Lyons, Publisher of University Press of America, to whom we express appreciation.

JACOB NEUSNER
for the editors

PART ONE

SOCIAL STUDIES:
ANCIENT ISRAEL, CHRISTIANITY,
AND JUDAISM

Sociohistorical Research
and the Contextualization
of Biblical Theology

MICHAEL LAFARGUE
University of Massachusetts/Boston

Howard Clark Kee has been a pioneer in insisting on the necessity of taking ancient social conditions into consideration when doing biblical interpretation and criticism. In part because of his influence a younger generation of scholars is now industriously at work on projects related to this theme.

But precisely because this field is relatively new, it appears to me that the implications of sociological research for biblical study have not been carefully thought through. This is especially true of the relation between the study of the social background of the Bible and the study of the theology of biblical authors. In this essay I would like to make some attempts at conceptual clarification concerning the relation of these two fields of study, and to offer some specific proposals as to the nature of the important contribution that sociohistorical reconstruction of the biblical milieu has to offer to the study of the theology of biblical authors.

TWO CONDITIONS FOR THE SERIOUS STUDY
OF BIBLICAL THEOLOGY

When I speak of the "study of the theology of biblical authors," I am speaking specifically of *theological* study of their theological views. Here I am essentially following Paul Tillich's "formal" definition of theology,[1] which implies that one can study a given body of theological thought from a number of different perspectives. One can study ideas about God, for example, from a psychological or sociological standpoint—or one can study them from a theological standpoint. My interest in this paper is in the latter, although what I want to speak of is the contribution that sociological study of biblical milieus has to make to this properly theological study. This focus on relevance to theology does not of course imply at all that sociohistorical reconstruction of biblical times is not also valuable simply in itself, or for other purposes.

My central opening point can be made by analogy. Suppose an American goes to live with a South American tribal group and wants to study their dances. She might study the dances from a number of different points of view: the psychological function they perform (as an outlet for nervous energy, say) or their sociological function (as helping to maintain a sense of group belonging). But she might also study them from the point of view of their aesthetic quality *as dance*. Two things would be necessary in such a study, which correspond to necessary elements in a properly theological study of biblical theology. First, the person would have to be someone who takes seriously the aesthetics of dance. Someone who is not sensitive to the aesthetic qualities of any dance, or who sees all dances as pretty much the same aesthetically, could not do a serious study of the aesthetics of tribal dances. Second, the person would have to make a great effort to adjust her personal aesthetic sensibilities and to put herself in a position actually to experience and appreciate the aesthetics of the tribal dances she is watching. Some case could be made that in a psychological or sociological study it is enough to know that dances have such and such an effect on the people, or *that* this group finds X features of the dance aesthetically pleasing. Plausible research of this kind might go on without the researcher's actually gaining the ability to experience personally and appreciate the aesthetic character of the dances. Whatever one might think of such completely "objective" psychological or sociological study, it seems obvious that a study of the aesthetics of the dances could not be seriously undertaken without empathic understanding, without what social scientists since Weber call *verstehen*.[2]

The same is true of the study of biblical theology from a theological point of view. For such study to be done adequately, the inquirer must be one who takes theology seriously as such—not necessarily Christian theology, of course, but the issue of what ultimately matters in life. And one vitally important step in this study would be precisely gaining an empathic (if perhaps vicarious) entrance into the theological point of view of the particular biblical book being studied.

The best description of what it means to "take theology seriously as such" is still found, I think, in Tillich's "formal" definition of theology as that knowledge which has to do with what is of ultimate concern.[3] Tillich's definition is one that offers a foundation for considering theological study analogous to the aesthetic study of dance: it constitutes theology as a serious subject in its own right (bodies of thought can genuinely be good or bad theologically), and yet in principal it makes possible a pluralistic view of this subject—that is, it makes it possible for there to be several different good theologies.[4]

I am deliberately omitting a third requirement for studying the Bible theologically, which many theologians would perhaps implicitly assume or actively insist upon. They might hold that to take seriously the theological study of biblical writings as such is to study them from the point of view of the one valid set of timelessly normative theological principles, whether this means deriving the principles from the Bible itself—as in so-called biblical theology—or whether it means evaluating biblical views in the light of normative principles derived from outside the Bible. This vision of the study of biblical theology is not, I think, compatible with the proposals offered below about the important contribution that sociohistorical reconstruction has to make to a theological study of the Bible.

On the present account, the ultimate purpose of the theological study of the Bible is basically "confrontational": we try to understand the particular theological views of biblical authors in their particularity because they offer an important challenge to our own views regarding what is of ultimate concern. On my view this challenge is of a dialogical kind, in that the outcome of the confrontation between the biblical authors' views and other views we have regarding ultimate concerns should not be predetermined. The theological views of any given biblical book may or may not prove to be decisively superior to those derived from elsewhere, or from our own experience.

CAUSAL FUNCTIONAL CONTEXTUALIZATION

The important modern insight that current theological study of the Bible has to take cognizance of is that cultural milieus may be radically different one from another, and that theology is a part of culture. Like every other aspect of culture, the meaning of theological ideas is determined contextually. Theological ideas get their meaning from the relation in which they stand to other elements of the cultural milieu of which they are a part.[5]

One important contribution of the Marxist tradition to this general insight is the perception that what constitutes a cultural milieu cannot here be restricted to "high culture," the kind of culture referred to when we speak of a "cultured" as opposed to an "uncultured" person. Cultural milieu as a meaning-giving context includes the entirety of the conditions under which people live insofar as these conditions influence their experience of the world. A person or group's cultural milieu includes, then, not only those aspects of their cultural heritage which are typically inculcated by specific "educational" projects—by parental education in proper behavior, church education in religious traditions, school education in the arts and science, education one might get from books, concerts, museums, and the like. It includes also such things as the material conditions under which people live, the way their psychological needs are met or not met, and their socioeconomic power relationships with other people and groups. The character of the world as experienced by any person or group is decisively shaped by all these material conditions no less than by the "spiritual" elements such as normative symbols, ideas, and institutions often thought of as "culture."

This, as I see it, is the general rationale for the necessity of taking into consideration socioeconomic conditions in a given biblical milieu when one is undertaking a theological study of a biblical book. But the very important question then becomes *how* we are to understand the relation between socioeconomic conditions of existence and the theological ideas that need to be understood "in the context" of these conditions. The difficulty I see in current thought on this issue is that those who are most insistent on the importance of material and socioeconomic factors in the biblical context also tend to see this relation along the lines of a "sociology of knowledge" that treats the relation as a causal or functional one.[6] On this model, concrete conditions "cause" people to have certain ideas, or ideas function instrumentally to cope with certain conditions or to further individual or group interests that are empirically definable in terms of these conditions. Thus it is thought that one has "understood" a given set of theological ideas when one has understood what caused people to formulate or to hold them, or when one has understood the function they have in furthering someone's concrete interests. In either case, the "context" for understanding ideas is conceived of as analogous to functioning physical systems like machines, in which one can speak of the way one element interacts in a causal fashion with other elements to produce some overall result. (Note that I am using "functional" here in a broad sense, not in the narrower sense in which one speaks today of the structural-functional model in sociological theory as opposed to the conflict-theory model preferred by Marxists. In this broader sense, revolutionary literature can be said to have a functional usefulness in furthering the revolutionary aims of one group, in conflict with what would be functional within the context of an established social system.)

Socioeconomic explanations of this kind do not take the views of the biblical authors seriously as theology. They do not strive for an "inside" empathic understanding of biblical views. Nor do they meet head-on the theology of biblical authors as a potential challenge to our own views about what ultimately matters. They assume a stance similar to that of the anthropologist who ignores the aesthetic qualities of tribal dance—and the way they might challenge her own aesthetic sensitivities—and focuses instead on the strictly functional relationship that tribal dances have to the concrete life of the tribal group she is studying.

Rather than taking these ideas themselves as a direct and head-on challenge to one's own views in the area of ultimate concern, the causal/functional model tries to get around behind these views, so to speak, and subsume them under some account of their causes or their functions. If one approves of their function (if one likes the fact that they are comforting, or that they encourage movements toward liberation), one might approve of them. But in any case, in judging these ideas according to other standards, one implies that the other standards are more ultimate than they. And this amounts to refusing to take them seriously *as theology*.

My claim here is not of course that causal/functional explanations of theological views are never valid in themselves. On the contrary, I think that there are probably no concrete cases of individuals or groups with an absolutely "pure" theology, in which functional considerations as described above play no part whatsoever. And if one is simply "counting heads" of concrete individuals and groups in history, it may well be that these considerations have outweighed all others in the majority of cases. But this should not be decided on an a priori basis. It is an empirical matter that ought to decided by weighing the available evidence in specific cases. To insist on using *only* causal/functional models when studying biblical or religious writings in general is to rule out a priori the possibility of discovering anything in the writings that could challenge one theologically. To insist on using only causal/functional models to explain the content of religious and ethical thought in general is to rule out the possibility that ethical or religious thought as such can have any substantive validity.

CONTEXTUALIZATION AND *VERSTEHEN*

But the causal/functional model does not provide the only way in which one can conceive of the relation between theological ideas and socio-economic elements of culture. There is also a way in which an understanding of the socioeconomic context can be an aid in empathic understanding. Let me illustrate using the example of alienation. Suppose for the moment that we can show with great probability that the community out of which the Gospel of Mark arose was very alienated socially. This might inform our understanding of the Gospel of Mark in two different ways. A strictly functional account might focus on the way in which, for example, various elements of this Gospel might simply be an expression of alienation (might be caused by alienation) or might function as a strategy for lessening the anxiety or for furthering the interests particular to an alienated group.

But one could also use alienation as a context for understanding in a different way. That is, one could focus on the fact that an alienated person experiences the world in a certain way. Her entire experience of the world is shaped by her alienated condition. The world as experienced by her is different from the world as experienced by a nonalienated person. Not only so, but the actual character of the way alienation shapes any particular group's experience is due to the particular factors causing the alienation, and other particular conditions under which it occurs. Therefore, to see the world as a particular alienated person sees it requires not only that we think of her world picture as an alienated one in a general sense but that we take into consideration also the particular factors and conditions that have gone into her particular alienation.

My ultimate point is that the *meaning* that certain theological ideas have for a given person has to be understood in the context of that person's world picture as a whole. And if the character of the world as experienced by a given person or group is significantly shaped by alienation, then it is important even for a properly theological understanding of those ideas that we understand the particular character of that alienation.

Along these lines, one might consider, for example, whether there is a close connection between the anti-Pharisee polemic in Mark and those passages which implicitly praise a distancing from family ties (e.g., 1:16–20; 3:21, 31–35; 10:28–31; 13:12–13). The anti-Pharisee polemic may reflect the lack of meaning felt in participation in some "officially" constituted Jewish community, and lack of meaningful family life may be a necessary background for the contrast between devotion to the kingdom and devotion to one's family. These might be closely linked in the experience of an alienated person, and if this is so it ought to structure the way we read the Gospel as well.

In this kind of contextualization, the knowledge that some particular biblical author has an alienated world picture, and a knowledge of the socioeconomic factors that brought about the alienation, are essentially aids in empathic understanding. On this basis, the ultimate usefulness of socioeconomic reconstruction of a biblical milieu *for a theological study of the Bible* is that it provides us with an essential aid for imaginatively entering into the point of view of the authors we are studying, vicariously experiencing the world as they experienced it. We ought to use our knowledge of particular alienating conditions in this milieu in order actively to try to put ourselves in the place of a person who exists under these conditions and to imagine what the world looks like from this perspective. This is essential for an understanding of that person's theology, because a person's theological views are part of her world picture and cannot be understood apart from her relation to other significant elements in that world picture.

CONTEXTUALIZATION AND TRANSCENDENCE

One might object to the distinction made above, on the grounds that meaning is not separate from function. The meaning that a particular idea has for a given person is not independent of the way it functions for the person in the context of psychological needs and social setting. The fact that an idea is felt as comforting, for example, or as an inspiration to liberatory action is part of the meaning that it has for the person involved.

I think this is true. It is not my position that function and meaning never influence each other. I want to argue only that there is an important distinction to be made between them. One way the distinction shows itself is in the above-mentioned fact that understanding meaning requires empathic understanding whereas an account of function does not. Another essential difference can be brought out by a brief discussion of how the present discussion relates to the notion of transcendence, particularly as this notion is used in Barthian theology.

There are two aspects in the notion of transcendence in Barth. Barth insists, first, that the transcendence of Christian theology consists in the potential it has to stand as a *challenge* to the conventional social atmosphere of a culture. He emphasizes this transcendent element over against what he sees as liberal theology's tendency to become simply a support for the existing European sociocultural order. In this respect, the transcendent is the opposite of what is functional vis-à-vis a given social order. But an emphasis on transcendence in this sense leads Barth to connect it with another sense of "transcendence," which I want to suggest is really a separate notion: the idea that "transcendent" means "absolute." In this second sense, what is transcendent has its meaning completely in itself and escapes the general principle enunciated above that all theology is part of some particular culture and that the meaning of all theological notions is bound up with their relation to other aspects of that culture.

On the present account, transcendence in this second sense, transcendence-as-absoluteness, is impossible. But transcendence in the first sense is not necessarily connected with absoluteness, and transcendence in this first sense is one important characteristic that makes a given theology a good theology. Theologies can be subjected to critical examination, and one issue they ought to be examined on is the degree to which their constituent elements *merely* serve to further some empirically definable interest, whether this be the interest of an individual, a society, or a revolutionary group within a society. Better theologies are those which give less emphasis to this consideration, and give expression instead to what it is that people ought to be in service to.

Ideas can indeed have a purely functional value, and this means that the people who hold them stand in a using relation to the ideas. It is possible for an individual to believe in an afterlife entirely because it is psychologically comforting to do so. Leaders in a society may encourage belief in God primarily because this makes people more obedient to authority and thus helps ensure the smooth functioning of the society. A revolutionary leader may promote hope in future rewards, utopian or supernatural, primarily because this helps motivate people to work for her cause. The thought or writing of a given person on ultimate questions might be most decisively shaped by the instrumental usefulness that this thought or writing serves in maintaining some given concrete psychological or political state of affairs, or in developing or enhancing the socioeconomic power of some particular group. In these cases, the ideas are in service to some other purposes. This is not necessarily bad in itself, but insofar as these ideas are being used to serve extrinsic purposes, they lack transcendence. They may be good as propaganda, but they are not good as theology.

This using relation is opposite to the kind of relation people ought to have to realities, values, or norms that have a claim on them. And what is transcendent in a given theology is constituted precisely by this kind of reality. That is, a given theology has a transcendent character for some particular group when it presents a given group with something *intrinsically* good which deserves that they *put themselves in service to it or to its realization.* "Transcendent" in this sense is the polar opposite of "instrumental." (Seen in this context there is a close similarity between Barth's emphasis on the transcendence of Christianity over against *Kulturprotestantismus* and the criticism of the Frankfurt school against the modern domination of "instrumental" reason.)[7]

On this account, transcendence in any given theology is a matter of degree. In the concrete, most normative ideas are probably formulated and held partly because of the intrinsically good reality they represent and partly because they serve some concrete interests of the individual or group holding them. But one can also speak of a possible differentiation of these two shaping and motivating factors. And greater emphasis can be given to one or the other of these factors in the formulation of a theology and in the way it is put into practice. A theology is more transcendent the more it differentiates between the good in itself and our service to it, on the one hand, and what has instrumental value for us, on the other. One test, then, of the degree of transcendence present in any theology is the degree to which it has the potential for becoming *dys*functional in relation to empirically definable psychological or sociological interests. Sacrifice of such interests is, of course, not called for on all occasions, but if a theology is so bound up with particular interests that it can never call on people to go beyond those interests or to sacrifice them in service to what is good in itself, to this extent it lacks transcendence.

I think a good case can be made that many biblical writings contain theologies with a high degree of transcendence in this sense. This is one important reason they deserve to be studied theologically. But the issue as to whether this is so, and the degree to which it is so, is a matter that should be established by argument rather than decided either way in an a priori fashion.

SEMIOTIC CONTEXTUALIZATION

My mention here of the "good in itself" and "service to the good" may conjure up for some a so-called Platonic theology, which advocates being in service to intellectual Ideas with supposedly timeless validity, suspended in heaven above the relatively "unimportant" details of concrete everyday life. The defense of such a theology is not at all my intention. A pivotal point in this essay is in fact that there is a crucial difference between the notion of the good in itself and the notion of "timeless" ideas, norms, or values. The distinction between the timeless good and the variable good is not at all the same as the distinction between the good in itself and what is instrumentally good. The fact that it may be necessary to conceive of the transcendent good differently in different ages and cultures does not mean that all concepts of the good are instrumental and not transcendent, in the first sense mentioned above.

The argument here can be put in other terms by further developing the comparison made earlier between theology and aesthetics. The relationship between some particular movement of an individual in a dance to the "context" of a total dance performance is different from the relationship between one part of a car engine to the entire engine ensemble it is part of. A leap in the air has a meaning when it is seen in the context of a formal ballet different from the meaning it has when seen in the context of a Comanche war dance. The meaning of the same act differs from context to context. But this variation in aesthetic meaning is due to a "semiotic" relationship between different elements of the dance. And semiotic relationships are fundamentally different in kind from the functional relationships between physically interactive parts of a machine. Again, one crucial difference can be seen in the fact that perceiving semiotic relationships requires an act of *verstehen* whereas one could program a computer to "understand" the functional relationship between one part of a motor and the rest of the motor as a physical interactive system geared to a certain output.

A central part of my argument, then, is that all notions and perceptions related to what is good in itself, including the transcendent good, are decisively conditioned by the particular cultural context in which they are perceived. But the relation of these perceptions to this context is analogous to the semiotic relation between elements of a dance and the total aesthetic performance, or between the individual words of a sentence and the sentence as whole. They are not analogous to the functional relationship between parts of a motor and the total physical performance or output of the motor. A theory of what is good in itself ought to be integrated into a semiotic account of culture and meaning such as that worked out in Umberto Eco's *Theory of Semiotics*.[8]

This semiotic account of contextualization makes it possible for theologies to have a genuinely transcendent grounding that is yet not timeless and independent of cultural contexts. That is, on this account "transcendence" itself is a thoroughly relational term. It is just that the relation in question is not a functional but a semiotic one.

To summarize my argument thus far then: Sociohistorical reconstruction of biblical milieus has something very important to contribute to the theological study of the Bible, but the functional understanding of the relation of theology to social background is not the proper model to use in this context. The functional model eliminates methodologically and a priori the possibility of finding anything transcendent in theological writing and makes serious "theological" study (in Tillich's sense) impossible. But cultures are not only functional systems. They are also semiotic systems, in which the meaning of each element is determined by its semiotic relation to other elements in a total world picture. This total world picture is determined by socioeconomic conditions as well as by elements of "high culture," and we need to understand the socioeconomic conditions underlying biblical writings in order to understand their authors' total world picture. The transcendent elements of their theology are not "absolute" but get their meaning and definition from their semiotic relation to the rest of this world picture. They can be relationally defined in this semiotic way while still retaining their potentially "dysfunctional," challenging relation to psychological or social structures considered as strictly functional systems, pushing them beyond their limits to the realization of higher good.

THE PROBLEM OF RELEVANCE

The observations above concern the theological study of the Bible—the way we might come to understand and appreciate the greatness as theology of the views expressed there. They have generally ignored another key issue traditionally associated with theological study: that of the relevance of biblical theology to the modern situation. The account offered of the nature of contextualization in theology does however have some implications for this question as well, and I would like to offer some observations on this issue in closing.

The main point here is that the remarks about the necessity of contextualized understanding of any theology apply to the modern context as well. What this implies about the relevance of the Bible to the modern world is not primarily that we *ought* consciously to attempt changes in theological notions taken from the Bible in order to make them more relevant to the modern world. The more fundamental point is that, whether we are aware of it or not, the meaning of biblical ideas that might be incorporated in our theology is already decisively shaped by their relation to a world picture shaped by our own socioeconomic and cultural conditions. Steadfast adherence to the same theology held by the biblical authors is simply not a guaranteed possibility for us. To be fully honest we have to reckon with the possibility at least that our own world picture is semiotically structured in such a radically different way that even some of the central and essential themes of biblical theology simply cannot be given a central place in our own theology without serious distortion of the meaning they had in the biblical context. Studying the theology of the biblical authors can be a great stimulus and aid in doing theology ourselves in the modern context. But the two are essentially different enterprises.

To cite an example that is of course debatable but certainly plausible: A good argument could be made (*a*) that the model of the monarchic king has a central place in practically all of biblical theology, and (*b*) that certain aspects of the modern situation make this model out of place today. The model of the monarchic king fits in different ways into the theology of different biblical authors. In some biblical traditions the figure of God the king is allied with earthly authority figures. In others "we have no king but Yahweh" is allied with severe criticism of all institutional authorities. In Paul's First Letter to the Corinthians a very similar emphasis on Christ as the sole leader of the congregation is allied with a certain egalitarian emphasis, putting all actual members of the congregation basically on an equal footing.

Images related to this latter "prophetic" interpretation of divine kingship in the Bible play a central role in some modern attempts to draw direct lessons from the Bible for theory and praxis related to modern political situations. This line of thought and research has done a great service in recovering central and important elements of biblical theology forgotten in previous eras, which tended to see biblical theology either as a purely "spiritual" affair or as unquestionably and always on the side of law and order. But it tends to ignore the necessity of a *modern* contextualization of theology, by implicitly adopting the quasi-Platonic assumption that certain revolutionary biblical ideas are timelessly valid, normative in all cultural contexts. The authoritative relevance of these ideas for our situation and all situations is thus assured and need not be questioned. The only question is how one ought to apply them to the particular situation one is in.

The objection that I want to raise against this is that one's images concerning transcendent good, and the way one relates to transcendent good, are not separate from the character of one's concrete experience of good in everyday life. This is closely related to the earlier point about the "semiotic" nature of the relation between our theology and the remainder of our picture of the world as experienced. What is characteristic of semiotic relationships is that elements related semiotically are *mutually* defining. No one element in a painting, not even a perhaps overwhelmingly central image, can be regarded as having its meaning completely in itself, so that the meaning it has is unaffected by other parts of the painting and its relationship to them is completely one-way. Applied to theology, this means that the meaning that the central image of God has in biblical and traditional Christian theology is not something it has timelessly and in itself. It had the meaning that it had because it served as a central focus summing up some key ways in which people in Christian cultures encountered the good in their everyday life. Think, for example, of the key role played in these cultures by the experience of the call of a particular situation, experienced first of all as a call but then also readily conceivable as the call of God.

But one has to consider whether the basic character of our experience of the good is changed today. It is at least plausible that the mode described above, and other modes of encountering the good in everyday life, that once gave intense meaning to the image of God the king no longer have the central and dominant place in people's experience that they once had. In terms of the hierarchy of goods as people experience them, it is being displaced by other modes. One could point, for example, to the much more important role that intimacy or depth in personal relationships plays today in people's experience of what is most meaningful in life. People today look for and find intrinsic goodness in the richness of relationships developed for their own sake. Pursuing this kind of good requires attention to the varying concrete particulars of another person's experience and to the quality of the *process* of personal relating as such, independent of its content. The good and meaning of these relationships is the kind of good that is given a central place, for example, in the political ideals of some recent feminist thinkers[9] and earlier to some extent also in the anarcho-syndicalist tradition.

Can the image of a divine monarch, even in its prophetic and revolutionary interpretation, serve as a focal image summing up *this* mode of encounter with what is good in itself in its most intense and transcendent form? This does not seem to be so. The monarchic image seems to have had its traditional meaning in a context in which people's predominant experience of the good was as of something lying outside individual people and their concrete interactions—a set of goals, a cause, a charismatic leader, a set of norms. In a context in which people's experiences of good are shaped differently, such an image cannot have the meaning it once had. If the hypothesis about the modern world sketched above is true, what can serve as an image of transcendent good in the modern context may be radically different from the images we can find in the Bible.

My point here is not, of course, that the modern situation is certainly as I have pictured it or that the monarchic image is assuredly inappropriate in a good modern theology. My argument is that this *might* be the case, and unmoving adherence to certain images central to biblical theology ought not be allowed to exclude this possibility in an a priori way. A thoroughly contextualized theological awareness cannot simply take for granted the contemporary relevance of any given aspect of biblical theology. I am personally of the opinion that biblical theology does still challenge us in ways that we need to be challenged. But one cannot make the study of the Bible in its sociological milieu a simple substitute for open and careful sensitivity to the particular character of the present situation made known in one's own concrete experience and in reflection on it.

NOTES

1. Paul Tillich, *Systematic Theology* (Chicago: Univ. of Chicago Press, 1951), 1:11–15.

2. See *Understanding and Social Inquiry*, ed. F. R. Dalmyr and T. A. McCarthy (Notre Dame, Ind.: Univ. of Notre Dame Press, 1977), 1–11.

3. Tillich, *Systematic Theology* 1:11–15.

4. Tillich's formal definition *makes possible* a pluralism among views about what ultimately matters which is somewhat broader than the position he himself tended to hold, concerned as he still was with the problem of "absolutes." Tillich's view is made the basis for a broader pluralism in John F. Wilson's *Religion: A Preface* (Englewood Cliffs, N.J.: Prentice-Hall, 1982), 21–22.

5. Dennis Nineham's *The Use and Abuse of the Bible: A Study of the Bible in an Age of Rapid Change* (London: Macmillan & Co., 1976) elaborates this thesis in a very full and detailed way and faces very honestly the radical implications it has for modern attempts to use the Bible as a book of norms for today.

6. Norman Gottwald's "Socioeconomic Demythologization of Israelite Yahwism," e.g., leads to such statements as "Yahweh is the historically concretized, primordial power to establish and sustain social equality," "Yahwism was the function of communal egalitarianism. . . .Yahwism was the servomechanism to reinforce the social system" (*The Tribes of Yahweh: A Sociology of the Religion of Liberated Israel 1250–1050 B.C.E.* [Maryknoll, N.Y.: Orbis Books, 1979], 692-93).

7. See esp. Max Horkheimer, *The Eclipse of Reason* (New York: Oxford Univ. Press, 1947), and Herbert Marcuse, *One Dimensional Man* (Boston: Beacon Press, 1964).

8. Umberto Eco, *Theory of Semiotics* (Bloomington: Indiana Univ. Press, 1976).

9. See, e.g., Mary Daly, *Beyond God the Father: Toward a Philosophy of Women's Liberation* (Boston: Beacon Press 1973), and Sally Gearhart, "Womanpower: Energy Re-Sourcement," in *The Politics of Women's Spirituality,* ed. Charlene Spretnak (New York: Doubleday & Co., 1982), 194–206.

2

The Apocalyptic Rendering
of the Isaiah Tradition

BERNHARD W. ANDERSON
Boston University

Today scholars are beginning to move from analysis to synthesis in the interpretation of the Book of Isaiah. The established practice of separating the book into several discrete parts, each of which is viewed in isolation from the whole, is giving way to exploratory efforts to understand the overall unity and theological dynamic of the Isaiah tradition.[1] Indeed, it is an illuminating experience to lay aside most of the commentaries of the past and to read through in one sitting the Book of Isaiah with a kind of "second naiveté."[2]

Previous studies have shown that the Book of Isaiah is the end result of a long and complicated history of redaction. Undoubtedly Isaiah himself had a hand in the compilation of his prophecies dealing with the Syro-Ephraimitic crisis of 735–733 B.C.E. (Isa. 6:1—8:18) and the Judean revolt against Assyria in 705–701 (Isaiah 28—31). A case has been made for a later "Assyrian" or "Josianic" revision in the time of national renaissance when the Assyrian power was weakening at the end of the seventh century, and perhaps a subsequent "updating" in the early exilic period after the fall of Jerusalem in 587 B.C.E.[3] A further expansion of the Isaianic tradition occurred in the mid–sixth century B.C.E. in connection with the rise of Cyrus of Persia, at which time the poems of the so-called Second Isaiah were added. Possibly Isaiah 35, which contains many literary and thematic affinities with Second Isaiah, was composed to unite Second Isaiah (Isaiah 40—55) with the body of material associated with First Isaiah.[4] Finally, during the period of the Second Temple, in the late sixth century and the fifth century B.C.E., the Isaiah tradition was expanded with proto-apocalyptic materials found in Isaiah 55—56 (Third Isaiah)[5] and, perhaps a bit later, with apocalyptic supplements that abound in Isaiah 1—35, such as the apocalypse of Isaiah 24—27.[6]

17

In his commentary on Isaiah 1—39, Ronald E. Clements aptly remarks that "this development from prophecy to apocalyptic forms one of the most striking features in the literary growth of the book of Isaiah."[7] This insight, shared with other scholars, provides the starting point for this essay. My purpose, however, is not to trace the process of growth or history of traditions evident in the Book of Isaiah. Instead of reading the Isaiah tradition forward from the standpoint of the seminal preaching of Isaiah of Jerusalem, as we are accustomed to do, I propose to consider it from the viewpoint of its final apocalyptic *relecture* or rendering.[8] This study, though confined to the Old Testament field, is in line with the emphasis of Howard Clark Kee on the apocalyptic orientation of the "community of the new age" to which the Gospel of Mark was addressed.[9] Significantly, this Gospel opens by picking up an eschatological note from the prophecy of Isaiah about preparing the "way of the Lord" (Mark 1:3; cf. Isa. 40:3).

Methodologically, we shall look for major theological clues concerning the apocalyptic rendering within the last stages of the redaction of the book. In rereading the whole, special attention will be given to Third Isaiah (Isaiah 55—56) and to the small apocalypses found in the first part (Isaiah 24—27; 34—35). Moreover, we must consider a number of eschatological passages interspersed throughout the first part of the book, often introduced by the formula "in that day" or "in that time." Strikingly, this redactional cliché is found almost without exception in Isaiah 1—33, suggesting that this part of the book has undergone a social redaction.[10]

The task is ambitious at this stage of research; hence, it must be delimited as much as possible. It is not the purpose of this essay to discuss the history of the redaction of the Book of Isaiah or to inquire into the historical setting of the various layers of tradition. Such a study of the history of traditions within the Book of Isaiah is a legitimate investigation, which has already yielded important results. Nor is our concentration on the final "rereading" of the Isaianic tradition intended to imply that the apocalyptic rendering was necessarily superior to renditions of the message of Isaiah in previous social settings, whether in the time of the eighth-century prophet (the seminal message of Isaiah), in the time of Josiah and the decline of Assyrian power, in the peculiar historical circumstances of the Babylonian exile (Second Isaiah), or in the distressed social conditions of the Restoration. The modest purpose of this essay is to consider how the Isaianic tradition was finally reinterpreted in the theological style known as apocalyptic, which should be understood as prophecy in a new idiom.

THE COSMIC KING OF ZION

A proper place to begin is with the recognition of the centrality of Zion or the "City of God"—a motif that runs through all levels of tradition and one that is heavily accented in the final apocalyptic rendering. Zion—that is, Jerusalem regarded as the center of the land—is the pervasive symbol for the people who have been drawn into special relationship with Yahweh, the "Holy One of Israel." Yahweh has "established" Zion as a refuge for the afflicted (14:32; cf. 28:16), Yahweh of hosts "dwells" (*shôkēn*) on Mount Zion (8:18; cf. 18:7; 24:23), and the Divine Warrior will come to Zion as "Redeemer" (24:23; 59:20) and celebrate there a victory banquet in the presence of all the peoples (25:6–8). Beyond the tragedy of Israel's history lies the exaltation of Zion:[11]

> And you shall be called
> "City of Yahweh,
> Zion of the Holy One of Israel."
> Whereas you have been forsaken,
> despised, with none passing through,
> I will make you a pride for ever,
> and a joy for ages to come.
> You shall suck the milk of nations,
> and nourish at the breast of royalty;
> And you shall know that I, Yahweh, am your Savior,
> and your Redeemer, the Mighty One of Jacob.
> (Isa. 60:14b–16)

This apocalyptic good news to Zion stands in fundamental continuity with the Isaiah tradition from its inception. Isaiah of Jerusalem was profoundly indebted to a new style of theology or, perhaps one should say, a pattern of symbolization, in which the salvific institutions were monarchy and temple—the two institutions that were alien to Israel's ancient Mosaic tradition.[12] His message had a different theological ring from that of a "prophet like Moses" (Deut. 18:15–18). Prophets who stood in the Mosaic tradition, preeminently Hosea and Jeremiah, perceived their social world primarily in the light of a story in which the two crucial moments were Exodus and Sinai or, in a larger sense, the epic tradition extending from Exodus to Conquest. Jeremiah, for instance, indicted Israel for having forgotten the story of Yahweh's saving actions in bringing the people out of the land of Egypt and leading them into the promised land and for having turned to another god-story (the Baal mythos) to find their knowledge of God and their vocation as a people (Jer. 2:4–13). In this kind of preaching, the future is somewhat open-ended, depending on whether or not the people are faithful to their covenant responsibilities. Strikingly, Isaiah of Jerusalem did not make much, if anything, of this sacred story. Rather, his message was grounded transcendently in faith in Yahweh, the cosmic King, whose rule on earth is mediated through the reigning Davidic king (the anointed one, or messiah) and whose abiding presence is known and celebrated in the temple of Zion. It was in the temple that Isaiah caught a vision of Yahweh enthroned "high and lifted up" in the cosmic temple and received his commission to convey and interpret the King's sovereign decree to the mundane order (Isaiah 6). Since his message was not predicated on the contingencies of history or the precarious exercise of human freedom but rather on God's cosmic wisdom and power, it provided the basis for security and stability in the face of social change and the threat of chaos.

Undoubtedly Isaiah's message was profoundly influenced by the Jerusalem cult in which the people praised Yahweh as the cosmic Creator and King (Psalms 47; 93; 95—99) who has founded the earth securely upon the waters of chaos (Ps. 24:1) and who has likewise founded Zion securely as the symbol of God's abiding presence with the people (Psalm 46). The influence of this kingdom-of-God theology, with its twin convictions of Yahweh's election of the Davidic king and Yahweh's choice of the Jerusalem temple, may be sensed in the attack of Jeremiah, a "prophet like Moses," upon its abuses, as in his temple sermon (Jer. 7:1–15) or in his quotation of the people's lament:

> Is not Yahweh in Zion,
> Is her King not in her?
> (Jer. 8:19b)

It would be wrong to make too much of Isaiah's virtual silence about the Exodus-to-Conquest tradition. There are clear echoes of the Mosaic tradition in Isaiah's preaching, as Walther Eichrodt has shown.[13] Moreover, the reintroduction of the Exodus tradition in the poetry of so-called Second Isaiah and later phases of the Isaiah tradition (10:24–27; 63:11–14) was an appropriate interpretation of the received Isaianic tradition. It is noteworthy, however, that when the Exodus tradition was invoked in later stages of redaction there was a recrudescence of the mythical view found, for instance, in the Song of the Sea (Exod. 15:1–18). In mythopoeic language the Divine Warrior is portrayed as engaging in conflict with pharaonic hosts (described in chaos imagery), winning the victory that creates a people and bringing them in triumph to the sacred mount,

> the place, O Yahweh, which thou
> has made for thy abode,
> the sanctuary, O Yahweh, which thy
> hands have established.
> (Exod. 15:17 RSV)

At this sanctuary, Yahweh, the triumphant warrior, is acclaimed as King (Exod. 15:18).[14] This is precisely the pattern that occurs in Second Isaiah's Exodus typology: the opening of a way through the wilderness (Isa. 40:3–5), the divine *Chaoskampf* that re-creates a people (55:9–10), the jubilant march of this people to Zion (55:11) where they acclaim Yahweh, the Divine Warrior, as King (52:7-10). The same pattern is developed, if not so lyrically, in the apocalyptic rendition. In ancient days Yahweh "brought his people up from the sea," accompanied Moses with "his glorious arm," "led them through the deeps," and "gave them rest" (63:11-14). Echoing the motif of the path through the waters, a visionary announces that in the future a "way" will be prepared through obstacles (62:10):

> Behold Yahweh has proclaimed
>   to the end of the earth:
> Say to the daughter of Zion,
>   "Behold, your salvation comes;
>   Behold, [Yahweh's] reward is with him,
>   and his recompense before him."
> And they shall be called The holy people,
>   the redeemed of Yahweh;
> and you shall be called Sought out,
>   a city not forsaken.
>   (Isa. 62:11-12 RSV)

The apocalyptic rendering of the Isaiah tradition moves beyond Israel's horizon into the universal dimension of Yahweh's sovereignty over the nations and over the whole creation and thereby seeks to bring out the fuller meaning of Isaiah's announcement that Yahweh is enthroned as cosmic King and that Zion is the chosen place of Yahweh's presence. In vivid apocalyptic portrayals, Yahweh's judgment upon Zion, as announced by Isaiah, expands into a universal judgment upon all the inhabitants of the earth (24:14-20) and even the "host of heaven" (24:21-23), "for Yahweh of hosts will reign [$m\bar{a}l\bar{a}k$] on Mount Zion and in Jerusalem" (24:23). Further, the motif of the pilgrimage of the nations to Zion, where in the presence of the great King they will scrap their armaments and find peace and security (2:1-4; cf. Ps. 47:9), is enhanced with the picture of a great banquet for all the peoples that Yahweh will spread "on this mount" (25:6-8). Thus the whole Isaiah tradition elaborates a fundamental paradox: that if the peoples would know and worship the God whose sovereignty is universal, they must come to the symbolic "center."[15]

THE MYSTERY OF GOD'S KINGDOM

Consideration of the theme of Yahweh's cosmic kingship in Zion leads to another important issue in the apocalyptic rendering of the Isaiah tradition: the relation between the cosmic kingdom of God and the divine sovereignty in mundane affairs. A key metaphor for expressing the relation between the cosmic and mundane realms is the image of the King presiding in the heavenly council. In prophetic tradition this image appears in

Isaiah's temple vision (Isaiah 6), is echoed at the beginning of the poetry of Second Isaiah (Isa. 40:1–11), and figures significantly in Daniel's vision of the cosmic judgment of the ancient of days (Dan. 7:9–12). According to the metaphor, the enthroned heavenly King announces in the council the decree that determines the future of the world. The prophet of Yahweh is an exceptional ("called") person who has stood in the heavenly council, has overheard the council's deliberation, and has been delegated with the task of reporting the divine word to the people (6:8–13; Jer. 23:18–22)—the word that "stands forever" (40:8) because it expresses God's sovereign decree that shapes the future.

The apocalyptic theme of the "mystery" or "secret" of God's kingdom, which is found in early Christian tradition (Mark 4:11 and pars.), can be traced back to the prophetic notion of the divine council in which Yahweh announces the decree to be carried to the mundane sphere.[16] In later prophetic tradition, the mystery involves the timetable for the coming of God's kingdom (Dan. 2:29–30). In Isaiah's vision, however, it was the announcement of an impending devastation of the land (Isa. 6:11–12). The prophet spoke of the *opus alienum* that Yahweh was about to perform on Mount Zion (28:21–22). Yahweh's "strange work" was a work of wrath—a "decree of destruction" (28:22) or even an act of war against Zion, the very place chosen as Yahweh's abode (31:4). Contrary to the popular view (reflected in the lament of Jer. 8:19), the presence of the holy God in Zion was not an endorsement of accepted social values or of the royal game of power politics but a judgment on the whole social order. This is what it means to live in the presence of God, whose holiness is a consuming fire.[17]

> The sinners in Zion are afraid,
> trembling has seized the godless:
> "Who among us can dwell with the devouring fire?
> Who among us can dwell with everlasting burnings?"
> (Isa. 33:14 RSV)

One would think that as prophecy moved into apocalyptic, there would be an inclination to forget about the "wrath" of God and to concentrate on the merciful disposition of God toward Israel, leaving only the nations exposed to divine wrath. But this is not the case. The *dies irae,* which was the theme of Isaiah's preaching—for instance, in the powerful strophes on the imminent day of Yahweh in 2:6–21—affects the whole world, including Zion that represents the people of God. Israel must drink first the intoxicating cup of divine wrath and then pass it on to its oppressors (51:17–23). To be sure, the wrath of God is not the last word; this is evident preeminently in the apocalyptic reinterpretation of Isaiah's Song of the Vineyard (cf. 5:1–6; 27:2–5). Nevertheless, the wrath of God, which is inescapable because of glaring social injustices (see the "woes" in 5:8, 11, 18, 20, 21, 22; 10:1–4), is necessary for the purification of Zion so that it may become "the city of righteousness, the faithful city," that is, truly the city of God (1:24–26). In a late phase of Isaianic tradition, it is said that Israel's history exhibits the divine pathos of love and enmity:

> In all their troubles He was troubled,
> And the angel of His Presence delivered them.
> In His love and pity
> He Himself redeemed them,
> Raised them, and exalted them
> All the days of old.
>
> But they rebelled, and grieved
> His holy spirit;
> Then He became their enemy,
> And Himself made war against them.
> (Isa. 63:9–10 TNK)

This delicate balance of divine judgment and mercy, and its manifestation in human affairs, belong to the "strange work" of God in human history.

Isaiah's attempt to communicate the vision and the audition received in the heavenly council to the mundane sphere met with human resistance, as evident from the gloomy view expressed in the account of his call (6:9–10). Set in their ways and given to riotous living, the people "never give a thought to the plan of Yahweh, and take no note of what He is designing" (5:12 TNK). Despite the people's blindness and deafness, however, Yahweh has a "plan," is doing a "work" (5:19)—and this theme runs like a red thread through the woven tapestry of the Isaiah tradition. When Yahweh has completed "his work on Mount Zion and Jerusalem," the pride of Assyria will be humbled (10:12). In a later phase of tradition the downfall of Assyria is seen in the perspective of Yahweh's purpose ('ēṣā) that embraces the whole earth:[18]

> Yahweh of hosts has sworn:
> "As I have planned,
>   so shall it be,
> And as I have purposed,
>   so shall it stand,
> that I will break the Assyrian in my land,
>   and upon my mountains trample him under foot;
> and his yoke shall depart from them,
>   and his burden from their shoulder."
> This is the purpose that is purposed
>   concerning the whole earth;
> and this is the hand that is stretched out
>   over all nations.

For Yahweh of hosts has purposed,
   and who will annul it?
His hand is stretched out,
   and who will turn it back?

            (Isa. 14:24–27 RSV)

The same theme was picked up later when Babylonia was seen in the context of God's overruling purpose. "The word of our God," announced in the heavenly council, "stands forever" (40:8; cf. 46:10); that word, when it goes forth from Yahweh's mouth, does not return empty but "will accomplish that which I purpose" (55:11). Hence, it is folly to resist what God has planned long ago (22:11) or to make plans as though God did not discern (28:24). Yahweh, the transcendent and holy God, before whom man-made idols pale into nothingness, has the wisdom to "foretell the end from the beginning" and the power to execute the purpose envisioned. This is the premise of the "argument from prophecy" that looms large in Second Isaiah's proclamation of the incomparability of the God of Israel (Isa. 41:21–29; 43:9–13; 44:6–8, 24–28; 45:20–25; 46:5–13; 48:3–16).

Wisdom exerted a great influence on the transformation of prophecy into apocalyptic, although not to the extent advocated by Gerhard von Rad, who initially maintained that apocalyptic is primarily related to the wisdom tradition, not prophecy.[19] In a wisdom parable (28:23–29), which seems to express later reflection on Isaiah's message,[20] we are told about the farmer who, taught by God, knows that there is a time for plowing up the ground and a time for planting seed; and at threshing time, he does not crush the grain (i.e., display wrath) forever.

This also comes from Yahweh of hosts;
   he is wonderful in counsel,
   and excellent in wisdom.

            (Isa. 28:29)

The implication is that God's affairs of plowing and sowing, of threshing and harvesting, are conducted according to a plan. The plan, however, is hidden to human perception, whether that of sages or princes (19:11–15). Indeed, God's wisdom confounds the plans of a powerful nation (19:3). For God's ways are not our ways, nor are God's thoughts our thoughts (55:8–9).

Given the mystery of God's sovereignty over the times, it is understandable that in the history of the tradition there would be a shift in emphasis: from word to vision. The primary task of a prophet was to proclaim the word into the present situation—a word that demanded to be heard because of the shock of God's future. Hence the designation of the message of Isaiah as "vision," *ḥāzôn,* in the superscription to the book is "rather unexpected," as noted in a recent commentary, especially since the superscription at the head of chapter 2, which introduces the first collection of Isaiah's oracles, used the term "word," *dābār*.[21] Admittedly, not too much should be made of this linguistic shift, for prophets also had visions and dreamed dreams: (Jer. 23:25–29). The designation of Isaiah's prophecy as "vision" is even more striking, however, when one considers that the first chapter of Isaiah is a summarizing introduction to the prophecy of Isaiah, even to the Book of Isaiah as a whole.[22] Certainly, "vision" is appropriate for the apocalyptic rendering of the Isaiah tradition in which the futuristic aspect of God's plan becomes prominent. "From a message about the immediate future," R. E. Clements observes, "prophecy has come to be understood as a mysterious disclosure of a divine mystery given centuries in advance."[23]

Furthermore, the shift from oral preaching to writing upon a scroll (i.e., to "scripture") led to an increasing emphasis upon the futuristic, and even the predictive, aspect of prophecy. Isaiah's decision to "bind up the testimony, to seal the teaching" among his disciples (8:1, 16) was an appeal to the future in a time when Yahweh was "hiding his face" from Israel (8:17). It was not just the hiddenness of God, however, but even more the unresponsiveness of the present generation that prompted depositing a permanent literary witness:

Now, go, write it down before them on a tablet,
　And inscribe it upon a scroll,
That it may be for a future day,
　A witness forever.
For it is a rebellious people,
　Faithless children,
Children who refused to hear
　the teaching of Yahweh;
Who said to the seers [rô'îm],
　"Do not see,"
To the prophets [ḥôzîm],
　"Do not prophesy truth to us;
Speak to us nice things,
　Prophesy delusions."

(Isa. 30:8–10)

In the final analysis, however, the inability to hear Yahweh's word is held to be not just a defect of the will, that is, hardheartedness or the refusal to see or believe (as in the case of King Ahaz, Isa. 7:12). Rather, the defect is fundamentally epistemological, owing to the gulf separating human wisdom from the wisdom of God. As suggested by an "in that day" passage (29:17–24) that clearly has an apocalyptic flavor, the problem will be overcome only by a "new creation":

In that day the deaf shall hear the words of a book,
    and out of their gloom and darkness the eyes of
the blind shall see.
(Isa. 29:18)

At the eschatological banquet, we read in the Isaiah apocalypse, Yahweh will destroy on "this mountain" (i.e., Zion) "the covering that is cast over all peoples, the veil that is spread over all nations" (25:7). On Mount Zion there will be a vision of God, the enthroned King, like that beheld by Moses and the leaders of Israel on the top of Mount Sinai (24:23b; cf. Exod. 24:9–11).

Thus the mystery of God's purpose is inaccessible to human beings apart from revelation that is perceived in prophetic vision; and even this prophetic witness, when written down in the "scroll of Yahweh" (34:16), is cryptic, for the scroll has to be unsealed (cf. 29:9–11). Accordingly the prophecy of the restoration of Judah, under the code name Ariel, meaning "mountain of God," reaches a climax with the announcement that Yahweh has drugged the prophets and covered the heads of the seers so that they cannot perceive Yahweh's purpose. The apocalyptic interpretation of the divine mystery is given in the supplementary words

> The vision [ḥāzûth] of all of this has become to you like the words of a sealed book. If it is handed to someone who can read, saying, "Read this," he will say, "I can't, because it is sealed." And if it is handed to someone who cannot read, saying, "Read this," he will say, "I can't read." (Isa. 29:11–12)

This is not a far cry from the view found in the apocalypse of Daniel about the disclosure in the heavenly council of the divine decree that is so cryptic that even the seer Daniel needs the help of an angelic interpreter (Dan. 7:16).

THE TRIUMPH OF THE DIVINE WARRIOR

Yahweh's plan, according to the apocalyptic rendering of the Isaiah tradition, is to act so that all nations will see the "righteousness" (vindication) or "salvation" of Zion.

> For the sake of Zion I will not remain silent,
>   for the sake of Jerusalem I will not be quiet,
> Until her vindication goes forth as a gleam,
>   and her salvation like a flaming torch.
> Nations shall see your vindication,
>   and every king your glory.
> And you shall be called by a new name,
>   which the mouth of Yahweh will bestow.
> (Isa. 62:1–4)

26

The theme of the vindication of Zion, which belongs to the celebration of Yahweh's kingship, was deeply rooted in the Jerusalem cult. This is evident in a song of trust (Ps. 74:12–17) lodged in the center of a lament in which an appeal is made to Yahweh to "remember Mount Zion, where you have dwelt." Apparently the poet speaks of Zion's being located in the center of the earth, the *axis mundi*.

> Yet God my King is from of old,
>   working salvation in the middle of the earth.
> (Ps. 74:12)

The poet then goes on to recall the mythical battle of ancient times when Yahweh divided the sea, crushed the heads of Leviathan on the waters, and established the order of creation (vv. 13–17). The battle of the divine warrior against the powers of evil assumes more and more importance in the history of the Isaiah tradition: in Second Isaiah (Isa. 51:9–11), in Third Isaiah (59:15b–20; 63:2–6), and above all, in the apocalyptic levels (27:1; 34:5–8).

The reason for this is to be found in a changing perception of the magnitude and pervasiveness of the power of evil, a changing perception that resulted from the terrible catastrophes that shook the foundations of Israel's world. Isaiah of Jerusalem, like the prophet Amos a few years before him in the eighth century, perceived that the problem of evil was located in the rebellious will of the people. Indeed, this is the Isaianic theme that is sounded in the introduction to the book:

> Hear, O heavens, and give ear, O earth;
>   for Yahweh has spoken!
> "Children have I reared and nurtured,
>   but they have rebelled against me.
> The ox knows its owner,
>   and the ass its master's crib,
> but Israel does not know [recognize Yahweh],
>   my people does not behave perceptively."
> (Isa. 1:2–3)

In this perspective, shared essentially by all the classical prophets, suffering is a form of divine "discipline" or correction. Catastrophe can be a form of therapy if it breaks a false allegiance, an inauthentic way of life, and provides the opportunity for a redirection of the will, a change of course (1:18–20). Then there may emerge from the crucible of suffering a new community, a just society (1:24–26; cf. 32:15–19; 58:8–14).

The emphasis on practicing justice in accordance with the righteousness of God's cosmic order was never surrendered in the history of the Isaianic tradition. An exquisite witness of this is found in a passage from Third

Isaiah which delineates the sort of "fast" that is acceptable to the holy God: to be sensitive to the needs of others and to act to overcome oppression (58:1–12). There was a strong tendency, however, to shift from the people as a whole, in whom there is no health (1:4–6), to the "sinners" within the people (57:20–21; 65:11–12; 66:24). In this view, the purification of Zion did not involve the whole community, the body politic, but only the "wicked" in distinction from the "righteous." This view is evident in a passage in the introduction to the Book of Isaiah which seems to represent a later, perhaps Deuteronomistic, redactional phase (1:27–31):[24]

> Zion shall be redeemed by justice,
>> and those in her who repent, by righteousness.
> But rebels and sinners shall be destroyed together,
>> and those who forsake Yahweh shall be condemned.
>> (Isa. 1:27–28)

Nevertheless, the prophetic view of suffering as deserved punishment for sin was tried in the balance and found wanting. This is evident from the prophecy of Habakkuk, which reflects the traumatic world crisis connected with the downfall of Assyria and the rise of the Babylonian Empire. The prophet does not doubt that Yahweh has ordained this brutal empire for chastisement (Hab. 1:12); to this extent there is agreement with Isaiah's view of the previous Assyrian regime as the "rod of Yahweh's anger." But the new threat from the north appeared to exceed all bounds, as though an avalanche of chaos were sweeping over the nations. Accordingly, Isaiah's expostulation with God begins, in the style of a lament, with a protest about violence (ḥāmās) and the cry "How long?"

> O Yahweh, how long shall I cry for help,
>> and you do not hear?
> or cry to you, "Violence!"
>> and you will not deliver?
> Why do you make me see wrongs
>> and look upon trouble?
> Destruction and violence are before me;
>> strife and contention arise.
>> (Hab. 1:2–3)

It is noteworthy that the priestly recension of the flood story, which probably received its final form in this general period, is introduced with the announcement that "the earth was filled with violence" (Gen. 6:11).

The Isaiah tradition, especially in its apocalyptic rendering, is concerned not only with the problem of sin but also with the problem of violence—violence that victimizes Israel and corrupts the whole human scene. Isaiah's portrayal of the Assyrian menace introduces an element of mystery. The Assyrian emperor, not knowing that he is only an instrument of God, is filled with boastful pride and his mind harbors "evil plans" (10:7). This happens when any nation achieves power, whether Midian (10:26), Moab (16:6), Egypt (19:11–15), Assyria (30:29–33; 37:22–24), or Babylonia (14:3; 47:6–7). Indeed, there seems to be a wild streak running through human history. The Babylon oracle in Isa. 13:1–16, for instance, suggests that a powerful nation is a front for a mysterious power of evil that defies explanation. The tyrant, whatever his national identity, conforms to the type portrayed in a powerful poem redolent of Canaanite mythology, who grasps for equality with God. He aspires to have a place on the "mount of assembly" along with gods such as *Helal* ("Day Star") and *Shahar* ("Dawn") and even to usurp the throne of God:

> How you are fallen from heaven,
>   O Day Star, son of Dawn!
> How you are cut down to the ground,
>   you who laid the nations low!
> You said in your heart,
>   "I will ascend to heaven;
> above the stars of God
>   I will set my throne on high;
> I will sit on the mount of assembly
>   in the far north;
> I will ascend above the heights of the clouds,
>   I will make myself like the Most High."
> But you are brought down to Sheol,
>   to the depths of the Pit.
>   (Isa. 14:12–15 RSV)

The human problem, then, is not simply sin, which may be overcome by divine discipline and forgiveness, but radical evil, which must be exorcised from history.[25] Accordingly, in the transition from prophecy to apocalyptic there was, as Paul Hanson observes in his study of Third Isaiah, a "growing indifference to the concrete events of plain history" and a "flight into the timeless repose of myth."[26] More and more the message of Isaiah was detached from its moorings in the political realities of Israel's history and was lifted into the symbolic world view of apocalyptic, in which the kingdom of God is in opposition to the powers of evil that oppress and crush people.

Hence, in the various levels of the Isaianic tradition, Yahweh is portrayed as the mythical Divine Warrior. In Isaiah's message during the eighth century, Yahweh's battle is against Zion (1:24–26). In a series of powerful poems, Isaiah announced that Yahweh's anger against Israel has not abated "and his hand is outstretched"—to strike (5:25; 9:11, 17, 21; 10:4). In a later level of tradition the divine hand is "stretched out over all the nations" and cannot be turned back (15:26–27). And in apocalyptic interpretation the outstretched hand takes on a fuller meaning: it is the "high hand and outstretched arm" that will save a victimized people from the "fury of the oppressor" (51:13). The Divine Warrior comes to vindicate Israel, his sword "sated with blood."

> For Yahweh has a day of vengeance,
>> a year of recompense for the cause of Zion.
>>> (Isa. 34:8)

Yahweh is portrayed as marching mightily from Edom in crimson garments, for when there was no one to help, "my own arm brought me the victory" (63:5).

Of special interest is the poetic use of the ancient myth of the Divine Warrior's combat against the powers of chaos. The imagery of the myth is evident in the portrayal of the *Völkerkampf,* the gathering of the nations for what is called the "war upon Mount Zion" (29:5–8).[27] In one passage, which may reflect the time of Assyria's decline, we are told that Yahweh will rebuke (*gā'ar*) these powers of chaos as at the time of creation (cf. Ps. 104:7) and will rule as triumphant King over the "roaring" of the floods (cf. Ps. 93:3–4):[28]

> Ah, the thunder of many peoples,
>> they thunder like the thundering of the sea!
> Ah, the roar of nations,
>> they roar like the roaring of mighty waters!
> The nations roar like the roaring of many waters,
>> but he will rebuke them, and they will flee far away,
> chased like chaff on the mountains before the wind,
>> and whirling dust before the storm.
> At evening time, behold, terror!
>> Before morning, they are no more!
> This is the portion of those who despoil us,
>> and the lot of those who plunder us.
>>> (Isa. 17:12–14 RSV)

In the poetry of Second Isaiah the myth of the Divine Warrior's battle against the chaos monster is used to portray the divine victory that once created—and will once again create and redeem—a people and enable it to march triumphantly to Zion (51:9–11). And an apocalyptic passage, which echoes linguistically the Canaanite myth of the Divine Warrior's victory over the chaos monster, speaks of Yahweh's ultimate conquest of the power of evil:

> In that day Yahweh with his hard and great and strong sword will punish Leviathan the fleeing serpent, Leviathan the twisting serpent, and he will slay the dragon that is in the sea. (Isa. 27:1 RSV)

This exorcism will result in liberation from oppression, suffering, and the power of death (25:6-8). Israel will be given "rest from your pain and turmoil and the hard service with which you were made to serve" (14:3).

In apocalyptic perspective, the triumph of the Divine Warrior is a consolation, first of all, for the afflicted and oppressed people of Israel:

> As a mother comforts her son
> So I will comfort you;
> You shall find comfort in Jerusalem.
> (Isa. 66:13 TNK)

For, to recall the theme treated earlier, the cosmic King is present in Zion. The God who is far off (transcendent) is also near (immanent):

> For thus says the high and holy One
>> who inhabits eternity,
>> whose name is holy:
> I dwell in the high and holy place,
>> and also with those of a humble
>> and contrite spirit,
> to revive the spirit of the humble,
>> and to quicken the hearts of the contrite.
> (Isa. 57:15)

Comfort in affliction is also the theme of the prose expansion in 30:19-26, where it is promised that the people of Zion will weep no more. Yahweh once gave them "the bread of adversity and the water of affliction," but the time is coming when the meaning of it all will no longer be hidden—when eyes will be open to see divine salvation and ears will hear the word of God. In the apocalyptic scenario, the new age will be characterized by marvelous fertility (30:23-26), the ingathering of the dispersed to Zion (60; 17:12), and security and peace (33:20-24). Above all, there will be no more violence in Zion:

> Violence shall no more be heard in your land,
>> devastation or destruction within your borders;
> you shall call your walls Salvation,
>> and your gates Praise.
> (Isa. 60:18)

The salvation of Zion, however, is not confined to the healing of Israel's wounds. To be sure, the centrality of Zion in the divine purpose is not surrendered at any point in the Isaianic tradition. Again and again it is said that the nations will be subdued (30:28), that they will behold Yahweh's "zeal" for Israel (26:11), and that they will bring their tribute to Zion (18:17b; 60:5-7, 16:17). The destiny of the nations, however, is somehow tied up with the vindication of Zion. They too will receive advantage from

Israel's suffering for its sins and from Yahweh's final conquest of the powers of evil and chaos. In Second Isaiah's poetry this was the prophetic implication of the humiliation and exaltation of Israel, the Suffering Servant who is commissioned to perform a task—to announce the victory of Yahweh, the Divine Warrior.[29]

Accordingly, in the apocalyptic rendering of Isaiah's message the imagery of the New Exodus becomes more inclusive, at least in some passages. Echoing the language of Second Isaiah, it is said that there will be a highway, along which the redeemed will return with shouting to Zion (35:8–10). But the eschatological road through the wilderness will not be just a Sacred Way for Israel—from Assyria, as at the time of the Exodus (11:16), or from Babylonia (40:3–4), or from Egypt (27:12–13). The particularity of Zion, paradoxical though it may seem, does not exclude the universality of Yahweh's saving purpose:

> In that day Israel will be the third with Egypt and Assyria, a blessing in the midst of the earth, whom Yahweh of hosts has blessed, saying, "Blessed be Egypt, my people, and Assyria the work of my hands, and Israel my heritage." (Isa. 19:24 RSV)

This is in line with the vision, found in the oracles of both Isaiah (2:1–4) and Micah (4:1–4), of the pilgrimage of the nations to Zion. In apocalyptic vision the divine triumph over evil, and hence the cessation of violence, will mark the beginning of a completely new age, a New Zion, indeed a New Creation:

> For behold, I am going to create a new heaven
>   and a new earth;
> the former things shall not be remembered,
>   they shall never come to mind.
> So, be glad and rejoice for ever
>   in what I am creating.
> For I am going to create Jerusalem as a joy,
>   and its people as a gladness.
> I will rejoice in Jerusalem,
>   and be glad in my people.
> No more will be heard in it the sound of weeping,
>   and the cry of distress.
>   (Isa. 65:17–19)

WAITING FOR GOD

In the apocalyptic rendering of the Isaiah tradition, the New Age is not just "one far-off divine event to which the whole creation moves" (Tennyson); rather, the kingdom of God, or in Isaianic language, the "Day of Yahweh," is "near" (13:6). Despite evidences to the contrary, the triumph of God over the powers of sin, chaos, and death will occur speedily and inevitably.

It has often been observed that Isaiah of Jerusalem was the great prophet of faith. In the Syro-Ephraimitic crisis, when Judah's two northern neighbors, Ephraim and Syria, attempted to force it into an anti-Assyrian coalition, he appealed to King Ahaz to calm down and not to practice a foreign policy based on the politics of anxiety. God is in control, he affirmed, so why not relax and see things in perspective! "If your faith is not sure [*ta'amînû*]," he said, in a play on words that defies translation (7:9b), "your throne will not be secure [*tē'āmēnû*]." In a later political crisis, when Judah was tempted to take refuge from the Assyrian threat by entering into alliance with Egypt, he also called for a steady faith that relied upon the overruling purpose of God:

> For thus said my Lord God,
>   the Holy One of Israel,
> "You shall triumph by stillness and quiet;
>   your victory shall come about
> Through calm and confidence."
>   (Isa. 30:15 TNK)

Isaiah's call for faith in the divine purpose was—and still is—an almost impossible demand in times of world crisis, when military force seems to be the practical course of action. Still, his message of faith, which ran up against human impatience, was remembered and even further emphasized in subsequent Isaianic tradition. The word to King Ahaz was strengthened by the addition of a chronological comment that in another sixty-five years the aggressive northern kingdom Ephraim would be shattered (Isa. 7:8b)—a note added in the next century when Isaiah's prophecy was fulfilled. In the retrospective view of faith, history provides evidences that God is in control, that God's word accomplishes its intended purpose.

Nevertheless, in any time faith has to cope with the hiddenness of God and to agonize over the question of whether, in the face of the injustices of the world, God's ways are just. The problem of theodicy is heard already in the lament of the people cited in Second Isaiah's majestic poetry (40:27). Having no other helper, the minority who are victimized by power turn to Yahweh in trust (26:4–7) and cry out for liberation from the "fury of tyrants" (25:4). Their cry is heard in the laments of the Psalter and in the complaints found now and then in the Isaianic tradition: "Where is your zeal, your power?" (64:15). When uttered by the prophet Isaiah, the cry "Yahweh, how long?" expressed frustration about the difficulty of communicating the divine message to a people that refused to hear. The same cry, however, had a different ring in later phases of the tradition, when Israel, faced by evil on a world scale, agonized over the time limit of God's judgment.

The apocalyptic answer to the cry "How long?" is "Not long!" "In a little while," according to a passage that has an apocalyptic ring, "the humble shall have increasing joy" and "the tyrant shall be no more" (29:17–24). God's people should have no fear of Assyria, we read in a supplemental passage that interprets Yahweh's decree of judgment upon the house of Israel, for "very soon" Yahweh's wrath will have spent itself and Yahweh "will wield his staff as he did over the Egyptians by the sea" (10:24–26). Indeed, according to some passages, the divine timetable is set. "In three years, fixed like the years of a hired laborer," Moab's decline will occur (16:13–14). Tyre will vanish from memory "for seventy years, equaling the lifetime of one king" (23:15–18). Passages like these, which anticipate the deterministic view of later apocalyptic, express faith's confidence that God is firmly in control of events.

> Hide but a little moment,
> until the indignation passes.
> For lo!
> The Lord shall come forth from his place
> To punish the dwellers of the earth
> For all their iniquity;
> And the earth shall disclose its bloodshed
> And shall no longer conceal its slain.
> (Isa. 26:20b–21 TNK)

Hence, it is important to "search and read" the Scripture—"the book of Yahweh" (34:16)—"for his mouth has spoken."

In the apocalyptic rendering of the Isaiah tradition, the theme of "waiting for Yahweh" has dynamic meaning. This note was sounded by Isaiah in the time when he resolved to "bind up and seal" the testimony as an appeal to a future generation: "I will wait for Yahweh who is hiding his face from the house of Jacob and I will hope in him" (8:17). The motif of waiting for God, and specifically for the demonstration of the justice of God's ways, is found in all levels of Isaianic tradition: early (Isa. 30:18; 33:2), middle (Second Isaiah, 40:31; 49:23; 51:5), and late (Third Isaiah, 56:9; 60:9) or apocalyptic (25:9; 26:8). It is noteworthy that the same verbs of waiting are found in psalms of lament in which a suppliant, praying in a time when Yahweh's "face" is hidden, waits through the times of darkness for Yahweh's act that brings relief from distress and liberation from injustice (Pss. 25:3, 5, 21; 27:14; 37:7, 9; 62:1, 5; 69:6; 130:5; cf. the Song of Thanksgiving, Ps. 40:1). "Watchman, what of the night?" (Isa. 21:11–12). The meaning of waiting through the night until the coming of morning is clear in an "in that day" passage:

> It will be said in that day,
> Lo, this is our God;

> we have waited for him that he might save us;
> This is Yahweh—we have waited for him;
> let us be joyful and rejoice in his salvation!
>
> (Isa. 25:9)

When read in apocalyptic perspective, the familiar passage at the conclusion of Isaiah 40 takes on a fuller meaning. Unfortunately, many people still quote the passage according to the King James Version, which renders the verb "wait for," *qiwwā*, as "wait upon," which in English means "to call or visit (especially a superior), in order to pay one's respects, ask a favor, etc." (*Webster's New World Dictionary*). But in the Book of Isaiah, "waiting for God" has a dynamic meaning. Reflecting the situation of the people's lament and thus the issue of theodicy (see 40:27), the verb means to look forward to the future when the triumph of God will be manifest.

> Even youths shall faint and be weary,
> young people shall fall exhausted;
> but those who wait for Yahweh shall renew their strength,
> they shall mount up with wings like eagles,
> they shall run and not be weary,
> they shall walk and not faint.
>
> (Isa. 40:30–31)

Those who raise the lament "How long?" are given the assurance that the future belongs to God and that deliverance is coming soon, sooner than one might think. Such faith prompts people who live in God's promise to stand on tiptoe, as it were, waiting eagerly for God's future.

The early Christian community, like the covenanters of Qumran, engaged in an apocalyptic rereading of the book of Isaiah. This is especially true in the Gospel of Mark. According to this evangelist, Jesus' preaching opened with an announcement of the imminence of God's triumph: "The time is fulfilled, and the kingdom of God is at hand. . ." (Mark 1:15). In this Gospel, God's salvation, however, is not only deliverance from the bondage of sin, as in the story of the healing of the paralytic (Mark 9:1–8), it is also deliverance from the terrible powers of evil and chaos at work in human history. Accordingly, Mark, in the spirit of apocalyptic writers, portrays the Messiah as the Divine Warrior who wages warfare against the kingdom of Satan and announces the imminent triumph of the Son of Man.

NOTES

1. The question of the unity of the Book of Isaiah was reopened by Brevard Childs's canonical approach in *Introduction to the Old Testament as Scripture* (Philadelphia: Fortress Press, 1979), 325–38. The discussion has been pursued fruitfully by, e.g., Ronald E. Clements in "The Unity of the Book of Isaiah,"

Interpretation 36 (1982): 117–19, and "Beyond Tradition History: Deutero-Isaianic Development of First Isaiah's Themes," *Journal for the Study of the Old Testament* 31 (1985): 95–113); by Walter Brueggemann in "Unity and Dynamic in the Isaiah Tradition," *Journal for the Study of the Old Testament* 29 (1984): 89–107; and by Rolf Rendtorff in "Zur Composition des Buches Jesaja," *Vetus Testamentum* 35 (1984): 295–320. See also *Reading and Preaching the Book of Isaiah,* ed. Christopher R. Seitz (Philadelphia: Fortress Press, 1988).

2. Rereading with a "second naiveté," as Karl Barth expresses it, is discussed in my "Tradition and Scripture in the Community of Faith," *Journal of Biblical Literature* 100 (1981): 5–21; see esp. p. 16.

3. A redaction in Josiah's reign is advocated by Hermann Barth in *Die Jesaja-Worte in der Josiazeit* (Neukirchen-Vluyn: Neukirchener Verlag, 1977) and by J. Vermeylen in *Du prophète Isaïe à l'apocalyptique,* 2 vols., Etudes bibliques (Paris: Librairie Lecoffre, 1977). Ronald E. Clements (*New Century Bible Commentary on Isaiah 1–39* [Grand Rapids: Wm. B. Eerdmans, 1980], 3–8) also advocates a "Josianic redaction," as well as a later updating in the years immediately after 587 B.C.E. A "structural overview" of the book as a whole is given by Marvin A. Sweeney in "Isaiah 1–4 and the Post-exilic Understanding of the Isaianic Tradition" (Ph.D. diss., Princeton Theological Seminary, 1983), 90–239.

4. O. H. Steck, *Bereitete Heimkehr,* Stuttgarter Bibelstudien 121 (Stuttgart, 1985).

5. Paul Hanson, *The Dawn of Apocalyptic* (Philadelphia: Fortress Press, 1975).

6. See, among others, William R. Millar (*Isaiah 24—27 and the Origin of Apocalyptic,* Harvard Semitic Monograph Series 11 [Missoula, Mont.: Scholars Press, 1976]), who dates the little apocalypse to the period of the exile (the last half of the sixth century B.C.E.).

7. Clements, *New Century Bible Commentary on Isaiah 1—39,* 22.

8. *Relecture* is the term used by Vermeylen in *Du Prophète Isaïe.*

9. Howard C. Kee, *Community of the New Age: Studies in Mark's Gospel* (Philadelphia: Westminster Press, 1977; rev. ed., Macon, Ga.: Mercer Univ. Press, 1983).

10. Not all of these passages (at least thirty-six, according to my count) come from the final proto-apocalyptic or apocalyptic stages. The formula "in that day" is found in some of Isaiah's poetry (e.g., 2:5–21).

11. Unless otherwise indicated, the author is responsible for translations. TNK stands for *Tanakh,* a translation of the Jewish Publication Society.

12. See N. Poulssen, *König und Tempel im Glaubenszeugnis des Alten Testaments,* Stuttgarter Biblischer Monographien 3 (Stuttgart, 1967). For discussions of Zion theology, see Bennie C. Ollenburger, *Zion, the City of the Great King: A Theological Investigation of Zion Symbolism in the Tradition of the Jerusalem Cult,* JSOT Supplement Series (Sheffield, Eng.: JSOT Press, 1987); and Jon D. Levenson, *Sinai and Zion: An Entry into the Jewish Bible* (New York: Winston-Seabury Press, 1985), esp. 89–194.

13. Walther Eichrodt, "Prophet and Covenant," in *Proclamation and Presence,* Festschrift G. H. Davies, ed. John I. Durham and J. R. Porter (Richmond: John Knox Press, 1970), 167–88. See also Levenson, *Sinai and Zion,* 187–217.

14. See Frank M. Cross, "The Song of the Sea and Canaanite Myth," in *Canaanite Myth and Hebrew Epic: Essays in the History of the Religion of Israel* (Cambridge:

Harvard Univ. Press, 1973), 112–44. The influence of the mythical pattern—chaos battle, kingship, palace (temple)—on the poetry of Second Isaiah is discussed by Tryggve N. D. Mettinger in "In Search of the Hidden Structure: YHWH as King in Isaiah 40—55," *Svensk exegetisk årsbok* 51–52, Festschrift B. Gerhardsson (1986-87): 148–57. For further treatment of the *Chaoskampf* in Israelite tradition, see my *Creation versus Chaos: The Reinterpretation of Mythical Symbolism in the Bible* (New York: Association Press, 1967; Philadelphia: Fortress Press, 1987) and "Exodus Typology in Second Isaiah," in *Israel's Prophetic Heritage,* Festschrift James Muilenburg (New York: Harper & Row, 1962), 177–95.

15. See Mircea Eliade, "The Symbolism of the Center," in *Cosmos and History: The Myth of the Eternal Return* (New York: Harper & Bros., 1959), 12–17.

16. See Raymond Brown, *The Semitic Background of the Term "Mystery" in the New Testament,* Facet Books (Philadelphia: Fortress Press, 1968).

17. This subject is explored further in my "'God with Us'—In Judgment and in Mercy: The Editorial Structure of Isaiah 5—10 (11)," in *Canon, Theology, and Old Testament Interpretation,* Festschrift Brevard Childs, ed. Gene M. Tucker, David L. Petersen, and Robert R. Wilson (Philadelphia: Fortress Press, 1988).

18. R. E. Clements assigns this passage to the "Josianic redaction." He discusses the importance of the theme of Yahweh's "plan" or "counsel" in the Isaianic tradition in an essay on the Book of Isaiah in the reference work *The Books of the Bible* (New York: Charles Scribner's Sons, forthcoming).

19. Gerhard von Rad, *Old Testament Theology,* vol. 2 (New York: Harper and Row, 1965), 303–8. He qualified his view somewhat in a *Sonderausdruck* (1965) of the German ed., pp. 315–37.

20. A number of commentators assign this passage to a later stage of the redaction of Isaiah: to the time of Josiah (Hermann Barth, in *Die Jesaja-Worte,* and Clements, in *New Century Bible Commentary on Isaiah 1—39*) or to apocalyptic interpretation (O. Kaiser, in *Isaiah Thirteen to Thirty-nine: A Commentary,* Old Testament Library [Philadelphia: Westminster Press, 1974]).

21. Joseph Jensen, O.S.B., *Isaiah 1—39,* Old Testament Message 8 (Wilmington, Del.: Michael Glazier, 1984), 38.

22. Georg Fohrer, "Jesaja 1 als Zusammenfassung der Verkundigung Jesajas," *Zeitschrift für die alttestamentliche Wissenschaft* 74 (1962): 251–68.

23. Clements, *New Century Bible Commentary on Isaiah 1—39,* 22. In *Isaiah One to Thirty-three,* Word Biblical Commentary (Waco, Tex.: Word Books, 1985), John D. W. Watts also attempts to read the whole book from the alleged standpoint of its completion ca. 435 B.C.E. and to regard it as a dramatic vision of God's "strategy" for Israel, who is called to "be separate from the state, a spiritual gathering of those who would serve God in spirit and in truth." This final reading sounds suspiciously like a Christian vision, and a sectarian one at that.

24. See, e.g., H. Wildberger, *Jesaja 1—12,* Biblischer Kommentar (Neukirchen-Vluyn: Neukirchener Verlag, 1972), 56–57, 66–67; and Clements, *New Century Bible Commentary on Isaiah 1—39,* 36–37.

25. I have discussed this issue more broadly in "Sin and the Powers of Chaos," in *Sin, Salvation, and the Spirit,* ed. Daniel Durken, O.S.B. (Collegeville, Minn.: Liturgical Press, 1979), 71–84.

26. See Hanson's discussion of "myth and history," in *Dawn of Apocalyptic,* 126–34.

27. For an illuminating discussion of the use of the chaos myth in the Jerusalem cult, see Tryggve N. D. Mettinger, "Fighting the Powers of Chaos and Hell—Towards the Biblical Portrait of God," *Studia theologica* 39 (1985): 21–38.

28. Howard C. Kee, in an essay ("The Terminology of Mark's Exorcism Stories," *New Testament Studies* 14 [1968–69]: 232–46) also appreciated by Mettinger ("Fighting the Powers"), shows that the motif of rebuking (*gā'ār*) the powers of chaos persists into the New Testament, esp. the Gospel of Mark, where Jesus "rebukes" the demons (Mark 1:25; 3:12) and calms the unruly waters (4:35–41).

29. See Edgar W. Conrad, "The Community as King in Second Isaiah," in *Understanding the Word,* ed. J. T. Butler, E. W. Conrad, and B. C. Ollenburger (Sheffield: JSOT Press, 1985), 99–111; see also Conrad's *Fear Not, Warrior: A Study of 'al tira' Pericopes in the Hebrew Scriptures,* Brown Judaic Studies (Chico, Calif.: Scholars Press, 1985), chaps. on Isaiah.

3

The Onset of Sects in Postexilic Judaism: Neglected Evidence from the Septuagint, Trito-Isaiah, Ben Sira, and Malachi

ALEXANDER ROFÉ
The Hebrew University of Jerusalem

Scholarly contributions throwing light on the history and nature of the Jewish sects during the Second Commonwealth are innumerable.[1] To my knowledge, however, most of them follow one course, that is, the perusal of direct information about the sects derived from Josephus, Qumran writings, the New Testament, and rabbinic sources. Consequently, the scholarly discussion has centered on the period beginning with the Maccabean revolt, and possible antecedents in the Persian and early Hellenistic ages have remained a matter for conjecture and contention. The present paper endeavors to supplement the mentioned "classical" sources with further evidence gleaned from late biblical and apocryphal sources. In this way, perhaps, the study of the beginnings of the Jewish factions, enriched by new data, will be based on more solid foundations.

It is well known that Josephus, in book 13 of his *Antiquities,* pars. 171–73, first points out the existence of the three sects—Pharisees, Sadducees and Essenes—when reporting on the rule of Jonathan the Maccabean (153–143 B.C.E.). This statement, which may at first seem anachronistic, is aptly confirmed by the Qumranic, that is, Essenian, *Covenant of Damascus* (5.20–6.11, 7.9–8.13), as well as by the proto-Qumranic *Book of Jubilees* (23.23–26), which with various allusions trace the beginnings of their sect to the crisis precipitated in 168 B.C.E. by the decree of Antiochus IV Epiphanes.

The crisis provoked by Antiochus Epiphanes, considered by itself, does not look a plausible starting point for the formation of the three sects. Quite the opposite: the common religious persecution should have led to, if anything, a reconciliation between the diverse factions in Judaism, excluding, of course, that of the Hellenized Jews. Therefore, if the sects appear as having taken shape by the mid–second century B.C.E., one is allowed to infer that the religious schism within Judaism had already existed latently earlier in the Hellenistic period, between 333 and 168 B.C.E. Hence, Antiochus's persecution and the revolt of the Maccabees seem only to have contributed to the evolution of the rivalry, causing it to erupt in political reality. This contribution is easily explained: the crisis of Antiochus IV had totally subverted the old regime of Judea—the hegemony of the Sadokite priests, the regulations of the cult as well as those of public observance. Consequently, all Jewish religious parties—the ruling one and those dissident— found themselves all at once paradoxically equalized, all forbidden, all illegal, all equal in the struggle against Macedonian oppression. Later on, when the tide turned in favor of the Jews, from 153 on, all factions scrambled, trying to impose their principles and practices in both temple and state religion, now officially recognized even by the Seleucid power.[2] Thus it seems only natural that the religious schism would explode soon after the first Maccabean victories, much as it is legitimate to look for its roots in the preceding century or centuries. This hypothesis, attractive as it may sound, must be corroborated by the relevant biblical and apocryphal texts.

Let us begin with the dyad Sadducees-Pharisees. There is an indication, neglected but reliable in my opinion, that the divergences between Sadducees and Pharisees in cultic questions already existed in the third century B.C.E. It is offered by the Greek text of 1 Sam. 7:6.

The Masoretic text reads:

ויקבצו המצפתה

וישאבו מים
וישפכו לפני ה'

ויצומו ביום ההוא
ויאמרו שם חטאנו לה'

They assembled at Mizpah,

drew water
and poured it out before the Lord;

they fasted on that day
and confessed their sins to the Lord.[3]

"Before the Lord" is said about a ritual act:[4] the water is dedicated to him, presumably upon the altar. The Greek faithfully follows the Hebrew text, but having translated the words "and poured it out before the Lord," it adds three words that equal one in Hebrew: ἐπὶ τὴν γῆν = ארצה (onto the earth).

This is self-contradictory. One does not pour water "before the Lord" onto the earth, one pours it on the altar! But if we recall the divergences between Pharisees and Sadducees about the libation of water on the temple's altar during the festival of Sukkot—how the former prescribed the ritual while the latter denied its legitimacy, throwing the water down to the floor whenever they could[5]—then the inconsistency is explained. Indeed, the words "onto the earth" did not obtain in the original Hebrew text, nor were they added by the translator or by the Greek copyists, since they were not familiar with the details of worship at the temple of Jerusalem; the word ארצה probably existed in the Hebrew *Vorlage* of the Septuagint; it had been introduced there by a Saducean scribe bent on denying the Pharisees all evidence from Scripture for their custom of water libation on the altar during the fall festival.[6]

The historical implications of this text are quite clear. Since the Greek translation of the Book of Samuel was made around the end of the third century,[7] and its *Vorlage* certainly contained the "Saducean" correction, here lies a piece of evidence, small but significant, that in the third century, well before the crisis of Antiochus IV, the divergences that in time characterized the Saducean-Pharisaic polemic already existed in Jerusalem.[8]

The roots of the Pharisaic-Saducean dissidence lie, however, much deeper. It was Abraham Geiger who noted, some 130 years ago, that Isaiah 66:3 contains a clear denunciation of the Jerusalem priesthood.[9] This is how I suggest translating the verse:[10]

> The slaughterer of the ox strikes a man
> the sacrificer of the sheep immolates a dog
> the presenter of meal offering cuts a swine
> the offerer of incense blesses an idol.

To slaughter oxen, to sacrifice sheep, to present a meal offering, to offer incense—all these were priestly functions or became such in the course of time. It is the priests, then, who are here denounced by the prophet.

If we relate this interpretation, which in my opinion is the only one to make sense of the verse, to the identification of Trito-Isaiah as the fifth-century author of the last thirteen chapters of the Book of Isaiah,[11] we obtain evidence that at that early date there was already a marked opposition to the priestly supremacy in Jerusalem. And when we link this passage with other invectives of Trito-Isaiah and with additional sources from that period—Malachi, Nehemiah, and the author of the Book of Ezra—a clear picture emerges. We see these authors, who define themselves as "servants of the Lord" (Isa. 54:17; 65:9, 13–16; 66:14), "fearers of the Lord" (Mal. 3:16, 20), "who fear the word of the Lord" (Isa. 66:2, 6; Ezra 9:4; 10:3), who profess to meekness (Isa. 61:1) and humility, being oppressed (Isa. 57:15; 66:2),[12] in a continuous polemic against the aristocracy and priesthood of Jerusalem.

This polemic has a social background, as becomes clear not only from the antagonism between poor and well-to-do but also from the social dia-tribe of Trito-Isaiah (Isaiah 58) and the debt remission proclaimed by Nehemiah (Nehemiah 5);[13] yet at the heart of the matter lies a religious antagonism, as the priestly aristocratic party is repeatedly charged with its idolatrous practices (Isa. 66:3; cf. 65:3–5) and intermarriage (Mal. 2:10–12; Ezra 9, 10; Neh. 13:23–28). This is not, however, merely a question of abiding by the law, because most of the charges refer to transgression of the Torah not in its literal but in its wider sense:[14] The Torah forbade inter-marriage with the seven peoples of Canaan; Ezra, Nehemiah, and Malachi extended the interdict to the neighboring peoples of their times. The Torah forbade agricultural labor on Shabbat; Nehemiah and Trito-Isaiah con-demned trading on that day as well. One is confronted here with a new interpretation of the Torah, an interpretation through analogy which later became the hallmark of the Pharisaic-rabbinic halakah. Where did this trend originate? We can only surmise on the basis of Ezra's and Nehemiah's place of origin in the eastern Diaspora of Mesopotamia and Persia. Here, after a century and a half of exile, a new type of Judaism has come into being: it is characterized by its ability to reinterpret the law, adapting the old rules of an agricultural society to a new reality of artisans and merchants. Besides, it stands out by the solidarity of its religionists, typical of a com-munity in exile. This feature comes to the fore in Nehemiah's diatribe on the remission of debts (Nehemiah 5). This same solidarity leads to the exclusion of foreigners, hence to the objection of foreign wives, not on the ground of purity but as a principle of faith. This is demonstrated by the subsequent institution of proselytism, about to appear (Isa. 56:1–8), thus completing the double aspect of Judaism—as a nation and a religion.

Thus, in my opinion, we may trace back the origins of the two main Jewish trends that oppose each other in the Second Commonwealth to the fifth century B.C.E. On the one hand, one finds the aristocracy of Jerusalem, headed by the Sadokids, which in time will take shape as the Sadducean party, and on the other hand, the popular movement that inherited the traditions of Jewish communities in exile and seeks therefore to separate itself from the foreigners (*bdl*, nif. in Ezra 6:21; 9:1; 10:8, 11; Neh. 9:2; 10:28; 13:3; as against Isa. 56:3). In the course of time they will become known as Pharisees, "separated," from the verb *prš*, which is the Aramaic and late Hebrew equivalent to the biblical Hebrew *bdl*. The identification of these two movements in the fifth century has already been suggested in the past;[15] the contribution of this paper lies in trying to describe them more clearly, using the evidence from Trito-Isaiah.

Much less is known about the origins of the Essenes, to be identified with the sect of Qumran. Some features of this denomination—its developed angelology, its concept of dual predestination by which the world is divided into sons of light and darkness—may be traced back to Iranian influences operating in the late Persian and early Hellenistic age.[16] All this is not very helpful, however, in dating the beginnings of the sect. More promising, and hence deserving closer attention, are some references to Essenian views extant in Jewish sources of the fourth and third centuries B.C.E. We start with a passage from Ben Sira (Sir. 15:11–20):

> Do not say: "From God is my transgression,"
> for that which He hates made He not.
> Do not say: "It is He that made me stumble,"
> for there is no need of evil men.
>
> . . . .
>
> God created man from the beginning
> and placed him in the hand of his own inclination.[17]

In this saying one may find reaction to the idea of predestination, characteristic of the Essenes. But the passage lacks a very essential element of Essenian doctrine: the absolute dual predestination. Rather, one finds here a particular predestination for a specific action of sin committed by an individual at a certain moment. Probably Ben Sira challenges here the Stoic concept of fate that reached him by means of some popular Hellenistic philosophy. In the same way, further on (16:16—17:24), Ben Sira seems to contend against another trend in Greek philosophy: the Epicurean denial of any interest of the divine in the human world.[18]

More significant is the question of the calendar, because as has been rightly observed, especially by S. Talmon,[19] differences in praxis deriving from divergent calendars determined unity or schism within Judaism much more than theological variances. The Essenes followed a quasi-solar calendar of 364 days, fifty-two exact weeks per year, implying an exact recurrence of the various festivals on determined weekdays. The *Book of Jubilees*, which first expounds this quasi-solar calendar—as opposed to the official Jewish moon calendar (see below)—accordingly rephrases the narrative about the creation of luminaries. Whereas in Gen. 1:14–15 one reads that both lights "will function as signs [לאתת], and for the appointed times [ולמועדים] and for the days and years," *Jubilees* 2.9 appoints the sun alone to be a great sign in the world, for the days and the Shabbats, for the months and the times, for the weeks and the jubilees, and for all the dates of the year. The significance of this passage has been duly recognized by modern scholars. What, on the other hand, seems to me not to have been noticed so far is the contradictory relation of *Jubilees* and Ben Sira, especially as shown by the new Massada text published by Yadin.[20] Indeed, Ben Sira says (Sir. 43:6–7),

וגם ירח יאריח עתות
ממשלת קץ ואות עולם
לו מועד וממנו חג
וחפץ עשה בתקופתו

Also he made the moon to conduct times,
a government of periods and eternal sign
hers is the feast, from her the solemnity
the [divine] will she fulfills with her revolution.

From this short quote from Ben Sira, as reconstructed on the basis of the various texts, we learn what the calendar followed in Jerusalem at the end of the third century B.C.E. was: undoubtedly a lunar one. But there is more to it. Clearly, Ben Sira too modifies the concept expressed by Gen. 1:14–19: It is not the sun and moon together that serve as signs for the appointed times; rather it is the moon only. She conducts times, dominates period; she is an eternal sign; from her the festivals are derived. In my opinion, it becomes clear that Ben Sira is here polemizing against an adverse tendency we may define as proto-Essenian. This is not surprising, if one takes into account the 365 years assigned to Henoch in the canonical Genesis (5:23) or the remarks that state the length of the flood (7:11; 8:14) as one year and ten days, that is, exactly 364 days! Even without fully adhering to the hypothesis of A. Jaubert concerning the priestly calendar,[21] there is enough evidence in late biblical literature for the importance attributed to the solar calendar. The Essenian movement was thus already lurking in Judea by the third century B.C.E.

One other point of correspondence between the literature of the Essenes and that of the dominant Jewish groups in early Hellenistic times is the use of the terms "fathers" and "sons."

Jubilees 23.9–32 contains a sermon that is of the utmost importance for the history of the Essenian sect. Among other things, it says (v. 16) that

the sons shall convict their fathers and their elders of sin and unrighteousness, and of the words of their mouth and the great wickedness which they perpetrate.

Then in v. 26:

In those days the sons shall begin to study the laws, and to seek the commandments and to return to the path of righteousness.

By using these terms of "sons" against "fathers" the sect defines itself as a revolutionary group, albeit pretending only to restore the ancient order. The innovative character is also demonstrated by the idea, recurring quite often in Essenian writings, that old age brings about the loss of reason (*Jub.* 23.11). This concept does indeed appear in late layers of the Hebrew Bible, such as the speech of Elihu (Job 32:7–9), yet it is the Essenian sect that brings it to its extreme conclusions by ruling that no elderly people, beyond sixty, will be admitted to the sect's council (e.g., *Damascus Covenant* 10.7–10). This proves, in my opinion, that the quarrel of "sons against fathers" does not just mean one-time social anarchy but describes the essential character of Essenism at its inception: a breaking away from the tradition of the Jewish majority represented by the authority of the elders.[22]

It is worth noting that the older Jewish parties seem indeed to have used the term "fathers," *'abot,* to designate their spiritual leaders and authorities: Ben Sira, in his *šebaḥ 'abot 'olam* includes his contemporary, the Sadokite high priest Shimeon, son of Johanan; and exactly the same term occurs in rabbinic literature, defining a different kind of authority, that of the first "pairs" down to Hillel and Shammai.[23] A consistent use of the term "fathers" by two contrasting currents in the Hellenistic period—the Jerusalem establishment on the one hand and the proto-Essenians on the other—thus seems well established.

Yet, the real antipode to *Jubilees* 23 is to be found in Malachi 3:22–24:

> Observe the law of my servant Moses, whom I charged at Horeb with statutes and judgments for all Israel.
> Lo, I send you the prophet Elijah before the coming of the great and terrible day of the Lord.
> He will turn the heart of fathers to sons and that of sons to fathers, lest I come and smite the land, a ban!

Let us try to understand these verses in their cohesion.[24] The passage, distinct from the words of the prophet Malachi,[25] forms the conclusion of the prophetic canon. Indeed, v. 22 interprets the Prophets in the light of the Torah: their contents, both stories and speeches, have, according to this conclusion, one main idea: the observance of the Torah. This, indeed, was the order given to Joshua at the beginning of the corpus (Josh. 1:8);[26] this also is the interpretation of the prophetic message in the main editorial homily of the Deuteronomistic author (2 Kings 17:13).

Then, in v. 23 the coming of Elijah is announced. He is taken to be the selfsame messenger of the Lord whose coming Malachi proclaimed in 3:1: "Lo, I send my messenger." Yet the messenger of the Lord of hosts according to Mal. 2:7 is a priest. Therefore, the coming messenger announced by Malachi in 3:1 is described in the following verses (vv. 2–4) as an ideal priest about to purge the priesthood of Jerusalem.[27] It follows that the conclusion of the canon (Mal. 3:22–24), while substituting Elijah for the "messenger" of Mal. 3:1, already sees him as a priest.[28] This is a first step toward the identification of Elijah with Pinehas, current in Jewish legend.[29] Thus we may explain the logical relation between v. 22 and v. 23: if Elijah is the ideal future priest, his role will be to interpret the law, since interpreting the law is an essential attribute of the priests, also mentioned by Malachi.

> For the lips of the priest guard knowledge and men seek law at his mouth; for he is a messenger of the Lord of Hosts. (Mal. 2:7)

"Thus keep the law," says this author, "and if doubts arise about its interpretation, do not worry; shortly Elijah will come, the ideal priest, to give you the right teaching!"[30]

These doubts, however, were by no means trivial: they amounted to dissidence between "fathers" and "sons," between a traditional school and a reform movement. And while in *Jubilees* 23 it is reform speaking, here in Mal. 3:24 tradition answers.[31] As usual, traditionalists, the old school, speak in the name of unanimity and concord; indeed, concord is required here, in the wish voiced that hearts will turn one to the other. Elijah, the ideal priest, is coming to reestablish unity within Judaism. How necessary this mission is we are told in the concluding words: "Lest I come and smite the land, a ban!" Here obtains an interesting case of midrashic interpretation: the amplification of a ruling through analogy. In Deut. 13:13–19 the smiting of a whole population by ban was the punishment for an apostate city; now this measure will be applied by the Lord himself to all of Israel, not on account of idolatry, which has already disappeared, but because of the dissensions and schisms that threaten to rend the people of Israel.

When was this conclusion of the canon of the Prophets composed? One cannot tell exactly. But we can say that Ben Sira, around 200 B.C.E., already knew it, since he paraphrases it in Sir. 48:10. Taking into account the content of this portion of the canon, one may assume that the conclusion was written around 300 B.C.E., at the beginning of the Hellenistic era. And the sect of the "sons" is already existent, even quite numerous, if the author considers it a danger to the unity of the people.

The anticipation of the coming of Elijah in the conclusion is meaningful because of another aspect as well. The author of the concluding verses no longer expects the appearance of further prophets. This is why he sets his hopes on the return of a prophet of former generations who by his long-recognized authority will restore legal and religious unity within Israel.[32] This awareness of the failing of inspiration in Israel has indeed later been considered by two distinct sources—Josephus and the Midrash[33]—as the primary reason that books composed after the Persian period were not reckoned canonical. Thus, the announcement of the return of Elijah well befits the conclusion of a major portion of the canon. On the other hand, the cessation of inspiration ties in with the emergence of a new, revolutionary sect. When inspiration is denied, a major source of authority within a confession is dried up. The contesting of all accepted tradition is apt to follow.

NOTES

1. A critical survey of scholarship has been offered by J. Neusner in *The Rabbinic Traditions about the Pharisees before 70*, vol. 3 (Leiden, 1971), 320–68.

2. For the ensuing strife in Hasmonean times, see L. I. Levine, "The Political Struggle between Pharisees and Sadducees in the Hasmonean Period" (Hebrew), in *Jerusalem in the Second Temple Period: A. Schalit Memorial Volume* (Jerusalem, 1980), 61–83.

3. Translations from the Hebrew Bible here and below have been adapted from the NJPS.

4. N. Rabban ("Before the Lord" [Hebrew], *Tarbiz* 23 [1951–52]: 1–8) understands the expression in too narrow a sense: "by the ark."

5. Cf. *m. Sukk.* 4.9; *t. Sukk.* 3.16; *b. Sukk.* 48b. Here too belongs the law against the one who steals the cup (of libation): *m. Sanh.* 9.6. See also the story, reported by Josephus, of how the people revolted in the temple against Alexander Jannaeus while he was officiating at the feast of Sukkot (*Ant.* 13.372).

6. The Pharisaic beliefs are also expressed in *m. Roš. Haš.* 1.2; *t. Roš. Haš.* 1.12; *b. Roš. Haš.* 16a. Their magic-sympathetic character has often been noted. See, e.g., R. Patai, *The Water* (Hebrew; Tel Aviv, 1936), 48–63.

7. See H. St. J. Thackeray, *A Grammar of the Old Testament in Greek*, vol. 1 (Cambridge, 1909), viii–x.

8. An analogous case, of a sectarian correction in the text of Isaiah, was discussed by I. L. Seeligmann in "Δεῖξαι αὐτῷ ψῶs" (Hebrew with English abstract), *Tarbiz* 27 (1957–58): 127–41.

9. A. Geiger, *Urschrift und Übersetzungen der Bibel* (Breslau, 1857), 56.

10. I have tried to substantiate this translation in my "Isaiah 66:1–4: Judean Sects in the Persian Period as Viewed by Trito-Isaiah," in *Biblical and Related Studies Presented to Samuel Iwry*, ed. A. Kort and S. Morschauser (Winona Lake, Ind.: Eisenbrauns, 1985), 205–17.

11. A. Kuenen, not B. Duhm, was the first to recognize that the last portion of Isaiah did not originate with Deutero-Isaiah; see A. Kuenen, *Historisch-critisch onderzoek van de boeken des Ouden Verbonds*, 2d ed., vol. 2 (1886; Amsterdam, n.d.), 134–50; German trans: *Historisch-Kritische Einleitung in die Bücher des Alten Testaments*, part 2, *Die Prophetischen Bücher* (Leipzig, 1892), 128–44. Biblical criticism has oddly neglected this great Dutch scholar. Yet I nurture no doubt that the prophecy of Trito-Isaiah does not begin with Isaiah 56, as maintained by Duhm, but with Isaiah 54.

12. The presence of the same terms in several late psalms may fit in with the picture drawn here of this incipient movement.

13. On this topic, see the chap. dedicated to Nehemiah in M. Smith's *Palestinian Parties and Politics That Shaped the Old Testament* (New York: Columbia Univ. Press, 1971).

14. See H. D. Mantel, "The Sadducees and the Pharisees," in *Society and Reli-*

gion in the Second Temple Period, ed. M. Avi-Yonah and Z. Baras, World History of the Jewish People 3 (Jerusalem, 1977), 99–123, 346–51.

15. See V. Aptowitzer, *Parteipolitik der Hasmonäerzeit im rabbinischen und pseudoepigraphischen Schrifttum* (Vienna, 1927), xxii–xxv; O. Holtzmann, "Der Prophet Maleachi und der Ursprung des Pharisäerbundes," *Archiv für Religionswissenschaft* 29 (1931): 1–21; L. Finkelstein, *Ha-Perushim ve-Anshe Keneset Ha-Gedolah* (with English summary; New York, 1950); and Mantel, "Sadducees and the Pharisees." S. Zeitlin ("The Pharisees: A Historical Study," *Jewish Quarterly Review* n.s. 52 [1961]: 97–120) pushed the origin of the two parties back to the 6th cent., the Pharisees originally being the followers of Zerubabel, the Sadducees of the high priest. In my opinion, however, this view is not well founded.

16. See S. Shaked, "Qumran and Iran: Further Considerations," *Israel Oriental Studies* 2 (1972): 433–46; and R. N. Frye, "Qumran and Iran: The State of Studies," in *Studies for Morton Smith at Sixty,* ed. J. Neusner, part 3 (Leiden, 1975), 167–73.

17. Translations from apocryphal books have been adapted from *Apocrypha and Pseudepigrapha of the Old Testament,* ed. R. H. Charles, 2 vols. (London: Oxford Univ. Press, 1913).

18. Thanks are due to Professor Abraham Wasserstein (Jerusalem), who kindly advised me on this matter.

19. S. Talmon, "The Calendar Reckoning of the Sect from the Judean Desert," in *Scripta Hierosolymitana,* vol. 4, *Aspects of the Dead Sea Scrolls,* 2d ed. (Jerusalem, 1965), 162–99.

20. Y. Yadin, *The Ben Sira Scroll from Masada* (Jerusalem, 1965).

21. A. Jaubert, "Le calendrier des Jubilés et la secte de Qumran: Ses origines bibliques," *Vetus Testamentum* 3 (1953): 250–64.

22. That the denial of the authority of the elders is revolutionary in character has been pointed out to me by Professor Yehoshua Arieli (Jerusalem). Dr. Alessandro Catastini (Leghorn, Italy) called my attention to the polemic of "youngsters" against "elders" as the hallmark of the LXX recension of Susanna. L. H. Schiffman ("Purity and Perfection: Exclusion from the Council of the Community in the *Serekh Ha-'edah,*" in *Biblical Archaeology Today* [Jerusalem, 1985], 373–89) seems to have unduly minimized the difference between the Pharisaic and Qumranic attitudes toward the authority of elderly people.

23. See H. Albeck, *Commentary on the Mishnah: Seder Neziqin* (Hebrew; Jerusalem and Tel Aviv, 1953), 348–49; and the references in *m. 'Ed.* 1.4; *b. B. Qam.* 30a; *y. Hag.* 2.2. In *t. Ṭ. Yom* 1.10 the term *'abot hari'šonim* is applied to later *tanna'im.*

24. The unity of the passage is indeed denied by K. Elliger (*Das Buch der zwölf kleinen Propheten,* vol. 2, 5th ed., Das Alte Testament Deutsch [Göttingen, 1964]) and W. Rudolph (*Haggai . . . Maleachi,* Kommentar zum Alten Testament [Gütersloh, 1976], a.l.).

25. Cf. the arguments of J. M. P. Smith in *Commentary on the Book of Malachi,* International Critical Commentary (Edinburgh, 1912), a.l.

26. Cf. Rudolph, *Haggai . . . Maleachi,* in the nn. to Mal. 3:22.

27. I cannot subscribe to the sharp critical analysis of A.S. van der Woude in "Der Engel des Bundes, Bemerkungen zu Maleachi 3, 1c und seinem Kontext," in

Die Botschaft und die Boten: Festschrift für H. W. Wolff (Neukirchen-Vluyn, 1981), 289–300.

28. That the messenger of the Lord in Mal. 3:1–5 is a priest has already been noted by B. V. Malchow in "The Messenger of the Covenant in Mal. 3:1," *Journal of Biblical Literature* 103 (1984): 252–55. As for the priestly extraction of Elijah it is already taken for granted in *b. B. Meṣ* 114a–b.

29. This equation, based on their common role as zealots of the Lord, is mentioned in *Tg. Ps.-J.* to Exod. 6:18; Num. 25:12; Deut. 30:4. Sir. 48:10 paraphrases Num. 25:4 in his praise of Elijah. Plausibly he was already acquainted with the midrashic identification of the two fighters against Baal.

30. Aliter B. de Vries, "The Prophet Elijah in Biblical Eschatology" (Hebrew), *A. Biram Volume* (Jerusalem, 1956), 82–86. In de Vries's opinion, the sending of Elijah, the messenger of the Lord, follows the pattern set by Exod. 23:20-33.

31. The correspondence between *Jub.* 23.9–32 and Mal. 3:24 has already been noted by E. Sellin in *Das Zwölfprophetenbuch, übersetzt und erklärt,* 2d and 3d eds., Kommentar zum Alten Testament (Leipzig, 1930), 618.

32. Cf. A. B. Ehrlich, *Randglossen zur hebräischen Bibel,* vol. 5 (1912; Hildesheim, 1968), 363.

33. Josephus *Contra Appionem* 1.7–8; *Midr. S. 'Olam Rab.* 30.

4

Bandits in Galilee:
A Contribution to the
Study of Social Conditions
in First-Century Palestine

SEÁN FREYNE
Trinity College, Dublin

Scholarly opinion has been less than enthusiastic in its response to S. F. G. Brandon's thesis about the revolutionary nature of the ministry of Jesus of Nazareth.[1] Nevertheless, it is quite surprising to find how frequently even those who are utterly opposed to Brandon's reconstruction assume that one of the presuppositions on which his case is argued, namely, that first-century Galilee was the seedbed of Jewish revolutionary ideas, is an accurate assessment of the social conditions there. Thus Martin Hengel in his major reconstruction of the Jewish revolutionary movement practically equiparates Galileans and revolutionaries.[2] J. H. Yoder, whose portrait of Jesus is the very antithesis of Brandon's, sees the pacifist Jesus opting for this radically different alternative against the backdrop of violent revolution as a very acceptable alternative.[3] Others too speak of a revolutionary Galilee, as though the matter were settled definitively, yet no hard data are produced to substantiate the position.[4]

Recent archaeological work has underlined the need to distinguish various subregions of Galilee, based on the evidence of the material remains of the Roman period.[5] Such divisions are presupposed in Jewish sources also on the basis of climatic (*m. Šeb.* 9.2) or geophysical differences (Josephus *War* 3.35–43). The need for such precision is all the more urgent, it would seem, when one attempts to assess the social conditions that existed in first-century Palestine at the same time. Again without going into any detail, the literary sources—Tannaitic literature, Josephus, the New Testament—make it quite clear that various differences between Galileans and Judeans prevailed in the period. In discussing the revolutionary situation of Galilee, therefore, our first task is to sketch briefly the prior history of the province, both political and religious, paying special attention to those factors that might suggest a rather different social ethos there from that of Judea.

The need for such attention to regionalism as a factor in discussing first-century C.E. Palestinian revolutionary ideas is called for in the light of some recent articles by Richard A. Horsley which focus on banditry as a social phenomenon, thereby opening up a new perspective on Jewish nationalist aspirations in the period.[6] If banditry is not just a breakdown of law and order but an act of social protest, attention must be given to the circumstances in which such factors occur if our assessment of the available data is to be accurate and well founded. This approach of Horsley has the advantage of drawing attention to a very specific social matrix within which a revolutionary ideology could ferment and receive concrete expression. It must be seen as a major advance on general statements about apocalyptic moods of a purely theological nature giving rise to Zealot-type revolts, with little or no concern being given to the social situation within which such millennial attitudes emerge.

Although the use of social-scientific theory can undoubtedly aid our reading of ancient texts by posing new and more realistic questions, there is still need for great sensitivity in applying developed models to highly complex situations about which we are only partially informed. It would be ironic if, having dismantled one construct, the Zealots, we were to replace it by another, that of social banditry. In fairness to Horsley, his work, appearing in a number of carefully documented articles, does clearly differentiate between prophetic liberation movements, messianic-style movements, and banditry, in first-century Palestine. The following discussion, therefore, is offered not as a criticism of his overall project but rather as a refinement of his conclusions based on my own studies of the Galilean social world. I hope it will serve as a fitting tribute to Howard Clark Kee, whose pioneering work in the application of social theory to early Christianity has always been conscious of the need to test theory against the actual data we possess from any given situation.

GALILEAN AND JUDEAN EXPERIENCE: SOME CONTRASTS

Judea's history in the Persian and early Hellenistic periods was largely determined by a concern to establish political and religious identity over against its Samaritan neighbors, and we need not here enter into the details of this difficult time.[7] What is important for our purposes is that the struggles of the period played a very real, if sometimes neglected, part in shaping Jewish attitudes for the subsequent encounter with Hellenism. By contrast to the newly established temple state, Galilee was and remained part of the Persian province of Samaria (see 1 Macc. 10:30), having been initially included in the Assyrian province of Megiddo after the first deportation of 731 B.C.E. (see 2 Kings 15:29).[8]

What is remarkable about this long history of administrative isolation is that it does not seem to have succeeded in disrupting Galilean loyalty to Jerusalem as the proper cultic center, even when syncretistic, if not downright pagan, influences were at work in its immediate environment. Unfortunately, scanty information makes it impossible to substantiate this claim in detail, yet as A. Alt has convincingly argued, it is by far the most plausible explanation of the few pieces of information at our disposal for the Persian period[9] and best explains subsequent loyalties as they emerge two centuries later at the time of the Hellenistic reform (see 1 Macc. 5:13, 21–23). It is possible to speculate on the reasons for this attachment: the northern provenience of the Deuteronomic reform; possible migrations to the north in the wake of the first Babylonian deportations; the presence of an old Israelite peasant stock that was undisturbed through the centuries, whose interest in Jerusalem may paradoxically have been developed as a result of its own fortunes under the Assyrians. Whatever the complex pattern of relationships may have been, it is sufficient for our present purposes to note that the new cult center on Mount Gerizim neither at its inception nor subsequently was able to attract Galilean support even though administratively it was part of the larger province for which the new shrine might have been expected to serve as the natural religious focal point.

Emil Schürer's influence as a historian of Judaism can be seen in the almost universally accepted view of the Hasmonean conquests of the north as the re-Judaization of Galilee, thereby ignoring the older attachments suggested in the previous paragraph.[10] When the evidence for this understanding of the situation is examined, it can be seen to be tenuous indeed. The reference to "Galilee of the Gentiles" at 1 Macc. 5:15 should be seen as part of the archaizing tone of this work, based on Isa. 8:23, rather than as an ethnographic description of the province as a whole, since the geographic indications of the episode make clear that it was localized in the neighborhood of the gentile cities of the coastal plain. Subsequently Josephus's account of the northern campaigns of Aristobulus and Alexander Janneus (*Ant.* 13.104, 322; *War* 1.76) is lacking in any detailed information about the Galilean hinterland beyond the attacks on Samaria and Scythopolis and their territories. Josephus must rely on Strabo's citation of Timagenes—not the most reliable of sources for Palestinian affairs or topography—concerning the defeat and forced circumcision of the Itureans (*Ant.* 13:318–19). But this can hardly be construed as the Judaization of the whole of pagan Galilee, given the nature of the Itureans' advance and the likely extent of their penetration into Upper Galilee.[11]

This is not to suggest that Hellenism had made no inroads into Galilee either as a cultural force or as an economic power in the 150-odd years between Alexander's conquests and the attempted reform of the Jewish religion by Antiochus Epiphanes. The Zenon papyri testify that even the heart of Galilee was not immune to such influences, irrespective of where precisely we locate Beth Anath.[12] What is debatable, however, is the impact such economic developments and technical skills were likely to have had on the old indigenous population's patterns of beliefs, given the overall policies of the Ptolemaic overlords when dealing with the peasants in Egypt and the outcome of interaction between Greek and Semite at the lower levels of the social stratum, even in more sophisticated urban environments of the East.[13]

Galilee, then, entered the new Hasmonean state freely, one might say enthusiastically, in view of the older cultic loyalties that were now enshrined in the administrative divisions of the restored kingdom. Yet this new situation was to give rise to new tensions, as a native landowning aristocracy emerged who were now the social oppressors, though ostensibly at least sharing a common faith with the peasants struggling to retain some meager links with the land.[14] This situation may help to explain the apparently anomalous reactions within the province when, on the one hand, the last of the Hasmoneans appears to have had considerable support there in his struggles to regain the kingdom, yet on the other, we repeatedly hear from Josephus that "all Galilee" was now on the side of Herod. Since this confrontation has a direct bearing on the question of brigandage in Galilee, we shall defer a detailed discussion of the evidence until the next section, but it is not without significance to note here that shortly before the arrival of the young Herod as *stratēgos* of Galilee, an aristocratic form of government had been established at Sepphoris as part of Gabinius's carve-up of the Jewish state (*Ant.* 14.91; *War* 1.170). Apparently even the Romans could not ignore the social realities that had emerged within the province, yet they considered that the native aristocracy should be trusted with the management of affairs without any reference to Jerusalem or its cultic significance.

After Herod's initial struggle for his kingship, Galilee recedes from the picture, though we do hear of the planting of Babylonian Jews in neighboring Trachonitis as a means of dealing with the wholesale banditry that was present in the region of the deposed Iturean chieftain Zenodorus (*Ant.* 15.342–43, 360–61; 17.24–25). This alone might suggest that Galilee was relatively peaceful during his reign, and the fact that we hear of new disturbances at Sepphoris after his death does not necessarily mean that throughout his reign the province as a whole was seething beneath the surface with nationalistic fervor, seeing that there were similar disturbances elsewhere throughout the kingdom (*Ant.* 17.269–85; *War* 2.55–65). The long and relatively peaceful reign of Antipas in Galilee was to shield the province from Roman procuratorial rule for almost half a century, and even though the worst excesses came later, it is natural to suppose that the polarization of attitudes toward Rome had already taken place in Judea at a much earlier stage than in the northern province. Too much should not be made of the apparent absence of any protest similar to that mounted by Judas the Galilean in Judea on the occasion of the census there in 6 C.E. when at last Galilee was incorporated into the Roman provincial system upon the death of Agrippa I in 44 C.E. Apparently some special administrative arrangement was made, if Tacitus's rather garbled statement about Galilee's being in the charge of Cumanus and Samaria under Felix has any element of truth in it (*Ann.* 12.54).[15] Yet at most this can only have been a temporary arrangement, since at the outbreak of the great revolt in 66 C.E. the strongly Romanophile Sepphoris had to appeal to the governor of Syria repeatedly for help, which was forthcoming only after considerable delay (*Life* 30.346, 373, 394), and as governor appointed by the provisional government, Josephus did not encounter any problems from a Roman presence within the province.[16]

By way of conclusion to this brief sketch of Galilean history we may point to some contrasts with the Judean situation which would seem to have relevance for a discussion of social banditry as a religious phenomenon in our next section. For one thing, no appeal can be made to the fanaticism of new converts to Judaism as a way of documenting allegedly radical religious attitudes in Galilee. If anything, it was in Judea in close proximity to the temple that the more rigorous adherents of Jewish faith were to be found, since it was there that the *beney geholāh* had made their home after the return from Babylon. Neither can the possible radicalization of Jewish faith in the wake of the persecutions of Antiochus Epiphanes be seen to have the same force in Galilee as in Judea, since it was to Jerusalem itself and its immediate environs that the brunt of the Syrian offensive was likely to have been directed. Certainly there were social tensions in Galilee between rich and poor (i.e., landowners and tenants, etc.) and between city and country, but there seems no reason for suggesting that these were any more acute there than elsewhere, and there is considerable likelihood that in fact they were less pressing. At least the glimpses we get of Galilean social life in the reign of Antipas, even from the Gospels, or later from Josephus's *Life,* do not suggest a peasantry totally disaffected and ready for the millennial holy war that would overthrow the agents of repression and exploitation.[17] This is not to suggest an idyllic picture of harmonious relations, but the attitudes of the peasant farmers of the Gischala region who were less than enthusiastic for the confrontation with Rome because of the arrival of the harvest (*War* 4.84), may not be altogether untypical of the general scene. Josephus intimates that the period of the later procurators saw a widespread increase of banditry, and certainly there seems every reason to suspect that there was a strong social and religious component to this phenomenon, given the corruption and venality of the procurators and the disregard for Jewish religious sensibilities.[18] Yet even in these circumstances it is striking how frequently such outbursts took place in Judea rather than Galilee, climaxing in the "invasion" of Jerusalem by bandits (*sicarii*) from the country who made common cause with the rebellious lesser clergy of the temple (*War* 2.425–29).[19]

BANDITRY IN GALILEE

The period from Herod's rise to power up to the first revolt against Rome, 48 B.C.E.–66 C.E., will be our special focus in discussing banditry in the Galilean context. Other material from the Gospels and later rabbinic sources could be introduced, but for different reasons this information is, to say the least, problematical. Consequently, we shall content ourselves with developing a profile from Josephus, paying special attention to those points at which banditry is clearly in evidence. It is from those expressions that we can hope to see more clearly how banditry fits the pattern of social relations within the province, and we can safely extrapolate from these details to the wider picture.

Herod and the Galilean Bandits

The first occurrence of banditry in Galilee mentioned in our sources concerns the *archilēstēs* Hezekiah whom the young Herod pursued and executed without consulting the Jerusalem Sanhedrin (*War* 1.204–15; *Ant.* 14.158–70). At first sight, this figure appears to be a classic example of social banditry, since it is explicitly stated that the people of Syria were overjoyed at his removal and hailed Herod as a peacemaker and liberator (*War* 1.205; *Ant.* 14.160). One of the characteristics of the social bandit, according to Horsley, is that his activity is never directed against his own people who support and protect him.[20] Does Hezekiah really fit this role?

In assessing the range and significance of Hezekiah's influence in Galilee, perhaps the reaction at his death is the clearest indication. One might reasonably expect there to have been an outcry in Galilee had his activity had the popular support and backing that a social brigand could rightly expect from his own people. Yet even though Josephus's accounts of the episode have considerable differences at this point, they concur that Jerusalem was the place where the outcry took place.[21] Thus in *Antiquities* we hear that *hoi en telei tōn Ioydaiōn* were disturbed at the rise of Antipater and his sons to power, one example of which was Herod's action in Galilee and the reputation both he and Phasael were acquiring (*Ant.* 14.163). A little later we read that *hoi prōtoi tōn Ioydaiōn* incited Hyrcanus to take some action against Herod for his highhanded behavior (*Ant.* 14.165ff.). The only possible suggestion of a Galilean reaction in this account is the statement that before coming to Jerusalem to answer the charges against him, Herod "settled the affairs in Galilee as he thought was to his best interest" (*Ant.* 14.169). This general statement, however, can hardly be construed to mean that Herod had to deal with a wide-scale popular uprising but rather must mean that he made arrangements for his own safe withdrawal to the province, should the trial in Jerusalem not work out to his advantage. This interpretation is confirmed by the more explicit statement of *War* 1.210 that Herod went up to Jerusalem with a strong military escort after first posting garrisons in Galilee. Furthermore, the *Antiquities* account mentions the mothers of the murdered men going to the temple to arouse the ire of the king and the people against Herod. Even when this episode is interpreted to mean that the women were Galileans who made the pilgrimage for this specific purpose, as Horsley believes, it is still highly significant that the account presupposes the absence of any spontaneous burst of outrage against Herod within the province. Nor is there the slightest hint elsewhere in Josephus's narrative that "the people regarded the brigands as honourable men" or that "they were on good terms with the people in Galilee."[22]

Who then were Hezekiah and his followers, and what was their social position in Galilee? Earlier we spoke of the Hasmonean nobility that emerged within the province in the wake of the conquests of the north, and of the fact that a real social gap existed between them as the new landowners, replacing their Seleucid counterparts, and the peasants, which the sharing of a common faith could not altogether bridge.[23] It is sometimes assumed that the population as a whole was pro-Hasmonean because Galilee was later the center for Antigonus, the representative of the ousted Hasmoneans and their Parthian allies when Herod sought to establish himself as king. This judgment needs to be carefully weighed, however, against the social background just mentioned. There certainly was some Hasmonean support there, but the strong impression one gets is that it was localized in the region of Sepphoris. At least that was the situation a decade after the Hezekiah affair, as we shall presently see. Furthermore, it should be noted that Hezekiah's attacks were directed against the Syrians, and this fact must also be assessed when judging the nature of his actions. Were he a social bandit attempting to right the wrongs inflicted on the Galilean peasantry, one could have expected his activity to be directed against the more immediate social oppressors within the province, namely, the Hasmonean aristocratic landowners, whose support Gabinius was prepared to draw on when establishing his temporary council at Sepphoris.

The explanation for the attacks on the Syrians may come from the decrees of Caesar, which Josephus has recorded and which reflect certain developments that had been taking place in the north since Pompey's takeover and the subsequent carve-up of the Jewish territory by Gabinius. Caesar decreed that "Hyrcanus [whom he restored as ethnarch of the whole Jewish territory] and his children should rule over the Jewish nation and enjoy the fruits of the places given them" (*Ant.* 14.196), and a *senatus consultum* confirming this decree is more specific: "The places, lands and farms, the fruits of which the Kings of Syria and Phoenicia, as allies of the Romans, were permitted to enjoy by their gift, these the senate decrees that the ethnarch Hyrcanus shall have" (*Ant.* 14.205). Furthermore, provision was to be made for the publication of these decrees in the various cities, with explicit mention of Tyre and Sidon (*Ant.* 14.195–97). Clearly these decrees presuppose encroachment by Syrian and Phoenician local rulers on what could legally be described as Jewish territory, and obviously some large estates had been taken over, presumably along the border area and in Upper Galilee. These encroachments and their legitimation by the Romans, which Caesar was now repudiating, probably took place after the battle of Tarichaeae (significantly in Galilee) sometime after 53 B.C.E. The defeat of the triumvir Crassus by the Parthians at Carrhae was the signal for Peitholaus, a Jerusalem Hasmonean, to attempt to restore Aristobulus, but he was defeated by the governor of Syria, Cassius Longinus, with disastrous results, thirty thousand men reputedly being sold into slavery (*Ant.* 14.119–20; *War* 1.180). This episode, barely recorded by Josephus, must have had serious social repercussions especially among the Galilean Hasmonean nobility, and it is to their ranks that we must assign Hezekiah, whose acts of banditry were therefore not performed in favor of the Galilean peasantry but were reprisals for the loss of his own possessions and presumably those of other nobles also. Against this conclusion it might be objected that the Galilean mothers would scarcely have appealed to Hyrcanus had Hezekiah and his followers been supporters of Aristobulus.[24] But it should be remembered that it was influential Jerusalem Jews who were the most vocal against Herod, no doubt because they saw in Hezekiah's fate a threat to their own position, even as supporters of Hyrcanus. The purge of the Hasmonean nobles after he had established himself as king (*Ant.* 15.5–6) clearly demonstrates that they had every right to be fearful.

Subsequent events in Galilee would seem to confirm this reading of the Hezekiah episode. We again hear of bandits in the province on the occasion of Herod's struggles against Antigonus from 39 to 37 B.C.E., and of Herod's repeated efforts to oust them. In the ten years since Herod's first encounter with the brigands, an Herodian aristocracy had in all probability begun to replace the Hasmonean one, and this explains the continuing tensions within the province. We repeatedly hear, on the one hand, that "all Galilee

57

except for a few inhabitants" were on his side, or statements of similar import (*Ant.* 14.395, 417, 430; *War* 1.291, 307, 315), only to be subsequently informed, on the other, that the brigands in the caves of Arbela had not been ousted (*Ant.* 14.133; *War* 1.316) or that his supporters had been thrown into the lake (*Ant.* 14.452–53; *War* 1.330). Horsley has attempted to distinguish two quite separate groups in these reports—the rebel garrisons of Antigonus and the bandits who engaged in social brigandage—because the former are never designated by the latter term by Josephus (*Ant.* 14.431ff./*War* 1.314ff.; *Ant.* 14.450/*War* 1.326).[25] But apart from the fact that such passages as *Ant.* 14.413–16/*War* 1.304ff. presuppose a full-scale military operation by Herod against the men in the caves who opposed his army, "combining the experience of seasoned warriors with the daring of the brigands," there is an inherent improbability in the distinction. Surely, with the outcome of the overall struggle still uncertain, Herod would not have spent so much energy in attempting to oust the brigands if he did not see in them very real enemies and a serious threat to his cause. Indeed, Josephus explicitly says that Antigonus's garrison had fled from Sepphoris (*Ant.* 14.414; *War* 1.304), and the caves of Arbela, where the terrain was difficult, were suited to guerrilla-style activity against the Herodians who had taken over their lands in Lower Galilee. Furthermore, the fact that Josephus tells the story of the old man who resisted Herod with a Maccabean-style act of defiance shows that for him at least, the "brigands" were upholders of an older tradition that was being threatened by Herod and his class.[26]

Our argument has been that the brigands who appear in Galilee at the beginning of Herod's reign do not fit the category of social bandits, at least as described by Horsley. Their activity is not directed toward vindicating the oppressed peasantry but is motivated rather by animosity toward those who were about to usurp their social position as large landowners within the province. This conclusion would appear to receive interesting confirmation from the revolt of Judas, son of Hezekiah, at Sepphoris after Herod's death in 4 B.C.E. If, as seems likely, his revolt was an attempt to restore the Hasmonean kingship,[27] we have a clue to the background of his father also and Herod's opposition to him. It is significant that the *Antiquities* account says that having armed his followers, he engaged in plundering, that is, in adopting similar tactics to those of his father and others of their ilk opposed to the Herodian aristocracy that had replaced them within the province (17.271–72, 288). Their banditry can be described as social in that it represents the last efforts of a dying social class to regain its former position of wealth and status within Palestinian life. But this does not mean that they were representative of or supported by the peasantry whose social oppressors they once had been.

Banditry in Galilee prior to the First Revolt

We have already mentioned the increase of banditry in Palestine during the second period of procuratorial rule, that is, from 44 to 66 C.E., climaxing in the open revolt against Rome in 66, when the country bandits from Judea joined forces with the city rebels. On one occasion, at least, during the procuratorship of Cumanus (i.e., 48–52 C.E.) Galileans were directly involved because of a border incident with the Samaritans, which led to a wholesale confrontation between Jews gathered in Jerusalem for the festival and the Samaritans (*Ant.* 20.118–37; *War* 2.232–46). A brigand leader, Eleazar, the son of Deineus, was summoned to the aid of the Jews, and he and his followers pillaged Samaritan villages before returning to their strongholds (*echuroi topoi*) after appeals of the Jerusalem religious and aristocratic leaders for peace had prevailed. It is not stated that Eleazar was a Galilean, but the fact that he operated in the border region—probably along the Via Maris that went through the Great Plain—and was prepared to vindicate the rights of Galileans suggests the possibility of social banditry in Galilee at this point at least, if not earlier. The figure and tactics of John of Gischala from the revolt period might also appear to support such a suggestion, despite Josephus's well-known desire to vilify him,[28] for it may not be just coincidence that his arrival in Jerusalem after the failure of the Galilean campaign led to an alarming increase of banditry in the city (*War* 4.121–37). Fortunately, we are in a position to assess the extent and nature of Galilean banditry for the period with more precision from Josephus's *Life,* which gives a first hand account of Galilean conditions in the immediate pre-66 period.

Instead of discussing the social roles of characters such as John of Gischala or Jesus son of Sapphias, who are never directly called bandits in *Life,* we shall examine those passages where bandits are explicitly mentioned within the Galilean context: *Life* 77–78 (Josephus makes a deal with the bandits); *Life* 105–11 (Jesus, the brigand chief from the borders of Ptolemais, aids Sepphoris against Josephus); *Life* 126–31, 145–46 (the highwaymen of Dabaritta, later called bandits, stir up resentment against Josephus as a traitor); *Life* 175 (Josephus must hide his true feelings about the Roman power because of the bandits); *Life* 206 (the Galileans fear they will be prey to the bandits should Josephus resign his office). Even a cursory glance at this list shows that banditry would now seem to have taken on political and social overtones in Galilee also, and we must attempt to evaluate its significance and extent, allowing for Josephan apologetic concerns. Before drawing any conclusions, however, it is necessary to look at each passage in more detail, taking account also of the parallels in *War,* when such exist.[29]

At *Life* 77–78 Josephus is detailing the measures that he took to pacify Galilee in relation to his stated intention of preparing for war with Rome while adopting wait-and-see tactics (*Life* 29). Josephus does not consider that he can disarm the bandits. Clearly they have considerable resources, and in view of the overall context of the passage—Gischala and John's independent behavior—it may be safely presumed that they operated on the borders between Upper Galilee and Tyre, a no-go region that was in perpetual turmoil (cf. *War* 4.105–6). The fact that John, Josephus's deadly opponent in both accounts, had acquired a mercenary army for himself in this region (*Life* 371; *War* 2.588, 4.84, 86) may explain Josephus's attempt to "buy off" these particular brigands at the expense of the Galilean populace, having convinced the latter that they would otherwise suffer from their pillaging. Josephus certainly had a mercenary army of his own subsequently also (*Life* 159; *War* 2.583–84),[30] quite independently of his Galilean militia, which was occasionally summoned to his support, though the suggestion is that his mercenaries were non-Jewish, at least in part. Later (*Life* 206–7), we hear that should Josephus abandon his charge in Galilee, the natives feared that they would suffer from the pillaging of the bandits. This particular statement has all the appearance of apologetic self-defense, coming as it does in a context where he relates his "supernatural" dream as the reason for staying on to confront the Romans (*Life* 208–9). Accordingly, it would be unfair to conclude that these Galilean bandits were actually harassing the local country people, something that would have excluded them from the role of social bandits in Horsley's terms. Nevertheless, the fact that they could support *either* Josephus *or* John as mercenaries scarcely justifies viewing them as a form of pre–political rebellion, possibly even sharing some apocalyptic ideas. Their leverage came from the need for aspirants for control of Galilee to have a strong military force, and they were able to play off the various aspirants to power, especially the Jerusalemite Josephus and the native John.

The next mention of bandits in Galilee would seem to confirm this suggestion. We hear of the brigand leader Jesus from the borders of Ptolemais being hired by the people of Sepphoris to do away with Josephus (*Life* 104, 111). The conclusion of the story fits with one of the overall themes of *Life*—Josephus's moderation and restraint in dealing with Galilean affairs—even when it seems to run counter to another motif of the work, namely, his desire to pacify the situation. In this regard one does not expect to hear that he would allow Jesus to reassemble his former force, and one could easily infer that either Josephus was able to do very little about the bandit situation or in reality he wished to obtain further support for himself. At all events the episode is instructive of the bandits' attitudes. The fact that they were prepared to support Sepphoris, an avowedly Roman town and consequently hated by the Galileans at large, shows the fickleness of their motives and the lack of any genuine concern for Galilean causes, social or religious. Equally significant is the fact that once again they changed sides so readily.[31]

The third important instance of banditry recorded in *Life* has at first sight more promise for Horsley's thesis. Some young men from the border post of Dabaritta waylaid the wife of Ptolemy, Herod's overseer, as she traveled with a large retinue along the Great Plain, and they brought their spoils to Josephus at Tarichaeae. We can see much more clearly here the pattern of social banditry, since presumably the lady was seen as a symbol of both Roman oppression and aristocratic domination, issues that were calculated to arouse the wrath of the socially oppressed within the province. It comes as no surprise then to hear that the affair was further exploited by those elements which saw in Josephus a moderate who was not prepared to employ the possibilities for revolt to the full. Thus we meet Jesus son of Sapphias, from Tiberias, at Tarichaeae espousing the religious ideals he had previously propagated in his native city on the occasion of the destruction of Herod's palace (*Life* 134–35, 66–67). And even when Josephus succeeded in allaying the fears that he was a traitor, further disturbances were instigated by a combination of the brigands and those who had promoted revolution (*stasis, Life* 145). This combination seems to have surfaced at Tiberias in particular, possibly due to the fact that Jesus was from the destitute classes (*Life* 35, 66) and so may have shared common social roots with the country brigands. It is significant that we hear that some (*tines*) Galileans joined in the sack of Herod's palace with him. Even though Josephus would have liked to brand Justus a revolutionary also, he later recognized that despite their mutual animosities, neither he nor Justus had anything in common with the brigands or their associates. At the same time he admitted that these latter played a significant role in Galilean life at that juncture, and that caution was called for in dealing with them (*Life* 175).

This survey of banditry in Galilee on the eve of the great revolt would seem to call for caution in judging its social significance in view of the different manifestations we have examined. Insofar as the bandits engage directly in the struggle against Rome, they certainly do not take the initiative in marshaling the population at large for revolt. Rather they are prepared to be "used" by the various individuals striving for control of the Galilean situation: the Jerusalem aristocrat Josephus, the native entrepreneur John of Gischala, and perhaps the only genuine Zealot leader in the province, Jesus son of Sapphias. Their willingness to function as mercenaries, thereby creating further difficulties in terms of support and pay for their own people, must also be evaluated in any discussion of their social role and motivation. Finally, the fact that Jesus, the brigand leader from the borders of the Ptolemais district, was prepared to support the Sepphorites against Josephus no matter how halfhearted Josephus was in preparing for the revolt shows that not every manifestation of banditry can be judged social banditry, even when the province as a whole was supposedly in the throes of the great struggle with Rome.

SOCIAL BANDITRY AND
SOCIAL CONDITIONS

Our examination of the explicit references to banditry in Galilee over a period of more than a hundred years has not revealed the consistent sort of picture we might have expected if the social situation there was such as is presumed by those who consider the province to have been the seedbed of Jewish revolutionary ideas based on social oppression throughout the period. By way of substantiating this view we shall apply the criteria for social banditry that have been suggested by Horsley to both the Galilean and Judean situations, judging the extent to which these are verified in each province. Clearly we can only here suggest the broad outlines that such an inquiry might take, and we shall confine ourselves to the immediate pre-revolt period. Then, if ever, the endemic situation in such area should come clearly into focus as the nation prepared itself for the confrontation with Rome.

The first condition is a state of economic depression and social unrest due to repressive measures of an alien regime which are perceived as unjust and intolerable. It would be difficult to find an area of the ancient world where this criterion did not apply in some measure, yet Horsley and others have rightly stressed the fact that Palestine was a particularly glaring example of such conditions in the period of the early empire.[32] Clearly many people lived on the borderline between penury and banditry, a fact graphically illustrated by the concern that the Jewish authorities showed on the occasion of the affair over Caligula's statue: the agricultural strike that developed throughout the country meant that the demands of the Roman tribute could not be met, and this would give rise to a wholesale banditry (*Ant.* 18.272–74).[33] Though it is a matter of degree, Galilee seems to have fared better than Judea in this regard. Perhaps the incident of the burning of the official records of debts (*archaiai*) in Jerusalem is as good an indicator as any of this contrasting situation. One of the first acts of the country Judean bandits on entering Jerusalem was to destroy any official record of debts, thereby setting the rich against the poor (*War* 2.247–48). Galilee too had such banking records, lately transferred from Tiberias to Sepphoris, to the economic advantage of Sepphoris (*Life* 38). Yet, strangely, we never hear of any attack similar to that in Jerusalem, despite the animosity that the Galilean populace felt for Sepphoris, so frequently referred to by Josephus. We certainly hear of border pillaging in Galilee: Jesus on the Ptolemais border; John on the imperial granaries of Upper Galilee, and the young men of Dabaritta on the borders of the Great Plain. To these acts we can add the destruction of Herod's palace at Tiberias. Yet when all these acts are weighed against the sustained practice of banditry in Judea proper, we can only conclude that the social conditions in the north were less pressing and ultimately less conducive to social banditry than in the south, something that is all the more remarkable in view of the fact that Galilee as a whole could be regarded as border country.

Second, we are told that social bandits enjoy the support of the peasant people who can distinguish between them and actual criminals. In the Galilean context this criterion certainly would seem to apply to those Galileans who supported Jesus in his act of pillaging Herod's palace in Tiberias (*Life* 66). These can be technically described as a "hidden rural proletariat" who were prepared to make common cause with their urban cousins of the destitute classes.[34] Presumably they had the tacit support of the villagers, though mention of the highwaymen of Dabaritta arousing the ire of the villagers in the Tarichaean region by suggesting that Josephus was about to betray their country to the Romans (*Life* 129, 132, 149) suggests caution. Sometimes an unprotected peasantry has to succumb to the nearest source of pressure without necessarily sharing its point of view. At Gischala, however, the situation would appear to be different. We hear that the country people there were less than enthusiastic for the revolt because of their farming obligations but were constrained to action by John and his close followers (*War* 4.80–84). If there is any truth in the report of John's callous manipulation of the oil monopoly (*Life* 74–75; *War* 2.591–92), we can perhaps understand the reasons for their reticence, and subsequent events would seem to have proved their judgment correct (*War* 4.106–11). Josephus's account of the judicial system he inaugurated is clearly meant to bolster his self-image (*Life* 79; *War* 2.570–71), yet it suggests the continued existence of procedures for dealing with law and order even in a national crisis, something that sharply contrasts with the general breakdown in Jerusalem and Judea in the same period. On the whole, then, it would seem once again that the Galilean situation was more "normal" than that of the south, where the combination of the Jerusalem populace and the bandits from the country is repeatedly affirmed. Even allowing for Josephan polemical concerns, the picture of the Galileans that emerges from both *Life* and *War* suggests a cautious peasantry and not one that has joined with the bandits in a full-scale peasant revolt.[35]

Third, the bandit rights wrongs, even to the point of helping the poor and needy with the spoils and conducting an independent judicial system in behalf of the peasants. There is very little additional evidence for Galilee under this heading, but the reluctance of the highwaymen to share their spoils with the Jerusalem populace for the restoration of the walls of the holy city was less than altruistic. John of Gischala's entrepreneurial activities are also lacking the kind of benevolence one might have expected toward his own people. Josephus is at pains to stress his own exemplary conduct in such matters (cf., e.g., *Life* 63, 80ff., 298), yet the fact that later he can be accused of sharp practices in relation to the booty from the destruction of Herod's palace (*Life* 285–97) suggests that he may not have been totally innocent. We have already mentioned the burning of the Jerusalem records of debts as indicative of the social conditions in the south, something that is graphically portrayed also by the activity of Simon bar Giora with his campaign of attacking the wealthy and proclaiming freedom for slaves throughout the Judean countryside before joining the other revolutionaries in Jerusalem (*War* 2.652; 4.507–8). Both incidents suggest that the character of the banditry in this region had a much greater social component than in Galilee where, one suspects, personal greed and selfishness were operating.[36]

Finally, there is the religious aspect of social banditry, representing as it does the divine justice that is actively engaged in bringing about the new order that is hoped for. Within the Galilean context the only overt religious motivation is that of Jesus of Tiberias who, despite Josephus's animosity, comes across as the kind of person that best fits this particular characteristic of the social bandit. Because of his influence at Tiberias it is not surprising to find two thousand of his townsmen fleeing to Jerusalem, presumably for religious reasons in the wake of the fall of their own city (*Life* 354). Nor can we exclude religious motivation from John's flight, especially in view of his previous contacts with such Jerusalem religious authorities as Simeon ben Gamaliel (*Life* 189–93). In this regard the impiety attributed to him by Josephus must be seen as further examples of John's vilification for personal reasons (cf. *War* 5.562–65; 7.263–64). It is significant, however, that we can attribute religious motivation to none of the other manifestations of banditry in the province. Even in the two instances cited, the lack of support for places other than their own native cities makes it clear that neither was fired with any great motivation for righting the wrongs of the people at large, and the episodic nature of the Galilean campaign as a whole suggests that there was no unifying religious principle that might have welded a scattered peasantry into an effective resistance movement. The absence of even the slightest suggestion of messianic pretensions in any of the Galilean leaders, bandit or other, is again in striking contrast with the Judean situation. Undoubtedly the Jerusalem temple served as the focal point for the religious aspirations of the Jerusalem populace and the Judean peasantry, as no doubt it had also done for Galilean pilgrims on the occasion of the great national festivals.[37] In the Galilean village communities, however, this motivating force was remote or inaccessible, except for the more daring (cf. Mark 13:14), "distracted" as the people were "with talk of revolt" (*War* 2.589). For our present discussion it is noteworthy that none of the individuals who surfaced in Galilean life was able to bridge the gulf that existed between the hopes that the cult center engendered and the daily circumstances, as the inhabitants awaited the Roman onslaught. Those scattered incidents of banditry that we have encountered within the province seem least capable of functioning in such a role.

This rapid survey confirms our previous conclusions. Social banditry and peasant revolts of millennial inspiration may indeed offer interesting typologies for a discussion of first-century Palestinian aspirations, but the results of our investigation suggest that they are more applicable to Judea (in the narrow sense) than to Galilee. Their usefulness in discussing the conditions in the latter province is to point out that despite the fact that the Galileans shared a common faith with their brothers in the south, regional factors and a historicopolitical and sociocultural character played a very important part in determining their understanding and expression of their beliefs.

NOTES

1. S. F. G. Brandon, *Jesus and the Zealots* (Manchester: Manchester Univ. Press, 1971). Cf. the reviews of M. Hengel in *Journal of Semitic Studies* 14 (1969): 231–40; and E. Lohse in *Novum Testamentum* 12 (1970): 78.
2. M. Hengel, *Die Zeloten*, 2d ed. (Leiden: E. J. Brill, 1976), 57–61, 322.
3. J. H. Yoder, *The Politics of Jesus* (Grand Rapids: Wm. B. Eerdmans, 1972).
4. See my "The Galileans in the Light of Josephus' *Vita*," *New Testament Studies* 26 (1980): 397–413.
5. E. Meyers, "Galilean Regionalism as a Factor in Historical Reconstruction," *Bulletin of the American Schools of Oriental Research* 21 (1976): 93–101.
6. R. A. Horsley, "Josephus and the Bandits," *Journal for the Study of Judaism in the Persian, Hellenistic, and Roman Period* 10 (1979): 37–63; idem, "Ancient Jewish Banditry and the Revolt against Rome," *Catholic Biblical Quarterly* 43 (1981): 409–32. For purposes of this article, I have not been able to use Horsley's most recent statement of his views in *Bandits, Prophets, and Messiahs: Popular Movements at the Time of Jesus* (in collaboration with J. Hanson; New York: Winston-Seabury, 1985).
7. Cf., e.g., A. Alt, "Die Rolle Samarias bei der Entstehung des Judentums," in *Kleine Schriften zur Geschichte des Volkes Israels*, 3 vols. (Munich, 1953–64), 2:316–37; E. Bickerman, *From Ezra to the Last of the Maccabees: The Foundations of Post-Biblical Judaism* (New York: Schocken Books, 1962), 43; and R. J. Coggins, *Samaritans and Jews: The Origins of Samaritanism Reconsidered* (Oxford: Basil Blackwell, 1975).
8. E. Fohrer, *Die Provinzeinteilung des assyrischen Reiches* (Leipzig, 1920), 56–

61. On the question of Galilee's administrative relations with Samaria in the Persian period, see M. Avi-Yonah, *The Holy Land from the Persian to the Arab Conquests: An Historical Geography* (Grand Rapids: Baker Book House, 1966), 25, 44–45.

9. A. Alt, "Zur Geschichte der Grenze zwischen Judäa und Samaria," in *Kleine Schriften* 2:346–62, esp. 359, n. 2.

10. E. Schürer, *Geschichte des jüdischen Volkes in Zeitalter Jesu Christi*, 3 vols. (reprint, Hildesheim, 1971), 1:275–76, 2:9–12.

11. For a more detailed discussion of this report for Galilean history, see S. Freyne, *Galilee from Alexander to Hadrian: A Study of Second Temple Judaism* (Wilmington, Del.: Michael Glazier, 1980), 43–44.

12. See V. Cherikover, *Palestine under the Ptolemies: A Contribution to the Study of the Zenon Papyri*, Mizraim 4, 5 (New York: G. E. Stechert & Co., 1937), 45ff.; and Freyne, *Galilee from Alexander to Hadrian*, 138–45.

13. For an example of such Hellenization in the immediate environs of Galilee, see E. Bickerman, "Sur une inscription grecque de Sidon," in *Mélanges syriens offerts à M. R. Dussaud* (Paris, 1939), 91–99.

14. Freyne, *Galilee from Alexander to Hadrian*, 156–70.

15. For a discussion of the problems of reconciling the accounts of Tacitus and Josephus concerning this episode with relevant recent bibliography, see M. Stern in *Compendia Rerum Judaicarum ad Novum Testamentum: The Jewish People in the First Century*, 2 vols., ed. M. Stern and S. Safrai (Philadelphia: Fortress Press; Assen: Van Gorcum, 1974–76), app. 2, 1:374–76.

16. *Life* 73 speaks of John of Gischala *en tē autoy eparchia*, which may indicate that he had a role in the Roman administration of the province.

17. Horsley, "Josephus and the Bandits," 60–63.

18. For details, see Freyne, *Galilee from Alexander to Hadrian*, 73–74.

19. We hear of the procurator Felix's punishing the populace for their complicity with the brigand chief Eleazar (*War* 2.253); the *sicarii* from Jerusalem are called a *heteron eidōs lēstōn* (*War* 2.254–57); the *lēstai* were united with the revolutionaries at the start of the revolt, according to *Life* 28; *War* 4.131–61 speaks of the many brigands from the country who joined the Zealots in the temple as the Romans advanced on Jerusalem after concluding the Galilean campaign. In all these instances we see the widening social base of the bandits and their increasing involvement with others in the revolt.

20. Horsley, "Josephus and the Bandits," 45.

21. There is no reference to the entreaties of the Galileans' mothers and the speech of Samias in the *War* account (cf. *Ant.* 14.172–74). The whole account in *Ant.* is more favorable to Hyrcanus, who secretly advises Herod to flee, having simply postponed the trial, whereas in *War* he acquits him. These differences are due in part to different sources but also to the differing tendencies of the two works, the former being pro-Hasmonean and the latter pro-Herodian.

22. Horsley, "Josephus and the Bandits," 53-55; idem, "Ancient Jewish Banditry," 421-22. In this latter case a general theory that peasants will appeal to a central religious authority in favor of the bandits whom they see as their just protectors is used to explain the Galilean mothers' appeals in the temple against Herod. It seems gratuitous to call the mothers of the murdered men Galilean peasants, as though the peasantry as a whole was outraged. Besides, it is highly

improbable even in light of the theory. The weak Hyrcanus was unlikely to have wanted to vindicate Galilean peasants' wrongs at the expense of Antipater's son, so an appeal for divine retribution would scarcely have been directed to him.

23. Freyne, *Galilee from Alexander to Hadrian*, 162-63, 181, 186-87.

24. Thus Horsley, "Josephus and the Bandits," 54, esp. n. 53, where he cites Hengel's *Die Zeloten*, 320-21, as also recognizing the problem of identifying Hezekiah as a follower of Aristobulus.

25. Horsley, "Josephus and the Bandits," 56, esp. n. 56; idem, "Ancient Jewish Banditry," 413.

26. For the tradition history of this particular story and its significance in Jewish martyrologies, see F. Loftus, "The Martyrdom of the Galilean Troglodytes (B.J. 1:312-313)," *Jewish Quarterly Review* 66 (1976): 212-23. Horsley's theory does not sufficiently explain the rise of banditry in Galilee prior to Herod's advent. He assumes that they were allowed to "roam free" as "no major threat to the social order of Galilee." This suggestion is not very helpful, however, in explaining the zeal with which the young Herod moved against them. Did they suddenly become a threat, and if so, to whom?

27. Freyne, *Galilee from Alexander to Hadrian*, 214-16. R. A. Horsley ("Popular Messianic Movements around the Time of Jesus," *Catholic Biblical Quarterly* 46 [1984]: 471-95) sees my suggestion about various recognizable forms of kingship as being based on the false supposition that "the peasantry had no messianic ideas of their own and were incapable of producing their own leadership" (483 n. 32). He does not seem to acknowledge that my suggestion is based on the fact that Judas, son of Hezekiah, was from Sepphoris, which I consider to have been a Hasmonean stronghold. Josephus's *Life* makes it quite clear that the peasantry could distance itself from Sepphoris and its attitudes (see below, n. 31). The fact that the Hasmonean claims on the high priesthood were regarded as illegitimate by the Hasidim and their heirs has no bearing on the matter, since the figure of John Hyrcanus, a "good" Hasmonean, could be invested with messianic traits (*Ant.* 13.299).

28. John is never called a bandit in *Life* despite his frequent confrontations with Josephus, whereas *War* 2.584-94 portrays him as both a brigand and a tyrant. This suggests that *lēstēs* can be used as a derogatory term by Josephus even when it does not fit the social conditions, despite Horsley's censure ("Josephus and the Bandits," 37-39) of Hengel's treatment.

29. S. Cohen's *Josephus in Galilee and Rome: His Vita and Development as a Historian* (Leiden: E. J. Brill, 1979) is the outstanding study of the relationship between *Life* and *War* and the historiographical merits of both works.

30. For details, see Freyne, *Galilee from Alexander to Hadrian*, 82-83. I do not agree, however, with Cohen's conjecture (*Josephus in Galilee and Rome*, 241-45, 255 n. 104) that this makes Josephus himself a Zealot.

31. On the relationship between Sepphoris and the Galileans, esp. during the revolt, see Freyne, *Galilee from Alexander to Hadrian*, 122-28.

32. Horsley, "Josephus and the Bandits," 60-61. See S. Applebaum, "The Zealots: The Case for Revaluation," *Journal of Roman Studies* 61 (1971): 155-70, esp. 167-68. For a Marxist interpretation of the relevant factors, see H. Kreissig, *Die sozialen Zusammenhänge des judäischen Krieges* (Berlin, 1970). In a later study, M. Hengel ("Zeloten und Sikarier," in *Josephus-Studien: Festschrift für Otto Michel*, ed.

O. Betz, M. Hengel, and K. Haacker [Göttingen: Vandenhoeck & Ruprecht, 1971], 175–96, esp. 181–82) has emphasized the social aspect of the Zealot movement more so than in his earlier study. See also M. Goodman, "The First Jewish Revolt: Social Conflict and the Problem of Debt," *Journal of Jewish Studies* 33 (1982): 416–27. Goodman correctly emphasizes the contrast between Judean and Galilean situations in regard to landownership. Horsley's account in "Ancient Jewish Banditry" (pp. 416–18) lacks precision on the question of Galilean ownership patterns. In this regard, Josephus's *Life* once again gives a rather different picture of the Galilean peasantry and their concerns.

33. Cf. above, n.19, where various references are listed in which bandits from the surrounding countryside and the people of Jerusalem are considered to have been in close liaison. In addition, see *War* 2.264–65, where brigands and impostors are said to have been engaged in destroying the homes of the wealthy in Judea and harassing those of the peasantry who were reluctant to join them. Even if it is argued that *pasa Ioydaia* in this notice includes Galilee (a possible meaning given Josephan usage), it is strange that we find no evidence of its social aftermath in *Life*, with the possible exception of the reference to the people of Sepphoris being in danger of being pillaged by the Galileans because they had made overtures to Cestius Gallus, the governor of Syria. Yet the Galileans are never described as bandits.

34. Freyne, *Galilee from Alexander to Hadrian*, 235–36.

35. Ibid., 243–44.

36. See above, nn.20, 32.

37. E.g., Luke 13:1–4; *Ant.* 17.254; *War* 2.43. For the religious significance of events in Judea, see Freyne, *Galilee from Alexander to Hadrian*, 231–33.

5

The Social Class
of the Pharisees in Mark

ANTHONY J. SALDARINI
Boston College

The purpose of this study is to locate the Pharisees among the other groups and parts of first-century Palestinian society. Hence, the modern category of class, despite all the problems associated with its definition and its use in reference to antiquity, can be of some help. Class is here used in its wider and less precise sense as a designation for a person's social status (prestige) and political power as well as economic power in society. Max Weber associated class with one's economic situation and possibilities, status with one's place in the social system according to law (estate) and one's prestige, and party with the political power of one's group. But these areas of life, wealth, status, and power overlap considerably, and many more variables conspire to give a person or a group its place, role, and limitations in society. S. N. Eisenstadt, in his study of social differentiation and stratification, notes that recent studies have shown decisively that a multidimensional approach to strata formation is necessary to take into account the complexities of society and the variations in cultures. The bases of what some call class, status, and party are different in other societies.[1]

After some general remarks are made on the sociology of groups such as the Pharisees, Mark's portrayal of the Pharisees will be analyzed. This study recognizes that no one of the sources that speak of the Pharisees (Josephus, the four Gospels, and various works of rabbinic literature) is historically reliable in itself. Only a critical study of each source can lay the groundwork for a historical reconstruction, and even then many questions will probably remain unanswered because of a lack of data.

Many modern and ancient groups are cited as analogies for the Pharisees. Rabbinic literature interprets them simply as rabbis who have great control over Jewish society, but this anachronistic view dates from the third to sixth centuries and tells us more about the social place of rabbis in Palestine and

Babylon then than it does about the first-century Pharisees. Christians usually treat the Pharisees as a specialized religious organization or sect separate from politics and society, on the analogy of a monastic group, withdrawn movement, or religious order. But since religion in antiquity was fully embedded in political society, the Pharisees can be conceived of as a sect only if one thinks of some modern sects that are very active in the political and social life of their countries.[2] Some have compared the Pharisees to Greek associations, but these associations were so varied that little new can be hypothesized concerning the Pharisees on the basis of this diffuse body of evidence, except to say that such organizations were very common.[3] Others have identified them as a school like the Greek philosophical schools, but these schools, too, varied greatly in their nature.[4] Greek associations and schools would have been greatly adapted to a Jewish context, and so the general models are severely limited in their usefulness for predicting the probable nature of the Pharisees. Though it is probable that the Pharisees had a coherent group structure with some norms for membership, a system of leadership, a program for training new members, and regular meetings for socializing and decision making, we do not know what those internal arrangements were.

Through Josephus and the Gospels we can get a view from the outside, that is, some indication of the Pharisees' place in society, their roles, influence, power (if any), and relationships with other parts of society. Josephus, who is interested in the governing class of Judaism and the political fortunes of the whole nation, mentions the Pharisees only on about twenty occasions, mostly when they are striving to gain power at times of social change. They are one of many groups and coalitions competing for power and influence in Jewish society, and they are not part of the governing class but dependent on them. In the categories of G. Lenski, they are retainers, that is, people who do not have independent wealth or power but who are not part of the virtually powerless lower classes who engage mostly in farming and a few other physically demanding occupations. Retainers have specialized capacities and are put at the service of the governing class as bureaucrats, lower officials, educators, advisers, soldiers, religious functionaries, and the like.[5] The governing class in Palestinian Judaism consisted of the chief priests in Jerusalem, the leaders of the prominent, wealthy (landowning) families, the family of Herod and families allied with them, and perhaps prominent regional leaders. This type of "aristocratic" government was typical in the Greco-Roman world. There was no independent middle class with a political and economic base independent from the upper classes. The retainers, who fulfilled the specialized bureaucratic and educational functions of the middle class today, were dependent on the wealthy upper classes. It should also be added that over ninety percent of the population belonged to the lower classes, and most engaged in farming. The gap between the upper and lower classes was enormous, with education and specialization limited to the upper classes. For most farmers the only way to move was down to the landless peasantry.

The Pharisees are very prominent in the Gospels because they are the opponents of Jesus, but this prominence does not mean that they were the most powerful leaders of Judaism. They were not members of the governing class; quite the opposite. Because Jesus was a minor religious figure in his lifetime and would hardly have been noticed by the Jerusalem authorities, or when eventually noticed, would not have been a focus of their attention—his day-to-day opponents would have been of a lower level—local leaders would have confronted Jesus in a competition for influence among the people.[6] Village leaders were usually the more wealthy landowners and members of old and prominent families that had achieved distinction in some way. Also, local government officials (if perceived as acting for the village), literate people, and local priests would have been part of the leadership. The Pharisees were probably part of this local leadership in Galilee, but not coterminous with any part of it. They could not develop their own interpretation of Judaism and propagate it among the people if they were full-time lower-class peasants. They must have been dependent for their livelihood on the priests and temple, the wealthy leaders of society, or Herod Antipas in Galilee. Some may have been small landowners themselves. They probably were influential among the people because they functioned as middlemen between the people and the upper echelons of society.

MARK

Mark mentions the Pharisees a limited number of times, less often than Matthew. They are mentioned alone in five cases, and in all instances they are in conflict with Jesus.[7] The scribes and Pharisees are mentioned together on two occasions when they are in conflict with Jesus (2:16; 7:1, 5).[8] The Pharisees are also linked with the Herodians twice (3:6; 12:13) in more political matters.[9] The social class and status of the Pharisees and their relationships to society can be determined by their geographical location and the issues they deal with in Mark. I am not assuming that Mark's presentation of the Pharisees is historically accurate. Rather, I am examining whether his picture of Jewish society and the Pharisees is consistent in itself and with wider first-century evidence. Its historical probability can only be determined by a wider study.

Mark places the Pharisees in Galilee on all occasions except one, when the Pharisees and Herodians are sent to Jesus in Jerusalem to entrap him.[10] The Pharisees meet Jesus at Capernaum and other rural towns (3:2, 6; 7:1,

5) and in many, often indeterminate, places (2:18, 24; 8:11; 10:2). In contrast with Josephus, who shows the Pharisees as closely linked with the leadership in Jerusalem, Mark sees them as active only in Galilee. They do not lack alliances and connections with other groups, for they plot with the Herodians (3:6), join the scribes in conflict with Jesus, and have some scribes in their midst (2:16). They even appear in Jerusalem once, but this may be due to the literary arrangement of Mark.[11] This does not eliminate the possibility of the Pharisees being active in Jerusalem, but it does render Mark's testimony uncertain.[12]

Further information concerning the nature and social position of the Pharisees can be deduced from the issues they discuss with Jesus. The Pharisees dispute with him over fasting (2:18), Sabbath observance (2:24; 3:2), and divorce (10:2). The scribes and Pharisees dispute with him over purification of hands (7:1), and the scribes of the Pharisees question his eating with sinners (2:16). The Pharisees also question Jesus' authority by demanding a sign (8:11). In concert with the Herodians, the Pharisees try to trap Jesus in a political matter, the question of Roman taxes (12:13), and they enter into a plot with the Herodians against Jesus.

Jacob Neusner has argued that the New Testament polemic against the Pharisees' concern with ritual purity, agricultural tithes, and Sabbath observance accurately reflects their program for Judaism in the first century.[13] These issues suggest to Neusner that the Pharisees were primarily a religious sect or table-fellowship group and not a politically active force. As we have seen in our analysis of Jewish society, however, a group with sectlike practices need not be cut off from political life, since religion is embedded in political society. Jerome Neyrey has analyzed all Mark's comments concerning purity, using Mary Douglas's anthropological studies to show that the purity rules in Mark function as boundary-setting mechanisms for the community.[14] Thus the Pharisees were the defenders of a certain kind of community, and Jesus challenged the Pharisees' vision of community by attacking their purity regulations concerning washing and food as well as Sabbath practice. The effect of Jesus' teaching was to widen the community boundaries and loosen the norms for membership in his community. Jesus thus created a new community outside the Pharisees' control and quite naturally provoked their protest and hostility.[15]

Jesus and the Pharisees did not argue over theological issues that were of interest to a limited number of Jews but rather competed for control over the community. The Pharisees were recognized leaders in the Galilean community, according to Mark. This means that they had recognition in the community and influence, if not power, with the people and other leaders of the community. Jesus, who was from a lower-class artisan family (perhaps landless peasants), did not have the social standing, honor, and influence to command respect as a teacher, as his return to Nazareth shows (6:2–3). Those who knew him dismissed him as a local carpenter without any community standing or recognition as wise or powerful. His family was an ordinary one, and his new claim to teaching authority and special standing in the community was rejected out of hand.[16] Mark explains the embarrassing lack of acceptance in Nazareth by the proverbial saying that "a prophet is not without honor, except in his own country, and among his own kin, and in his own house" (6:4).[17] Jesus was excluded from the society of his own town but went on to attain new status, honor, and influence in the other towns of Galilee through his own works and those of his followers (see the rest of Mark 6). In Mark's narrative this provoked the attack of the Pharisees and scribes over purity regulations and control of the community in chapter 7, a conflict that fits first-century society very well.

Another aspect of Jesus' relationship to the people is implied by his emergence as a leader of the people. Jesus did not occupy a socially recognized role that would give him power or influence because of his social status. Jesus attained his leadership role for some people in society by developing a reputation. His reputational authority derives from his successful criticism of the legitimate authorities and his ability to persuade people to follow his standards for Jewish society.[18] By interpreting Jewish custom and law and teaching the people how to live as Jews, Jesus also assumes a position as patron of the people and mediator between the people and God. As a patron of the people, Jesus cares for them and brings them that which they cannot get for themselves in return for a personal bond of loyalty and support. A patron-client relationship is a voluntary alliance between two unequal persons that is often long-lasting and diffuse; by this relationship the patron and client each commit themselves to exchange favors and come to each other's aid in a time of need.[19] Jesus brings healing, exorcism, guidance, and the promise of further security and prosperity (the kingdom of God), as well as an assurance of God's approval. In doing this he is again challenging the Pharisees who have been the guides of the people though less powerful than Jesus.[20] Jesus and the Pharisees also act as competing brokers for the people. When a patron helps his clients to deal satisfactorily with powerful people beyond his world, he acts as a broker. Both Jesus and the Pharisees offer guidance in dealing with God by interpreting his will and pointing out when certain actions will earn his pleasure or displeasure. The Pharisees in their relations with the scribes who have Jerusalem connections and with the Herodians who have control in Galilee show that they are attempting to keep the peace and make society run smoothly in conjunction with the national authorities.

Because the Pharisees in Mark have relationships with other groups in society, enter into a political alliance with the Herodians against Jesus (3:6), and with the Herodians put Jesus to the test at the instigation of the Jerusalem leaders (12:13), they act like a well-connected political-interest group, of which the scribes of the Pharisees (2:16) may be the Jerusalem representatives. The *interest group,* one of the most common types of voluntary association, is organized on the basis of shared and distinctive interests among the members. A *political-interest group* seeks to convert its interests into public law or gain control over social behavior.[21] In modern terminology, political-interest groups are also pressure groups. Since the Pharisees' religious views are integral to the way Jews live in Palestine, they seek to control or influence, as much as possible, the political, legal, and social factors that might determine the social practices and views of the community. Groups, such as the Pharisees, which have power and influence usually seek to label as deviant competing groups such as Jesus and his followers. The give-and-take of political, social, and religious life and the struggles for power among dominant and deviant groups explain many of the conflicts among Jewish groups in Palestine.

In Mark's Gospel, as in Josephus's history of the first century, the Pharisees are a religious-interest group with political goals, but they are not a dominant group. Mark's Pharisees are not based in Jerusalem, contrary to Josephus, but the dominant social pattern remains. The Pharisees exercise influence on the people and compete with Jesus for control. They confront Jesus concerning his teaching, and they object to Jesus' challenge to tradition. They speak of Sabbath and food laws. This suggests that the Pharisees are a group with a specific interpretation of certain laws and practices which has social recognition. They seek influence and resultant control among the people as religious experts, and in this quest they compete with Jesus. Because in antiquity, political authority is thoroughly enmeshed with religious teaching, practice, and authority, they enter into political alliances with the Herodians and are associated with the scribes, who do have some political control. They are members of the retainer class, involved in community guidance and leadership, even if not in an official capacity. They have community standing according to the prevailing system of prestige and honor, and they probably function as patrons and brokers for the people, even if they have lost direct political power. Consequently, they play a minor role in the national drama, especially in Galilee, where Jerusalem's influence is attenuated.

Even if Mark does not know much about the historical Pharisees or scribes, as Michael Cook argues,[22] he does reproduce the dominant social pattern of ancient society and place the Pharisees at the edges of the governing class. They are a political-interest group that is out of power. Consequently, they are not seen as active in Jerusalem, and their sphere of action is in the towns of Galilee. Though we cannot be certain that Mark and his sources give us a completely accurate picture of the Pharisees as a strong community force in Galilee in the early and middle first century, their general role in Jewish society is intrinsically probable.

NOTES

1. S. N. Eisenstadt, *Social Differentiation and Stratification* (Glenview, Ill.: Scott Foresman, 1971), 81–83. See also Jonathan H. Turner, *Societal Stratification: A Theoretical Analysis* (New York: Columbia Univ. Press, 1984), esp. chaps. 4 and 8. Turner supports Eisenstadt in the claim that the class and status system is determined by a series of complex factors, and he criticizes Gerhard E. Lenski (see below, n. 5) because, after distinguishing many complex factors, he lumps them together as a composite and too simple phenomenon (pp. 57–58). In fact, as we shall see, Lenski emphasizes the complexity of the stratification system implicit in class and status.

2. Bryan Wilson (*Magic and the Millennium* [London: William Heinemann, 1973]) shows that several types of sects are very active politically.

3. See the huge variety of organizations culled from Greek inscription by Franz Poland in *Geschichte des griechischen Vereinswesens,* Fürstlich Jablonowskischen Gesellschaft zu Leipzig 23, der historischen-nationalökonomischen Sektion 38 (Leipzig: Teubner, 1909).

4. No one (*pace* Ellis Rivkin, *A Hidden Revolution* [Nashville: Abingdon Press, 1978]) has proved that the Pharisees were primarily a learned, philosophical-like group. On the diversity of Greek philosophical schools, see Stanley Stowers, "Social Status, Public Speaking, and Private Teaching: The Circumstances of Paul's Preaching Activity," *Novum Testamentum* 26 (1984): 59–82.

5. Gerhard E. Lenski, *Power and Privilege: A Theory of Social Stratification* (New York: McGraw-Hill, 1966), 243–48.

6. "Influence" is used in the precise sense developed by Talcott Parsons in *Politics and Social Structure* (New York: Free Press, 1969), 405–29, esp. 416. The influential person is considered to be a reliable source of information or judgment concerning the information and thus is able to influence the judgment and actions of others. Influence is contrasted with power, which is the ability to carry out one's will against opposition, i.e., secure the performance of actions by others against their will, usually with the threat of sanctions.

7. Mark 2:18; 2:24; 3:2; 8:11, 15; 10:2. Mark 3:2 says "they" were watching Jesus in the synagogue in order to accuse him. Context both before this story and at the end, where the Pharisees conspire with the Herodians against Jesus, indicates that the Pharisees are meant, at least in the Markan context.

8. Michael Cook's contention (*Mark's Treatment of Jewish Leaders* [Leiden: E. J. Brill, 1978]) that these instances are redactional is gratuitous. A textual variant in Mark 9:11 also links the Pharisees with the scribes.

9. The scribes are mentioned alone on seven occasions (Mark 1:22; 3:22; 9:11; 9:14; 12:28, 32; 12:35; 12:38). They are linked with the chief priests and elders five times (8:31; 11:27; 14:43; 14:53; 15:1) and with just the chief priests an additional four times (10:33; 11:18; 14:1; 15:31). Finally, to round out the picture, the chief

priests are mentioned alone five times (14:10; 15:3; 10, 11, 31). The chief priests and the whole Sanhedrin are mentioned in 14:55. In addition, the high priest and his household are mentioned a number of times in the Passion story. The chief priests, scribes, and elders occur together from chap. 8 on, esp. in chaps. 11–15, where they are concerned with the death of Jesus.

10. The Pharisees are in Galilee in Mark 2:16, 18, 24; 3:2, 6; 7:1, 5; 8:11; 10:2. They, with the Herodians, are in Jerusalem only in 12:13. They are described in 7:3 and 8:15 in a Galilean setting.

11. In chap. 12, just before the arrest of Jesus, Jesus meets a series of his opponents: the Pharisees and Herodians (12:13), the Sadducees (12:18), and a friendly scribe (12:28). Jesus then concludes with an attack on the scribes (12:35–40) and implicitly on the temple authorities, the priests, when he says that the temple will be destroyed (13:1–2). It is likely that Mark brings the Pharisees—and possibly the Herodians—into this context to create a complete roster of Jesus' opponents just before the arrest and crucifixion.

12. Cook (*Jewish Leaders*) argues that the Pharisees in the early part of Mark and the scribes in the latter part are really the same group called by different names in different sources. His thesis presumes Rivkin's analysis of the Pharisees and depends on a rather arbitrary source analysis.

13. Jacob Neusner, *From Politics to Piety* (Englewood Cliffs, N.J.: Prentice-Hall, 1973), chap. 4. Neusner has also shown ("'First Cleanse the Inside,'" *New Testament Studies* 22 [1976]: 486–95) that the dispute over cleaning the inside or outside of the cup in Mark 7 reflects a genuine first-century controversy over ritual purity. Note that in 7:3–4, Mark says that "the Pharisees, and all the Jews, do not eat unless they wash their hands, observing the tradition of the elders." He notes, in addition, that they wash when they come in from the marketplace and they also wash pots and cups, etc. Mark seems here to be explaining a Jewish practice that is not peculiar to the Pharisees but more widely accepted, and he may be implying that the Pharisees' practice concerning washing was widely accepted among Jews in the first century.

14. Jerome Neyrey, "The Idea of Purity in Mark's Gospel," *Semeia* 35 (1986): 91–128.

15. Joanna Dewey (*Markan Public Debate: Literary Technique, Concentric Structure, and Theology in Mark 2:1—3:6*, SBLDS 48 [Chico, Calif.: Scholars Press, 1980], 120–21, 188–90) argues that healing and eating are two issues that link the early chaps. of Mark together and connect to the ultimate condemnation of Jesus. She thus attributes the function of these themes to Markan redaction. These literary conclusions do not address or deny the traditional nature of the controversies over purity nor their probability as first-century issues between Jews and the Jesus movement.

16. The competition for honor and community standing in antiquity required that anyone who claimed more prestige or authority than that recognized by the community should compete for that position and defeat anyone who challenged him.

17. Lacking honor (*atimos*) is mentioned in the Gospels only here and in the parallel in Matt. 13:57. Honor (*timē*) is used in the Johannine version of the saying (John 4:44). Luke 13:33 has another version of this saying. (In Matt. 27:6, 9, *timē* is

used in its other meaning, "price.")

18. Bruce Malina, *Christian Origins and Cultural Anthropology* (Atlanta: John Knox Press, 1986), 118–19.

19. Carl H. Lande, "Introduction: The Dyadic Basis of Clientelism," in *Friends, Followers, and Factions,* ed. Steffen W. Schmidt et al. (Berkeley and Los Angeles: Univ. of California Press, 1977), xiv, xx. For additional data, analysis, and bibliography, see S. N. Eisenstadt and Louis Roniger, "Patron-Client Relations as a Model of Structuring Social Exchange," *Comparative Studies in Society and History* 22 (1980): 42–77; idem, *Patrons, Clients, and Friends: Interpersonal Relations and the Structure of Trust in Society* (New York and Cambridge: Cambridge Univ. Press, 1984); and Ernest Gellner and John Waterbury, eds., *Patrons and Clients in Mediterranean Societies* (London: Gerald Duckworth & Co., 1977).

20. Though miracles are not attributed to the Pharisees in the Gospels, Josephus does say that they could or at least claimed to predict the future for their clients (*Ant.* 17.2.4 [43]). Such claims were normal for religious leaders.

21. E. Pfuhl, *The Deviance Factor* (New York: D. Van Nostrand, 1980), 122.

22. Cook, *Mark's Treatment.*

6

Social Typification and the Classification of Ancient Letters

STANLEY K. STOWERS
Brown University

Two handbooks on letter writing that classify letters into types have survived from antiquity.[1] The *Typoi Epistolikoi,* falsely attributed to Demetrius of Phalerum (hereafter, Demetrius), discusses twenty-one types,[2] and the *Epistolimaioi Charactēres,* transmitted under the name of either Libanius or Proclus (hereafter, Libanius), enumerates forty-one types.[3] Papyrus exercises in letter writing from Egypt also attest to the practice of dividing letters into types.[4] The bilingual *Bologna Papyrus,* for instance, consists of eleven model letters of various types which had probably been copied from a handbook by a student.[5] Such handbooks were probably used by some teachers of rhetoric and by those who trained professional letter writers. In spite of much skepticism on the part of some scholars, studies have shown that extant letters do tend to fall into types, especially when the writers were well educated.[6]

I wish to show that the handbooks reflect a widespread approach to the classification of Greek and Latin letters through the typification of social interactions. In describing types of letters the handbooks do not specify formal rhetorical-literary features or stylistic traits but picture a typical social interaction that could be transacted through letters. I believe that this socially oriented perspective of the handbooks can provide a healthy corrective to the narrowly form-critical approach to letters that has been dominant in New Testament studies.

The concept of social typifications has been used most productively in the sociology of knowledge.[7] So, for instance, Peter Berger and Thomas Luckmann summarize,

> The social reality of everyday life is thus apprehended in a continuum of typifications, which are progressively anonymous as they are removed from the "here and now" of the face-to-face situation. At one pole of the continuum are those

others with whom I frequently and intensively interact in face-to-face situations—my "inner circle," as it were. At the other pole are highly anonymous abstractions, which by their very nature can never be available in face-to-face interaction. Social structure is the sum total of these typifications and of the recurrent patterns of interaction established by means of them. As such, social structure is an essential element of the reality of everyday life.[8]

It is appropriate to honor Howard Clark Kee as the pioneer in the use of the sociology of knowledge for New Testament studies.

The ancient letter was a genre that strongly typified the interaction between persons, precisely because it fictionalized personal presence. As Jacques Derrida has recently reminded us, there is a strong tradition in the West of attempting to ground truth and legitimacy in the speech of those who are personally present to one another.[9] Such "primary" speech is often supposed to be beyond or lie beneath the typification and artificiality of writing. The classical tradition gave the letter a privileged position because it was supposed to be not literature but a second-best means of communicating personal presence. The modern romantic tradition has perpetuated exactly the same understanding. For Adolf Deissmann the real letter was remote from literature. He likened it to a telephone call, the personal presence of those who are physically separated. Both the epistolary handbooks and ancient letters themselves belie this fantasy of a privileged personal presence unmediated by the structures and typifications of language and its closest written approximate, the letter.

Writing does differ from speech in at least two ways.[10] First, it tends to eliminate guarantees to privacy. Writing may become "permanent" and public in a way that speech usually does not. Second, there are important communicative aspects of personal presence that are not a part of writing, for example, inflection, tone, gesture, overt emotional behavior. The letter is writing: it has no guarantee of privacy or secrecy; it has no "context of personal presence" to help fix meaning. And yet, unlike most literature, it is written in the form of direct address. Ancient theorists said that authors were to write their letters as if they were speaking face to face with the recipient.[11] The letter fictionalizes personal presence. Thus ancient letters were largely constituted by the literary typification of social situations where two or more people interacted, usually in face-to-face encounters.

The handbooks' approach to the generic specification and taxonomy of letters is best seen in the brief "definitions" and sample letters they provide for each type. For the blaming letter Demetrius writes,

The blaming type [*memptikos*] is one that undertakes not to seem to be harsh. For example:
Since time has not yet permitted you to return thanks for the favors you have received, (your failure to do so) is not the reason why I supposed it well not to

mention what you have received. And yet you will (continue to) be annoyed with us, and impute words (to us). We do, then, blame you for having such a disposition, and we blame ourselves for not knowing that you are such a man. (4.5–11)[12]

Libanius says,

The blaming kind [*memptikē*] is that in which we blame someone.
The blaming letter. You did not act well when you wronged those who did good to you. For by insulting your benefactors, you provided an example of evil to others. (15.17–16.1, 22.4–6)[13]

It is clear that Demetrius and Libanius are not using a conception of genre as a complex combination of formal, structural, stylistic, and thematic characteristics. We are not dealing with anything comparable to Aristotle's generic description of drama and epic, or even Horace's discussion of poetic types in the *Ars poetica*. The definitions that the handbooks give are too bare, and the sample letters too sketchy, for this method of classification. One could, of course, agree with the suggestion made by some that Demetrius and Libanius did not fulfill their tasks very well.[14] Scholars have been surprised to find missing from the handbooks clear definitions in terms of formal features and characteristic *topoi*.

A more adequate approach is to note that the "descriptions" and sample letters are chiefly occupied with depicting social situations. A social situation occurs when people participate in their social world at a particular point in time. A social situation can best be described by using modern sociological concepts such as those of role, role expectation, social structure, status, action, and motivation-legitimation. Analyzing a social situation is akin to analyzing an episode in a narrative. The descriptions and sample letters in the handbooks provided an outline of the essential elements of episodes that could be rendered as letters. One finds a plot, actors who are to occupy certain roles, a point of view, motivations, and resolutions.

Both Demetrius's and Libanius's letters of blame indicate that the writer and recipient are to exhibit a certain type of role relationship. The writer in a letter of blame is a benefactor who expects honor from the recipient in return for benefactions. The honor is due him because of his social role. Thus it is a relationship of superordinate (writer) to subordinate (recipient), or of equals. Several specific social roles would fit this type, for example, patron-client, friendship, parent-child. Only a superordinate or, in some instances, an equal has the right to demand honor and to give blame when the other party fails to return the proper respect. In both of the handbooks the recipient has not only failed to honor his benefactor but has actually displayed dishonor. In Demetrius the recipient in the sample letter has displayed annoyance or dislike for the writer, at least partly, by falsely imputing words to his benefactor. In Libanius the recipient has committed some kind of strong insult (*hubrizein*) against his benefactor.

The action the writers perform is that of blaming. Blaming is the opposite of praising. The former removes honor from the person's account, thus reducing his or her social status. It is by virtue of the writer's superordinate position in society that he can blame the recipient. Blame, however, is a mild form of rebuke. Demetrius explains that in using it one tries not to seem too harsh. Unlike the use of harsher forms of rebuke (e.g., *loidoria, oneidizein,* and sometimes *epitimēsis*), the use of blame supposes that the writer already has a positive social relationship with the recipient and that he wants to maintain that relationship. So the patron wants to rebuke his client but does not want their relationship to end. He wants only to restore the relationship by causing the client to return the honor that is properly due the patron. The letter of blame implies the threat that the patron will make his rebuke public. When the blaming is made fully public, the social status of the client will have been lowered.

When people participate in a social situation, they are implicitly and unconsciously "agreeing" with the social system and its goals. The maintenance of this social fabric is legitimation. In letters, the order is legitimated when the writer provides motivations and gives reasons to which the recipient agrees. The handbooks provide samples of such reasons and motivations as are appropriate to the social situation that is typified in each kind of letter. This act of commending the social world is much less explicit in the two sample letters of blame than in other sample letters. In both cases the blame is sanctioned when the writer suggests that the recipient has entered into some kind of negative relationship with the social order. Demetrius suggests that the recipient's character is epitomized by his failures toward his benefactor. In other words, the recipient's character does not measure up to the role he exercises in society. Libanius says that by insulting his benefactor, the recipient has provided an example (*paradeigma*) of evil for others. In each case, the writer indicates that the recipient has stepped out of his proper place in society. The writer hopes that the recipient will be compelled by the logic of the order and regularize his relationship to the writer and society.

Ancient theorists of letter writing denied that the letter was a type of literature and asserted that it was instead a substitute for personal presence.[15] The handbooks follow this fiction of personal presence in their specification of letter types. They describe each type of letter by sketching a social situation with its characteristic action and social relationships. In the letter, social situations that normally occur in face-to-face encounters are rendered as literature. The handbooks typify those social situations in their descriptions and sample letters. These sketches served letter writers like plot outlines to be used on appropriate occasions.

In the introduction to his handbook, Demetrius describes precisely this process:

> According to the theory that governs epistolary types [*typōn*], Heraclides, they can be composed from a great number of generic patterns [*eidōn*], but arise from among those which always fit the particular circumstance [of the letter writing situation]. . . . I have taken it upon myself, by means of certain generic categories [*ideōn*], to organize and set forth both the number of distinctions between them and what they are, and have sketched a sample, as it were, of the arrangement of each kind [*tēs hekastou genous taxeōs*], and have, in addition, individually set forth the fundamental logic [*logon*] for each of them. (1.1–11)[16]

Demetrius explains what he intends to do, and the corresponding theory, with clarity and concision.[17] The theory of epistolary types requires that the writer compose according to generic patterns that must fit the circumstances of the author's particular situation in writing. Demetrius's discussions of types make it clear that the "author's particular situation" would include his social relationship to the recipient of the letter, the current status of the relationship, and the particular occasion for writing. Demetrius intends to describe and distinguish these types of letters by, first, sketching a sample of how each type is arranged and, second, commenting on the logic of the type.

The method of taxonomy found in the handbooks of Demetrius and Libanius is far from unique. It is an approach to classification employed widely in the rhetorical tradition. That tradition was virtually unanimous in defining the three *genē* of rhetoric by means of social contexts and characteristic activities of speech within those contexts. In the judicial genre the speaker's objective was to persuade a judge or jury of the justice or injustice of some act. The ideal context for the deliberative genre was the political council or civic assembly, where the speaker pled for the expediency or inexpediency of a certain course of action. The setting for the epideictic genre was a number of typical social occasions such as weddings, birthdays, departures, and funerals.[18] The speaker clarified and reinforced what was considered honorable and dishonorable in the culture by praising and blaming persons and things—for example, cities or seasons—which were significant to the occasion in question.

Epictetus (*Diss.* 3.23.33–34) speaks of three philosophical genres. He vehemently opposes a confusion of the sophist's epideictic display with philosophical protreptic, because epideictic cannot accomplish the purposes of the philosopher in the philosophical school. Epictetus understands that there is a confusion of kinds (*charaktēres*). The purposes of two different social contexts have been confused: sophistic entertainment in the theater and exhortation in the philosopher's class are incommensurable.[19] Epictetus defines genre in terms of purposes to be accomplished within particular social situations.[20]

In the case of rhetoric's three *genē* and Epictetus's *charactēres* of speech, like Demetrius's *typoi* and Libanius's *charactēres*, generic description and taxonomy are accomplished by delineating actions appropriate to specific social situations. The classification of speech and literature according to characteristic social occasion is understandable in light of the practice of tracing genres back to Homer. Grammarians and rhetoricians attempted to find models for every form of rhetoric and literature in Homer.[21] Menander Rhetor says,

Among the many genres which the divine poet Homer taught us he did not neglect the genre [*eidos*] of monody. For he has conferred monodic speeches on Andromache, Priam and Hecuba which are fitting for each of their characters, as if he wished to demonstrate to us that he was not ignorant of these things. We must therefore take our starting point from the poet and elaborate them as we understand the principle [*to theōrēma*] as the poet has handed it down to us. (434.11–18)[22]

This view of the Homeric heroes as exemplars of rhetorical skills was ancient—dating at least to the fifth century B.C.E.—and became ubiquitous.[23] Homer was the Bible for everything that was considered characteristic of genuinely Greek social life. The *theōrēma* that Homer provided for Menander was like Demetrius's and Libanius's description of letter types. It was the bare sketch of a characteristic social occasion involving an appropriate act of speech. For both epistolary theorists and Menander, this *theōrēma* was the fundamental generic logic that could be used as the basis for rhetorical elaboration through the employment of the techniques of amplification and the selection and development of *topoi*.

In both handbooks the model or sample letters consist only of a few terse lines setting forth the gist of the reasoning that the type involves. Most often the model letter takes the form of an enthymeme, a rhetorical syllogism. Thus Libanius's insulting letter:

The insulting letter. If you had been a noble person you would have had many genuine friends, but now that you are [so] bad, in all likelihood you have no friend at all. For every sensible person always hastens to flee from someone foul. (28.27–30)

If the user of the handbooks had studied rhetoric or even merely the *progymnasmata*, he would know how to elaborate each part of the syllogism in the model letter. Both the educated and the less educated letter writer would be reminded of the logic of the social code involved in performing some action—for example, praising, thanking, commending, rebuking, requesting—by means of a letter. Most often the sample letters involve the ancient institution of friendship and some kind of praising or blaming, shaming or honoring. This is not surprising since the letter-writing tradition had intimate connections with Greek friendship and the occasional nature of letter writing gave it many parallels to epideictic, the rhetoric of praise and blame.

Many of the types in the handbooks have corresponding genres in epideictic rhetoric.[24] The following types of letters from the handbooks are clearly epideictic: blaming (*memptikos*), commending (*systatikos*), ironic (*eirōnikos*), censorious (*epitimētikos*), admonishing (*nouthetētikos*), thanking (*eucharistikos*), invective (*psektikos*), friendly (*philikos*), praying (*euktikos*), threatening (*apeilētikos*), reproaching (*oneidistikos*), consoling (*paramythētikos*), insulting (*hubristikos*), praising (*epainetikos*), reproving (*elenktikos*), maligning (*diablētikos*), grieving (*lypētikos*), erotic (*erōtikos*), congratulatory (*syncharētikos*), diplomatic (*presbeutikos*). These letters involve types of praise and blame as they were understood in epideictic rhetoric. The many types of blame also reflect the influence of the popular and philosophical hortatory traditions.[25] In contrast, only two types of letters clearly belong to judicial rhetoric, the accusing and the apologetic letter. The advising letter (*symbouleutikos*) is most clearly deliberative.

Since epideictic is the rhetoric of occasional speaking and occasionality is the hallmark of the letter, this correspondence is not surprising. Furthermore, the social code plays an equally central role in both the specification of epideictic genres and types of letters. The farewell speech (*propemptikon*), for example, consists of someone departing on a trip and someone who has a positive social relationship with the traveler addressing him in ways appropriate to the particular social relationship. Menander Rhetor says (395.4–30) that the farewell speech is adaptable to three different relationships. If the speaker is socially superior to the traveler, he should give advice. If they are equals, that is friends, the speaker should display his affection for the traveler. In the farewell speech of a social inferior to a superior, the speaker is to praise the traveler. Demetrius says that the friendly letter is written between social equals except in the case of officials in high positions who write as if they were friends even if they are not social equals.[26] His reproachful letter depicts the master of a household taking his client or freedman to task and presupposes some kind of hierarchical relationship.[27] In both the epideictic and epistolary types, characteristic actions or speech acts within typical social contexts are essential to generic specification, the taxonomy of subtypes within the larger genre.

Scholars of ancient epistolography have been impressed by the disparity between the papyri and the literarily transmitted letters.[28] Some have even denied that the types of the handbooks reflect the reality of practice at all.[29] I suggest that the cause of this skepticism lies at least partly in a failure to grasp or appreciate the ancient method of conceiving epistolary genres. Instead, scholars have sought to analyze letters in terms either of structure and form or characteristic *topoi* and phraseology. Both approaches are too reductionistic. Studies of structure and form have focused almost exclusively on the formulaic elements of the prescript and conclusion of letters.[30] Only this material has seemed to be uniquely epistolary. According to this approach the body is merely the message to be communicated. But ancient epistolary theorists and the handbooks saw things quite differently: they have virtually nothing to say about the prescript and conclusion but focus on the so-called body.[31] The body is not mere information to be communicated but rather a medium through which a person performs an action or a social transaction with someone from whom he or she is physically separated.[32] Viewed from this ancient perspective, an elaborate letter of commendation written by a highly educated person and a crude commendation by a barely literate Egyptian peasant are essentially of the same genre because they are both attempting to effect the same social transaction. The elaborations of the one letter make it cultured and aesthetically pleasing, not of a different genre.

The second scholarly approach has also been reductionistic. Most notably, Heikki Koskenniemi and Klaus Thraede have studied characteristic *topoi* and phraseology.[33] They have focused on clichés and language from the tradition of Greek friendship, which was, of course, very important to the letter-writing tradition: educated writers in antiquity tended closely to identify the letter with friendship. But as a glance at the types of the handbooks and the types represented in extant letters clearly shows, it is misleading to reduce the letter genre to the friendly letter. It is perhaps helpful to say that the friendly letter was to letter writing as the encomium of a person was to epideictic. The ancients considered the most characteristic expression of epideictic to be the speech that praised an honorable or worthy person. The epideictic division of rhetoric even became known as encomium and panegyric. Not every subgenre of epideictic, however, involved praise of an honorable person. The encomium of a person was the model, but there were many other kinds of praising and blaming and varied social occasions within epideictic.[34] Similarly, the letter of friendship was considered to be the most characteristic expression of letter writing, but in fact both the papyri and the literary corpus are characterized by numerous types.

By understanding the ancient approach to classification, its relation to social circumstance and educational level, it will be possible to understand better the relationship between the papyri and the literarily transmitted letters. To a large extent the writers of the handbooks were describing practice when they divided the letter into many types. If this is the case, then why have scholars of ancient letter writing failed to find the types of the handbooks among ancient letters? Researchers have clearly identified and studied only the friendly letter and the letter of recommendation among either the papyri or the literarily transmitted letters.[35]

It seems to me that two factors often make it less than obvious that the types of the handbooks are represented among the letters. First, the types as described in the handbooks are ideals that greatly simplify actual practice. These authors knew that the types were frequently mixed and combined. Libanius even provides the "mixed letter" as his last type.[36] It is a letter of praise and blame. Thus scholars must look for letters of mixed types and not just the pure ideals.

Second, educational level is an essential factor in several respects. The rhetorical elaboration of a letter makes it look very different from the same type in its barest form. The papyri make up a sample that is representative of the culture and society of some small Egyptian towns. We have large numbers of letters from illiterate and barely literate people who often had to employ a relative or professional writer. Most of these people did not participate at all in the ancient literary culture. For this reason we would not expect to find certain kinds of letters among the papyri, except rarely. So, for instance, I have not yet found a parenetic letter. To write a parenetic letter required knowledge of the moral-precept tradition and the ability to present traditional models of moral character through various rhetorical techniques.[37] I have, however, discovered very simple hortatory letters that one might describe as the poorly educated man's version of the parenetic letter.[38] Similarly, the few letters of consolation among the papyri are quite different from the literarily transmitted examples of that type, which employ the *topoi* of the consolatory tradition that were taught in the *progymnasmata* and in epideictic rhetoric.[39] On the other hand, the mundane types such as requesting, replying, reporting, and inquiring are not found—at least in comparably simple forms—in proportionately large numbers among the literary letters, which by definition were letters of some special merit making them worthy of preservation.

There are more types represented among both the papyri and the literarily transmitted letters than have usually been thought. I cannot here argue each case, but I have selected a sampling of types to propose as illustrations (excluding those mundane types which are obviously well represented among the papyri): praising, blaming, advising, admonitory, thanking, supplicatory, and threatening.[40] In each case it was not difficult to find examples among both the papyri and the literarily transmitted letters which seem to fit the specifications of the handbooks.[41] The handbooks and their method of classification allow us to understand letter writing on a large scale as a dynamic and complex system of activities and social transactions which could be carried out by separated people. The handbooks specify genre by describing a characteristic action performed in a typical social situation. Thus they contain a sort of implicit sociology of letter writing. The attempt to view Hellenistic and Roman letters through categories based only on form and structure or *topoi* and phraseology is reductionistic and leads to the view that the papyri and the literarily transmitted letters have almost nothing in common. The ancient approach to classification reflected in the handbooks, student exercises, and comments by theorists allows us to see how the same kinds of language acts and social transactions were attempted by people of different social and educational levels. The method of generic specification found in the handbooks provided both for the taxonomy of letters into many types and for a flexibility of style and occasionality in composition.

NOTES

1. *Demetrii et Libanii qui feruntur Topoi Epistolikoi et Epistolimaioi Charakteres*, ed. V. Weichert (Leipzig, 1910). Introduced and translated by Abraham Malherbe in "Ancient Epistolary Theorists," *Ohio Journal of Religious Studies* 5 (1977): 3–77.

2. L. Brinkmann, "Der älteste Briefsteller," *Rheinisches Museum für Philologie* 64 (1909): 310–17; *Demetrii et Libanii*, ed. Weichert, 1–12; and B. Olsson, *Papyrusbriefe aus der frühesten Römerzeit* (Uppsala, 1925), 7–9. Demetrius's handbook in its present form is dated between 200 B.C.E. and 300 C.E. by various scholars, but the handbook almost certainly originated before 100 C.E.

3. Libanius's handbook is variously dated between the 4th and 6th cents. C.E.: H. Hinck, "Die *Epistolimaioi Characteres* des Pseudo-Libanios, *Neue Jahrbücher für Philologie und Paedagogie* 99 (1869): 537–62; J. Sykutris, "Proklos peri epistolimaiou," *Byzantinisch-neugriechische Jahrbücher* 7 (1928–29): 108–18; and H. Rabe, "Aus Rhetoren-Handschriften," *RhM* 64 (1909): 296ff.

4. U. Wilcken, *Urkunden der Ptolemäerzeit* 1 (Berlin and Leipzig, 1927), nos. 110, 111, 144, 145; W. Schmid, "Ein epistolographisches Übungstück," *NJhb* 145 (1892): 692–99; H. Koskenniemi, *Studien zur Idee und Phraseologie des griechischen Briefes bis 400 n.chr.* (Helsinki, 1956), 57–59; and A. Erman, *Die Literatur der Aegypten* (Leipzig, 1923), 252, 257, 260.

5. *Papyri Bononienses* 1, ed. and comm. O. Montevecchi (Milan, 1953); and Malherbe, "Ancient Epistolary Theorists," 9–10, 42–55.

6. For attempts to classify papyrus and nonpapyrus letters into types, and observations about the difficulties involved, see Rabe, "Aus Rhetoren-Handschriften," 291 n.2; Brinkmann, "Der älteste Briefsteller," 311–17; *Demetrii et Libanii*, ed. Weichert, xix–xx; Olsson, *Papyrusbriefe*, 7–10; M. M. Wagner, "A Chapter in Byzantine Epistolography: The Letters of Theodoret of Cyrus," *Dumbarton Oaks*

Papers 4 (1948): 119–81; and S. Stowers, *Letter Writing in Greco-Roman Antiquity* (Philadelphia: Westminster Press: 1986). For skepticism about the influence of the handbooks on practice, see below, n. 29.

7. Georg Simmel, *The Sociology of Georg Simmel,* ed. and trans. Kurt H. Wolff (New York: Free Press, 1950), 352–55 and elsewhere; and Alfred Schutz, *On Phenomenology and Social Relations: Selected Writings* (Chicago: Univ. of Chicago Press, 1970), 111–22, 200–235. See also Peter Berger and Thomas Luckmann, *The Social Construction of Reality* (Garden City, N.Y.: Doubleday & Co., 1966), 28–34.

8. Berger and Luckmann, *Social Construction,* 33.

9. Jacques Derrida, *Of Grammatology* (Baltimore: Johns Hopkins Press, 1977).

10. Simmel, *Sociology,* 352–55.

11. See Malherbe, "Ancient Epistolary Theorists," 15.

12. Ibid., 31.

13. Ibid., 71.

14. Koskenniemi, *Studien zur Idee und Phraseologie,* 61–63.

15. See Malherbe, "Ancient Epistolary Theorists," 15; and Koskenniemi's discussion of *parousia,* in *Studien zur Idee und Phraseologie.*

16. I have modified Malherbe's translation.

17. Discussion of Demetrius's stated theory and plan in this paragraph is strikingly absent from the modern expositions of epistolary theory. Koskenniemi (*Studien zur Idee und Phraseologie,* 54–63) and K. Thraede (*Grundzüge griechischrömische Brieftopik* [Munich, 1970] 25–27) are interested only in what the handbook has to say about the friendly letter.

18. T. Burgess, *Epideictic Literature,* Chicago Studies in Classical Philology 3 (Chicago: Univ. of Chicago Press, 1902); V. Buchheit, *Untersuchungen zur Theorie des Genos Epideiktikon* (Munich, 1960); and *Menander Rhetor,* ed., trans. and comm. D. A. Russell and N. G. Wilson (New York and London: Oxford Univ. Press, 1981).

19. See Epictetus *Diss.* 3.23.30–32, where the lecture room of the philosopher is compared to a hospital. The point is made several times in the discourse.

20. Francis Cairns, *Generic Composition in Greek and Roman Poetry* (Edinburgh: Edinburgh Univ. Press, 1972), 6. Cairns shows that social situation is central to some kinds of generic classification in antiquity and not to others.

21. See George Kennedy, "The Ancient Dispute over Rhetoric in Homer," *American Journal of Philology* 78 (1957): 23–42; L. Radermacher, "Artium Scriptores: Reste der voraristotelischen Rhetorik," in *Oesterreiches Akademie der Wissenschaften, Philosophisch-historische Klasse, Sitzungsberichte* 227/3 (Vienna, 1951), 3–103; and Cairns, *Generic Composition,* 34–35.

22. My translation.

23. Cairns, *Generic Composition,* 6.

24. Cf. the following lists of epideictic genres: Burgess, *Epideictic Literature,* 105–13, 187; and Quint. *Inst.* 3.4.3.

25. Stowers, *Letter Writing,* 91–152.

26. *Demetrii et Libanii,* ed. Weichert, 2 (19–23), 3 (1–5).

27. Ibid., 4 (14–19).

28. By far the most influential proponent of this gulf between the two bodies of letters was Adolf Deissmann (*Light from the Ancient East* [New York: Harper &

Bros., 1927]), who proposed the widely influential distinction between the "letter" and the "epistle."

29. C. W. Keyes, "The Greek Letter of Introduction," *American Journal of Philology* 56 (1935): 31–44. Cf. Koskenniemi, *Studien zur Idee und Phraseologie,* 61–63.

30. E.g., Otto Roller, *Das Formular der Paulinischen Briefe* (Stuttgart, 1933); Paul Schubert, *Form and Function of the Pauline Thanksgiving* (Berlin, 1939); Carl Bjerkelund, *Parakalō* (Oslo, 1967); and Chan-Hie Kim, *Form and Structure of the Familiar Greek Letter of Recommendation,* SBLDS 4 (Missoula, Mont.: Scholars Press, 1972).

31. It is also significant that ancient editions of letter collections frequently delete or abbreviate the opening and closing formulas.

32. Philostratus *De epist.* (Kayser ed., 258 [23–26]) shows how ancients thought about letters in terms of activities: "Whether we grant something or make a request, whether we agree with someone or disagree, whether we express love, we shall more easily prevail if we express ourselves with clarity of style" (Malherbe, "Ancient Epistolary Theorists," 41, modified). Furthermore, when he discusses examples of the best letter writing, he divides his examples into classes of activity, i.e., of philosophers, military commanders, and leaders of state.

33. Koskenniemi, *Studien zur Idee und Phraseologie,* and Thraede, *Grundzüge.*

34. See Stowers, *Letter Writing,* 77–152.

35. On the friendly letter, see Koskenneimi, *Studien zur Idee und Phraseologie;* and on the letter of commendation, Keyes, "Greek Letter of Introduction," and Kim, *Form and Structure.*

36. *Demetrii et Libanii,* ed. Weichert, 34 (1–5).

37. On the parenetic letter, see Abraham Malherbe, "Exhortation in First Thessalonians," *Novum Testamentum* 25 (1983): 238–56; idem, "Hellenistic Moralists and the New Testament," in *Aufstieg und Niedergang der römischen Welt,* ed. W. Haase (Berlin, forthcoming), 2:26; and Benjamin Fiore, "The Function of Personal Example in the Socratic and Pastoral Epistles" (Ph.D. diss., Yale Univ., 1982).

38. *W. Chr.* 10; *P. Oxy.* 744, 3057, 3069.

39. *P. Oxy.* 115, 1874; *P. Grenf.* 2.36; *P. Wisc.* 44. On consolation, see R. Kassel, *Untersuchungen zur griechischen und römischen Konsolationsliteratur* (Munich, 1958). On Christian consolation, see R. C. Gregg, *Consolation Philosophy* (Cambridge, Mass.: Philadelphia Patristic Foundation, 1975).

40. For some of these types among the papyri, see J. L. White and K. A. Kensinger, "Categories of Greek Papyrus Letters," *Society of Biblical Literature 1976 Seminar Papers,* ed. G. MacRae (Missoula, Mont.: Scholars Press, 1976), 79–91.

41. Praise: *P. Lond.* 1244; *P. Oxy.* 1860; *P. Jews* 1925, 1956, 1927; Plato *Ep.* 12; Fronto *Ad M.Caes* 2.2, 4.1; Apollonius of Tyana *Ep.*; Socratics *Ep.* 20; Pliny *Ep.* 4.18; Cyprian *Ep.* 39; Basil *Ep.* 17, 50; Synesius *Ep.* 60, 71, 117; Augustine *Ep.* 58; Theodoret *Ep.* 60, 71. Blame: *P. Oxy.* 1067, 1348, 2595; *P. Fay.* 112; *UPZ* 1.59; *C. P. Jud.* 2.444; *P. Par.* 47; *P. Mert.* 112, 115; Apollonius of Tyana *Ep.* 46; Crates *Ep.* 32; Basil *Ep.* 12; Synesius *Ep.* 8, 23, 46, 138. Advice: *CPR* 20; *P. Oxy.* 299, 531; *P. Bon.* 1, 3, 4, 11, 12; Isoc. *Ep.* 1; Plato *Ep.* 6, 7, 8; Cicero *Ad fam.* 15.4; Pliny *Ep.*

1.23, 6.29, 7.9; Crates *Ep.* 12, 22, 25; Socratics *Ep.* 29; Fronto *Ad amic.* 2.11; Pliny *Ep.* 7.1, 9, 17; Augustine *Ep.* 228. Admonition: *SB* 6263; *P. Teb.* 1.23; *P. Oxy.* 938; *UPZ* 144; Cicero *Ad fam.* 5.14; Pliny *Ep.* 9.5; Diogenes *Ep.* 17; Crates *Ep.* 8, 10, 26, 30, 32; Anacharsis *Ep.* 2.8; Socratics *Ep.* 34; Basil *Ep.* 261; Synesius *Ep.* 143. Thanking: *P. Oxy.* 811; *SIG* 1.384; Pliny *Ep.* 9.24, 10.2, 89; Apollonius of Tyana *Ep.* 11; Jerome *Ep.* 4.1; Ruricius 2.53; Synesius *Ep.* 9, 14. Supplicatory (*metamelētikos;* cf. Demetrius's *axiōmatikos*): *BGU* 846; *P. Heid.* 1.6; Basil *Ep.* 59, 60; Theodoret *Ep.* 96. Threatening: *P. Tebt.* 2.424; *P. Hib.* 55, 59; *P. Flor.* 162; *P. Oxy.* 1295, 1839; *P. Fay.* 135; Pliny *Ep.* 1.15; Diogenes *Ep.* 38; Cyprian *Ep.* 40; Jerome *Ep.* 137.

7

Beyond Myth,
after Apocalypse:
The Mishnaic Conception of History

JACOB NEUSNER
Brown University

The framers of the Mishnah, a late-second-century law code that, along with the Hebrew Bible, forms the foundation of Judaism as we know it, present us with a kind of historical thinking quite different from the one they, along with all Israel, had inherited in Scripture. The legacy of prophecy, apocalypse, and mythic history (*Heilsgeschichte*) handed on by the writers of the books of the Old Testament exhibits a single and quite familiar conception of history seen whole. Events bear meaning—God's message and judgment. What happens is singular—therefore, an event to be noted—and points toward lessons to be drawn for where things are heading and why. If things do not happen at random, they also do not form indifferent patterns of merely secular, social facts. What happens is important because of the meaning contained therein. That meaning is to be discovered and revealed through the narrative of what has happened.

So for all forms of Judaism until the Mishnah, the writing of history is a form of prophecy. Just as prophecy takes up the interpretation of historical events, so historians retell these events in the frame of prophetic theses. And out of the two—historiography as a code of mythic reflection, prophecy as a means of mythic construction—emerges a picture of future history, that is, what is going to happen. That picture, framed in terms of visions and supernatural symbols, in the end focuses, as much as do prophecy and history writing, upon the here and now.

The upshot is simple. History consists of a sequence of one-time events, each singular, all meaningful. These events move from a beginning somewhere to an end at a foreordained goal. History moves toward eschatology, the end of history. The teleology of Israel's life finds its definition in eschatological fulfillment. Eschatology therefore constitutes not a choice *within* teleology but a definition *of* teleology. History done in this way then

91

sits enthroned as the queen of theological science. Events do not conform to patterns. They form patterns. What happens matters because events bear meaning, constitute history.

Now, as is clear, such a conception of mythic and apocalyptic history comes to realization in the writing of history in the prophetic pattern or in the apocalyptic framework, both of them mythic modes of organizing events. We have every right to expect such a view of matters to lead people to write books of a certain sort rather than of some other. In the case of Judaism, obviously, we should expect people to write history books that teach lessons or apocalyptic books that through pregnant imagery predict the future and record the direction and end of time. And in antiquity that kind of writing proves commonplace among all kinds of groups and characteristic of all sorts of Judaisms but one.

The Mishnah, which I shall identify in a moment, contains a very few tales, and no large-scale conception of history. It organizes its system in nonhistorical and socially unspecific terms, lacking all precedent in prior systems of Judaism and in prior kinds of Judaic literature. Instead of narrative, it gives description of how things are done, that is, descriptive laws. Instead of reflecting on the meaning and end of history, it constructs a world in which history plays little part. Instead of narratives full of didactic meaning, it provides lists of events so as to expose the traits that they share and thus the rules to which they conform. The definitive components of a historical-eschatological system of Judaism—description of events as one-time happenings, analysis of the meaning and end of events, and interpretation of the end and future of singular events—none of these commonplace constituents of all other systems of Judaism (including nascent Christianity) of ancient times finds a place in the Mishnah's system of Judaism.

So, as we shall see, the Mishnah finds no precedent in prior Israelite writing for its mode of dealing with things that happen. The Mishnah's way of identifying happenings as consequential and describing them, its way of analyzing those events it chooses as bearing meaning, its interpretation of the future to which significant events point—all those in context were unique. Yet to say that the Mishnah's system is ahistorical could not be more wrong. The Mishnah presents a different kind of history. More to the point, it revises the inherited conception of history and reshapes that conception to fit into its own system. When we consider the point of the biblical myth, the force of its eschatological and messianic interpretation of history, the effect of apocalypse, we must find astonishing the capacity of the Mishnah's framers to think in a different way about the same things. As teleology constructed outside the eschatological mode of thought in the setting of the biblical world of ancient Israel, it proves amazing. Let me now show some of the principal texts that contain and convey this other conception of how events become history and how history teaches lessons.

THE MISHNAH

When the temple of Jerusalem fell to the Babylonians in 586 B.C.E., Israelite thinkers turned to the writing of history to explain what had happened. From that time onward, with the composition of the Pentateuch and the historical books—Joshua, Judges, Samuel, and Kings—to teach the lessons of history, and the prophetic and apocalyptic books first to interpret and then to project those lessons into the future, Israel explained the purpose of its being by focusing upon the meaning of events. The critical issue then was salvation: from what? for what? by whom? In that context, the belief in a supernatural man, an anointed savior or messiah, formed a natural complement to a system in which teleology took the form of eschatology. Israelites do their duty because of what is happening and of where events will lead. All things point to a foreordained end, presenting the task of interpreting the signs of the times. No wonder, then, that, when the temple of Jerusalem fell to the Romans, in 70 C.E., established patterns of thinking guided writers of Judaic apocalypse to pay attention to the meaning of history.

The character of the Israelite Scriptures, with the emphasis upon historical narrative as a mode of theological explanation, leads us to expect all forms of Judaism to evolve as a deeply historical and messianic religion. With all prescribed actions pointed toward the coming of the Messiah at the end of time, and all interest focused upon answering the historical-salvific question "How long?" Judaism from late antiquity to the present day presents no surprises. Its liturgy evokes historical events to prefigure salvation; prayers of petition repeatedly turn to the speedy coming of the Messiah; and the experience of worship invariably leaves the devotee expectant and hopeful. Just as rabbinic (now-normative) Judaism is a deeply messianic religion, secular extensions of Judaism for their part have commonly proposed secularized versions of the established pattern of focus upon history and interest in the purpose and denouement of events. Teleology once more takes the form of eschatology embodied in messianic symbols and given expression in mythic, historical narrative.

Yet for a brief moment a vast and influential document presented a kind of Judaism in which history did not define the main framework, in which the issue of teleology took a form other than the familiar eschatological one, and in consequence, in which historical events were absorbed through their trivialization in taxonomic structures into a nonhistorical system. In the kind of Judaism at hand in this document, messiahs did figure. But these "anointed men" played no *historical* role. They undertook a task quite different from that assigned to Jesus by the framers of the Gospels. They were merely a species of priest, falling into one classification rather than some other.

The Mishnah, ca. 200 C.E., is a strange corpus of normative statements which we may, though with some difficulty, classify as a law code or a schoolbook for philosophical jurists. The difficulty of classification derives from the contents of the document, which deal with topics to which in the main we should be reluctant to assign the title of law. Composed in an age in which, on the Roman side as well, people were making law codes, the Mishnah presents a systematic account of the life of Israel, the Jewish people in the land of Israel. The Mishnah comprises sixty-three tractates covering six categories of activity. These begin, first, with rules for the conduct of the economy—that is, agriculture—with special attention to the farmers' provision of priestly rations. Second come rules for various special holy days and seasons, with special attention to the conduct of the sacrificial service and life of the temple cult on such occasions, and corresponding conduct in the home. Third are rules governing the status of women, with particular interest in the transfer of a woman from the domain of one man to that of another. Fourth is a code of civil laws, covering all aspects of commercial, civil, and criminal law, and offering a blueprint for an Israelite government based on the temple in Jerusalem and headed by a king and a high priest. Fifth, we find rules for the temple's sacrificial service and for the upkeep of the temple buildings and establishment, with emphasis upon the life of the cult on ordinary days. Finally, the Mishnah details taboos affecting the cultic life, in the form of unclean things and rules on how to remove their effects.

This brief account of the document points toward its principal point of interest: sanctification. At issue is the life of Israel under the aspect of holiness, lived out in relationship to the temple and under the governance of the priesthood. What has been said indicates also what the document neglects to treat: salvation, that is, the historical life of the Jewish nation— where it is heading and how it is to get there. The Mishnah omits all reference to its own point of origin, thus lacking a historical account or a mythic base: this represents a shift from Scriptures' myths for the Mosaic codes. The framers of the code likewise barely refer to Scripture itself, rarely produce proof texts for their own propositions, and never imitate the modes of speech of ancient Hebrew as do the writers of the Dead Sea Scrolls at Qumran. They hardly propose to explain the relationship between their book and the established Holy Scriptures of Israel. The absence of sustained attention to events and a doctrine of history serves also to explain why the Messiah as an eschatological figure makes no appearance in the system of the Mishnah and in no way defines its teleology.

Accordingly, the later decades of the second century, after the defeat of Bar Kokhba, witnessed the composition of the Mishnah, a vast book, later received as authoritative and turned into the foundations of the two Talmuds, one composed in Babylonia, the other in the land of Israel, which define Judaism as we know it. If, then, we ask about the context in which this foundation document of the rabbinic canon came into being, we find ourselves in an age that had witnessed yet another messianic war, fought by Israel against Rome, this under Bar Kokhba, from 132 to 135. That war, coming three generations after the destruction of the temple, aimed to regain Jerusalem and rebuild the temple. It seems probable that Bar Kokhba in his own day was perceived as a messianic general, and the war was imagined to come at the expected end of time, the eschatological climax to the drama begun in 70. If so, the character of the Mishnah, the work of the survivors of the war, proves truly astonishing. Here, as I said, we have an immense, systematic, and encompassing picture of the life of Israel in which events scarcely play a role, in which history rarely intervenes. The goal and purpose of it all find full and ample expression with scarcely a word about either the end of time or the coming of the Messiah. In a word, the Mishnah presents us with a kind of Judaism possessed of an eschatology—a theory of the end—without a messiah, as teleology beyond time. When the point of insistence is sanctification, not salvation, in the Mishnah, we see the outcome.

So this great document, created by survivors and their disciples, contains a rich stash of question marks. Its authors tell us nothing about theological context—about the character and authority of the document, why they have made it, or what they want people to do with it. They ignore the entire antecedent literary heritage of Israel, referring only occasionally to Scripture but never to any other writing. The generative issues persistently addressed throughout the Mishnah's discourse concern sorting out matters of doubt, plotting the way in which conflicts between valid principles are resolved, and, in all, examining the way in which things reach their proper classification. These deeply philosophical questions take up problems of potentiality and actuality, intention and deed, the genus and the species, mixtures of various kinds, and similar perennial issues of thought. Inquiry comes to full exposure in discussion of arcane topics, most of them rarely if ever addressed in previous Israelite writings except, in varying measure, in Scripture itself.

THE USES AND MEANING OF HISTORY
IN THE MISHNAH

By "history" I mean not merely events but how events are organized and narrated so as to teach lessons, reveal patterns, tell us what we must do and why, what will happen to us tomorrow. In that context, some events contain richer lessons than others; the destruction of the temple of Jerusalem teaches more than a crop failure, being kidnapped into slavery more than stubbing one's toe. Furthermore, lessons taught by events—"history" in the didactic sense—follow a progression from trivial and private to consequential and public. The framers of the Mishnah explicitly refer to very few events, treating those they do mention with a focus quite separate from what happened—the unfolding of the events themselves. They rarely create or use narratives. More probative still, historical events do not supply organizing categories or taxonomic cl·ssifications. We find no tractate devoted to the destruction of the temple, no complete chapter detailing the events of Bar Kokhba, nor even a sustained celebration of the events of the sages' own historical lives. When things that have happened are mentioned, it is neither in order to narrate nor to interpret and draw lessons from the event. It is either to illustrate a point of law or to pose a problem of the law—always en passant, never in a pointed way.

So when sages refer to what has happened, this is casual and tangential to the main thrust of discourse. For example, the "men slain at Tel Arza" (by the Romans?) come under discussion only because we have to decide whether they are to be declared legally dead so their wives may remarry (*m. Yebam.* 16.7). The advent of Gentiles to Jerusalem (in 70?) raises the question of whether we assume a priest's wife has been raped (*m. Ketub.* 2.9). A war comes into sight—not named, not important—only because of a queen's vow, taken when her son goes off "to war" (*m. Nazir* 4.1). Famous events, of enduring meaning, such as the return to Zion from Babylonia in the time of Ezra and Nehemiah, gain entry into the Mishnah's discourse only because of the genealogical divisions of Israelite society into castes among the immigrants (*m. Qidd.* 4.1). Where the Mishnah provides little tales or narratives, moreover, they more often treat how things in the cult are done in general than what in particular happened on some one day. For instance, there is the tale of the burning of the red cow (*m. Parah,* chap. 3) or of the purification of the *mesora* of Lev. 13:2ff. (*m. Neg.,* chap. 14). The names of temple officers are catalogued (*m. Šeqal.* 51.1). But we learn no more about them than the jobs to which they were assigned. Allusions to famous events even within sages' own circles do not demand detailed narration (as to *m. Kelim* 5.10). It is sufficient to refer casually to well-known incidents. Narrative, in the Mishnah's limited rhetorical repertoire, is reserved for the narrow framework of what priests and others do on recurrent occasions and around the temple. In all, that staple of history, stories about dramatic events and important deeds, in the minds of the Mishnah's jurisprudents provides little nourishment. Events, if they appear at all, are treated as trivial. They may be well known but are consequential in some way other than is revealed in the detailed account of what actually happened.

Sages' treatment of events, as we shall now see in detail, determines what in the Mishnah is important *about* what happens. Since the greatest event in the century and a half—from ca. 50 C.E. to ca. 200—in which the Mishnah's materials came into being, was the destruction of the temple in 70 C.E., we must expect the Mishnah's treatment of that incident to illustrate the document's larger theory of history: what is important and unimportant about what happens. The treatment of the destruction occurs in two ways.

First, the destruction of the temple constitutes a noteworthy fact in the history of the law. Why? Because various laws about rite and cult had to undergo revision on account of the destruction. The following provides a stunningly apt example of how the Mishnah's philosophers regard what actually happened as being simply changes in the law:

m. Roš Haššana 4.1–4

4.1   A. On the festival day of the New Year which coincided with the Sabbath—

      B. in the Temple they would sound the *shofar*.

      C. But not in the provinces.

      D. When the Temple was destroyed, Rabban Yohanan ben Zakkai made the rule that they should sound the *shofar* in every locale in which there was a court.

      E. Said R. Eleazar, "Rabban Yohanan b. Zakkai made that rule in the case of Yabneh alone."

      F. They said to him, "All the same are Yabneh and every locale in which there is a court."

4.2   A. And in this regard also was Jerusalem ahead of Yabneh:

      B. in every town which is within sight and sound [of Jerusalem], and nearby and able to come to Jerusalem, they sound the *shofar*.

      C. But as to Yabneh, they sound the *shofar* only in the court alone.

4.3   A. In olden times the *lulab* was taken up in the Temple for seven days, and in the provinces for one day.

      B. When the Temple was destroyed, Rabban Yohanan ben Zakkai made the rule that in the provinces the *lulab* should be taken up for seven days, as a memorial to the Temple;

      C. and that the day [the sixteenth of Nisan] on which the *omer* is waved should be wholly prohibited [in regard to the eating of new produce] (M. Suk. 3.12).

4.4   A. At first they would receive testimony about the new moon all day long.

      B. One time the witnesses came late, and the Levites consequently were mixed up as to [what] song [they should sing].

      C. They made the rule that they should receive testimony [about the new moon] only up to the afternoon offering.

      D. Then, if witnesses came after the afternoon offering, they would treat that entire day as holy, and the next day as holy too.

E. When the Temple was destroyed, Rabban Yohanan b. Zakkai made the rule that they should [once more] receive testimony about the new moon all day long.

F. Said R. Joshua b. Qorha, "This rule too did Rabban Yohanan b. Zakkai make:

G. 'Even if the head of the court is located somewhere else, the witnesses should come only to the location of the council [to give testimony, and not to the location of the head of the court].'"

The passages before us leave no doubt about what sages selected as important about the destruction: that it produced changes in synagogue rites.

Second, although the sages surely mourned for the destruction and the loss of Israel's principal mode of worship, and certainly recorded the event of the ninth of Ab in the year 70 C.E., they did so in their characteristic way: *they listed the event as an item in a catalogue of things that are like one another and so demand the same response. But then the destruction of the year 70 no longer appears as a unique event.* It is absorbed into a pattern of like disasters, all exhibiting similar taxonomic traits, events to which the people, now well schooled in tragedy, knows full well the appropriate response. So it is in demonstrating regularity that sages reveal their way of coping. Then the uniqueness of the event fades away, its mundane character is emphasized. The power of taxonomy in imposing order upon chaos once more does its healing work. The consequence was reassurance that historical events obeyed discoverable laws. Israel's ongoing life would override disruptive, one-time happenings. So catalogues of events, as much as lists of species of melons, served as brilliant apologetic by providing reassurance that nothing lies beyond the range and power of ordering system and stabilizing pattern.

m. Ta'anit 4.6–7

4.6 A. Five events took place for our fathers on the seventeenth of Tammuz, and five on the ninth of Ab.

B. On the seventeenth of Tammuz (1) the tablets [of the Torah] were broken, (2) the daily whole offering was cancelled, (3) the city wall was breached, (4) Apostemos burned the Torah, and (5) he set up an idol in the Temple.

C. On the ninth of Ab (1) the decree was made against our forefathers that they should not enter the land, (2) the first Temple and (3) the second [Temple] were destroyed, (4) Betar was taken, and (5) the city was ploughed up [after the war of Hadrian].

D. When Ab comes, rejoicing diminishes.

4.7 A. In the week in which the ninth of Ab occurs it is prohibited to get a haircut and to wash one's clothes.

B. But on Thursday of that week these are permitted,

C. because of the honor due to the Sabbath.

> D. On the eve of the ninth of Ab a person should not eat two prepared dishes, nor should one eat meat or drink wine.
> E. Rabban Simeon b. Gamaliel says, "He should make some change from ordinary procedures."
> F. R. Judah declares people obligated to turn over beds.
> G. But sages did not concur with him.

I include m. Ta'an. 4.7 to show the context in which the list of m. Ta'an. 4.6 stands. The stunning calamities catalogued at 4.6 form groups, reveal common traits, and so are subject to classification. Then the laws of 4.7 provide regular rules for responding to, coping with, these untimely catastrophes, all in a single classification. So the raw materials of history are absorbed into the ahistorical, supernatural system of the Mishnah. The process of absorption and regularization of the unique and one-time moment is illustrated in the passage at hand.

Along these same lines, the entire history of the cult, so critical in the larger system created by the Mishnah's lawyers, produced a patterned—therefore, sensible and intelligible—picture. As is clear, everything that happened turned out to be susceptible of classification once the taxonomic traits were specified. A monothetic exercise, sorting out periods and their characteristics, took the place of narrative, to explain things in its own way: first this, and then that, and in consequence, the other. So in the neutral turf of holy ground, as much as in the trembling earth of the temple mount, everything was absorbed into one thing, all classified in its proper place and by its appropriate rule. Indeed, so far as the lawyers proposed to write history at all, they wrote it into their picture of the long tale of the way in which Israel served God: the places in which the sacrificial labor was carried on, the people who did it, the places in which the priests ate the meat left over for their portion after God's portion was set aside and burned up. This "historical" account forthwith generated precisely that problem of locating the regular and orderly which the philosophers loved to investigate: the intersection of conflicting but equally correct taxonomic rules, as we see at m. Zebah. 14.9 below. The passage that follows therefore is history so far as the Mishnah's creators proposed to write history—the reduction of events to rules forming compositions of regularity, and therefore meaning:

m. Zebaḥim 14.4–8, 14.9

> 14.4 I A. Before the tabernacle was set up, (1) the high places were permitted, and (2) [the sacrificial] service [was done by] the first born [Num. 3:12–13; 8:16–18].
> B. When the tabernacle was set up, (1) the high places were prohibited, and (2) the [sacrificial] service [was done by] priests.
> C. Most Holy Things were eaten within the veils, Lesser Holy Things [were eaten] throughout the camp of Israel.

14.5 II A. They came to Gilgal.
   B. The high places were permitted.
   C. Most Holy Things were eaten within the veils, Lesser Holy Things, anywhere.

14.6 III A. They came to Shiloh.
   B. The high places were prohibited.
   C. (1) There was no roof-beam there, but below was a house of stone, and hangings above it, and (2) it was "the resting place" [Deut. 12:9].
   D. Most Holy Things were eaten within the veils, Lesser Holy Things and second-tithe [were eaten] in any place within sight [of Shiloh].

14.7 IV A. They came to Nob and Gibeon.
   B. The high places were permitted.
   C. Most Holy Things were eaten within the veils, Lesser Holy Things, in all the towns of Israel.

14.8 V A. They came to Jerusalem.
   B. The high places were prohibited.
   C. And they never again were permitted.
   D. And it was "the inheritance" [Deut. 12:9].
   E. Most Holy Things were eaten within the veils, Lesser Holy Things and second-tithe within the wall.

14.9 VI A. All the Holy things which one sanctified at the time of the prohibition of the high places and offered at the time of the prohibition of the high places outside—
   B. lo, these are subject to the transgression of a positive commandment and a negative commandment, and they are liable on their account to extirpation [for sacrificing outside the designated place, Lev. 17:8–9; *m. Zebaḥ.* 13.1A].
   C. [If] one sanctified them at the time of the permission of high places and offered them up at the time of the prohibition of high places,
   D. lo, these are subject to transgression of a positive commandment and to a negative commandment, but they are not liable on their account to extirpation [since if the offerings had been sacrificed when they were sanctified, there should have been no violation].
   E. [If] one sanctified them at the time of the prohibition of high places and offered them up at the time of the permission of high places,
   F. lo, these are subject to transgression of a positive commandment, but they are not subject to a negative commandment at all.

The inclusion of *m. Zebaḥ.* 14.9, structurally matching *m. Taʿan.* 4.7, shows us the goal of the historical composition. It is to set forth rules that intersect and produce confusion, so that we may sort out confusion and make sense of all the data.

The upshot may now be stated briefly. The Mishnah absorbs into its encompassing system all events, small and large. With them the sages accomplish what they do with everything else: a vast labor of taxonomy, an immense construction of the order and rules governing the classification of everything on earth and in heaven. The disruptive character of history—one-time events of ineluctable significance—scarcely impresses the philosophers. They find no difficulty in showing that what appears unique and beyond classification has in fact happened before and so falls within the range of trustworthy rules and known procedures. Once history's components, one-time events, lose their distinctiveness, then history as a didactic intellectual construct, as a source of lessons and rules, also loses all pertinence.

So lessons and rules come from sorting things out and classifying them, that is, from the procedures and modes of thought of the philosopher seeking regularity. To this labor of taxonomy, the historian's way of selecting data and arranging them into patterns of meaning to teach lessons proves inconsequential. One-time events are not what matters. The world is composed of nature and supernature. The repetitious laws that count are those to be discovered in heaven and, in heaven's creation and counterpart, on earth. Keep those laws, and things will work out. Break them, and the result is predictable: calamity of whatever sort will supervene in accordance with the rules. But just because it is predictable, a catastrophic happening testifies to what has always been and must always be, in accordance with reliable rules and within categories already discovered and well explained. That is why the lawyer-philosophers of the mid–second century produced the Mishnah: to explain how things are. Within the framework of well-classified rules, there could be messiahs, but no single Messiah (in Christian theological terms, *Geschichte*, but no *Historie*).

Up to now I have contrasted "history" with "eternity," and framed matters in such a way that the Mishnah's system appears to have been ahistorical and antihistorical. Yet in fact the framers of the Mishnah recognized the pastness of the past and, hence, by definition, laid out a conception of the past that constitutes a historical doctrine. But it is a different conception from the familiar one. To express the difference, I point out that for modern history writing what is important is to describe what is unique and individual, not what is ongoing and unremarkable. History is the story of change, development, movement, not of what does not change, develop or move. For the thinkers of the Mishnah, historical patterning emerges as, today, scientific knowledge does—through taxonomy, the classification of the unique and individual, the organization of change and movement within unchanging categories. That is why the dichotomy between history and eternity, change and permanence, signals an unnuanced exegesis of what was in fact a subtle and reflective doctrine of history. That doctrine proves entirely consistent with the large perspectives of scribes, from the ones who made omen series in ancient Babylonia to the ones who made the Mishnah. That is why the category of salvation does not serve but the one of sanctification fits admirably.

MISHNAH'S COMPLEMENT:
APOCALYPSE IN TOSEFTA

Sometime between 200 and 400 a corpus of materials in the language and style of the Mishnah was collected to complement the teachings of the Mishnah. This corpus, the Tosefta, was framed in the same period as the founding of the two great Talmuds, one of the land of Israel, the other of Babylonia. But it adhered closely to the modes of organization and of thought of the Mishnah, and hence serves as a suitable answer to the question, What happened next? For there are two answers, the one at hand, the other in the two Talmuds. A separate account of the latter is required. But the Tosefta's collectors organized and expressed information just as did those of the Mishnah, and they did so in order to say pretty much the same things. That is why it is appropriate to conclude this account of the Mishnah by taking one step outward and beyond.

We close our inquiry with a stunning example of how in the Tosefta the system constructed by the founders of the Mishnah treats already-available historical-apocalyptic materials of Scripture. The passage at hand shows us what the Tosefta's authorities, sometime a century after the Mishnah, do with the most historical of all scriptural materials, apocalypse. The climax of scriptural historiography comes in apocalyptic interpretations of natural symbols in terms of concrete historical events, and of events in terms of symbols. Such interpretation is provided by the visionaries in the Book of Daniel. To appreciate the Mishnah's power, we see the Tosefta's transformation of the apocalyptic vision, following the entire discussion in context. What we see is the interpretation of the apocalyptic vision of history wholly in terms of what happens within the circles of sages' debates—a truly stunning metamorphosis out of history entirely and into the realm of philosophers:

t. Miqwa'ot 7.11

A. A cow which drank purification-water, and which one slaughtered within twenty-four hours—
B. This was a case, and R. Yose the Galilean did declare it clean, and R. Aqiba did declare it unclean.
C. R. Tarfon supported R. Yose the Galilean. R. Simeon ben Nanos supported R. Aqiba.
D. R. Simeon b. Nanos dismissed [the arguments of] R. Tarfon. R. Yose the Galilean dismissed [the arguments of] R. Simeon b. Nanos.
E. R. Aqiba dismissed [the arguments of] R. Yose the Galilean.

F. After a time, he [Yose] found an answer for him [Aqiba].

G. He said to him, "Am I able to reverse myself?"

H. He said to him, "Not anyone [may reverse himself], but you [may do so], for you are Yose the Galilean."

I. [He said to him,] "I shall say to you: Lo, Scripture states, *And they shall be kept for the congregation of the people of Israel for the water for impurity* (Num. 19:9).

J. "Just so long as they are kept, lo, they are water for impurity—but not after a cow has drunk them."

K. This was a case, and thirty-two elders voted in Lud and declared it clean.

L. At that time R. Tarfon recited this verse:

M. "*I saw the ram goring westward and northward and southward, and all the animals were unable to stand against it, and none afforded protection from its power, and it did just as it liked and grew great* (Dan. 8:4)—

N. "[This is] R. Aqiba.

O. "*As I was considering, behold, a he-goat came from the west across the face of the whole earth, without touching the ground; and the goat had a conspicuous horn between his eyes.*

P. "*He came to the ram with the two horns, which I had seen standing on the bank of the river, and he ran at him in his mighty wrath. I saw him come close to the ram, and he was enraged against him and struck the ram and broke his two horns*'—this is R. Aqiba and R. Simeon b. Nanos.

Q. "*And the ram had no power to stand before him*'—this is R. Aqiba.

R. "*But he cast him down to the ground and trampled upon him*'—this is R. Yose the Galilean.

S. "*And there was no one who could rescue the ram from his power*'—these are the thirty-two elders who voted in Lud and declared it clean.'"

In the sages' debates, Daniel's vision of the kingdoms now is turned into an account of the class of titans. The history of nations, their wars and kings and victories, moves from the world of material reality to the realm of mind constructed in the fantastic law systems of the Mishnah and the Tosefta. History in the ordinary sense of the word is not merely rejected or ignored. It is transformed. The process inaugurated in the Mishnah's reduction of unique events to their monothetic taxa and absorption of these events within a system of predictable classification here reaches its climax. People who know what history really consists of will then recognize that sages make history. They make history in the thoughts they think and the rules they lay down. In such a context as this, there is place for neither history nor an end of history, nor will the Messiah find his services required.

ESCHATOLOGY WITHOUT MESSIAH, TELEOLOGY BEYOND TIME

At issue is the direction of eschatology in the foundation document and its continuations. It is not merely whether, or how frequently, the figures of the Messiah and Elijah make an appearance, how often the "days of the Messiah" come under discussion, or how many references we find to the "end of days" or events we regard as historical. We focus upon how the system laid out in the Mishnah takes up and disposes of those critical issues of teleology worked out through messianic eschatology in other, earlier versions of Judaism. These earlier systems resorted to the myth of the Messiah as Savior and Redeemer of Israel, a supernatural figure engaged in political-historical tasks as king of the Jews, even a God-man facing the crucial historical questions of Israel's life and resolving them: the Christ as king of the world, of the ages, of death itself. Even though the figure of a Messiah does appear, when the framers of the Mishnah speak of the Messiah, they mean a high priest designated and consecrated to office in a certain way, and not in some other way. The reference to "days of the Messiah" constitutes a given, a conventional division of history at the end time but before the ultimate end. But that category of time differentiated plays no consequential role in the teleological framework established within the Mishnah. Accordingly, the Mishnah's framers constructed a system of Judaism in which the entire teleological dimension reached full exposure with scarcely a hint of a need to invoke the person or functions of a messianic figure of any kind. Perhaps, in the aftermath of Bar Kokhba's debacle, silence on the subject served to express a clarion judgment. I am inclined to think so. But for the purpose of our inquiry the main thing is the simple fact that I have expounded and illustrated.

The issue of eschatology, framed in mythic terms, draws in its wake the issue of how, in the Mishnah as the foundation document of Judaism, history comes to full conceptual expression. History as an account of a meaningful pattern of events, making sense of the past and giving guidance about the future, begins with the necessary conviction that events matter, one after another. The Mishnah's framers present us with no elaborate theory of events, a fact fully consonant with their systematic points of insistence and encompassing concern. Events do not matter, one by one. The philosopher-lawyers exhibited no theory of history either. Their conception of Israel's destiny in no way called upon historical categories of either narrative or didactic explanation to describe and account for the future. The small importance attributed to the figure of the Messiah as a historical-eschatological figure therefore fully accords with the larger traits of the system as a whole. Let me speak with emphasis: *If what is important in Israel's existence is sanctification, an ongoing process, and not salvation, understood as a one-time event at the end, then no one will find reason to narrate history.*

That is why, at the end, we come to the absurdity of the reduction of an apocalyptic vision of the wars of great empires to the paltry dimensions of an academic argument about nothing of material consequence. Were it not for the document's prevailing seriousness, we might be inclined to see Rabbi Tarfon's reading of Dan. 8:4 as a remarkably subtle and ironic judgment, a joke. But so far as I know, it was not a joke. The disproportion between Daniel's images and Tarfon's interpretation strikes us. But it struck no one before us. What we learn from the Tosefta is the way forward, from the Mishnah onward, as it was explored by some in the third and fourth centuries. So, as I said, the Tosefta tells us what people might have done.

But we realize full well that the Tosefta does not point toward the character of Judaism as it was to emerge from late antiquity: richly eschatological, obsessed with the Messiah and his coming, engaged by the history of Israel and the nations. The Tosefta, in line with the Mishnah, allowed no glimpse at a doctrine of Israel's history and destiny, because the framers had nothing to show. But Judaism at the end did indeed provide an ample account and explanation of Israel's history and destiny. These emerged as the generative problematic of Judaism, just as they framed the social reality confronted by Jews wherever they lived. So to seek the map that shows the road from the Mishnah, at the beginning, to the fully articulated Judaism at the end of the formative age in late antiquity, we have to look elsewhere. For as to the path from the Mishnah through the Tosefta—this is not the way people took.

It could never have been the way, because, in my view, the Mishnah with its documents of continuation and succession proposed to ignore the actualities of the social condition of Israel. The critical issues confronting the Jewish nation emerged from its sorry political condition. In the most commonplace sense of the word, these were *historical* issues. Any sort of Judaism that pretended the history of Israel could be reduced to lists of events sharing the same taxonomic traits, and that the destiny of Israel might be absorbed into an essentially imaginary framework of sanctification attained through the human heart and mind, demanded what the Jewish nation could not give. For people could not pretend to be other than who they were and what they were. Israel constituted a defeated people, driven from its holy place, yet reminded, every time they opened their ancient Scriptures, of God's special love for them and of their distinctive destiny among nations. Israel lived out an insufferable paradox between God's word and world, between promise and postponed fulfillment. So the critical issue confronting any sort of Judaism to emerge in late antiquity reached definition and attained urgency in the social reality, the everyday experience, of Israel. When? By whom? To the Jewish nation history proved very real indeed. The political question of Israel's destiny settled by the myth of the promise of the Messiah's coming salvation—a concrete national and historical salvation—could not be wished away. It demanded response: How long, O Lord? So, as is clear, the Mishnah's system would have to undergo revision and reformation. The labor of renewal would demand fresh and original thinkers—exegetes of a remarkably subtle capacity.

PART TWO

LITERARY STUDIES:
PAUL

8

Acts of the Apostles as a Historical Source

GERD LUEDEMANN
University of Göttingen

In 1897, Adolf von Harnack wrote a sentence that has ever since evoked a great deal of discussion. With respect to the evaluation of the sources of earliest Christianity, Harnack wrote, we are at present caught up in a movement back to ecclesial tradition about these sources.[1] This situation was especially applicable to a source that Harnack considered to stand alongside Paul's letters and Eusebius's church history as a pillar for historical knowledge about early Christianity, namely, the Acts of the Apostles. In three brilliant monographs, Harnack presented proof for his statement and its relevance to Acts. These were *Luke the Physician* (1907), *The Acts of the Apostles* (1909), and *New Studies to the Acts of the Apostles* (1911).[2] These volumes mark the end of nineteenth-century critical research into Acts,[3] research that had begun in the work of Ferdinand Christian Baur. After a hesitant start, Baur examined the historical information in Paul's letters alongside that of Acts and came to the conclusion that a "comparison of these two sources [necessarily] leads to the opinion that, in the light of the great differences between the two presentations, historical truth can reside only on one side or the other."[4] This keynote, struck in the introduction to his book on Paul from the year 1845, is then applied to, or argued for, each chapter of Acts in part 1 of the book.[5] This is where Baur treats the "life and work of the apostle Paul." Since he follows the sequence of Acts in this part of his study, there results a sort of commentary about Acts that has the main purpose of ferreting out its historical elements. The methodological criteria for determining them are comparison with the letters of Paul, the history of religions, literary criticism, and tendency criticism. The comparison between the historical parts of Acts and the Pauline letters especially led Baur to conclude that only a few sections in Acts have positive historical value. On the other hand, the history of religions and tendency criticism reveal

109

the value of Acts to be great indeed:[6] with them he concludes that Acts was written in the second century to reconcile the opposing parties of Paulinists and Judaists.[7] This thesis was then adopted by Albert Schwegler and Eduard Zeller,[8] two of Baur's students who later achieved renown as classical philologists. Both Schwegler and Zeller set a large and firm question mark behind Acts as a historical source. Furthermore, Baur's type of criticism of Acts was brilliantly displayed in 1870 when Franz Overbeck, a member of the Tübingen school in the allegorical sense, revised W. M. L. de Wette's commentary.[9] Overbeck does differ from Baur with respect to the purpose of Acts: according to him the author was almost completely unaffected by the old parties and wrote as a gentile Christian who freely transferred the ecclesial situation of his own time into the primitive apostolic period.[10] In the actual historical work on the text of Acts, however, and in the conviction that early Christianity must be investigated on a purely historical basis, Overbeck and Baur see eye to eye.[11] Overbeck surpasses Baur in refining—or introducing—source criticism,[12] but his opinion of the historical value of Luke's presentation is as low as that of his predecessor.[13]

It would be wrong, however, to give the impression that the type of criticism of Acts presented by Baur and Overbeck was generally acclaimed in the nineteenth century. Rather the opposite was the case. Their position became the object of recurrent critique from both the learned and the unlearned.[14] Nevertheless, it must be admitted that for decades the Tübingen approach, and particularly its detailed exegesis, formed the generally acknowledged point of departure for liberal critical analysis of Acts[15]—that is, until precisely from among this circle Harnack delivered the forceful counterstroke. After pronouncing the verdict cited earlier that early ecclesiastical tradition was enjoying a growing assessment of reliability in the eyes of research, Harnack published his brilliant three-volume apology of Luke in 1906–11 and there asserted the opposite of virtually everything that the Tübingen scholars and the liberal theologians following them[16] had said about the historical value of Acts. First of all—as one might expect—ancient Christian tradition[17] is right in saying that Luke, the companion of Paul, is the author of both the Gospel of Luke and Acts. He announces himself as such in the "we" passages, which, together with all the other parts of the second half of Acts, present historically correct reports of what he himself has witnessed. The report of events in Acts 1—12, to which Luke naturally was not an eyewitness, derives from various sources of diverse quality.

Thus the difference between Harnack and Baur's school in evaluating the historical value of Acts could hardly be greater, and we may describe the Tübingen school and Harnack as the two major poles in research into Acts, between which, of course, at the turn of the century there were many variations. Baur, Overbeck, and Harnack seem to me still to be the great antipodes, as a short glance at the study of Acts after Harnack reveals.

Harnack's line was continued by Alfred Wikenhauser and no less than Eduard Meyer.[18] For Meyer the authorship of Luke, the companion of Paul, had been definitely established, and Acts is "one of the most important historical works preserved from antiquity."[19] (Volume 3 of his work *Ursprung und Anfänge des Christentums* basically offers a "history" of early Christianity on the basis of Acts.)[20] Strong support for Harnack's evaluation of Acts is found to the present day, especially in the Anglo-Saxon sphere.[21] Finally, sections of contemporary German research manifest that the evaluation of the historicity of Acts is in an upward trend, and the most recent statements of Martin Hengel reveal that Harnack's analysis of Acts is indeed a resource for current research.[22]

The line of Baur and Overbeck continues mainly in literary critical work such as the studies of Julius Wellhausen,[23] which leave Acts behind in bits and pieces, almost losing sight of the question of the historical value of the traditions and sources recovered from Acts. Here, too, belong the studies by Martin Dibelius,[24] which successfully tested style criticism on Acts, and large stretches of North American research, which under the direction of Henry Cadbury, Kirsopp Lake, and F. J. Foakes Jackson established a milestone in the critical investigation of Acts with the five-volume work *The Beginnings of Christianity* and in which the secondary character of Acts was emphasized by such scholars as John Knox and Donald Riddle.[25] Redaction-critical investigation of Luke's two-volume work, especially Acts, should also be mentioned here.[26] While the concern of this type of study was, above all, to become Luke's reader, it needs to be critically remarked that, contrary to the intention of the founders of such investigation, the currently thriving redaction criticism has not seldom led to an almost total neglect of the question of the historicity of the reports in Acts.

This neglect is due, on the one hand, to an overgrown skepticism about everything that Luke wrote and, on the other hand, to the conviction that reconstructing history is theologically questionable because only the kerygma is truly of importance. Contrary to this neglect of history, I would emphasize that since the advent of historical thinking, reconstruction of early Christian history is *necessary* in order to understand early Christian writings. Since Luke himself regards Acts as a historical report about early Christianity (see Luke 1:1–4), we have to address systematically the question of the historical value of this document.

In that respect, the first question to be asked, "Was the author of Acts an eyewitness?" is of such importance that it must be treated here once again.

If it is answered positively, then Acts should be placed next to the letters of Paul and should be considered virtually a *primary source*. If the author was not an eyewitness, then Acts should be regarded as a *secondary source* and its historical value considered much lower than that of the primary source, the Pauline letters.[27]

But what criteria can lead us to a clear-cut decision on this question? One possible approach would be to compare the theologies of Paul and Acts and especially of Paul in Acts.[28] If there prove to be major differences, then it could be concluded that the author of Acts could not have been a companion of Paul. This approach must be left to one side, however, for theological differences between Luke and Paul are likely to be very unreliable criteria for the resolution of our question. Furthermore, one must take into account that even Paul's contemporaries understood his theology in very divergent ways (cf. Rom. 3:8 and, on the other hand, 1 Corinthians 6:12; 8) and that in the following period his theology was only superficially apprehended (2 Peter 3:15). For these reasons, we cannot rule out the possibility that a companion of the historical Paul is responsible for the so very non-Pauline theology of the two Lukan volumes.[29]

Viable approaches to the solution of the problem should be sought solely in *historical* considerations. Along this line, one argument that has been brought against the thesis that Luke was an eyewitness refers to the fact that Luke has omitted some conflicts that Paul's letters reveal to have been decisive. It is said, for example, that Luke mentions neither the gentile Christian Titus, whose circumcision was a disputed point at the Jerusalem conference, nor the crises in the Pauline congregations that are documented in the letters. Such arguments, however, are not likely to be convincing. The author of Acts did not write *sine ira et studio*. An impartial reading of Acts readily reveals that Luke knew more than he reported. That is to say, it is certain that Luke left out certain details—for example, the execution of the apostle, or the delivery of the collection during Paul's last visit to Jerusalem—owing to the particular intentions. The absence of such details cannot be used as a persuasive argument against the thesis that Luke was an eyewitness.[30] Satisfactory arguments against that thesis are most likely to be based only on historical statements that disclose total personal ignorance of Paul on the part of the author of Acts.

Let us test this criterion. Among the happy coincidences for Pauline research is that the extant sources allow *certainty* with regard to the number of times that the apostle traveled to Jerusalem as a Christian. Galatians 1:15–24 excludes any additional journey between the first visit (vv. 15–16) and the second trip, to the Jerusalem conference (2:1–10). The report of the agreement for the collection (Gal. 2:10) and the history of the collection in the Pauline congregations give convincing force to the thesis that Paul was in Jerusalem only one other time, namely, to deliver the collection. That is, it is virtually certain that Paul was in Jerusalem only *three times* as a Christian.[31] Acts, in contrast, reports no less than five trips to Jerusalem (Acts 9; 11; 15; 18:22; 21). It seems impossible that Luke could have been a companion of Paul and simultaneously susceptible to such a mistake. This inaccuracy rather proves Luke to be an author who evidently had no personal knowledge of the life of the apostle. One should also expect that in case of a companionship with Paul, Luke would have told us more about the early Paul.

But there is also another passage that leads to the conclusion that the author of Acts belongs to a later era. In the prologue of the Gospel—a prologue that should be taken to apply to both volumes—Luke differentiates three separate groups of witnesses: the eyewitnesses; those who have composed written reports of the events; and himself as author of the two-volume work dedicated to Theophilus. Two things are clear from the prologue: (1) Luke had predecessors and employed their reports in his work; that is, he is using tradition(s) as he writes. Thus, in the Gospel he employs at least Mark and the sayings source. (2) Luke probably belongs to the third generation. This last point also speaks against the thesis that Luke was a companion of Paul. The thesis that Luke was an eyewitness will therefore have to be left to one side, even though one must acknowledge that research has too quickly dismissed this assumption.[32]

I have already briefly indicated above that Luke knew more than he reported and that he employed traditions in the composition of his two-volume work. Where did these traditions come from? Who passed them on to Luke? How can they be reconstructed? With regard to the origin of the traditions in the Pauline part of Acts, we are faced with three possibilities:
1. Luke knew and used only the letters of Paul.
2. Luke had access only to traditions other than the Pauline letters.
3. Luke used both the letters and the traditions.
To aid in accomplishing the task we have set for ourselves, each possibility needs to be evaluated. We shall begin with the first and ask, Did the author of Acts know and use Paul's letters?

The assumption that Luke knew the letters of Paul is a well-founded hypothesis, which becomes all the more persuasive the later Luke's two-volume work is dated. If Luke belongs to the third Christian generation, as I suggested above, then in light of the fact that he understands himself as a student of Paul or—expressed more carefully—that he stands within the sphere of Pauline tradition (for otherwise I cannot explain the extensive portrayal of Paul), his awareness of the existence of Paul's letters is almost certain.[33] The question then is not whether Luke *knew* the letters of Paul but whether he *used* them in composing his work.

This question can be answered only if traces of the use of Paul's letters can be established with certitude.[34] In short, we must search for agreements between Acts and the letters and then ask whether these agreements are best explained by the assumption that the letters were employed in writing Acts. In what follows we shall review the most important reasons supporting the assumption that Luke used Paul's letters:[35]

1. Most of the places and areas mentioned in Acts as stations of Paul's activity also recur in the corpus Paulinum.[36]
2. The agreement of 2 Corinthians 11 with Acts 9 regarding Paul's daring flight from Damascus is even more striking because both reports break off at the same point, with Paul being let down in a basket through the city wall.
3. The stations in Paul's journeys in Acts disclose surprising coincidence with the stations that can be reconstructed on the basis of the letters. In each case Paul travels from Philippi through Thessalonica and Athens to Corinth (cf. Acts 17 and 1 Thessalonians 2—3).
4. The names of Paul's co-workers in Acts generally agree with similar information in Paul's letters.

Each of these points draws attention to considerable agreement, but not a single one of them brings convincing proof that Luke used Paul's letters, and the question arises whether these observations are more adequately explained by the assumption that Luke used traditions deriving from the area missionized by Paul, traditions the age, origin, and place of which remain to be determined.

In order to avoid biasing the results, it is best to use the word "tradition" in a broad sense. In the remainder of this article, "tradition" means both written sources and oral information.[37] Thus, our question about the historical value of Acts must be reformulated. We must not ask about the value of Acts itself but about the value of the *traditions* Luke has reworked. If Luke himself does not have any personal knowledge of the events he describes, then it would be nonsensical to determine the historical value of Acts by analyzing the story level of the text. Luke's activity as an author— this we can already say—consists of coupling traditions with one another. For us this means that our *first* task must be the separation of redaction and tradition. The *second* task will then be the determination of the historical value of the recovered tradition.

The isolation of tradition in Acts, however, is faced with considerable difficulties. The reasons for this difficulty lie in the literary character of Acts and in the fact that, in contrast to the situation with Luke's Gospel, almost none of the materials used in Acts (the *Vorlagen*) have been preserved elsewhere. The literary character of Acts often prevents the classical methods of literary criticism from attaining reliable results. Word statistics are only partially useful, for Luke has transformed—or at least tried to transform—all of the material into his own language. Observation of tensions in the text does not necessarily direct us to pre-Lukan material, for such tensions might be attributed to the author's conscious attempt at varying his style.[38] Although I do not want to question the value of these two methodological steps, the limitations just mentioned as well as the fact of Luke's editorial reworking of the traditions should be emphasized once more. But on the other hand, Lukan language and style cannot be taken as proof that Luke did not use traditions.

In this article we will, of course, be able to analyze only a few selected texts. It is not without reason that the passages have been taken from the part of Acts that deals with Paul, for here there is relatively often the possibility of advancing redaction-critical and historical analysis by comparison with the Pauline letters. The following texts will be examined:

(a) Acts 18 (Paul in Corinth)

(b) Acts 17—18; 18—19; 27 (the routes of Paul's journeys)

(c) Acts 21 (Paul in Jerusalem)

We shall proceed by determining first the meaning of each text at the redactional level, then the content of its traditional character, and finally the historical value of the individual traditions.

Paul in Corinth (Acts 18:1—17)

The pericope reports Paul's mission in Corinth, which is first carried out weekly in the synagogue and then later in the neighboring house of Titius Justus. Silas and Timothy arrive from Macedonia and find Paul, who during his stay in Corinth has been working with the couple Aquila and Priscilla. (The couple had been forced to leave Rome because of the edict of Claudius and had come to Corinth.) It is here in Corinth that the famous "trial" of Paul before the proconsul Gallio, who dismisses the accusations of the Jews against Paul (Acts 18:12–17), takes place.

Redactional features are quite obvious in this section: Paul's preaching in the synagogue every Sabbath (the connection with the Jews) and the positive portrayal of Gallio, the Roman proconsul, whose attitude is presented as an example of how the Romans (in contrast to the Jews) behave or should behave toward Christians. The fact that these themes find numerous parallels in Acts reveals that these aspects derive from Luke.

Otherwise, the report seems to reflect *tradition*. This is the case with Paul's employment by Aquila and Priscilla in Corinth shortly after Claudius's edict against the Jews, with the arrival of Silas and Timothy from Macedonia, with Paul's preaching in the house of Titius Justus, with the conversion of Crispus (the ruler of the synagogue), with a "trial" before

Gallio, and with the activity of Sosthenes as ruler of the synagogue. Not linguistic considerations but rather the *concreteness* of these reports leads to the conclusion that this material is traditional.

The question now arises whether Acts has chronologically located these traditions correctly and whether the traditions all derive from one and the same visit by Paul to Corinth. This twofold question should probably be answered in the negative for the following three reasons:

1. The pericope discloses a break between v. 11 and v. 12. Verse 11 concludes with a temporal reference: Paul remained in Corinth for eighteen months. Then new material begins. It is introduced with the words "When Gallio was proconsul of Achaia . . ." Thus, even on a purely external showing, the two units are disparate.

2. Verse 8 knows a Crispus as ruler of the synagogue. Verse 17, in contrast, has Sosthenes in this position. Since it is highly probable that the office of a ruler of the synagogue was exercised by only *one* person, each unit probably refers to a different period of time.[39]

3. The chronological references contained in the traditions belong to periods separated from each other by approximately ten years. The expulsion of Jews from Rome, mentioned in v. 2, took place in the year 41. The major part of recent scholarship is in agreement as to that. Gallio, however, was in office in the years 51–52.

At this point and in confirmation of the above analysis, it should be noted that Luke habitually reports on Paul's mission by grouping together into one narrative all the pieces of information known to him. If Paul visits the same place more than once, Luke reports it only summarily.[40] This observation makes it necessary to locate chronologically anew each of the traditions that can be recovered. This observation also stands in accord with the earlier analysis of Acts 18, where we concluded that this passage contains traditions that derive from different visits to Corinth. One of the traditional units probably derives from the year 41, since Paul worked with Aquila and Priscilla during his initial mission in Corinth. The other unit reflects the years 51–52, when Gallio was proconsul of Achaia.

If we evaluate the historical veracity of the traditions, we can ascertain that they have a high historical value. Paul's connection with Aquila and Priscilla during the founding visit in Corinth, which is also evident from the letters (1 Cor. 16:19b) is confirmed by the report in Acts, as is the fact that Silas and Timothy reached Paul during the initial mission in Corinth. This is the case because Silas and Timothy were probably closely connected with the Macedonian brethren who, according to 2 Cor. 11:9, brought Paul financial aid when he was in Corinth (cf. 1 Thess. 3:6). With regard to the years 51–52, a stay in Corinth different from the founding mission may also be determined from the letters. This visit belongs in the period of the great collection, which the apostle undertook in accordance with the agreement at the Jerusalem conference. If what has been said already indicates that the traditions of Acts 18 are of high historical value, then this index would increase even more if John Knox's and my own proposed early dating of the initial Pauline mission should prove to be correct. For in that case a traditional part of Acts 18 would preserve chronologically correct information about Paul's arrival in Corinth. His arrival would indeed have taken place during the year in which Claudius expelled Jews—including Aquila and Priscilla—from Rome, that is, the year 41. The same historical value to which the traditions in Acts 18 attain could not, of course, be acknowledged for the Lukan redaction. Insofar as Luke would have transferred the initial mission in Corinth to the period after the Jerusalem conference and would have unified into one narrative, events that were actually separated by more than ten years, he would be responsible for dating the Pauline mission to Greece about a decade too late.

Travel Routes

Luke presents Paul's mission as a journey that achieves its goal in Rome. The journey leads Paul from the place of his conversion near Damascus to Damascus itself (Acts 9:8), from there to Jerusalem (9:26), then to Cilicia (9:30, "Tarsus"), then to Antioch (11:26) and Jerusalem (11:30), and thereafter onto the so-called *first* missionary journey (chaps. 13—14) through Cyprus and South Galatia back to Antioch. Next comes the third trip to Jerusalem (15:3-4), followed by the so-called *second* missionary journey (15:40—18:22) from Antioch through Asia Minor and Greece back to Jerusalem. Finally, the same stations are visited on the so-called *third* missionary journey (18:22—21:15). At the end occurs the dangerous voyage to Rome (chaps. 27—28).

On the one hand, the journeys of Paul are a Lukan mode of presentation to illustrate the spread of the gospel from Jerusalem to Rome. They are paralleled by the journey of Jesus (the Lukan travel narrative, Luke 9:51—19:28), the redactional character of which may be demonstrated by a comparison with Mark. On the other hand, traditions can be recovered at the following three points:

1. We recall that the order of stations in 1 Thessalonians 2—3 and Acts 17 (Philippi, Thessalonica, Athens, Corinth) has sometimes led to the conclusion that Luke made use of the letters of Paul. Even though this thesis provided unsatisfactory for the known reasons, the fact that called forth this thesis, namely, the remarkable correspondence in the list of stations, nevertheless deserves to be explained. In my judgment, the best explanation is that Acts 17 is based on a *traditional* list of stations (an itinerary).

2. Acts 18 presents a trip from Ephesus to Caesarea, then to Jerusalem, and from there to Antioch, Phrygia, the region of Galatia, and Ephesus. Julius Wellhausen once described the peculiar character of this journey in these words:

> From Ephesus, to Caesarea, up to greet the brethren, down to Antioch, then back through Galatia and Phrygia. With plans made at a moment's notice and reported in telegraphic style, no American could have done it better.[41]

In my judgment, the epitomic character of this report, which covers a journey of more than a thousand miles, speaks for the assumption that our passage indeed contains traditional material at this point, for otherwise it is "not apparent why the author would have invented this entire list and then have treated it so cursorily."[42]

3. Acts 27 presents a dangerous voyage. Verses 9–11, 21–26, 31, and 33–36, which are concerned with Paul as a prophet of misfortune and a savior in time of need, may be separated out. There remains the report of a shipwreck and the successful escape from it. Wellhausen's conclusion seems irrefutable: in Acts 27, Luke has employed a non-Christian source and has expanded it by adding the figure of Paul.[43]

We can now formulate a historical judgment of the three traditions about the journeys which we have isolated:

1. With regard to the journey in Acts 17—18: The tradition here can claim historical value insofar as the order of the stations agrees with the one given in the letters. First Thessalonians 2—3 make it likely that when Paul missionized Greece, he came from Philippi through Thessalonica and Athens to Corinth. But one must again be critical with respect to Luke's chronological placement of this journey. On the basis of Paul's own witness and—as may already be said here—owing to the chronological correspondence of the expulsion of Jews from Rome and the initial mission in Corinth (Acts 18:2), it is probable that this initial journey took place ten years earlier than Acts reports. It would have to be placed—if one wanted to maintain the order of Acts—between Acts 10 and 11.

2. With regard to the journey in Acts 18—19: Our results on Acts 18—19 will be similar to those on Acts 17—18. Paul's own witness makes it likely that the apostle undertook a journey from Greece to Jerusalem that agrees with the order of stations in Acts 18.[44] To this extent the tradition is historically valuable. There are, however, serious reasons to doubt the accuracy of the journey's chronological placement. Its present placement assumes that in the middle of his journey to organ-

ize the collection, Paul undertook a trip to Palestine—which being a distance of over a thousand miles, would have been an exasperating detour. In agreement with many others, I consider this impossible. Nevertheless, the historical value of this tradition becomes apparent when one transfers the journey to its historical place as that can be reconstructed from Paul's letters. The tradition then accurately reports of the journey from Greece to Palestine that Paul undertook in order to participate in the Jerusalem conference (Galatians 2).[45]

3. With regard to the journey in Acts 27: Compared with the trips already discussed, a different picture emerges for the voyage in Acts 27. Although it is certain that Paul traveled to Rome after his last visit in Jerusalem (*1 Clement* 5), the report of the voyage does not stand in any genetic relationship with Paul's trip to Rome. For Luke himself probably adopted the report of this voyage from a literary model. It should thus be designated a product of his reading and be considered nonhistorical.

Paul in Jerusalem (Acts 21)

Acts 21 reports Paul's arrival in Jerusalem. Here he finds lodging in the house of the Hellenist Mnason and receives a warm welcome from James and the elders, to whom he relates the success of the mission to the Gentiles. James nevertheless advises Paul to manifest his loyalty to the law by assuming responsibility for a Jewish ritual, because Christians who are zealous for the law have heard about the apostle to the Gentiles that he teaches all the Jews who dwell among the Gentiles to forsake Moses, telling them not to circumcise their children or live according to the Jewish customs. Paul follows this advice.

The section just described bears clear marks of Lukan redaction: Paul maintains good relations with the congregation in Jerusalem and with James, its leader. Similarly, Paul transgresses the law in not a single point up to the end. By his participation in a Jewish ritual, Paul even openly documents that he upholds the law.

There are two things that call for attention:

1. In v. 17 the *entire* congregation greets Paul and his companions. But in the following the many zealous brethren who have heard the hostile rumors are distinguished from the entire congregation. (Do they not belong to the congregation?)

2. It is strange that there are any rumors at all about Paul's criticism of the law, especially since the portrayal of Paul in Acts provides absolutely no foundation for such rumors. Thus the inference seems likely that both the mention of Christians who harbor reservations about

Paul and the report of Paul's proclamation about the law are pieces of tradition that the author of Acts has transformed in accordance with his theology but was unable to eliminate completely.

What about the historical value of such a tradition? In my judgment it should definitely be estimated as high, for the content of Acts 21:21 is confirmed by the witness of Paul's letters. Admittedly, his proclamation concerning the law does not correspond with the principles outlined in Acts 21:21. Paul wanted all, both the Jews and the Gentiles, to remain in their own states (1 Cor. 7:17–20). But in practice, the predominately gentile Christian Pauline congregations (cf. Gal. 3:11ff; 6:15; 1 Cor. 1:19) had left this noble principle behind. The minority of Jewish Christians and their children in the Pauline congregations seem to have actually been estranged from the Mosaic law.

Acts 21:21 is thus definitely a historically reliable statement about what was actually occurring in the Pauline congregations.

The other part of the tradition in Acts 21, the existence of many anti-Pauline Jewish Christians in Jerusalem, should also be considered definitely historical. In Rom. 15:31, Paul himself indicates that the Christians in Jerusalem might not be receptive to him. Furthermore, we know from the letters that the anti-Pauline opposition in the Pauline congregations originated in Jerusalem.[46]

We can thus say that the Lukan report of Paul's arrival in Jerusalem in Acts 21 contains traditional material that should be considered both old and historical.

By way of conclusion we may review the course of the argument and formulate a few provisional perspectives on the historical value of the Acts of the Apostles.

We began with a survey of the turbulent history of research into the historical value of Acts. At the beginning stood the radical criticism of F. C. Baur; in the middle, the reversion toward tradition by Adolf von Harnack; and at the end, a polarity—on the one hand, redaction criticism with diminished interest in the historical question, and on the other hand, a rising tide of research that defends the historical reliability of Acts. In retrospect it can be said that on the question of the historicity of Acts, Baur and Harnack have remained the classic antipodes even to the present. It thus seemed best to make some decisions about the mutually exclusive positions of Baur and Harnack. For this purpose we critically addressed the alternative theses that the author of Acts was an eyewitness and that he employed the Pauline letters. The first thesis would imply that Acts would in general carry great historical value; the second would imply that Acts is of very little historical value. Both theses proved unacceptable, and instead we postulated that Luke in his composition had reworked other traditions to a larger degree than had been assumed. That meant that the question of the historicity of Acts could be adequately addressed only as the question of the historical value of the traditions that have been reworked therein. In accordance with this task we selected three different textual units and in each case posed questions regarding redaction, tradition, and historical veracity. Though only a small portion of Acts was analyzed, the results that we achieved seem to provide a basis for the following general inferences:

1. Acts remains an important source for the history of early Christianity alongside the letters of Paul.
2. This is because much of its content is historically reliable and provides information about primitive Christianity that goes beyond that contained in Paul's letters.
3. Of course, it must be added immediately that this judgment applies *only for the traditions* that have been reworked in Acts, the chronological framework of which must furthermore be reconstructed from the letters.
4. To this extent, a chronology developed solely on the basis of the primary source, the letters, is a necessary prerequisite for the isolation of traditions in Acts.
5. The recovered traditions often cannot be form-critically classified and furthermore can be reconstructed only in their basic outlines.
6. In reconstructing the traditions, one should in general give more consideration than has been customary to the effects of Luke's reading of extra-Christian material. Such effects are found in Acts 27 and were probably the influence elsewhere too.
7. A special problem is posed by the parts of Acts that were not treated in this article and that are not paralleled by a historical witness in Paul's letters. Their analysis is yet to be undertaken, but the manner in which traditions have been reworked in the Gospel and in the parts covered by the Pauline letters should provide valuable guidelines for this task. Owing to the thorough nature of Lukan redaction, it does admittedly seem to be a hopeless undertaking to try to reconstruct sources of a continuous nature for these parts. Here too only individual traditions are recoverable. In not a few cases judgments about their historicity will have a low degree of reliability because of the dearth of material for verification.
8. A critical analysis of Acts, with attention given to the question of the traditions it contains and the historicity of those traditions, has become an important task following the flood of redaction-historical studies of Acts. This is not a hopeless undertaking, as the examples above have shown.[47] Thus, the type of research that I have described

is a necessary preliminary task for a long-overdue history of early
Christianity.

NOTES

1. Adolf von Harnack, *Geschichte der altchristlichen Literatur bis Eusebius,* part
2, vol. 1, *Die Chronologie der Literatur bis Irenäus* (Leipzig: J. C. Hinrichs, 1897), x.
    2. Adolf von Harnack, *New Testament Studies,* vol. 1, *Luke the Physician, the
Author of the Third Gospel and the Acts of the Apostles,* trans. J. R. Wilkinson, ed. W.
D. Morrison (New York: G. P. Putnam's Sons; London: Williams & Norgate, 1907);
idem, *New Testament Studies,* vol. 3, *The Acts of the Apostles,* trans. J. R. Wilkinson
(New York: G. P. Putnam's Sons; London: Williams & Norgate, 1909); idem, *New
Testament Studies,* vol. 4, *The Date of the Acts and the Synoptic Gospels,* trans. J. R.
Wilkinson (New York: G. P. Putnam's Sons, 1911).
    3. See Arthur Cushman McGiffert, "The Historical Criticism of Acts in Ger-
many," in *The Beginnings of Christianity,* ed. F. J. Foakes Jackson and Kirsopp Lake
(London: Macmillan & Co., 1920–33), 2:363–95; Andrew Jacob Mattill, "Luke as a
Historian" (Ph.D. diss., Vanderbilt Univ., 1959), 20–206; Emmeran Kränkl, *Jesus,
der Knecht Gottes: Die heilsgeschichtliche Stellung Jesu in den Reden der Apos-
telgeschichte,* Biblische Untersuchungen 8 (Regensburg: Friedrich Pustet, 1972),
16–36; and W. Ward Gasque, *A History of Criticism of the Acts of the Apostles,*
Beiträge zur Geschichte der biblischen Exegese 17 (Grand Rapids: Wm. B. Eerd-
mans; Tübingen: J. C. B. Mohr [Paul Siebeck], 1975), 21–106.
    4. Ferdinand Christian Baur, *Paulus, der Apostel Jesu Christi—Sein Leben und
Wirken, seine Briefe und seine Lehre: Ein Beitrag zu einer kritischen Geschichte des
Urchristentums* (Stuttgart: Becher & Müller, 1845), 5. My trans.
    5. Ibid., 15–243; ibid., 2d ed., ed. Eduard Zeller, 2 vols. (Leipzig: Fues's Verlag,
L. W. Reisland, 1866–67), 1:19–272.
    6. Ibid. (1845), 13; (1866), 1:17.
    7. Ibid. (1845), 5–6; (1866), 1:8–9.
    8. Albert Schwegler, *Das nachapostolische Zeitalter in den Hauptmomenten seiner
Entwicklung,* 2 pts. in 1 vol. (Tübingen: L. F. Fues, 1846), 2:73–123; and Eduard
Zeller, *Die Apostelgeschichte nach ihrem Inhalt und Ursprung kritisch untersucht*
(Stuttgart: Carl Macken, 1854), 318.
    9. W. M. L. de Wette, *Kurze Erklärung der Apostelgeschichte,* 4th ed., rev. and
enl. Franz Overbeck, Kurzgefasstes exegetisches Handbuch (Leipzig: S. Hirzel,
1870).
    10. Ibid., xxxi; see also idem, "Über das Verhältnis Justins des Märtyrers zur
Apostelgeschichte," *Zeitschrift für wissenschaftliche Theologie* 15 (1872): 305–49;
and Paul Wilhelm Schmidt, "De Wette-Overbecks Werk zur Apostelgeschichte und
dessen jüngste Bestreitung," in *Festschrift zum 500-jährigen Bestehen der Uni-
versität Basel* (Basel, 1910), 32–33 (274–75).
    11. Franz Overbeck, *Über die Christlichkeit unserer heutigen Theologie,* 2d ed.,
rev. and enl. (Leipzig: C. G. Naumann, 1903), 4.
    12. Cf. Overbeck's remarks about the "we" passages (Wetter, *Kurze Erklärung
der Apostelgeschichte* [1870], xxxvii–lii).

13. For Overbeck's criticism of Acts, see also Johann-Christoph Emmelius, *Tendenzkritik und Formengeschichte: Der Beitrag Franz Overbeck zur Auslegung der Apostelgeschichte im 19. Jahrhundert,* Forschungen zur Kirchen- und Dogmengeschichte 27 (Göttingen: Vandenhoeck & Ruprecht, 1975).

14. For examples, see Gerd Lüdemann, *Paulus, der Heidenapostel,* vol. 2, *Antipaulinismus im frühen Christentum,* Forschungen zur Religion und Literatur des Alten und Neuen Testaments 130 (Göttingen: Vandenhoeck & Ruprecht, 1983), 27–31.

15. See Otto Pfleiderer, *Das Urchristentum: Seine Schriften und Lehren im geschichtlichen Zusammenhang,* 2d enl. and rev. ed., 2 vols. (Berlin: G. Reimer, 1902); Heinrich Julius Holtzmann, *Die Apostelgeschichte,* Hand-Commentar zum Neuen Testament 1, 2, 3d ed., completely rev. (Tübingen: J. C. B. Mohr [Paul Siebeck], 1901); Carl Heinrich von Weizsäcker, *The Apostolic Age of the Christian Church,* trans. from the 2nd rev. ed. J. Millar, 3d ed., 2 vols. (New York: G. P. Putnam's Sons; London: Williams & Norgate, 1899–1907).

16. For a criticism of Harnack, see Emil Schürer's review of *Lukas der Arzt* by A. von Harnack, in *Theologische Literaturzeitung* 31 (1906): cols. 405–8; and Heinrich Julius Holtzmann, "Harnacks Untersuchungen zur Apostelgeschichte," *Deutsche Literaturzeitung* 29 (1908): col. 1093–99.

17. Oldest text about 180: Irenaeus *Haer.* 3.1.

18. Alfred Wikenhauser, *Die Apostelgeschichte und ihr Geschichtswert,* Neutestamentliche Abhandlungen 8/3–5 (Münster: Aschendorff, 1921); and Eduard Meyer, *Ursprung und Anfänge des Christentums,* 3 vols., 1st–3d eds. (Stuttgart and Berlin: J. G. Cotta, 1921–23).

19. Ibid. 1:xiii.

20. For a criticism, see Martin Dibelius's review of *Ursprung und Anfänge des Christentums* by Eduard Meyer, in *Deutsche Literaturzeitung* 45 (1924): cols. 1635–43.

21. For an overview, see Gasque, *History of Criticism,* 251–66.

22. As representative, see Martin Hengel, *Acts and the History of Earliest Christianity,* trans. J. Bowden (Philadelphia: Fortress Press, 1980; London: SCM Press, 1979); idem, *Between Jesus and Paul: Studies in the Earliest History of Christianity,* trans. J. Bowden (Philadelphia: Fortress Press; London: SCM Press, 1983); and Jürgen Roloff, *Die Apostelgeschichte,* Das Neue Testament Deutsch 5 (Göttingen: Vandenhoeck & Ruprecht, 1981).

23. Julius Wellhausen, "Noten zur Apostelgeschichte," *Nachrichten der Gesellschaft der Wissenschaften in Göttingen—philologisch-historische Klasse* (1907): 1–21; idem, "Kritische Analyse der Apostelgeschichte," *Abhandlungen der Gesellschaft der Wissenschaften zu Göttingen—Philologisch-historische Klasse* n.s. 15/2 (1914).

24. Martin Dibelius, "Stilkritisches zur Apostelgeschichte," in his *Aufsätze zur Apostelgeschichte,* ed. Heinrich Greeven, Forschungen zur Religion und Literatur des Alten und Neuen Testaments 60 (Göttingen: Vandenhoeck & Ruprecht, 1951), 9–28.

25. F. J. Foakes Jackson and Kirsopp Lake, ed., *The Beginnings of Christianity,* part 1, 5 vols. (London: Macmillan & Co., 1920–33); John Knox, "'Fourteen Years Later': A Note on the Pauline Chronology," *Journal of Religion* 16 (1936): 341–49; idem, "The Pauline Chronology," *Journal of Biblical Literature* 58 (1939): 15–29;

idem, *Chapters in a Life of Paul* (Nashville and New York: Abingdon-Cokesbury Press, 1950; London: A. & C. Black, 1954); and Donald Wayne Riddle, *Paul, Man of Conflict: A Modern Biographical Sketch* (Nashville: Abingdon-Cokesbury Press, 1940).

26. See Hans Conzelmann, *The Theology of Luke*, trans. J. Bowden (New York: Harper & Row, 1969); idem, *Die Apostelgeschichte*, 2d ed., rev., Handbuch zum Neuen Testament (Tübingen: J. C. B. Mohr [Paul Siebeck], 1972); and Ernst Haenchen, *The Acts of the Apostles: A Commentary*, trans. B. Noble and G. Shinn (Philadelphia: Westminster Press; Oxford: Basil Blackwell, 1971).

27. For the methodological differentiation between primary and secondary sources, see Ernst Bernheim, *Lehrbuch der historischen Methode und der Geschichtsphilosophie: Mit Nachweis der wichtigsten Quellen und Hilfsmittel zum Studium der Geschichte*, 5th and 6th ed., rev. and enl. (Leipzig: Duncker & Humblot, 1908).

28. See Philipp Vielhauer, "On the 'Paulinism' of Acts," in *Studies in Luke-Acts: Essays Presented in Honor of Paul Schubert*, ed. L. E. Keck and J. L. Martyn (1966; Philadelphia: Fortress Press, 1980), 33–50.

29. See, correctly, Gerhard Schneider, *Das Evangelium nach Lukas*, 2 vols., Ökumenischer Taschenbuchkommentar zum Neuen Testament 3 (Gütersloh: Gerd Mohn; Würzburg: Echter Verlag, 1977), 1:33.

30. See Hildebrecht Hommel, "Neue Forschungen zur Areopagrede Acta 17," *Zeitschrift für die neutestamentliche Wissenschaft* 46 (1955): 145–78.

31. See Gerd Luedemann, *Paul, Apostle to the Gentiles: Studies in Chronology*, trans. F. S. Jones (Philadelphia: Fortress Press, 1984), 37 n.51, 147–48; and Robert Jewett, *A Chronology of Paul's Life* (Philadelphia: Fortress Press, 1979), 85–86, 95–96, and elsewhere.

32. Adolf von Harnack, *Neue Untersuchungen zur Apostelgeschichte und zur Abfassungszeit der synoptischen Evangelien* (Leipzig: J. C. Hinrichs, 1911), 21–28; and Dibelius, *Aufsätze*, 119.

33. See John Knox, "Acts and the Pauline Letter Corpus," in *Studies in Luke-Acts*, ed. Keck and Martyn, 279–87.

34. See Andreas Lindemann, *Paulus im ältesten Christentum: Das Bild des Apostels und die Rezeption der paulinischen Theologie in der frühchristlichen Literatur bis Marcion*, Beiträge zur historischen Theologie 58 (Tübingen: J. C. B. Mohr [Paul Siebeck], 1979), 165.

35. For an overview, see William O. Walker, "Acts and the Pauline Corpus, Reconsidered," *Journal for the Study of the New Testament* 24 (1985): 3–23, esp. 8–9.

36. See Lindemann, *Paulus im ältesten Christentum*, 165.

37. For the difficulties with using the term "tradition" in Acts, see Jacob Jervell, *The Unknown Paul: Essays on Luke-Acts and Early Christian History* (Minneapolis: Augsburg Pub. House, 1984), 69.

38. See James Hardy Ropes, "An Observation on the Style of S. Luke," *Harvard Studies in Classical Philology* 12 (1901): 299–305.

39. But note that in Luke, too, Sosthenes is leader of the synagogue about eighteen months (v. 11) after the conversion of Crispus.

40. This holds for Corinth (18:1ff.), although on his later journey Paul will stay here for three months (20:2–3). It is also true for Thessalonica (17:1ff.), where Paul

will spend time later (20:2), and for Philippi, where Paul will travel twice at a later point (20:2, 3–6); cf. Lystra (Acts 14:8–20, 21) and Ephesus (Acts 19; 18:19ff.).

41. Wellhausen, "Noten," 14.

42. Pfleiderer, *Das Urchristentum,* 514–15.

43. Wellhausen, "Noten," 18–19.

44. See Luedemann, *Paul, Apostle to the Gentiles,* 152–56.

45. That Paul himself reports that he and Barnabas went to Jerusalem (Gal. 2:1–2) is no conclusive argument against this thesis. Neither does Gal. 2:1–2 mention the place from which Paul and Barnabas left for Jerusalem, nor does it presuppose that they have worked together immediately before the conference.

46. See Lüdemann, *Paulus, der Heidenapostel* 2:103–65.

47. Cf. my forthcoming book, *Die Traditionen der Apostelgeschichte und ihr Geschichtswert: Ein Kommentar* (Göttingen: Vandenhoeck & Ruprecht, 1987). The present article is partly identical with the introductory chapter of that book.

9

Catalogues of Vices, The Apostolic Decree, and the Jerusalem Meeting

PEDER BORGEN
University of Trondheim

In several studies the present author has discussed aspects of Paul's Letter to the Galatians.[1] The analyses have been focused on the claim made by Paul's opponents that he preached circumcision (5:11) and pleased men (1:10). These points have also been related to the role played by the Jerusalem meeting (2:1–10) within the context of the letter and the conflict in Galatia.

Galatians 5:11

In Gal. 5:11, Paul says, "And I, brethren, if I am still preaching circumcision, why am I, despite this fact, persecuted? In that case the stumbling-block of the cross is done away with."[2] The conditional clause has the form of a real case. Thus, Paul's opponents had evidently been saying that he himself was still preaching circumcision. Commentators have had difficulties deciding on what basis the opponents made this claim.[3]

There is a good reason for raising anew the question whether the context of Gal. 5:11 can yield more information about Paul's preaching of circumcision. The question may be formulated in this way: Does Paul in this context reiterate ideas from his missionary preaching in Galatia, ideas that the opponents have misunderstood and misused in support of their circumcision campaign? In Gal. 5:19–21 Paul states explicitly that he repeats points from his previous preaching to the Galatians: "Now the works of the flesh are manifest, such as fornication, etc., respecting which I tell you beforehand, as I have already previously told you, that they who do such things will not inherit the Kingdom of God." In his preaching to the pagan Galatians, Paul spoke against the works of the flesh. With some variation in wording Paul repeatedly stresses this point in his preaching:

Gal. 5:13: εἰς ἀφορμὴν τῇ σαρκί
5:16: ἐπιθυμίαν σαρκός
5:17: ἡ . . . σὰρξ ἐπιθυμεῖ. . . .
κατὰ τῆς σαρκός
5:24: τὴν σάρκα. . . .
σὺν τοῖς παθήμασιν καὶ ταῖς ἐπιθυμίαις

Against this background the following hypothesis can be formulated: Paul refers pointedly to this topic taken from his previous preaching, because his opponents have claimed that in this way he preached circumcision to be the same as the removal of passions and desires. On what basis could they make this claim? The reason was that, among the Jews of that time, circumcision was understood to portray the removal of passions, desires, and evil inclination. In the works of Philo of Alexandria this interpretation of circumcision is very common, and he uses terminology similar to that which Paul uses in Gal. 5:13, 16, 17, 19, 24:

> *De migratione Abrahami* 92: τὸ περιτέμνεσθαι ἡδονῆς καὶ παθῶν πάντων ἐκτομὴν . . . ἐμφαίνει (receiving circumcision portrays the excision of pleasure and all passions).

> *De specialibus legibus* 1.305: περιτέμνεσθε τὴν σκληροκαρδίαν [Lev. 26:41; cf. Deut. 10:16], τὸ δέ ἐστι, τὰς περιττευούσας φύσεις τοῦ ἡγεμονικοῦ, ἃς αἱ ἄμετροι τῶν παθῶν ἔσπειράν τε καὶ συνηύξησαν ὁρμαί ("Circumcise the hardness of your hearts," that is, the superfluous overgrowths of the mind, which the immoderate appetites of the passions have sown and raised).

Of special interest is *Quaestiones in Genesin* 3.52, since here the term "flesh"—central to Paul—symbolizes the passions: "the flesh of the fore-skin, symbolizing those sensual pleasures and impulses [= ἡδονὰς καὶ ὁρμάς] which afterwards come to the body."[4] Although Philo has a dichotomic view of man, in these passages he does not make a sharp dualism between body and soul. He applies circumcision to both entities, so that both the body and the soul/mind/heart are to be circumcised.

In a similar way, we read in the Qumran writings, in 1QpHab 2.13, that the foreskin of the heart is to be circumcised in addition to the circumcision of the body, which seems to be taken for granted. A parallel to the thoughts of Paul and Philo occurs also in 1QS 5.5–6, where it says that the foreskin of the evil inclination is to be circumcised.[5] It is of importance that in 1 QpHab 2.13–14 this inclination leads to drunkenness, a vice that Paul includes among the works of the flesh in Gal. 5:21 (μέθαι, κῶμοι).

In *Migr.Abr.* 92, Philo shows that such ethical interpretations of circum-cision might lead to different attitudes and practices. Philo criticizes some Jews who, although they have the right understanding of the ethical mean-ing of circumcision, ignore the external observance of it. Philo himself stresses that the ethical ideas are of necessity tied to the external observance of bodily circumcision. Although Philo, according to *Quaestiones in Exodum* 2.2, gives heathens the status of proselytes on the basis of ethical circumcision of the pagan pleasures, he means that the observance of bodily circumcision is to follow.[6] In a similar way Paul's opponents have linked Paul's preaching against fleshly pagan desires closely to bodily circumcision: ethical circumcision is to be followed by obedience to the commandment to carry out bodily circumcision. The idea that the observance of circumcision should follow and complete ethical circumcision is supported by Gal. 3:3, where Paul writes, "Having begun with the Spirit, will you now complete with the flesh?" A. Oepke suggests that Paul's opponents in Galatia argued that the Galatians needed a supplement, needed a completion by obeying the law of Moses.[7] Circumcision played a basic role in this complete submission to the law. Thus, Paul's opponents—who appeared as his followers—said that he preached circumcision (Gal. 5:11).

Galatians 1:10b

The Judaizers, who worked among the Galatians, claimed that Paul preached circumcision, as they did themselves. This claim implied that Paul, like them, wanted the Christian congregations to conform to the Jewish community. In Gal. 1:10, Paul seems to deal with this matter: εἰ ἔτι ἀνθρώποις ἤρεσκον, Χριστοῦ δοῦλος οὐκ ἂν ἤμην ("If I still tried to please men, I would not be the slave of Christ"). H. Schlier, F. Mussner, and others rightly understand the sentence to be "biographical": ἔτι, "still," is then understood to refer to the time after Paul's call (1:13ff.)[8] When Schlier and Mussner specify what Paul refers to when he talks about pleasing men, their interpretations become more problematic. They maintain that Paul's opponents criticized him for pleasing men when he proclaimed a gospel free from circumcision and the other requirements of the law.[9] This interpretation of the opponents' criticism cannot be correct, however, since according to Gal. 5:11 they maintained that Paul still preached circumcision.

It must be remembered that Paul and the Judaizers formulate the same point in different ways. Hence, what Paul in a derogatory sense would call pleasing men, they would evaluate in a positive way: Paul wished to be accepted by the Jewish community after he had received the call to be an apostle.

When Gal. 5:11 and 1:10 are seen together, they give clues to the way the Judaizers claimed that Paul represented their own cause. They claimed that Paul continued (cf. ἔτι) to preach and practice circumcision after he received his call. In this respect, there was continuity between his teaching before and after he became an apostle. As has been shown in our analysis of

Gal. 5:11, the conformists had reason for their claim: Paul continued to draw on traditions about circumcision and related Jewish traditions. Accordingly, the conformists drew the conclusion that Paul wanted to be accepted by the Jewish community and please men by still advocating circumcision.

Some of the conclusions preached are

1. When Paul preached that the heathen Galatians should depart from the desires of the flesh and enter the society of those who serve and love each other, the Judaizers claimed that this was the ethical meaning of circumcision. Thus, Paul, in their view, still preached circumcision, and the task of these Judaizers was to persuade the Galatians to make bodily circumcision follow upon their ethical circumcision. By obedience to the commandment of circumcision the Galatian converts would make evident that they lived under the law of Moses. Thus, in the opinion of the Judaizers, Paul wanted to be accepted by the Jewish community and to please men by continuing to advocate circumcision.

2. But Paul objected to this misunderstanding and misuse of his preaching to the Galatians. For him their transition from the pagan desires of the flesh to a communal life in love was in an exclusive way tied to their being crucified with Christ, not to bodily circumcision and the jurisdiction of the law of Moses. Thus, Paul's service of Christ meant conflict with the Jewish communities: "If I still tried to please men, I would not be the slave of Christ" (Gal. 1:10). Christianity was not a nationally bound religious movement but cross-national in its nature.

In the present study, this understanding will be related to some of the more debated questions relative to the Jerusalem meeting. A further analysis of Paul's Letter to the Galatians may throw new light on the Jerusalem meeting and on the so-called apostolic decree in Acts 15:20, 29; 21:25.

PAUL'S REPORT ON HIS PREACHING
AT THE JERUSALEM MEETING

In our observations we shall not raise the historical questions about the Jerusalem meeting itself. Our concern here is with the role Gal. 2:1–10 plays in Paul's letter. This approach is akin to that of H. D. Betz in his commentary on the letter. He interprets the letter using a legal defense plea as a model in accordance with the recommended practice of various standard authorities on rhetoric.[10] We are, however, focusing on the actual issues in the controversy between Paul and his opponents and not on the formal rules of rhetoric.

The issue of circumcision is explicitly mentioned in Gal. 2:3: "Not even Titus who was with me and who was a Greek was compelled to be circum-

cised." Let us try to characterize in a precise way Paul's view and the view
the opponents held on this issue. Paul's reference to his preaching in Gal.
2:2 will serve as a point of departure. In Gal. 2:2, Paul writes, "And I laid
before them the gospel which I preach among the gentiles." A corresponding reference to Paul's preaching is found in Gal. 5:11: "If I still preach
circumcision . . ." Several observations indicate that these two formulations
refer to the same preaching by Paul.

1. The same technical term for preaching is used in both places: κηρύσσειν. Betz makes the following comment on Gal. 5:11:[11] "The language suggests that κηρύσσειν περιτομήν ("preach circumcision") is
   Paul's language, formulated in contrast to κηρύσσειν Χριστόν
   ("preach Christ"), his usual concept." This is probable, but a sharper
   distinction should be made between Paul's view and that of his opponents. The opponents represent the view that both phrases mean the
   same: to preach the gospel of Christ means to preach physical circumcision. Paul does not make this identification, however, but contrasts
   the two formulations.
2. In both Gal. 2:2 and 5:11 the Gentiles are the addressees of the
   preaching. In Gal. 2:2 there is an explicit reference to the Gentiles,
   and in 5:11 the preaching refers in particular to Paul's missionary
   activity among the Galatian Gentiles, although the attention here is
   focused on Paul's preaching since the time of his call.
3. Paul does not make a distinction between his preaching in Galatia and
   his preaching prior to the meeting in Jerusalem. His report from the
   Jerusalem meeting in Gal. 2:1–10 is rather meant to give support to
   his preaching in Galatia—that is, to counter the opponents' misunderstanding of it. Two observations in Gal. 2:1–10 demonstrate
   this:
   (a) In 2:5, Paul states that his action in Jerusalem was taken for the
       benefit of the Galatians—"in order that the truth of the gospel
       might remain with you."
   (b) The present tense used in Gal. 2:2 presupposes that Paul
       preached the same gospel before the Jerusalem meeting and since
       that time up to the writing of the letter: "Und schliesslich geht aus
       dem 'zeitlosen' Präsens κηρύσσω hervor, dass er dieses spezifike
       Heiden-Evangelium auch jetzt noch unter den Heiden verkündet
       und auch bei den Galatern verkündet (vgl. auch 1:11)."[12]

How can Gal. 2:2 and 5:11 refer to the same preaching by Paul? Both in
Gal. 5:11ff. and in Gal. 2:2ff. Paul objected to the misunderstanding and
misuse of his preaching to the heathen Galatians. Although he preached
Christ within the context of Jewish proselyte traditions, such as the catalogue of pagan vices (Gal. 5:19–21), he did not imply that the gentile

Christians should undergo physical circumcision and become citizens of the Jewish nation. In this polemic against the opponents and the Galatian churches, Paul tells them that he at the Jerusalem meeting presented the same gospel, exclusive of physical circumcision. The pillar apostles agreed with him.

Our conclusion is then the following: The problem Paul faced in Galatia was that he, in his preaching of the gospel of Christ, drew on the Jewish teaching about proselytes in which catalogues of pagan vices and physical circumcision were an integral part. Correspondingly, when Paul reported on his preaching of the gospel in Jerusalem, the following question was raised: When Paul preached Christ to the Gentiles within the context of Jewish proselyte traditions, did this mean that the Gentiles had to undergo physical circumcision and join the Jewish nation? Paul's opponents in Galatia, just like the opponents at the Jerusalem meeting, maintained that physical circumcision was basic. They claimed that Paul held this view as well. Paul, on the other hand, although drawing on the Jewish traditions about proselytes in his preaching, that is, that they were to turn away from pagan vices, did not intend for them physical circumcision and Jewish citizenship.

SOME CATALOGUES OF VICES
AND VIRTUES

Some of the proselyte traditions employed by Paul should be discussed in more detail. In this context, lists of vices and virtues illustrate the contrast between the pagan way of life and the Jewish and Christian way of life.[13]

In Gal. 5:19–21, Paul explicitly states that he repeats points from his previous preaching to the Galatians. These points are in the form of a list of vices. "Now the works of the flesh are manifest, such as fornication, etc., respecting which I tell you beforehand, as I have already previously told you, that they who do such things will not inherit the Kingdom of God." In his initial preaching, Paul spoke against the works of the flesh and exemplified such works by means of a catalogue of vices. Also elsewhere in his letters Paul uses catalogues of vices to illustrate the pagan way of life, which for the converts belonged to the past. For example, Paul addresses himself in 1 Cor. 6:9–11 to the readers who were cleansed and purged of the pagan vices:[14] "Do you not know that the unrighteous will not inherit the kingdom of God? Do not be deceived; neither the immoral, nor idolaters, nor adulterers, nor homosexuals, nor thieves, nor the greedy, nor drunkards, nor revilers, nor robbers will inherit the kingdom of God. And such were some of you. But you were washed, you were sanctified, you were justified in the name of the Lord Jesus Christ and the Spirit of our God" (RSV).

In the two lists of Gal. 5:19–21 and 1 Cor. 6:9–11 there is agreement in the wording at two points, namely, in the reference to idolatry (Gal. 5:20, εἰδωλολατρία; 1 Cor. 6:9, εἰδωλολάτραι) and to adultery (Gal. 5:19, πορνεία; 1 Cor. 6:9, πόρνοι). Apart from these two terms, there are a variety of words used, although some overlap in their meanings.

In the Jewish traditions, idolatry and sexual misdeeds are closely associated. Idolatry is, moreover, seen as the root of all vices. Thus, in the context of a catalogue of vices in Wisd. of Sol. 14:12—26, we read, "The devising of idols was the beginning of fornication, and the invention of them the corruption of life."[15] From Gal. 5:19–21 and 1 Cor. 6:9–11 it is evident that Paul in his preaching to the Gentiles made use of catalogues of vices to characterize the life from which they ought to depart, and which they as converts already had left behind. The themes of idolatry and fornication were central, and together with these, a variety of other vices were mentioned by him. Considering this variety, it is obvious that it is unwarranted to think in terms of a more fixed proselyte cathecism. Proselyte traditions had much more flexibility and variation.[16]

As a contrast to the catalogue of vices in Gal. 5:19–21, Paul in 5:22–23 offers a list of virtues to portray Christian life: "But the fruit of the Spirit is love, joy, peace, patience, kindness, goodness, faithfulness, gentleness, self-control." No corresponding characterizations of the new life are given in 1 Cor. 6:9–11, but in both places it is said that new life is based on the reception of the Spirit. From this it is evident that the virtues given in Gal. 5:22–23 exemplify the life in the Spirit which the pagan Corinthians were sanctified to partake in according to 1 Cor. 6:9–11. A further characterization of the new life is found in Gal. 5:13–14: the "freedom" to which the Galatians were called meant that they should serve as slaves to one another, "for the whole law is fulfilled in this one word, you shall love your neighbor as yourself" (Gal. 5:14, quoting Lev. 19:18).

The objection might be raised against the above analysis that in Jewish sources the use of catalogues of vices and virtues was not confined to traditions connected with proselytism. Neither does such a limitation apply to the love commandment of Lev. 19:18. There is truth in this objection, but it is sufficient for the purpose of the present study simply to document the fact that this material, besides having other uses, also served to describe to the proselytes the pagan background for their entry into the life of a proselyte.[17] Documentation of this is found in *Virt.* 180–82, where Philo says that the conversion of the pagans to monotheism serves as a basis for the new life exemplified by a catalogue of virtues: "For it is excellent and profitable to depart without backward glance to the ranks of virtue and abandon vice that malignant mistress; and where honour is rendered to the God who is, the whole company of the other virtues must follow in its train as surely as in the sunshine the shadow follows the body. The proselytes become at once temperate, continent, modest, gentle, kind, humane, serious, just, high-minded, truth-lovers, superior to the desire for money and pleasure. . . ." The parallelism between Gal. 5:22–23 and *Virt.* 182 is obvious. Some of the virtues are even direct parallels: Paul, ἀγάπη; Philo, φιλάνθρωποοι. Paul, χρηστότης; Philo, χρηστοί. Paul, ἐγκράτεια; Philo, ἐγκρατεῖς.

The first virtue listed in Gal. 5:22 is "love," ἀγάπη. As background for this virtue, Paul quoted the love commandment of Lev. 19:18 in Gal. 5:14. This indicates that the summary of the law in the love commandment had a place in the instruction of proselytes. The Babylonian Talmud Šabb. 31a supports this view. Here it is said that Hillel summed up the law of Moses in the Golden Rule. Hillel made this summary for a heathen whom he accepted as a proselyte. The Golden Rule was in turn so closely associated with the love commandment of Lev. 19:18 that in the Jerusalem Targum both are paraphrased together to render Lev. 19:18. Consequently, this use of the Golden Rule within the context of proselytism makes probable that the love commandment also was used within the same setting.

It remains to relate these observations made on catalogues of vices and virtues to the preceding discussion of Paul's report on the Jerusalem meeting in Gal. 2:1–10.[18] When Paul in Jerusalem reported on his preaching of the gospel to the Gentiles (2:2), his gospel comprised the Jewish proselyte tradition. His preaching included catalogues of vices which served to illustrate the pagan way of life and catalogues of virtues which exemplified the new life in the spirit (Gal. 5:19–23). The similar lists given by Paul in other letters show that various catalogues were used by him, and not only one form. The question debated in Jerusalem was, then, whether such proselyte traditions could be separated from physical circumcision and Jewish citizenship. According to Paul, "Those . . . who were of repute added nothing to me." This meant that they did not add the requirement of physical circumcision to Paul's preaching of Christ within the context of Jewish proselyte traditions.

JEWISH PROSELYTE TRADITION—
NOT APOSTOLIC DECREE

This analysis of Paul's presentation of the Jerusalem meeting within the context of the Galatian controversy, and his use of catalogues of vices and virtues in this connection, throws light on the use of a catalogue of vices in Acts 15:20, 29, and 21:25, often called the apostolic decree.

The apostolic decree is in various manuscripts presented in two different main versions, the Alexandrian and the Western.[19] The Alexandrian version of Acts 15:20 reads, "to abstain from the pollutions of idols, and unchastity and from what is strangled and from blood." The Western version omits "what is strangled" and adds the Golden Rule in Acts 15:20 and 15:29. Thus, in 15:20 the Western text reads, "to abstain from the pollutions of idols, and unchastity and blood; and all things they do not want happening to them, do not do towards others."

This "decree" has been much debated among New Testament scholars. In general it is understood as a decree that, according to the author of the Acts, was impressed upon the gentile Christians to make possible full social intercourse between Gentiles and Jews in the churches. Consequently, scholars find that this decree contradicts Paul's report from the Jerusalem meeting in Gal. 2:6: "Those . . . who were of repute added nothing to me." Our hypothesis is that no such contradiction exists.

At the beginning of this century, A. Resch brought the apostolic decree into the discussion of the catalogues of vices in the New Testament.[20] According to him, the basis of the catalogues was the three vices of idolatry, adultery, and murder. The original form of the apostolic decree consisted of these three points, according to Resch, and the many catalogues of vices in the New Testament were elaborations of this apostolic decree. But Resch's hypothesis has several weaknesses. The textual support for Resch's suggested original form of the decree is weak. His derivation of the many catalogues of vices in the New Testament from this decree is too mechanical and seems to be too much of a historical simplification.

After Resch the apostolic decree has been largely ignored in the discussion of the catalogues of vices in the New Testament.[21] Instead, the decree has largely been understood against the background of Leviticus 17 and 18 and the Noahittic commandments, or in the light of rabbinic teachings about the deadly sins, idolatry, adultery, and murder.[22] Although Resch's hypothesis as such cannot be maintained, it is pertinent to ask again if the apostolic decree should not be included among the New Testament catalogues of vices and be interpreted on that basis.

In comparison with the catalogues in Gal. 5:19–21 and 1 Cor. 6:9–11, the catalogue in Acts 15:20, 29, and 21:25 is quite short. The Alexandrian version in Acts 15:20 has four parts:

(a) Pollutions of idols
(b) Unchastity
(c) What is strangled
(d) Blood

The Western version consists of three parts:

(a) Pollution of idols
(b) Unchastity
(c) Blood

Furthermore, the Golden Rule is added.

Such short catalogues of vices are not uncommon, however. Ephesians 5:5 has three (or four) parts:

(*a*) Fornicator
(*b*) Impure person
(*c*) One who is covetous, i.e., (*d*) an idolator

Five (six) parts are found in Col. 3:5:

(*a*) Unchastity
(*b*) Impurity
(*c*) Passion
(*d*) Evil desire
(*e*) Covetousness, which is (*f*) idolatry

Revelation 22:15 lists six parts:

(*a*) Dogs
(*b*) Sorcerers
(*c*) Fornicators
(*d*) Murderers
(*e*) Idolators
(*f*) Everyone who practices falsehood

In 2 Cor. 12:21, three parts are listed:

(*a*) Impurity
(*b*) Unchastity
(*c*) Licentiousness

Acts 15:20, 29, and 21:25, with a list of four—or three—parts, fits very well into the pattern of short catalogues. Moreover, there are parallels, and even close agreements, between the catalogue in Acts and several of the other short lists: Idolatry and unchastity occur in Acts 15:20, 29; 21:25; and in Rev. 22:15, as well as in Col. 3:5 and Eph. 5:5. Murderers in Rev. 22:15 (οἱ φονεῖς; cf. Rom. 1:29) parallel blood(shed) (τὸ αἷμα) in the Western version of the catalogue in Acts. The Alexandrian version has the same term "blood," τὸ αἷμα, but here it may refer to the eating of blood.[23] It is significant that the longer catalogues in Gal. 5:19–21 and 1 Cor. 6:9–11 also list idolatry and unchastity in close agreement with Acts 15:20, 29; 21:25. These two vices are central in Jewish characterizations of the pagan way of life.

Thus, both the numbers of vices and the kind of vices listed support the hypothesis that Acts 15:20, 29, and 21:25 do not render a specific apostolic decree, but the list of vices in these verses is to be ranked together with the many other catalogues of vices, especially those which characterize the pagan way of life.

The function of the catalogue of vices in Gal. 5:19–21 and of the one in Acts 15:20, 29 will be analyzed further, since both passages are connected with the Jerusalem meeting. The analysis above of Gal. 2:1-10 showed that Paul's preaching in Galatia was the same as his preaching of the gospel prior to the Jerusalem meeting, about which he reported at the meeting. This means that he preached Christ all the time within the context of Jewish proselyte traditions. Included in such traditions were catalogues of pagan vices, such as the one in Gal. 5:19-21. The Gentiles were to turn away from such vices when they became Christians. Correspondingly, the catalogue of vices in Acts 15:20, 29, and 21:25 does not constitute an apostolic decree but exemplifies the kind of Jewish proselyte instruction that was part of the Christian preaching. The issue both in Acts 15 and in Gal. 2:1-10 and 5:11-26 can be formulated in this way: Should and could the Christians, when using Jewish proselyte teachings (exemplified by a catalogue of pagan vices from which the gentile converts were to turn away), neglect the requirement of physical circumcision and the integration of gentile converts into the Jewish nation? From Gal. 2:6 we learn that "those who were of repute" in Jerusalem did not add the requirement of physical circumcision to Paul's preaching of Christ within the context of Jewish proselyte traditions. He had excluded physical circumcision from this teaching, and "those who were of repute" agreed with him. The conclusion is that neither the catalogue of pagan vices in Acts 15:20, 29, and 21:25 nor the catalogue of vices in Gal. 5:19-21 is in contradiction with Gal. 2:6.[24] Both list pagan vices from which the Gentiles were to turn away according to Jewish and Christian proselyte instruction. Such catalogues therefore were part of the missionary preaching and teaching that were taken for granted before, during, and after the Jerusalem meeting. Thus, at the meeting it was decided that this preaching, including such catalogues of vices, should continue without physical circumcision's being required.

Several observations support the view that the catalogue of vices (the apostolic decree) in Acts 15:20, 29, and 21:25 has its place in traditions related to the institution of proselytism in Judaism:

1. The catalogue of vices from which the gentile Christians were to abstain spells out the implications inherent in the conversion of the Gentiles. The term ἐπιστρέφειν (Acts 15:19) is a term commonly used to denote the conversion of a Gentile.[25]

2. The catalogue of vices from which they were to abstain is not presented as a burden to be laid upon the gentile Christians.[26] The burden (παρενοχλεῖν, Acts 15:19) is to be interpreted as the requirement of physical circumcision. Thus, the joyful message (Acts 15:31) sent to the churches in Antioch, Syria, and Cilicia was that the "Christian proselyte" preaching of abstention from pagan vices did not imply physical circumcision (Acts 15:23-29). The phrase ἡμῖν πλέον μηδὲν ἐπιτίθεσθαι ὑμῖν βάρος πλὴν τούτων τῶν ἐπάναγκες in Acts 15:28 is

to be understood accordingly. The meaning is not that some burden (though not so great as circumcision) is to be laid on the Gentiles but that no burden at all is to be imposed.[27] In the teaching of the Christian proselytes, the abstention from pagan vices was to be kept while the requirement of physical circumcision was to be abandoned.

3. The various versions of the catalogue of vices in Acts 15:20, 29, and 21:25 have features that clearly tie them to Jewish proselyte traditions. In the various versions it is said that the Gentiles are to abstain from idolatry and adultery, two points that, as we have seen, are also central in the proselyte catalogues in Gal. 5:19–21 and 1 Cor. 6:9–11. Moreover, the version in the Alexandrian text (counseling abstention from the pollution of idols and from fornication, and from things strangled, and from blood) draws on points from Lev. 17:8, 10ff., 13; 18:6ff.,[28] which refer to the proselytes, according to Jewish exegesis.[29]

4. Finally, the inclusion of the Golden Rule in the Western text is in agreement with the way in which Hillel, according to *b. Šabb.* 31a summed up the law of Moses in the Golden Rule. Hillel made his summary for a heathen whom he accepted as a proselyte. This use of the Golden Rule is, moreover, parallel to Paul's application of the love command (Lev. 19:18) to the Christian "proselytes" in Galatia (Gal. 5:13–14). In Jewish tradition the Golden Rule was so closely associated with the love commandment, that in the Jerusalem Targum both are paraphrased together to render Lev. 19:18.[30]

How can it be explained that there are two versions and several variant readings of the catalogue of vices in Acts 15:20, 29, and 21:25? The reason is that the catalogue is no apostolic decree made at the Jerusalem meeting but a representative example of Jewish proselyte traditions already used in the Christian preaching and teaching of "Christian proselytes." Thus, the decision taken at the Jerusalem meeting did not have the definite wording of a decree but said that such proselyte teachings should be taught and practiced independently of physical circumcision. Thus, in later reports from the meeting, such as the ones in Acts 15:20, 29; 21:25; and Gal. 2:1–10—seen together with Gal. 5:11–26—the actual wording of such catalogues of pagan vices varied, but the points against pagan worship and unchastity were stable elements.

One major problem remains to be solved: How can one explain the point against "what is strangled" in the Alexandrian version, and that the author includes Paul among those who stood behind it? The apostles and the elders, together with the whole church at Jerusalem, sent Judas and Silas with Paul and Barnabas to Antioch to deliver to the church there the message that was agreed upon at the meeting (Acts 15:22–35). According to his letters, Paul was quite liberal as to the Jewish dietary laws and even limited the prohibition against eating pagan sacrificial meat to the actual participation in the cultic sacrificial acts themselves. Different interpretations of these letters have been suggested by scholars. C. K. Barrett thinks that Paul's liberal views about eating articles of food that had been offered in pagan sacrifice contradict the requirements of the apostolic decree (see 1 Corinthians 8; 10). He claims that it is difficult to believe that Paul was present when the decree was drawn. According to Barrett, the Cephas group in Corinth attempted to introduce into the church at Corinth the Jewish Christian orthopraxy of the decree.[31] Correspondingly, some scholars think that the men who came from James to Antioch (Gal. 2:11ff.) brought the decree and demanded that it be put into effect.[32]

These suggestions do not explain how a *decree* agreed upon at the Jerusalem meeting could lead to such completely opposite views and practices. The answer is that the catalogue against pagan vices in Acts 15:20, 29, and 21:25 was not a decree. The meeting in Jerusalem took up only the issue of "Christian proselytes" and circumcision. The decision was that Jewish proselyte tradition should be taught without the inclusion of physical circumcision. The numerous other problems involved in the complex and varied Jewish teachings addressed to proselytes were not taken up. The conflict about table fellowship in Antioch (Gal. 2:11ff.) and the controversies about dietary matters in Corinth (1 Corinthians 8; 10) show that dietary matters had not been decided upon at the Jerusalem meeting. The application of Jewish dietary regulations to the Christian proselytes became an issue both at Antioch and in Corinth, and probably also elsewhere.[33]

Our analysis indicates that the explanation of the two versions and the variant readings in Acts 15:20, 29, and 21:25 should be based on two observations:

1. In Acts 15 and in 21:25 the Jerusalem meeting and the present of the authors are seen together, just as Paul includes what was said at the Jerusalem meeting in his argument with his opponents in Galatia.
2. The Jerusalem meeting separated the requirement of physical circumcision from the Christian use of Jewish proselyte traditions, such as the catalogues against pagan vices. Thus, the many other problems which were present in these traditions were not taken up.

Thus, Jewish proselyte traditions were used continuously before, during, and after the Jerusalem meeting, and this meeting dealt with one specific point in this connection. These circumstances explain why we actually find in Acts 15 two main versions of a Jewish catalogue against pagan vices that was associated with the meeting: the Alexandrian version of Acts 15:20, etc., and the Western version of Acts 15:20, etc. Within these two main versions there are also several variant readings in manuscripts, patristic literature, and the like. The sample catalogue used at the Jerusalem meeting and brought into the letter sent to Antioch, Syria, and Cilicia (Acts 15:20-35) was then in some circles actualized along the lines of Leviticus 17—18 so as to specify dietary matters as in the Alexandrian version.[34] Both the men from James (Gal. 2:11ff.) and the persons in Corinth who advocated strict observance (1 Corinthians 8) were among those who after the Jerusalem meeting in particular activated the elements of dietary observances in the Jewish proselyte traditions. They even might have thought that Paul accepted such dietary observances, since at the Jerusalem meeting physical circumcision was the issue and this requirement was the only one removed from the Jewish proselyte traditions. Other circles interpreted the Jerusalem sample catalogue by emphasizing the pagan ethical vices, together with idolatry. The Western version of Acts 15:20, etc., listing three vices and the Golden Rule, is akin to the Pauline version built into Gal. 5:13-21 which consists of an extensive list of vices and the love command and also includes a proselyte catalogue of virtues (5:22-23).

CONCLUSIONS

The present analysis has sought to demonstrate that there was no apostolic decree decided upon at the Jerusalem meeting. In the Christian employment of Jewish proselyte traditions exemplified at the meeting by a catalogue against pagan vices (Acts 15:20, 29; 21:25; cf. Gal. 5:19-21; 1 Cor. 6:9-11), the requirement of physical circumcision was taken out, and thus the gentile converts were not required to become Jews and citizens of the Jewish nation. The exact wording of the sample catalogue used at the Jerusalem meeting is not preserved, but the renderings are found in later reports and documents. Thus, two versions can be identified: the Alexandrian version, with emphasis on ritual observance, and the Western version, which focuses upon ethical vices and virtues. The catalogues against pagan vices found in Gal. 5:(13f.,) 19-21, and 1 Cor. 6:9-11 give further documentation of the kind of (Jewish) proselyte traditions of which the catalogue in Acts 15:20, 29, and 21:25 is an example.

NOTES

1. See P. Borgen, *Paul Preaches Circumcision and Pleases Men, and Other Essays on Christian Origins* (Trondheim, 1983), 15-42, 75-97; idem, ed. *The Many and the One: Essays on Religion in the Graeco-Roman World Presented to H. Ludin Jansen* (Trondheim, 1985), 225-49.

2. See E. de Witt Burton, *A Critical and Exegetical Commentary on the Epistle to the Galatians* (Edinburgh, 1921), 287.

3. H. Schlier, *Der Brief an die Galater* (Göttingen, 1971), 238-39; and E. Haenchen, *The Acts of the Apostles* (Oxford, 1971), 480-81 and elsewhere.

4. R. Marcus, *Philo* (Loeb Classical Library), supp. 1:253, n. 1.

5. See E. Lohse, *Die Texte von Qumran* (Darmstadt, 1971).

6. See Borgen, *Paul Preaches Circumcision*, 17–18.

7. A. Oepke and J. Rohde, *Der Brief des Paulus an die Galater* (Berlin, 1973), 101.

8. Schlier, *Der Brief an die Galater;* and F. Mussner, *Der Galaterbrief* (Freiburg, 1974).

9. Schlier, *Der Brief an die Galater*, 42; and Mussner, *Der Galaterbrief*, 63.

10. H. D. Betz, *Galatians* (Philadelphia: Fortress Press, 1979).

11. Ibid., 268–69.

12. Mussner, *Der Galaterbrief*, 102.

13. Borgen, *Paul Preaches Circumcision*, 28, 81–82.

14. E. Kamlah, *Die Form der katalogischen Paränese im Neuen Testament* (Tübingen, 1964), 11–14, 178; A. Vögtle, *Die Tugend- und Lasterkataloge im Neuen Testament* (Münster, 1936), 224–25; and B. S. Easton, "New Testament Ethical Lists," *Journal of Biblical Literature* 51 (1932): 4–5.

15. Easton, "New Testament Ethical Lists," 1–3.

16. See Vögtle, *Die Tugend- und Lasterkataloge*, 3–4; and S. Wibbing, *Die Tugend- und Lasterkataloge im Neuen Testament* (Berlin, 1959), 4–7.

17. Borgen, *Paul Preaches Circumcision*, 28, 81–84.

18. Cf. P. Borgen, "The Cross-National Church for Jews and Greeks," in *The Many and the One*, ed. Borgen, 235–43.

19. See B. M. Metzger, ed., *A Textual Commentary on the Greek New Testament* (New York: United Bible Societies, 1975), 429–34; Haenchen, *Acts of the Apostles*, 468–72; H. Conzelmann, *Die Apostelgeschichte* (Tübingen, 1963), 84–85; J. Roloff, *Die Apostelgeschichte* (Göttingen, 1981), 225–28; and G. Schneider, *Die Apostelgeschichte*, vol. 2 (Freiburg, 1982), 189–92.

20. G. Resch, *Das Aposteldekret nach seiner ausserkanonischen Textgestalt untersucht* (Leipzig, 1905), 19–127. Cf. Vögtle, *Die Tugend- und Lasterkataloge*, 5–6.

21. See Vögtle, *Die Tugend- und Lasterkataloge;* Wibbing, *Die Tugend- und Lasterkataloge;* and Kamlah, *Die Form der katalogischen Paränese*.

22. See surveys in the works listed in n. 19 above.

23. See, among others, Conzelmann, *Die Apostelgeschichte*, 85.

24. See the survey in Haenchen, *Acts of the Apostles*, 468.

25. See Acts 9:35; 26:18; 1 Thess. 1:9.

26. See M. Dibelius, *Studies in the Acts of the Apostles* (New York: Charles Scribner's Sons, 1956), 97; and Haenchen, *Acts of the Apostles*, 449 n. 3.

27. See Haenchen, *Acts of the Apostles*, 453 n. 2.

28. See Conzelmann, *Die Apostelgeschichte*, 84–85; and Haenchen, *Acts of the Apostles*, 469.

29. F. Siegert, "Gottesfrüchtige und Sympatisanten," *Journal for the Study of Judaism* 4 (1973): 135. The LXX trans. makes Leviticus 17—18 refer to proselytes.

30. Borgen, *Paul Preaches Circumcision*, 82–84.

31. C. K. Barrett, "Things Sacrificed to Idols," *New Testament Studies* 11 (1965): 142–50.

32. D. Catchpole, "Paul, James, and the Apostolic Decree," *New Testament Studies* 23 (1977): 428–44.

33. Conzelmann, *Die Apostelgeschichte*, 85: "Gal 2:11 zeigen, dass das Problem

der Tischgemeinschaft von Juden und Heidenchristen auf dem Konzil noch nicht besprochen wurde."

34. Cf. F. Siegert, "Gottesfrüchtige und Sympatisanten": "Das Aposteldekret galt eben nicht christlichen Gottesfürchtigen, sondern aus den Heiden kommenden getauften Gemeindegliedern—wenn man so will, christlichen Proselyten." Siegert bases his argument on the LXX interpretation of Leviticus 17—18, in which the regulations for "strangers" have explicitly been applied to "proselytes."

10

Paul, Phoebe,
and the Spanish Mission

ROBERT JEWETT
Garrett-Evangelical Theological Seminary

In response to scholars like Howard Clark Kee who are exploring the social context of early Christianity, the awareness is dawning in current scholarship that Paul should be understood not simply as a theologian and a writer of letters but as a self-supporting missionary actively engaged in cooperative projects with a number of groups and individuals. Paul's social setting is as crucial for the understanding of a doctrinal letter like Romans as are the intellectual problems concerning the law, the bondage of the will, and the perceived threat to the sovereign rule of God posed by the refusal of some Jews to accept the gospel.

This study explores the social and business relations between Paul and a key person in the project to enlist Roman help in the Spanish mission. It proposes a new solution to the problem of the role of Phoebe in Rom. 16:1–2. To lay out the basis for this solution, we begin with the requests for hospitality and support that Paul makes in his diplomatic style in Rom. 15:24, 28, examining the challenge that Spain would have posed for the Pauline mission as a background for this request. A genuine question is confronted at the outset: Why did Paul actually need the support of the Roman churches in order to embark on the Spanish mission? In light of our findings on this question, I turn to the description of Phoebe and examine the details concerning her social status, ecclesiastical office, and projected mission in Rome. Finally, I would like to draw the strands of the evidence together that point toward Phoebe as the patroness of the Spanish mission.

THE REQUEST FOR AID AND THE PROBLEM
OF THE SPANISH MISSION

In Rom. 15:24, Paul refers to his plan to "see you in passing as I go to Spain, and to be sped forward on my journey by you, once I have enjoyed your company for a little." The implication of "see you" is actually "get acquainted,"[1] which is confirmed by the subsequent expression "enjoy your company." The significant qualification, however, should not be overlooked. To remain in Rome "for a little while" implies that Paul is not going to be a long-term burden. Perhaps the experience the Roman house churches have already had with itinerant missionaries who overstayed their welcome had left them wary and Paul's acquaintance with a number of former members of the Roman churches, as evident elsewhere in chapter 16, explains his diplomatic sensitivity at this point.

The crucial element in v. 24 in relation to the Spanish mission is the expression ὑφ᾽ ὑμῶν προπεμφθῆναι, which is perceived by commentators as something of a technical expression in early Christian missionary circles.[2] C. H. Dodd has a sure grasp of the implications when he writes,

> Thus the expression seems to have been almost a technical term with a well-understood meaning among missionaries. Paul is hinting that he would like the church of Rome to take some responsibility for his Spanish mission, so that he can start work in the west with their moral support at least, and possibly with some contribution from them in assistants or funds.[3]

Otto Michel writes that whoever is "sped forward" in this way "receives moral support and economic support" to carry out a particular mission.[4] The significance of these nuances will become apparent in a moment, but first a brief look at the second reference to the visit in 15:28. Here Paul says that after the offering has been delivered, "I shall go on by way of you to Spain." Again the temporary quality of his planned visit to Rome is emphasized, along with the hope to get acquainted in transit, and by implication, to involve them in the planning and support of the Spanish project.[5]

What was there about the Spanish mission that required such elaborate and tactful preparation? If, indeed, the entire Letter to the Romans is directly related to this project, why was it all necessary? Why did Paul not think it was feasible to start the mission in Spain as he had in Thessalonica or Corinth? Why not arrive without advance notice or preparation, commence preaching in a synagogue, find a local patron or patroness, and build a local congregation of converts? In light of information that has recently become available, we are now in a position to provide a more informed answer to this question. I suggest that the indications of missional strategizing and logistical arrangements in Romans were directly related to the peculiar religious, cultural, economic, and linguistic conditions in Spain.

The first matter on which new information is available relates to the presence of a Jewish population in Spain during the Julio-Claudian period. Ernst Käsemann and C. E. B. Cranfield assume the presence of Jewish communities in Spain, relying primarily on outdated information in Emil

Schürer and in Michel.[6] Evidence of a substantial Jewish settlement in Spain does not appear until the third and fourth centuries C.E., as W. P. Bowers has shown.[7] The indications of the practice of the Jewish religion in Spain are so sparse that it is not even included in the comprehensive survey of "oriental religions" by Antonio García y Bellido.[8] A trilingual inscription at Tortosa is cited by Michel as evidence of a Jewish population, but this also appears to stem from the second century C.E. at the earliest.[9] The reference to initial Jewish settlements in Spain found in the Talmud which were used by earlier researchers must, according to Bowers, "be traced back to the massive disruptions and relocations of Judaism in C.E. 70–135."[10] Bowers further points out that in the various listings in Jewish literature of the lands to which the Diaspora had spread prior to these enforced migrations, it always "stops short of the western Mediterranean beyond Rome."[11] Paul appears to operate on the same assumption as in Rom. 10:18, that while "the proclamation to the Jewish people has been completed," there is still a need "for a pioneer mission to Spain," which implies that there was no Jewish population there.[12] There seems to be little doubt that commentators, even those whose work has been completed after the publication of Bowers's article,[13] have been led astray by outdated information on this issue.

The lack of Jewish settlement in Spain would have posed several substantial barriers to Paul's previous missionary strategy. Not only would this eliminate the prospects of Jewish converts to the gospel but it would also rule out finding a group of God-fearers or proselytes in the Spanish cities to recruit as the initial core of Christian churches. There would be no initial interest in a messianic proclamation prepared by devotion to the Septuagint. The evidence of the oriental religions in Spain, including the Semitic residue from Phoenician and later Punic colonization, shows no trace of Hebrew influence.[14] The absence of synagogues eliminated the avenues that Paul had habitually used to establish a base of operations in the Greek cities of the east. There is a widespread consensus that despite the apologetic interests of the Book of Acts, it is realistic to expect that wherever possible he would begin his missionary activities in local synagogues and move to an independent base of operations after troubles erupted or patrons and patronesses emerged.[15] Without a synagogue as a starting point, the crucial contacts with appropriate patrons would be extremely difficult to make, especially for a handworker of Paul's social class.

The absence of synagogues would pose a related economic problem, because Jewish travelers often used such buildings as convenient hostels and places to develop business contacts. The studies by Ronald F. Hock[16] and J. Paul Sampley[17] reveal the role of these informal social contacts in providing the economic framework of Paul's self-supporting missionary strategy. In the case of Spain, prior arrangements for bases of operations and the recruitment of appropriate patrons would be required in the absence of the resources of local synagogues. Given the Roman domination of the economic resources in Spain and the high proportion of mines, industries, and estates directly owned and managed by the empire,[18] it would likely be necessary to approach this problem through persons close to administrators in Rome. The broad consequence of the lack of Jewish settlement is that the entire strategy of the Spanish mission needs to be reconceived.

When one inquires about the nature of the Spanish cultural situation during the period of Paul's intended mission, the commentaries on Romans are silent. It is eloquent testimony to the preoccupation with Rome and Jerusalem that the debate over Romans has never touched on what Paul states as the ultimate goal of his mission. But extensive information has long been available, most accessibly in M. Rostovtzeff's *Social and Economic History of the Roman Empire*.[19] He showed that the image of Spain as the most thoroughly Latinized colony of Rome was in need of revision, that large portions of the Iberian Peninsula were substantially untouched by the veneer of Roman civilization. The rural population in particular and the northern portions of Spain specifically remained apart from Greco-Roman culture. In general, he concluded, "Those who held Latin rights and were more or less romanized formed a small minority of the population of Spain, while the status of the rest remained the same as it had been before the 'thorough urbanization' of the country."[20] On the decisive question of the language spoken in Spain, the barriers to a Greek speaker like Paul were rather high. While Latin was spoken in the major cities, at least in part, and at times rather poorly, the "Iberians and Celt-Iberians of Spain spoke their own languages."[21]

A number of subsequent studies[22] and the extensive articles on the Latinizing of Spain in the *ANRW* confirm the general outlines of Rostovtzeff's summary.[23] At the time of the Roman conquest around 200 B.C.E., there were four main language groupings in Spain, the Indo-European languages in west-central and northwest Spain, the Iberian dialects in southern Spain and on the east coast, the Punic languages in the southern coastal area, and a wide range of primitive languages of obscure origin. In addition, there were three small pockets where Greek was used, on the east coast where colonies had been established in an earlier period.[24] Faced with this bewildering variety of languages, the Romans made no effort to create a multilingual administration or even to develop a translation service; they simply imposed a Latin system that was more rapidly accepted in the south and east than in the west and north.

The most fully Latinized area was Hispania Ulterior, or Baetica, where the native languages had largely been forgotten in the major cities by the

Augustan period and non-Latin inscriptions, as well as the minting of bilingual coins, had ceased. It was this province that had attracted the largest group of Italian immigrants[25] and produced most of the impressive cultural, political, and military leaders who rendered conspicuous service to the empire. A senatorial province since the time of Augustus, Baetica was ruled by a proconsul of praetorian rank, frequently selected from senators with roots and experience in Spain. This indicates the cultural niveau and significance of the province to the empire.[26] It was the most heavily urbanized portion of Spain, with ninety municipalities boasting some level of Roman privilege.[27] The presence of several famous Greek teachers in Baetica indicates the level of cultural aspiration of the elite. Even here, the local languages retained their hold in smaller cities and rural areas, and the pre-Roman city names remained in currency despite official renamings by Roman authorities.[28]

The other two provinces were Latinized only along the coastal areas, in major river valleys, and in isolated military and mining colonies. That leads specialists like Hartmut Galsterer to suspect an overstatement in Pliny's report that "all Spain" was given Roman citizenship under Vespasian.[29] Hispania Citerior, often referred to as Tarraconensis, was the largest colony in the empire and was ruled by an imperial legate of high rank, indicating its importance and prestige.[30] Lusitania was the least urbanized portion of Spain, ruled by a legate of lower rank.[31] Continued resistance against Roman rule was evident in the destructive Cantabrian War of 29–19 B.C.E. and in the refusal of a substantial portion of the population in Lusitania and Tarraconensis to abandon the worship of native deities in favor of the Roman pantheon. A large portion of the northern and western portions of the peninsula was not Latinized until long after Paul's time. The Iberian alphabet and dialects remained in use in the inner regions of Spain until they were gradually displaced by Christian missionizing in the sixth century and thereafter, with some regions retaining their linguistic distinctiveness until the Middle Ages.[32]

The situation in Spain presented Paul's missionary strategizing with formidable challenges on both the linguistic and the political levels. If he were to seek out the small remnants of Greek-speaking population, the mission would have little chance of spreading through the peninsula. Proclamation and instruction in Latin would be required, and there is no evidence that Paul was sufficiently fluent to carry this out without translators. Indeed, such resources would be difficult to develop, because the Hebrew Scriptures were not yet available in Latin, and the first evidence we have of Latin-speaking churches is in the middle of the second century.[33] Even the church in Rome remained Greek-speaking until the middle of the third century,[34] and elsewhere in the West the church was associated for centuries with Greek immigrants.[35] The translation of the gospel, the liturgy, and the instructional traditions into another idiom would be a substantial undertaking, especially in light of the fact that a range of additional translation resources would be required to reach beyond the restricted circle of Latin civilization in Spain. Given the resistance against Roman culture in large portions of Lusitania and Tarraconensis, it would probably not have appeared either feasible or promising to rely entirely upon the language of the conquerors. Since the Latinized urban centers functioned as outposts of Roman rule and civilization in ways quite different from the Greek-speaking portions of the empire where Paul had scored his earlier successes,[36] care would have to be taken to find local patrons who were not resented by the native population.

In sum, the Spanish mission required a level of planning and support that represented a quantum leap from the improvisational scheme of earlier Pauline missionizing. An indirect indication of the cultural barriers to be overcome was that in the wake of the failure of the missionary plan that Paul announced in Romans,[37] it was not until the second century that Christian communities could be established in Spain.[38] By that time there were Jewish immigrants in Spain who may have provided a basis for Christian missionizing which was lacking during Paul's lifetime.

THE RECOMMENDATION OF PHOEBE

You may be asking yourself at this point, What does all this have to do with Phoebe? We have no evidence that she came from Spain or that she spoke Latin. How can she have been relevant for the project of the Spanish mission?

The evidence about Phoebe is restricted to the brief recommendation Paul writes in the first two verses of Romans 16. Before this evidence can be examined, there is the text-critical question to resolve. Briefly stated, the problem is that the doxology of Rom. 16:25–27 is found in six different locations in the manuscripts of Romans, some of which eliminate chapter 16 entirely. It appears that Marcion circulated a version of Romans without either chapter 15 or 16. A widespread critical consensus that pertained until the late 1970s assumed that chapter 16 did not originally belong to Romans. Possibly it was sent as a letter of greeting to the Ephesian church, along with an extra copy of Romans,[39] or it was part of a farewell letter to Ephesus sent from Rome that was mistakenly included in the editing of Romans,[40] or it was created at the time of the publication of the letter in order to demonstrate Paul's close relations with the Roman church.[41] My initial adherence to a version of the Ephesian hypothesis[42] was undermined by the text-critical studies by Harry Gamble[43] and Kurt Aland,[44] who made compelling cases that the textual history is best explained by an original letter of sixteen chapters and that the combination of recommendation and greeting is appropriate as an ending of an extended letter. Equally compelling was the argument of Wolf-Hennig Ollrog, that the greetings in Romans 16 are actually highly inappropriate for the Ephesian setting, or for any other church where Paul had ministered for a substantial length of time.[45] The personal details concerning some of the persons he greets are formulated as if the congregation as a whole did not know of their accomplishments, which is strange if Paul's knowledge of them coincided with the congregation's knowledge. It sounds as if Paul is introducing and recommending them as reliable leaders in a congregation where neither he nor they were very well known. Other persons are named without any personal reference or intimate detail whatsoever, which seems absurd if Paul had worked with them for almost three years, as was the case in Ephesus. This is a significant observation, it seems to me, when one reflects on how such a lack of social and political finesse would have been received in a congregation like Ephesus, where Paul should have known everyone intimately. The greetings of Romans 16 are therefore much more suitable for an audience where Paul had never functioned as a missionary. Ollrog also points out that Romans 16 refers neither to Paul's past experience with the congregation nor to its future prospects, which is markedly in contrast with other letters addressed to congregations for which he felt responsible as a founder. These considerations forced me to recognize that the Ephesian hypothesis is far less adequate in explaining the peculiar content of Romans 16 than the traditional assumption that it was originally directed to the Roman congregation.

My subsequent study of the diplomatic genre of Romans[46] and of the rhetorical structure of the letter confirmed the appropriateness of the material in chapter 16, with the exception of the interpolation of 16:17–20[47] and the doxology of 16:25–27.[48] The authentic portions of chapter 16 are part of the peroration that begins with 15:14, which means that its contents are a crucial indication of the purpose of the letter. Since the chapter opens with the recommendation of Phoebe, the clarification of her role must therefore receive a very high priority.

Phoebe was a gentile Christian[49] from Cenchreae, the eastern port of Corinth.[50] The reference to her as "our sister"[51] indicates what Cranfield refers to as "membership in the Christian community."[52] It carries the nuance of her solidarity with Paul as well as with all other Christians in Rome and elsewhere. The expression "our sister who is[53] deaconess of the church in Cenchreae" has a legitimizing effect. Although earlier commentaries interpret the term διάκονος as signifying a subordinate role along the lines of the modern deaconess movements,[54] it now appears more likely that Phoebe functioned as the leader of the congregation. That διάκονος was an official title of church leadership has been shown by Ulrich Brockhaus and Bengt Holmberg,[55] and in light of the term's use in 1 Cor. 3:5; 2 Cor. 3:6; 6:4; 11:15, 23, to refer to missionaries including Paul himself, it is no longer plausible to limit Phoebe's role to philanthropic activities.[56] Elisabeth Schüssler Fiorenza contends that "the diakonos, like the synergos, therefore, is a missionary entrusted with preaching and tending churches. . . . It can be concluded, therefore, that Phoebe is recommended as an official teacher and missionary in the church of Cenchreae."[57] In light of the possessive qualification "deaconess of the church in Cenchreae," it seems more likely that she functioned as a local leader rather than as a missionary.

The second title associated with Phoebe confirms this impression of congregational leadership. In Rom. 16:2, Paul writes that "she has also been a patroness[58] to many, and also to me." The term προστάτις means "protectress, patroness, helper," and its masculine counterpart took on the technical sense of a legal patron.[59] Although the upper-class connotation of "patroness" runs counter to the subordinate implication traditionally seen in the term "deaconess," several commentators have pointed to its relevance in this context.[60] Käsemann argued on the ground of the lack of precise parallels to the legal use of the feminine term προστάτις that "women could not take on legal functions,"[61] but this does not stand up under the weight of newly discovered evidence. E. A. Judge points to a recently published papyrus from 142 B.C.E. referring to a woman's being appointed the legal προστάτις of her fatherless son.[62] Ramsay MacMullen's recent survey shows that women made up a "fifth of all rescript-addresses" in the Roman period and that "perhaps a tenth of the protectors and donors that collegia sought out were women. Honors paid to a patroness ob merita, or some similar hint, indicate how the game was played."[63] He concludes that "as a general rule, then, women as benefactors should be imagined playing their part personally and visibly, out in the open."[64] Other investigations of the archaeological evidence confirm this picture.[65] Recent studies by Gerd Theissen,[66] Holmberg,[67] Aloys Funk,[68] Jerome Murphy-O'Connor,[69] and Wayne A. Meeks[70] of the leading role played by upper-class benefactors in early Christian communities provide the social background of the description of Phoebe's status. The host or hostess of house churches was usually a person of high social standing and means, with a house large enough for the church to gather, who presided over the eucharistic celebrations and was responsible for the ordering of the congregation. The fact that Paul mentions Phoebe as a patroness "to many, and also to me" indicates the level of material resources that would qualify for this kind of leadership role. In light of this high social standing and Paul's relatively subordinate social position as her client,[71] it is preposterous that translations like the RSV render προστάτις as "helper."[72]

The key question in relation to Phoebe's recommendation is how to understand what Paul requests in her behalf. The expression αὐτὴν προσδέξησθε ἐν κυρίῳ ἀξίος τῶν ἁγίων implies welcoming her to Rome with full hospitality. Käsemann refers to the "secular sense" of προσδέχεσθαι, "of welcoming and offering lodging and help."[73] Cranfield protests against this secular interpretation on the grounds of the prominent use of "in the Lord"[74] but feels that the expression "worthy of the saints" is redundant. The fact that προσδέχεσθαι often appears in secular letters of recommendation with the connotation of hospitality for the bearer of a letter[75] indicates that Käsemann was on the right track. I think that the expression as a whole should be interpreted in light of Phil. 2:29, where προσδέχεσθαι is used, in reference to welcoming back the beloved Epaphroditus, for rolling out the red carpet. Edgar J. Goodspeed suggested that this welcome consisted primarily in the provision of respectable housing, which would probably not have been essential for a person of her means and status.[76] The expression implies rather that Phoebe should be received with honor suitable to her social class, her position as a congregational leader, her previous contributions to the Christian mission, and her role in the missionary project envisioned in Romans.

The second half of the request in behalf of Phoebe is to "provide her whatever she needs from you in the matter" (Rom. 16:2). This request is interpreted either in light of the use of πρᾶγμα, as referring to a personal transaction in business or law that brings Phoebe to Rome,[77] or in view of the indeterminate expression ἐν ᾧ ἂν ὑμῶν χρῄζῃ, as an open-ended request for aid.[78] The latter interpretation is far more likely correct, in view of the frequent use of this kind of expression in papyrus letters of recommendation.[79] Cranfield interprets this open-ended request in far too personal a manner, explaining that "in widely varying matters Phoebe could stand in need of their help; and in all such matters they are loyally to stand by their fellow-Christian."[80] It is far more likely that the "matter" that Phoebe will bring to Rome has an integral relation to the purpose of the letter and that Paul requests the congregation to provide whatever she needs to accomplish it. That Phoebe needs help with her business or legal affairs hardly seems plausible, given her stature as a patroness capable of giving aid to a number of early Christian missionaries. Her wealth and social status belie the pathetic descriptions by imaginative exegetes of her need for safe housing[81] or for Paul's intercession in the face of dire necessity.[82] But if such fantasies are abandoned, what is the content of Paul's request? It must have significance or else it would hardly have been mentioned as the opening request in the final series of personal greetings.

I believe a case can be made that Paul provides a direct hint in the wording of Rom. 16:2c: ". . . for she has also been a patroness to many, and also to me." The explanatory words καὶ γάρ follow immediately after the vague term πράγματι, thus specifying what is meant by the "matter." It is the matter of Phoebe's patronage. Phoebe has agreed to underwrite a project of vital significance to Paul and to the letter he is writing.[83] Since she is a missionary patroness "of many" and therefore a person of substantial wealth, the churches of Rome would have no fear that cooperation with her would require onerous financial obligations on their part. They would be honored by the prospect of involvement with a person of this social status.

PHOEBE'S ROLE IN THE
SPANISH MISSION

The suggestion I have to make about the role of Phoebe, therefore, is that she had agreed to cooperate with Paul as the patroness of the Spanish mission. Since that mission could not proceed in the manner of Paul's usual strategy, Phoebe agreed to travel to Rome while Paul was delivering the Jerusalem offering. Her task was to create the logistical base for the Spanish mission. The recommendation that Paul writes is thus a request that the Roman house churches cooperate with her in the patronage that this mission requires. The "matter" referred to in Rom. 16:2b is thus the patronage referred to in v. 2c. In light of the evidence that we have assembled about the peculiar requirements of the Spanish mission, I would suggest the following outline of the task that Phoebe would have to accomplish.

The Tasks of Phoebe's Patronage

1. In view of the practice of Greco-Roman epistolography, it is clear that the choice of a letter bearer was sometimes as crucial as the content of the letter. A trusted messenger would fill in the sensitive details and carry out the tasks envisioned in the letter. It is widely assumed that Phoebe was the bearer of Romans.[84] The likelihood of this assumption as well as the confidential role played by letter bearers is sustained and illustrated by Pseudo-Demetrius's example of a typical letter of recommendation:

> So-and-so, who is conveying this letter to you, has been tested by us and is loved on account of his trustworthiness. You will do well if you deem him worthy of hospitality both for my sake and his. . . . For you will not be sorry if you entrust to him, in any manner you wish, either words or deeds of a confidential nature. . . .[85]

Phoebe's primary task would thus be to present the letter to the several house churches in Rome and discuss its contents and implications with church leaders. She would attempt to achieve the aims of the letter, namely, the unification of the Roman house churches so that they would be able to cooperate in the support of the Spanish mission. Given the diversity of the several house churches alluded to in chapter 16,[86] this would have required formidable political skills on Phoebe's part. In view of the complexity of the argument of the letter, it would also have required substantial interpretive skills.

2. Convincing the independent house churches that Paul was a trustworthy partner for the Spanish mission project would not have been easy, given his previous involvement in controversial projects and conflicts. Christians of various orientations would have had reason to question the advisability of working with Paul. Conservative Jewish Christians would have known him as a radical advocate of the gentile mission and a chief opponent of the Judaizers. They would have heard reports of Paul's harsh encounter with Peter at Antioch, in which Paul had denounced Peter as hypocritical for refusing to eat with Gentiles. They would have been suspicious of Paul's strategy of acting like a Jew to the Jews and a Gentile to the Gentiles, wondering if Paul was reliable.

The house churches close to Roman governmental circles (Rom. 16:10–11) would have been concerned about Paul's history of difficulties with provincial authorities: the repeated imprisonments and the involvements with riots and other public disturbances in Pisidian Antioch, Iconium, Lystra, Philippi, Beroea, Corinth, and Ephesus. Cooperation with a controversial troublemaker might threaten the safety of the house churches in Rome or undermine the relationship of some of their leaders with other Roman authorities. These considerations would be particularly relevant in light of the crucial importance of Spain for imperial finances and the elements of resistance against Roman civilization in two of the three Spanish provinces. Although the repercussions about sponsoring subversive activities would have been felt most directly by Christians among the Narcissiani and the Aristobuliani who were administering imperial affairs in places like Spain, leaders of the other house churches in Rome would also have understood the risk.

Paul's sponsorship by an upper-class patroness like Phoebe would have gone far to answer the inevitable questions concerning Paul's reliability. Her wealth, social prestige, and legal status would serve as a kind of guarantee that his actions would remain within responsible limits and would afford him and the Roman church a measure of protection if he got into trouble. The churches at Rome could thus cooperate in the mission without undertaking its patronage, which meant that they would not become liable if Paul's history repeated itself. An additional mitigating factor that Phoebe likely would have pointed out was that the controversies related to Paul had largely been fomented by radical Jewish opposition to his mission, and the absence of a Jewish population in Spain might allow a less disruptive missional enterprise.

3. If Phoebe could succeed in the first two tasks, she would solicit the advice and counsel of the Roman house churches to find suitable resources for the mission in Spain. This would involve providing bases of operation in each of the three provinces for Paul and his missionary colleagues, finding logistical support for their travels and lodging, and recruiting translators capable of moving from Greek to Latin and the Iberian dialects. The most crucial decision, of course, would be the selection of the right contacts in Spain, because the lack of synagogues made it impossible for Paul to get acquainted with circles of gentile God-fearers before recruiting appropriate patrons for house churches. In this instance, the decisions would have to be made ahead of time and negotiations would be required to prepare the way before his arrival. If inappropriate local patrons were chosen, the entire mission would be jeopardized.

The List of Potential Allies in Rome

The long list of names in Rom. 16:3–15 has been a major puzzle to earlier researchers. Even the defenders of the integrity of the sixteen-chapter letter have been at a loss to suggest a plausible reason for the unprecedented number of greetings. I suggest that the greetings can be understood in relation to Phoebe's mission to prepare the way for Paul in the months prior to his expected arrival after the journey to Jerusalem. This list is comparable to a roster of potential campaign supporters that political operatives bring into a city as they begin to establish a campaign for their candidate. Since these persons are listed immediately after the reference to Phoebe's "matter," the greetings constitute the first stage of a recruitment process. These are diplomatic greetings, with clear political implications in relation to the proposal to cooperate with Paul in the Spanish mission, which Paul had outlined at the end of chapter 15. These names fall into several categories.

1. Close, personal friends and co-workers in the Pauline and other mission fields who now reside in Rome. Judging from the personal greetings and individual details, these persons include Prisca, Aquilla, Epaenetus, Mary, Andronicus and Junias, Ampliatus, Urbanus, Stachys, Apelles, Tryphaena and Tryphosa, Persis, and Rufus and his mother. Some of these persons appear to be closer to Paul than others, and the best guess is that most of them would have been refugees returning to the Roman churches that had been closed by the edict of Claudius. Others were simply persons now residing in Rome whom Paul had met in the earlier phases of his missionary activity. Some of these persons were Christians of very long standing: Andronicus and Junias were Jewish Christians who, according to

16:7, were converted prior to Paul's conversion. This means that they had been Christians at least since 34 C.E., more than twenty years prior to the writings of Romans.

2. The other persons greeted are leaders of Roman house churches whose identity is known to Paul through hearsay. On the basis of observations by Ollrog,[87] it is clear that many of the persons greeted had not been in personal contact with Paul. If he had known them personally, the lack of personal details, when compared with things said about other early Christian leaders, would have appeared impolite. These leaders include those of the house of Aristobolus, Herodian, those of the house of Narcissus, Asyncritus, Phlegon, Hermes, Patrobas, Hermas, Philologus, Julia, and Nereus and his sister, Olympas. Although Paul has not met these persons, the effect of naming them is honorific.[88] By singling them out, Paul in effect takes the first step toward recruiting them for Phoebe's patronage. In the ancient world, naming leaders had an important political function. In this particular situation, with the competition between leaders resident in Rome and those returning after the lifting of the edict of Claudius, the naming of competitors also has a politically significant bearing. The task of Christian tolerance in the form of mutual acceptance, so prominent a theme in Rom. 14:1—15:7, is thereby being advanced in the very chapter that traditional commentators have found irrelevant to the presumed doctrinal purpose of the letter.

The Evidence of Patronage

Although the plans for Paul's mission to Spain were interrupted and ultimately frustrated by the Jerusalem riot, his subsequent imprisonments, and his execution in Rome,[89] there are some indications that a patron was active in his behalf during this period. When Paul announces his travel plans in Rom. 15:24-28, he indicates no element of uncertainty about having sufficient means for passage to Jerusalem and back to Rome. Given the precarious state of his finances during the years prior to his journey (see Phil. 4:11-12; 2 Cor. 11:27) and the marginal economic situation of self-employed handworkers of Paul's type, it seems unlikely that he could have earned sufficient funds for these extensive journeys. In view of the elaborate arrangements visible in 2 Cor. 8:18-22 to avoid the charge of fraud in the collection and delivering of the Jerusalem offering,[90] it is difficult to believe that Paul was counting on using those funds for his own travel and living expenses. The most likely source of financial assistance was the person who Paul acknowledged in Rom. 16:2 had been playing the role of his patroness—Phoebe of Cenchreae.

There are also some curious details in Acts' account of Paul's arrival as a prisoner in Rome which point toward effective patronage in his behalf.

When Paul and his party arrived in Puteoli a week before their arrival in Rome, they had contacts with Christians there and were greeted by Christian delegations who traveled out from Rome to the Forum of Appius and to Three Taverns, which were sixty-five and fifty kilometers away from the city respectively. These encounters would have required advance arrangements involving not only the house churches in Rome and its surrounding area but also the Roman authorities in charge of the transfer of prisoners.[91] An influential person or persons must have ascertained or arranged that Paul's case would be handled with benign care so that his travel arrangement could be revealed in advance and visits allowed.[92] Finally, we are told, in Acts 28:16, 30, that Paul was able to live for two years under house arrest, which meant that he had to provide not only the rent for his lodgings but also for the upkeep of his guards.[93] That Paul could have worked out or afforded such arrangements on his own is inconceivable. The patronage of at least one wealthy and influential person would have been essential, not only to provide the resources that are directly visible in the two-year stay in Rome but also to work behind the scenes to ensure that the case against Paul remained inactive. In all these details, I think we are justified in suspecting the hand of the single person whom Paul introduces to the Romans as his patroness—Phoebe the deaconess of the church at Cenchreae.

NOTES

1. Otto Michel, *Der Brief an die Römer*, 12th ed. (Göttingen: Vandenhoeck & Ruprecht, 1963), 369.
2. Ibid.
3. C. H. Dodd, *The Epistle of Paul to the Romans* (London: Hodder & Stoughton, 1932), 229.
4. Michel, *Der Brief an die Römer*, 369.
5. For a discussion of the eschatological motivation of the Spanish mission, see Roger D. Aus, "Paul's Travel Plans to Spain and the 'Full Number of the Gentiles' of Rom xi 25," *Novum Testamentum* 21 (1979): 232–62.
6. Ernst Käsemann, *Commentary on Romans*, trans. G. W. Bromiley (Grand Rapids: Wm. B. Eerdmans, 1980), 398; C. E. B. Cranfield, *A Critical and Exegetical Commentary on the Epistle to the Romans* (Edinburgh: T. & T. Clark, 1979), 2:769; and Michel, *Der Brief an die Römer*, 369. The recent edition of Schürer abandons the notion of Jewish settlement in Spain prior to C.E. 300; see Emil Schürer, *The History of the Jewish People in the Age of Jesus Christ (175 B.C.–A.D. 135)*, rev. and ed. G. Vermes et al. (Edinburgh: T. & T. Clark, 1986), 3/1:84.
7. W. P. Bowers, "Jewish Communities in Spain in the Time of Paul the Apostle," *Journal of Theological Studies* 26 (1975): 400.
8. Antonio García y Bellido, *Les religions orientales dans l'Espagne Romaine* (Leiden: E. J. Brill, 1967), 1–20.

9. Michel (*Der Brief an die Römer*, 369 n. 2) cites this as evidence of Jewish communities in Spain during the Pauline period, but W. P. Bowers's recent survey indicates that the trilingual inscriptions at both Tortosa and Tarragona are dated by experts between the 2d and 6th cents. C.E. See Bowers, "Jewish Communities," 395–402.

10. Bowers, "Jewish Communities," 400.

11. Ibid., 401; Michael Stern's survey "The Jewish Diaspora," in *The Jewish People in the First Century* (Philadelphia: Fortress Press, 1974), 1:169–70 overlooks this lack of direct reference in Jewish sources and cites Rom. 15:28 as evidence that "it may be assumed that there already was a Jewish settlement in Spain during the Julio-Claudian period." Stern observes, however, that there is no "concrete evidence of Jewish settlements . . . in the Latin provinces of the empire," which surely should include Spain.

12. Bowers, "Jewish Communities," 402.

13. Most recent commentators appear unaware of the relevance of Bowers's study; cf. Roy A. Harrisville, *Romans* (Minneapolis: Augsburg Pub. House, 1980), 243–44; Ulrich Wilckens, *Der Brief an die Römer (Röm 12—16)* (Neukirchen-Vluyn: Neukirchener Verlag, 1982), 3:124, 128; and Paul J. Achtemeier, *Romans* (Atlanta: John Knox Press, 1985), 228–33. An exception is Dieter Zeller; see his *Der Brief an die Römer* (Regensburg: Friedrich Pustet, 1985), 14.

14. Cf. García y Bellido, *Religions orientales*, passim.

15. For evidence suggesting that the homes of patrons were the primary locus of the Pauline mission, see Stanley Kent Stowers, "Social Status, Public Speaking and Private Teaching: The Circumstances of Paul's Preaching Activity," *Novum Testamentum* 26 (1984): 68–73.

16. Ronald F. Hock, *The Social Context of Paul's Ministry: Tentmaking and Apostleship* (Philadelphia: Fortress Press, 1980), 29–42.

17. J. Paul Sampley, *Pauline Partnership in Christ: Christian Community and Commitment in Light of Roman Law* (Philadelphia: Fortress Press, 1980), 52–72, 81–87.

18. M. Rostovtzeff, *The Social and Economic History of the Roman Empire* (Oxford: Clarendon Press, 1926; citations from the 2d ed. rev. P. M. Fraser, 1957), 213–14. Cf. J. M. Blázquez (Martínez), "Roma y la explotación económica de la Peninsula Ibérica," *Las raices de España*, ed. J. M. Gómez-Tabanera (Madrid, 1967), 253–81.

19. Rostovtzeff, *Social and Economic History*, 211–15.

20. Ibid., 215.

21. Ibid., 213.

22. Carol H. V. Sutherland, *The Romans in Spain 217 B.C.–A.D. 117* (London: Methuen & Co., 1971); F. J. Wiseman, *Roman Spain: An Introduction to the Roman Antiquities of Spain and Portugal* (London: G. Bell & Sons, 1956), 63 ("It was only a small percentage of middle- and upper-class Spaniards who gained any direct contact with Rome and the Romans. It was only in the towns of Andalusia, the east coast and the Ebro valley that there was any marked transition to Roman manners and the Roman way of life, in the first century A.D."); T. R. S. Broughton, "The Romanisation of Spain: The Problem and the Evidence," *Proceedings of the American Philosophical Society* 103 (1959): 645–51; idem, "Municipal Institutions in

Roman Spain," *Cahiers d'histoire mondiale* 9 (1965): 129–40; P. Bosch-Gimpera, "Les soldats ibériques agents d'hellénisation et de romanisation," in *Mélanges d'archéologie, d'épigraphie et d'histoire offerts à Jérôme Carcopino* (Paris: Hachette, 1966), 141–48; and José Manuel Roldán Hervas, "De Numancia a Sertorio: Problemas de la romanización de Hispania en la encrucijada de las guerras civiles," in *Studien zur antiken Sozialgeschichte: Festschrift Friedrich Vittinghoff,* ed. W. Eck, H. Galsterer, and H. Wolff, Kölner historische Abhandlungen 28 (Cologne and Vienna: Böhlau, 1980), 157–78.

23. Antonio García y Bellido, "Die Latinisierung Hispaniens," *ANRW* 1/1 (1972): 462–91; Michael Koch, "Ausgewählte Bibliographie zur Latinisierung and Romanisierung Spaniens," ibid., 491–500; Antonio Tovar and José M. Blázquez Martínez, "Forschungsbericht zur Geschichte des römischen Hispanien," *ANRW* 2/3 (1975): 428–51.

24. García y Bellido, "Die Latinisierung Hispaniens," 463–66; the linguistic map he provides on p. 476 implies a larger importance for the Punic languages than in the earlier discussion. For a treatment of the cultural legacy of the Greek colonies, see Rhys Carpenter, *The Greeks in Spain* (1925; New York: AMS Press, 1971), and Antonio García y Bellido, *Factores que contribuyeron a la helenización de la España prerromana* (Madrid: Tipografía de Archivos, 1934).

25. See A. J. N. Wilson, *Emigration from Italy in the Republican Age of Rome* (Manchester: Manchester Univ. Press, 1966), 22–40.

26. See Géza Alföldi, *Fasti Hispanienses: Senatorische Reichsbeamte und Offiziere in den spanischen Provinzen des römischen Reiches von Augustus bis Diokletian* (Wiesbaden: Steiner, 1969), 294.

27. See Hartmut Galsterer, *Untersuchungen zum römischen Städtewesen in Spanien,* Madrider Forshungen 8 (Berlin: Walter de Gruyter, 1971), 65–68.

28. García y Bellido, "Die Latinisierung Hispaniens," 470–78.

29. Galsterer, *Untersuchungen,* 37–50.

30. See Alföldi, *Fasti Hispanienses,* 289–90.

31. Ibid., 293–94.

32. García y Bellido, "Die Latinisierung Hispaniens," Baldinger, *Die Herausbildung der Sprachräume auf der Pyrenäenhalbinsul* (Berlin: Akademie-Verlag, 1958), 43–51.

33. See W. H. C. Frend, *The Rise of Christianity* (Philadelphia: Fortress Press, 1984), 340.

34. See William H. C. Frend, *Town and Country in the Early Christian Centuries* (London: Variorum, 1980), xiii, 126.

35. See Frend, "A Note on the Influence of Greek Immigrants on the Spread of Christianity in the West," in *Town and Country,* xiii, 125–29.

36. See Werner Dahlheim, "Die Funktion der Stadt im römischen Herschaftsverband," in *Stadt und Herrschaft: Römische Kaiserzeit und hohes Mittelalter,* ed. F. Vittinghoff, Historische Zeitschrift n.s. 7 (Munich: Oldenbourg, 1982), 48–55.

37. That Paul was released from Roman imprisonment and pursued the mission to Spain is highly unlikely even if the evidence from the Pastorals is taken to be historical, for they reflect missionary activities in the East rather than in the West. See Robert Jewett, *A Chronology of Paul's Life* (Philadelphia: Fortress Press, 1979), 45f–46. O. F. A. Meinardus's survey of the evidence concludes that the accounts of

a Pauline mission in Spain are probably a "mere extension of an intent" ("Paul's Missionary Journey to Spain: Tradition and Folklore," *Biblical Archeologist* 41 [1978]: 62).

38. See R. Konetzke, "Spanien," in *Religion in Geschichte und Gegenwart*, 3d ed., 6:223; and Jewett, *Chronology*, 131–32.

39. Paul Feine created a compelling form of this hypothesis in "Die Abfassung des Philipperbriefes in Ephesus, mit einer Anlage über Rm. 16, 3–20 als Epheser-brief," *Beiträge zur Förderung christlicher Theologie* 20 (1916): 278–425. An account of the extensive early debate on this question is found in Rudolf Schumacher's *Die beiden letzten Kapitel des Römerbriefes: Ein Beitrag zu ihrer Geschichte und Erklärung* (Münster: Aschendorff, 1929), 61–66. The foremost British and American advocates of this view were T. W. Manson ("St. Paul's Letter to the Romans—and Others," *Bulletin of the John Rylands University Library of Manchester* 31 [1948]: 224–40; repr. in *The Romans Debate*, ed. K. P. Donfried [Minneapolis: Augsburg Pub. House, 1977], 1–16) and Edgar J. Goodspeed ("Phoebe's Letter of Introduction," *Harvard Theological Review* 44 [1950]: 55–57); recent advocates of this view include Willi Marxsen (*Introduction to the New Testament: An Approach to Its Problems*, trans. G. Buswell [Philadelphia: Fortress Press, 1968], 107–8), Gerhardt Friedrich ("Römerbrief," in *Religion in Geschichte und Gegenwart*, 3d ed., 5:col. 1138), Walter Schmithals (*Der Römerbrief als historisches Problem* [Gütersloh: Mohn, 1975], 138–47), and Helmut Koester (*Introduction to the New Testament*, vol. 2, *History and Literature of Early Christianity* [Philadelphia: Fortress Press, 1982], 138–39).

40. J. J. MacDonald ("Was Romans xvi a Separate Letter?" *New Testament Studies* 16 [1969–70]: 369–72) argues that the chapter matches several Greco-Roman paradigms for letters of recommendation. See also Hans-Martin Schenke, "Aporien im Römerbrief," *Theologische Literaturzeitung* 92 (1967): 881–84. Hans-Martin Schenke and Karl Martin Fischer (*Einleitung in die Schriften des Neuen Testaments* [Berlin: Evangelische Verlagsanstalt, 1978], 1:136–42) propose the provenience from Rome and suggest that the redactors mistakenly included it in with Romans.

41. See John Knox, *The Epistle to the Romans*, Interpreter's Bible 9 (Nashville: Abingdon Press, 1955), 365–68. For other versions of this scheme, though without the redactional motive suggested by Knox, see Paul Feine and Johannes Behm, *Einleitung in das Neue Testament*, 9th ed. (Heidelberg: Quelle & Meyer, 1950), 176; Hans Werner Bartsch, "Die historische Situation des Römerbriefes," in *Studia Evangelica*, ed. F. L. Cross (Berlin: Akademie-Verlag, 1968), 4:282; and Johannes Mueller-Bardorff, *Paulus* (Gütersloh: Gütersloher Verlagshaus, 1970), 16–18.

42. Robert Jewett, *Paul's Anthropological Terms: A Study of Their Use in Conflict Settings* (Leiden: E. J. Brill, 1971), 41–42.

43. Harry Gamble, *The Textual History of the Letter to the Romans: A Study in Textual and Literary Criticism* (Grand Rapids: Wm. B. Eerdmans, 1977), 31–95.

44. Kurt Aland, *Neutestamentliche Entwürfe* (Munich: Chr. Kaiser Verlag, 1979), 284–301.

45. Wolf-Hennig Ollrog, "Die Abfassungsverhältnisse von Röm 16," in *Kirche: Festschrift Günther Bornkamm zum 75. Geburtstag*, ed. D. Lührmann and G. Strecker (Tübingen: J. C. B. Mohr [Paul Siebeck], 1980), 221–44.

46. Robert Jewett, "Romans as an Ambassadorial Letter," *Interpretation* 36 (1982); 5–20.

47. See Robert Jewett, *Christian Tolerance: Paul's Message to the Modern Church* (Philadelphia: Westminster Press, 1982), 17–23, where a case for interpolation is developed in part out of suggestions by Knox and Schmithals. Ollrog presents a similar case in "Die Abfassungsverhältnisse," 229–34.

48. See Wilckens, *Der Brief an die Römer* 1:22–24.

49. Cranfield, *Critical and Exegetical Commentary,* 780: "That she was a Gentile Christian may be inferred from her name; for a Jewess would scarcely have had a name deriving from pagan mythology."

50. See R. Scranton, J. W. Shaw, L. Ibrahim, *Kenchreai . . .: Results of Investigations . . . for the American School of Classical Studies in Athens 1* (Leiden: E. J. Brill, 1978).

51. The textual variant ὑμῶν in P₄₆ A F G P pc it bo_ms is less strongly attested than ἡμῶν.

52. Cranfield, *Critical and Exegetical Commentary,* 780; Wilckens, *Der Brief an die Römer,* 131; and André Viard, *Saint Paul, Epître aux Romains* (Paris: Gabalda, 1975), 307.

53. The addition of καὶ after οὖσαν in Aleph* A C₂ D F G Ψ M latt sy sa is about as strongly attested as its deletion in the other manuscripts. The Nestle-Aland 26th ed. places it in brackets, indicating a divided vote, but it seems more likely to have been added for stylistic purposes. It has a slightly condescending effect, suggesting that her status as deacon improves her rank as a mere "sister," and thus is less likely to have originated with Paul than with later, more chauvinistic traditions.

54. See Charles Hodge, *Commentary on the Epistle to the Romans,* 2d ed. (Philadelphia: Claxton, 1866), 704: Phoebe was "a *servant,* . . . i.e., *deaconess.* It appears that in the apostolic church, elderly females were selected to attend upon the poor and sick of their own sex." Cf. William Sanday and Arthur C. Headlam, *A Critical and Exegetical Commentary on the Epistle to the Romans* (New York: Charles Scribner's Sons, 1895), 417; Hans Lietzmann, *The History of the Early Church* (London: Lutterworth Press, 1963), 1:146; and Michel, *Der Brief an die Römer,* 377. Current commentaries follow this general line, limiting Phoebe's activities to the "practical service of the needy" (Cranfield, *Critical and Exegetical Commentary,* 781) and "charitable care of the poor, sick, widows, orphans . . ." (Käsemann, *Commentary on Romans,* 410). Adolf Jülicher rejects this subordinate interpretation in *Der Brief an die Römer: Die Schriften des Neuen Testaments* (Göttingen: Vandenhoeck & Ruprecht, 1917), 2:330.

55. Ulrich Brockhaus, *Charisma und Amt: Die paulinische Charismenlehre auf dem Hintergrund des frühchristlichen Gemeindefunktionen* (Wuppertal: Rolf Brockhaus, 1972), 100; and Bengt Holmberg, *Paul and Power: The Structure of Authority in the Primitive Church as Reflected in the Pauline Epistles* (Philadelphia: Fortress Press, 1978), 99–102.

56. For the evidence liking the διάκονος role with "missionarische Verkündigungstätigkeit im weitesten Sinn," see Wolf-Hennig Ollrog, *Paulus und seine Mitarbeiter: Untersuchungen zu Theorie und Praxis der paulinischen Mission* (Neukirchen-Vluyn: Neukirchener Verlag, 1979), 73–74. Aloys Funk (*Status und Rollen in den Paulusbriefen: Eine inhaltsanalytische Untersuchung zur Religionssoziologie*

[Innsbruck: Tyrolia, 1981], 86, 112) refers to the "positiv bewertete institution-alisierte Rolle" that Phoebe exercised as the leader of the congregation.

57. Elisabeth Schüssler Fiorenza, *In Memory of Her: A Feminist Theological Reconstruction of Christian Origins* (New York: Crossroad, 1984), 171.

58. A late textual variant attested in F and G provides παραστάτις, "assistant," at this point, a term more appropriately linked to the widely cited RSV translation "helper" than προστάτις, which properly means "patroness."

59. W. Bauer, W. F. Arndt, and F. W. Gingrich, *Greek-English Lexicon of the New Testament,* 718.

60. Jülicher, *Der Brief an die Römer,* 330; Adolf Deissmann, *Paul: A Study in Social and Religious History* (Gloucester, Mass: Peter Smith, 1958), 240; Schumacher, *Die beiden letzten Kapitel,* 50; and Michel, *Der Brief an die Römer,* 377. See also the brief note by Margaret D. Gibson: "Phoebe," *Expository Times* 23 (1912): 281.

61. Käsemann, *Commentary on Romans,* 411.

62. E. A. Judge, "Cultural Conformity and Innovation in Paul: Some Clues from Contemporary Documents," *Tyndale Bulletin* 35 (1984): 21. The papyrus was published by Orsolina Montevecchi ("Une donna 'prostatis' del figlio minorenne in un papiro del II$_a$," *Aegyptus* 61 [1981]: 103–15). Montevecchi discusses the Phoebe parallel on p. 106.

63. Ramsay MacMullen, "Women in Public in the Roman Empire," *Historia* 29 (1980): 211.

64. Ibid., 212.

65. E. Lyding Will, "Women's Roles in Antiquity: New Archeological Views," *Science Digest* (March 1980): 35–39.

66. Gerd Theissen, *The Social Setting of Pauline Christianity: Essays on Corinth,* trans. J. H. Schütz (Philadelphia: Fortress Press, 1982), 69–120.

67. Holmberg, *Paul and Power,* 103–6.

68. Funk, *Status und Rollen,* 206–15.

69. Jerome Murphy-O'Connor, *St. Paul's Corinth: Texts and Archeology* (Wilmington, Del.: Michael Glazier, 1983), 153–66.

70. Wayne A. Meeks, *The First Urban Christians: The Social World of the Apostle Paul* (New Haven: Yale Univ. Press, 1983), 51–73.

71. Cf. Judge, "Cultural Conformity," 21: "Paul is acknowledging his social dependence upon Phoebe."

72. A modern commentator who comes closer to conveying the nuance of προστάτις in his translation is Charles K. Barrett, *The Epistle to the Romans* [New York: Harper & Bros., 1958], 283: "a protectress of many, and of me myself"), but he insists that Paul could not have been her client because he was free born, so that the "more general sense" of "protectress" is to be preferred to "patron."

73. Käsemann, *Commentary on Romans,* 411.

74. Cranfield, *Critical and Exegetical Commentary,* 781–82.

75. Chan-Hie Kim, *Form and Structure of the Familiar Greek Letter of Recommendation,* Dissertation Series 4 (Missoula, Mont.: Scholars Press, 1972), 76–77, 133.

76. The inattention to the class implications of προστάτις leads many commentators to the conclusion that the provision of housing was the major need that the

congregation in Rome would have to meet; e.g., see Goodspeed, "Phoebe's Letter," 55–57.

77. Michel, *Der Brief an die Römer,* 378; and Feine, "Abfassung," 148.

78. Käsemann, *Commentary on Romans,* 411.

79. See Kim, *Form and Structure,* 78–79, 133.

80. Cranfield, *Critical and Exegetical Commentary,* 782.

81. Goodspeed, "Phoebe's Letter," 56.

82. Frederic L. Godet (*Commentary on Romans* [Grand Rapids: Kregel, 1977], 448) cites Renan's romantic speculation that "this poor woman started on a wild winter journey across the Archipelago without any other resource than Paul's recommendation."

83. Schüssler Fiorenza suggests that the rationale of Paul's request was the "exchange law" of Greco-Roman patronage, according to which he "asks that the community of Rome repay Phoebe for the assistance and favors, which Paul owed her as her client" (*In Memory of Her,* 182, citing S. C. Mott, "The Power of Giving and Receiving: Reciprocity in Hellenistic Benevolence," in *Current Issues in Biblical and Patristic Interpretation,* ed. G. E. Hawthorne [Grand Rapids: Wm. B. Eerdmans, 1975], 60–72). It is not clear, however, why Paul would have expected that the Roman house churches, which owed nothing to him for their formation and growth, could have felt obligated to repay Phoebe in his behalf.

84. See Cranfield, *Critical and Exegetical Commentary,* 780: "It is highly probable that Phoebe was to be the bearer of Paul's letter to Rome." Most commentators who believe chap. 16 originally belonged to the letter draw a similar conclusion.

85. Abraham J. Malherbe, "Ancient Epistolary Theorists," *Ohio Journal of Religion* 5/2 (1977): 31.

86. See Hans-Josef Klauck, *Hausgemeinde und Hauskirche im frühen Christentum* (Stuttgart: Katholisches Bibelwerk, 1981), 21–30; and Joan M. Petersen, "House Churches in Rome," *Vigiliae Christianae* 23 (1969): 264–72.

87. Ollrog, "Abfassungsverhältnisse," 236–41.

88. Kim (*Form and Structure,* 140) suggests that "the salutations in Rom. 16:3–16 are actually oblique commendations." Cf. Ollrog, *Paulus und seine Mitarbeiter,* 191–93.

89. Cf. Jewett, *Chronology,* 45–46.

90. Cf. Hans-Dieter Betz, *2 Corinthians 8 and 9: A Commentary on Two Administrative Letters of the Apostle Paul* (Philadelphia: Fortress Press, 1985), 76–77, 143–44.

91. See William M. Ramsay, *St. Paul the Traveller and Roman Citizen* (London: Hodder & Stoughton, 1920), 344. Ernst Haenchen (*The Acts of the Apostles,* trans. from the 14th ed. [1965] B. Noble and G. Shinn [Philadelphia: Westminster Press, 1971], 719–20) was so impressed with the difficulties in logistics and command structure that he marks Acts 28:14a, 15–16 as Lukan additions. Haenchen does not consider the possibility of political influence in Paul's behalf to explain these details.

92. See Gottfried Schille, *Die Apostelgeschichte des Lukas* (Berlin: Evangelische Verlagsanstalt, 1983), 477.

93. For typical arrangements for house arrest under Roman law, see Theodor Mommsen, *Römische Staatsrecht,* 2d ed. (Graz: Akademische Druck, 1952), 2:317.

Paul, His Opponents
in 2 Corinthians 10—13,
and the Rhetorical Handbooks

J. PAUL SAMPLEY
Boston University

We have not inquired very much how people in Paul's time carried on their arguments, how they made their cases, and how they tried to persuade one another. Neither have we considered how people those days defended themselves against charges. This is all the more surprising because in the apostle Paul we encounter a polemicist and an apologist without equal in the literature of the early church.

The rhetorical handbooks from around the time of Paul provide us with the best basis for gaining insight into how people structured their arguments. Of course, Paul nowhere declares that he knows the rhetorical handbooks, but we do realize that they were standard fare in the education of schoolchildren in that time, and it is clear that Paul uses many of the devices they recommend.[1]

For the study undertaken here, contemporary rhetorical tradition is perhaps best exemplified by Cicero's *De inventione*. Another handbook, *Ad Herennium*, wrongly attributed to Cicero, also dates from the first century B.C.E. A third manual, Quintilian's *Institutio oratoria*, was probably written about three decades after Paul's death. From Cicero, through *Ad Herennium*, to Quintilian, we encounter relatively fixed rhetorical guidelines concerning particular ways in which one may cultivate good will (*benevolentia*) for one's own case and thereby detract from the support that a judge, jury, or audience will be willing to give to one's adversaries. In this paper we examine whether Paul knows and uses the specific rhetorical devices that the handbooks—taking Cicero as our touchstone—advise for winning good will for oneself and undercutting one's opponents.[2] When 2 Corinthians 10—13 is viewed in light of the rhetorical handbooks' suggestions, what features stand out? Does Paul employ the standard rhetorical devices for achieving good will?

I have chosen to test the matter in 2 Corinthians 10—13 for two reasons. The scope and cohesiveness of 2 Corinthians 10—13 render it an ideal test area. Also, as a fragment of an extended correspondence with the Corinthians, 2 Corinthians 10—13 has a broader context for interpretation of Paul's strife.[3]

Of the Corinthian correspondence, the most contentious piece is 2 Corinthians 10—13. Charge and countercharge bristle. Paul anticipates another visit to Corinth and lays down ground rules for that meeting: "This is the third time I am coming to you. Any charge must be sustained by the evidence of two or three witnesses" (2 Cor. 13:1). Paul hopes that what he writes will avert the confrontation (13:10).

CICERO AND GOOD WILL

Cicero recognizes that in a dispute, good will (*benevolentia*) is available from a number of sources and the effective orator will not overlook any of them but will attempt to orchestrate all of them to favor his own case. Although Cicero has a jury in mind, his observations hold equally well for an audience or even for the readers of a letter.

According to Cicero, there are four ways to cultivate good will: by references to (*a*) ourselves (*ab nostra*), (*b*) our opponents (*ab adversariorum*), (*c*) what we might call the jury (*ab iudicum persona*), and (*d*) the case or situation itself (*a causa*) (*De inv.* 1.16.22). For Cicero, the first three are the primary means. Cicero details how each of the ways may be pursued effectively. Our plan will be to examine each source of good will as detailed by Cicero to see whether or how fully Paul relies on such devices in 2 Corinthians 10—13.

Good Will by Reference to Ourselves

Cicero suggests four ways to gain good will from the audience by comments about ourselves:

> We shall win good-will from our own person if we [A.] refer to our own acts and services without arrogance; if we [B.] weaken the effect of charges that have been preferred, or of some suspicion of less honourable dealing which has been cast upon us; if we [C.] dilate on the misfortunes which have befallen us or the difficulties which still beset us; if we [D.] use prayers and entreaties with a humble and submissive spirit. (*De inv.* 1.16.22)[4]

A. We will derive good will "if we refer to our own acts and services without arrogance [*sine arrogantia*]." *Ad Herennium* concurs ("by praising our services without arrogance") but sheds some light on what might be considered such services: "revealing also our past conduct toward the republic, or toward our parents, friends, *or the audience*" (1.5.8; emphasis added).[5]

Indeed Paul frequently reminds the Corinthians of his "acts and services" in their behalf. He first preached the gospel to them (10:14b). The same point, but with a change of imagery, is made a few verses later (11:2). Further, he "preached God's gospel without cost to you" (11:7), without burdening anyone (11:9; 12:13–14, 16). Finally, the Corinthians were the beneficiaries of "signs and wonders and mighty works" that Paul did among them (12:12).

But Cicero warned that references to one's own "acts and services" must be made "without arrogance." On the one hand, Paul tries to steer clear of arrogance. At the outset he identifies himself with the "meekness and gentleness of Christ" (10:1), and later he boasts of his weaknesses (11:30; 12:9) and with irony reminds the Corinthians that he was "too weak" to take advantage of them (11:20–21; cf. 13:9).

On the other hand, Paul's boasting seems to violate Cicero's advice that arrogance will undermine the gains one may make with reference to one's "acts and services." Paul is in a quandary. Some people at Corinth have assailed him and his credentials. Cicero recognizes that such attacks cannot be ignored; one can gain favor by undercutting the "effect of the charges that have been preferred" (1.16.22). Personal attacks by people at Corinth must be refuted, but arrogance is to be avoided. That is Paul's dilemma. He takes three steps to diminish the degree to which his boasting will be taken as arrogance: (1) he employs the fool/madman model (11:16ff.; 13:11ff.);[6] (2) he claims that he is being forced to boast (12:11); and (3) he talks of himself in a third-person mode as the "man in Christ who fourteen years ago was caught up to the third heaven" (12:2ff.).[7]

In Paul's claim that he was forced to boast we come to the heart of Paul's predicament. If the Corinthians had related to Paul as he thinks they should have, *they would have commended him* (12:11) and he would not have been obliged to sing his own praises. Instead, they have ignored the "signs of a true apostle" that "were performed among you in all patience" (12:12) and have derogated him. Thus they have forced him to change the earlier pattern of abasing himself in order that they might be exalted (11:7). Though he knows he has proper grounds for boasting in the Lord's work through him, he has resisted boasting. But in the present circumstance he must boast (*kauchasthai dei,* 12:1). Then, he maintains that the Corinthians forced him to it (12:11). Quintilian recognizes a proper function for a digression (*excursio*) of this sort and maintains, "If we do introduce a digression, it must always be short and of such a nature that we give the impression of having been forced from our proper course by some uncontrollable emotion" (4.2.104).

Thus Paul's argument accords with the handbooks when he refers to his own "acts and services" in behalf of the Corinthians and when he takes steps to minimize the arrogance that some may impute. The charges against him, combined with the Corinthians' failure to recognize Paul as they should, force him to a digressionary boast.

B. Good will can also be garnered "if we weaken the effect of charges that have been preferred, or of some suspicion of less honourable dealing which has been cast upon us." Beyond the already-mentioned defense of his apostleship, Paul responds in chapters 10—13 to a range of other charges: (1) Paul is inconsistent in his dealings; he vacillates. When he is with them he is meek, even weak; when he is apart from them he is harsh (10:1). (2) Paul acts in a worldly fashion. He walks "according to the flesh" (10:2). Presumably, one may consider under this heading the various claims that Paul has robbed other churches (11:8), that he is interested in the Corinthians just for their wealth, and that he will resort to anything in his dealings with them, even fraud (12:16).[8]

The handbooks detail how to refute charges. Any charge must be met in one of three ways: (*a*) by a denial that the act was done, (*b*) by an admission that it was done and a defense of having done it, or (*c*) by a claim that the act was other than charged.[9]

The handbooks agree that it is best, if possible, to issue an unequivocal denial of the charge. When that cannot be done, the action may be defended as appropriate or necessary. For example,

> Milo is accused of killing Clodius. Either he did or did not do the deed. The best policy would be to deny the fact, but that is impossible. It is admitted then that he killed him. The act must then have been either right or wrong. We urge that it was right. If so, the act must have either been deliberate or under compulsion of necessity, for it is impossible to plead ignorance. (Quint. 7.1.34)

The third line of defense—to claim that the deed was other than charged—reclassifies the act. For example, it might be said that X did kill Y but treason was the alternative.[10]

In response to the various charges against him, Paul issues a flat denial to some, admits the partial truth of others, and redefines for the rest.

Flat denial. In a variety of ways, Paul directly rebuts the charge of inconsistency or vacillation. Paul reminds the Corinthians that he has consistently refused support from them even when he was with them and in need. And that pattern will continue, he pledges (11:9, 12).

Flat denials also meet the complaint that he acts one way when absent from them and another when with them. "Let such people understand that what we say by letter when absent, we do when present" (10:11). We see it also in 13:2: "I warned those who sinned before and all the others, and I warn them now while absent, as I did when present on my second visit."

Other charges also receive unambiguous denials. Paul wants "not what is yours" (12:14). Rather, he seeks the Corinthians themselves. On another matter, he denies that he is even capable of speaking or doing anything other than the truth (13:8; cf. 11:31; 12:6). Paul also categorically rejects the charge that he has overextended himself (10:4). That denial is supported further by the reminder that "we were the first to come all the way to you with the gospel of Christ" (10:4), "even to you" (10:13).

Paul directly refutes one more accusation: "I was crafty [*panourgos*, "ready to do anything"], you say, and got the better of you by guile [*dolos*, "deceit" or "fraud"]" (12:16). This charge may be the opponents' reshaping of an earlier Pauline claim that he had "become all things to all, that I might by all means save some" (1 Cor. 9:22). In 2 Corinthians 10—13, Paul responds that he never took advantage of the Corinthians—and furthermore, neither did Titus, whom Paul sent with the unnamed brother (12:17–18). Others have taken advantage of the Corinthians, he alleges, and even abused them, but Paul and his fellow workers never have.[11]

Admission of partial truth. The handbooks recognize that if the charge cannot simply be denied, it can be admitted if there are extenuating or exonerating circumstances. Accordingly, Paul responds to some charges by admitting that there is some truth to them and explains their significance in a way different from his opponents. For example, he concedes that he may be "unskilled [*idiotes*, a "lay person," "untutored"] in speaking" (11:16)—partially admitting to the propriety of the charge—but warns that the Corinthians should not confuse that weakness with a lack of knowledge.[12]

Another, similar charge is treated by Paul with a partial admission. He has been accused of weakness. At several points he admits that he is weak but turns his own admission of weakness into a testimony of God's power that works through him. Accordingly, he claims no power in himself—the Corinthians are partly right—but the power of God at work in him can be neither downgraded nor ignored. Paul cites his hardships and dangers as illustration that God's strength is made perfect in Paul's weakness (11:23–29; 12:5–10). "For the sake of Christ, then, I am content with weaknesses, insults, hardships, persecutions, and calamities; for when I am weak, then I am strong" (12:10). In fact, Paul claims that his weakness—to which some Corinthians point derisively—has actually served the Corinthians well: with blistering irony Paul says that he, unlike the people to whom the Corinthians admiringly turn in Paul's absence, has been too weak to take advantage of them (11:21).

Admission with redefinition. Finally, the handbooks recognize that a charge may be overturned by a redefinition. In such a situation, the defendant admits that something took place but clarifies that it was not what was charged. Paul has offended some Corinthians by accepting aid from Macedonia (see Phil. 4:10ff.) while at Corinth and while steadfastly refusing Corinthian support. Apparently some Corinthians have charged that Paul is "robbing" other churches (11:8). Paul does not deny the support. He simply redefines it as something other than robbery: "The brothers who came from Macedonia provided me with everything I wanted" (11:9 JB). In that verse Paul subtly but clearly makes the "brothers from Macedonia" the subject of the verb.[13] They supplied my needs. That he *received* support from Macedonia, yes; that in any sense he *took* it, no. Furthermore, the *Corinthians* were the beneficiaries of the aid because it enabled Paul to serve them: "I robbed other churches [you suggest] by accepting support from them [but the reason I did accept the aid was] in order to serve you" (11:8).

In remarks throughout 2 Corinthians 10—13, Paul seeks to gain the good will of the Corinthians by undercutting the effect of the charges that have been leveled at him. He defends as above suspicion his dealings with the Corinthians. But the rhetoricians realized that such proofs and disputations of charges were merely a part of the total effort to cause the judge, jury, or audience to decide in favor of the defendant.

Proofs, it is true, may induce the judges to regard

> our case as superior to that of our opponent, but the appeal to the emotions will do more, for it will make them wish our case to be better. And what they wish, they will also believe. (Quint. 6.2.5)

Appropriately, the next step in Cicero's advice for winning good will appeals to the emotions of the audience.

C. "We shall win good-will from our own person . . . if we dilate on the misfortunes which have befallen us or the difficulties which still beset us." *Ad Herennium* makes the same point: ". . . by setting forth our disabilities, need, loneliness, and misfortune" (1.5.8). Cicero calls for winning good will by reference to past and present difficulties. Paul looks to the past and catalogues his sufferings and hardships:

> But whatever any one dares to boast of—I am speaking as a fool—I also dare to boast of that. Are they Hebrews? So am I. Are they Israelites? So am I. Are they descendants of Abraham? So am I. Are they servants of Christ? I am a better one—I am talking like a madman—with far greater labors, far more imprisonments, with countless beatings, and often near death. Five times I have received at the hands of the Jews the forty lashes less one. Three times I have been shipwrecked; a night and a day I have been adrift at sea; on frequent journeys, in danger from rivers, danger from robbers, danger from my own people, danger from Gentiles, danger in the city, danger in the wilderness, danger at sea, danger from false brethren; in toil and hardship, through many a

sleepless night, in hunger and thirst, often without food, in cold and exposure. (11:21b–27)

He punctuates this lengthy expression of hardship with a declaration of indignation (11:29) and an oath as to his truthfulness (11:31). Then, as if to illustrate the list with one specific example, he tells of an event at Damascus. "The governor under King Aretas guarded the city of Damascus in order to seize me, but I was let down in a basket through a window in the wall, and escaped his hands" (11:32–33; cf. Acts 9:23–25).

Cicero indicates that good will may be obtained by reference not only to difficulties that have been encountered in the past but also to ones that persist into the present. Paul seizes this opportunity as well. "For the sake of Christ, then, I am content with weaknesses, insults, hardships, persecutions, and calamities" (12:10). This generalizing and comprehensive statement appears after his description of his continuing struggle with a disability, his thorn in the flesh (12:7–9). Paul's recounting of his personal difficulty—especially in the detail of its thrice-rejected appeal for its removal—highlights his own continuing "disabilities, need, . . . and misfortune" (*Ad Her.* 1.5.8).

Already in Chapter 11, Paul attaches to the lengthy list of past troubles and trials (11:21a–27) a statement about enduring problems: "And, apart from other things, there is the daily pressure upon me of my anxiety for all the churches" (11:28). Further, Paul identifies with the weaknesses and struggles of all Christians. When any believer stumbles, Paul burns over it (11:29). Not only has Paul suffered great and continuing difficulties in the past but he is also never without anxiety over the welfare of the churches and the individual Christians who compose them.

Before we turn to the next means of winning good will, one matter deserves further comment. There are two striking features about the list of hardships (11:21b–29). First is its length and comprehensiveness. Second, though it seems to win the good will of the readers, it is at the same time an attack upon Paul's opponents by a comparison that claims Paul has outdone whatever the adversaries may claim. What starts off as a comparison of status and lineage ("Are they Hebrews? So am I") becomes an assertion of Paul's superiority ("Are they servants of Christ? I am a better one"), and the evidence that supports the claim of superiority is the Ciceronian recounting of hardships ("with far greater labors, far more imprisonments, with countless beatings, and often near death," 11:23). The comparative form in which Paul casts this argument (cf. 11:21b) shows that Paul is not the only person who knows what the handbooks recommend. Paul's opponents also know about the appeal for good will by reference to one's difficulties, and Paul has heard of their claims in that regard.[14] It is perhaps by such a means that they have aggrandized their own status so that Paul mockingly calls them "superlative apostles" (12:11). Not only has he heard of their claims but he chooses to counter them by a more impressive list. And we no doubt learn about the Damascus escape by basket and the "thorn in the flesh" because Paul is following the rhetorical tradition in an effort to win his readers' support.

D. "We shall win good-will from our own person . . . if we use prayers and entreaties with a humble and submissive spirit." We have seen two matters in Paul's struggle with the Corinthians that make a "humble and submissive spirit" difficult for him to communicate. First, his status and power as an apostle have been under attack. Nowhere in his extant correspondence does Paul let such an attack go unanswered. In 2 Corinthians 10—13 Paul responds with his boast in Christ. Second, Paul's adversaries seem to have recited *their own* "acts and services" to the Corinthians and "dilated on their difficulties." In response, Paul has chosen, whether rightly or wrongly, to weigh his own services and difficulties over against those of his opponents and to declare "no contest." But Cicero says good will is gained by prayers and entreaties with a humble and submissive spirit.

Chapters 10—13 begin in that tone. Paul entreats (*parakalo*) them "by the meekness and gentleness of Christ" so that he will not be forced to a showdown of boldness when he arrives in Corinth (10:1–2). Prayerful entreaty reappears in 13:5 and runs through the remainder of the letter fragment. Paul prays for the Corinthians' improvement (*katartisis,* 13:9). Though he himself may seem to have failed, he prays "God that you may not do wrong . . . but that you may do what is right" (13:7). He hopes that the Corinthians "will find that we have not failed" (13:6), but whether he himself has failed or not is unimportant when compared with the Corinthians' improvement. Paul openly shares with the readers his fear that he may come to Corinth and "find you not what I wish" (12:20). With that he reports another concern: "I fear that when I come again my God may humble me before you" (12:21). The context suggests that his fear is not so much that he may be shown wrong or out of joint with God's purposes; he knows he can do nothing against the truth (13:8). Rather, he may be humbled by God and have to mourn "over many of those who sinned before and have not repented of the impurity, immorality, and licentiousness which they have practiced" (12:21). Although Paul boasts and counterattacks, he finally falls into line with Cicero's and the other handbooks' directions to gain further good will by prayers, entreaties, and demonstration of a humble spirit.

Good Will by Reference to Opponents

So far our analysis has restricted itself to Cicero's guidelines for winning good will by reference to oneself. But good will can also be garnered by undercutting one's adversaries, by making them appear ignoble and unworthy of fealty:

> Good-will is acquired from the person of the opponents if we can bring them into hatred, unpopularity, or contempt. They will be hated if some act of theirs is presented which is base, haughty, cruel, or malicious; they will become unpopular if we present their power, political influence, wealth, family connexions, and their arrogant and intolerable use of these advantages, so that they seem to rely on these rather than on the justice of their case. They will be brought into contempt if we reveal their laziness, carelessness, sloth, indolent pursuits, or luxurious idleness. (*De inv.* 1.16.22)[15]

As surely as Paul's adversaries followed the handbooks' advice by citing their own hardships and sufferings, so also they followed the manuals' guidelines by accusing Paul of base motives (he is more interested in personal gain and profit than in the Corinthians, 11:9), inconsistency (he is two-faced and vacillates, 10:1) and untrustworthiness (he robs other churches and is deceitful, 11:8; 12:16). Just as certainly Paul casts aspersions on his adversaries. In this contretemps both sides have availed themselves of the handbooks' suggestions.

Paul barrages his opponents with heavy accusations. They are "false apostles," workmen who accomplish their deeds by deceit or treachery (*dolios*, 11:13).[16] They masquerade as apostles of Christ (11:13). They make themselves out to be like Paul, to be working on the same terms that Paul does (11:12). Paul is not surprised (*ou thauma*) by the machinations of his adversaries, because he knows that Satan masquerades as an angel of light. Accordingly, it is no big surprise (*ou mega oun*) when Satan's servants pretend to be what Paul is in fact, namely, servants of righteousness (11:14–15). In a pithy, concise judgment, Paul confidently declares that God's verdict will surely come upon those false apostles: "Their end will correspond to their deeds" (11:15).

Paul chides the Corinthians because they did not discern for themselves the difference between the false apostles and him. Had they done so, Paul would have been commended by the Corinthians (12:11). Unlike the pretenders, Paul can declare, "The signs of a true apostle were performed among you in all patience, with signs and wonders and mighty works" (12:12). The Corinthians should have recognized that Paul was "not at all inferior to these superlative apostles" (12:11). Paul claims, however, that the Corinthians preferred the haughty, overbearing, even cruel, ways of the fake apostles. "For you gladly bear with fools, being wise yourselves! For you bear it if a man makes slaves of you, or preys upon you, or takes advantage of you, or puts on airs, or strikes you in the face" (11:19–20). Paul ironically contrasts his conduct with that of his opponents: "To my shame, I must say, we were too weak for that!" (11:21). In 11:19–20, Paul presents his adversaries' behavior as "base, haughty, cruel, or malicious" (*De inv.* 1.16.22) "by adducing some base, highhanded, treacherous, cruel, impudent, malicious, or shameful act of theirs" (*Ad Her.* 1.5.8).

Paul pursues the matter further. He is in a different class from his opponents, because they commend themselves and "measure themselves by one another" (10:12). That shows that they are "without understanding" (10:12). By contrast, Paul knows "it is not the man who commends himself that is accepted, but the one whom the Lord commends" (10:18).

Paul makes no explicit charge against his opponents along the line of laziness, idleness, sloth, or luxurious habits—as Cicero and *Ad Herennium* suggest. But the Corinthians surely know whether there is an implicit indictment for such behavior in Paul's persistent refusal to take any support from the Corinthians[17] even though they know that he has accepted aid from the Macedonians (11:9). His adversaries have taken advantage of the Corinthians in this regard (11:2). By contrast, Paul would rather "spend and be spent for your souls" (12:15).

In 2 Corinthians 10—13, Paul depicts himself as the true apostle who is genuinely anxious for the Corinthians' welfare. The masquerading apostles, by contrast, are portrayed as self-seeking persons who use their pretended authority to build themselves up at the expense of the Corinthians. If in fact good will may be won for one's case by discrediting the motives and actions of one's adversaries, Paul's treatment of his opponents qualifies as a strong attempt to recover good will toward himself and his gospel.

Good Will by Reference to the Audience

The audience, jury, or judge can be encouraged to support one's case by certain sorts of references to them:

> Good-will will be sought from the persons of the auditors if an account is given of acts which they have performed with courage, wisdom, and mercy, but so as not to show excessive flattery: and if it is shown in what honourable esteem they are held and how eagerly their judgment and opinion are awaited. (*De inv.* 1.16.22; cf. *Ad Her.* 1.5.8)

Paul certainly does not employ "excessive flattery" with the Corinthians in 2 Corinthians 10—13. Neither does he refer to any past actions of theirs that were marked by courage, wisdom, or mercy.

At this point, two factors complicate the matter of reference to audience. First, the audience to which Paul makes his appeal and from whom he hopes to receive renewed support—that very audience contains some who have chosen to follow Paul's opponents. The neat separation of opponents from judge, jury, or audience envisaged by the handbooks is not the situation that Paul faces. The case is more complex. Audience and opponents overlap. It is therefore not too surprising that Paul forgoes reference to their "acts which they have performed with courage, wisdom, and mercy." Second, Paul departs from the handbooks because his goal is not simply the Corinthians' approval of him or his vindication of himself. The stakes of Paul's rhetorical efforts with the Corinthians are much more to persuade them to "do what is right" (13:7). Paul "may seem to have failed" (13:7), he "may appear" not "to have met the test" (13:7). He hopes the Corinthians "will find out that we have not failed" (13:6), but of far greater importance to Paul is their "improvement" (13:9), that their obedience may be complete (10:6), that their faith may increase (10:15). Simply put, his rhetoric is subject to his gospel. Whereas the ultimate rhetorical goal of a self-defense would be to have the judge or audience side with the defendant, for Paul the ultimate goal is that the gospel function as fully as possible in the lives of the readers. Paul does hope that the Corinthians will come to a positive judgment about him, but he stands ready to sacrifice their opinion about him to the greater goal of their growth in the faith.[18]

Cicero says good will may be obtained from the audience "if it is shown in what honourable esteem they are held" (De inv. 1.16.22). Second Corinthians 10—13 offers mixed evidence on this matter. On the one hand, the Corinthians are called brethren (11:8; 12:18; 13:11) and even beloved (12:19). But we know from Paul's use of "brethren" that other believers are his brothers and sisters in Christ not because he holds them in high esteem but because Christ died for them. Paul knows the Corinthians are his brothers in Christ and reaffirms that relationship. He declares his love for them (11:11; 12:15). By these assertions he does indicate a deep commitment to them.

On the other hand, there are three points in the letter fragment where Paul expresses a fear that the Corinthians may too easily be swept away by a different allegiance (11:4, 19–20; 12:20). Paul thinks the Corinthians are on the wrong track. But he never wonders whether he loves them or whether they are still his brothers and sisters in Christ.

The final way in which Cicero suggests that good will may be cultivated by reference to the audience is "if it is shown . . . how eagerly their judgment and opinion are awaited" (De inv. 1.16.22). An index of Paul's eagerness to hear their judgment may be seen in his twice-mentioned anticipated visit (12:14; 13:1). He even states that he hopes the letter will bring them around and obviate any severe use of his authority in the Lord: "I write this while I am away from you, in order that when I come I may not have to be severe in my use of the authority which the Lord has given me for building up and not for tearing down" (13:10; cf. 10:8). Though he would not shy away from dealing with their charges against him face to face (13:1), he hopes that his letter will bring about an amendment not only in their attitude toward him (13:6) but also in their relationships with one another ("quarreling, jealousy," etc., 12:20). The starting point for such a change of heart proceeds from the question "Do you not realize that Jesus Christ is in you?" (13:5). If they grant that premise—and they must if they are to live according to the gospel that Paul preached to them—then it is imperative that they avoid wrong and "do what is right" (13:7).

Apparently some of the Corinthians have said that they would like some proof (*dokime*) that Christ was speaking in Paul (13:3). Paul's answer to that demand is twofold, the first part direct and simple, the second complex. First, for those who want proof, Paul warns that he will come to them and "will not spare them" (13:2). They will see the "power of God" at work in the "weak" Paul. Second, Paul in a masterly way turns the demand for "proof" back on the Corinthians. They want Paul to pass a test. But he deftly declares that *they* are the ones who now have the test before them: "Examine yourselves, to see whether you are in the faith. Test yourselves. Do you not realize that Jesus Christ is in you?—unless indeed you fail to meet the test!" (13:5). Paul prays to God that the Corinthians pass the test (13:6). He will know when he arrives at Corinth.

Good Will by Reference to the Case

As Cicero puts it, "Good-will may come from the circumstances themselves if we praise and exalt our own case, and depreciate our opponent's with contemptuous allusions" (*De inv.* 1.16.22). From *Ad Herennium* we see much the same: "From the discussion of the facts themselves we shall render the hearer well disposed by extolling our own cause with praise and by contemptuously disparaging that of our adversaries" (1.5.8).

Paul "praises and exalts" his own case in several ways. He uses terms of warfare and battle.[19] Though he walks in the world, the battle in which he is engaged has a scope that transcends the world. Similarly, the arsenal of his weapons surpasses the powers of this world. God's power is said to be working through Paul (10:4–5) . The importance and grandeur of Paul's case is further highlighted by claims of a special connection with God or with Christ, including unparalleled revelations, visions, and translations into God's presence, once even into the third heaven (12:1–5).[20] Finally, Paul's own case is affirmed as praiseworthy by making clear his special importance to the Corinthians. If the Corinthians might be likened to a pure virgin betrothed and presented to her one husband, Christ, Paul's special role should be designated that of matchmaker, best man, or father of the bride (11:2).

By contrast, Paul thinks his opponents show themselves to be nobodies who scurry around comparing themselves with one another and with others in hopes of finding some slight advantage over someone. They seize any minuscule difference as grounds for boasting and overblown claims. Paul's conclusion: "They are without understanding" (10:12). By comparison with Paul, however, they are not simply without understanding, they also lack the kind of *standing* that he has in the purposes of God and in Christ. In a comparison between the matchmaker in the marriage of the Corinthians with Christ and the servants of Satan who specialize in deceit, Paul depicts himself as the one who by word and deed deserves allegiance. Paul's "contemptuous allusions" (*De inv.* 1.16.22) tilt the scales against his opponents; his praise of his own standing and case is designed to weigh heavily for him.

Paul knows—and uses—the rhetorical traditions designed to persuade one's audience by undercutting one's opponents and by setting one's own case in its best light. And so do the intruders.

Our examination of Paul's indebtedness to certain recommended rhetorical conventions may help us understand some features of 2 Corinthians 10—13. We may now be able to understand why Paul presses his case so relentlessly and so hard, why Paul writes as if he is being forced to express himself as a madman or fool: his adversaries have been using the same rhetorical conventions against him—and with some success. They have attacked Paul by reference to his person, just as the handbooks recommend, by questioning his motives and his mode of operation. Further, by recitation of their own hardships and difficulties, they have appealed to the Corinthians in an effort to garner good will. Paul is stung by these charges and comparisons. And he is further hurt that some Corinthians have been swayed to support his opponents. As a result, he counters by pushing his own case even harder.

Paul employs the rhetorical conventions of his time as a means of guiding the Corinthian Christians onto what he considers a safer, more fruitful path. But as is the case with everything that Paul co-opts from his culture, Paul is no prisoner of the rhetorical conventions and practices of his time. He uses them when he thinks they may be of advantage to him in advancing the gospel and in seeking the Corinthians' "improvement," but he does not employ them in a rote or mechanical or simply self-serving fashion. For example, Quintilian contemplates that one might even be driven to use "falsehood if it seems to us that it is likely to advance our case" (4.1.33). Paul cannot and will not go that far (2 Cor. 11:31; 13:8). Similarly, though the handbooks urge the speaker to praise the noble works of the audience, when Paul is unable to cite such deeds he does not do so.

It is appropriate that Paul employs the rhetorical conventions only when they serve his purposes, because his purposes are not identical to those envisioned by the handbooks. In the manuals, the goal of the speaker is to win the favor or verdict of the judge, jury, or audience. In Paul's situation, the goal is to bring the hearers to a clearer understanding and fuller living of the gospel. In many ways 2 Corinthians 10—13 does read like a Pauline self-defense,[21] very much in line with what would be expected by anyone familiar with the handbooks. But in chapter 13, Paul departs significantly from standard rhetorical practice when he distinguishes his own fate from that of his audience, the Corinthians. He realizes that he may be judged to have been inadequate, weak, even a failure. He can abide that if the Corinthian Christians change course and begin what he terms "improvement," or growth in the faith. This observation can be cast in different terms. Paul's real concern is the gospel and its proper and powerful expression in the lives of the Corinthians. His primary purpose is not rhetoric itself, but like most educated citizens of the world in his time Paul uses rhetoric to achieve the goals toward which he strives. In 2 Corinthians 10—13 we encounter not gospel as occasion for rhetoric but rhetoric in service of the gospel.

NOTES

1. E. A. Judge ("Paul's Boasting in Relation to Contemporary Professional Practice," *Australian Biblical Review* 16 [1968]: 37–50) assesses the "place of rhetoric in antiquity" (pp. 42ff) as a context for his evaluation of Paul's boasting.

2. This study is not intended to diminish the importance of the issues pursued by Christopher Forbes in "Comparison, Self-Praise, and Irony: Paul's Boasting and the Conventions of Hellenistic Rhetoric," *New Testament Studies* 32 (1986): 1–30. Our purposes here are more narrowly focused.

3. If, as some would maintain, 2 Corinthians 1—7 had in fact been written after 2 Corinthians 10—13 and only placed in its present non-chronological position by a later redactor, we would be in a position to evaluate the outcome of Paul's rhetorical efforts in 2 Corinthians 10—13. See V. P. Furnish's argumentation in *2 Corinthians*, Anchor Bible (New York: Doubleday & Co., 1984), 35–54. Notice of P. Marshall's "Enmity and Other Social Conventions in Paul's Relations with the Corinthians" (Ph.D. Diss., Macquarie Univ., 1980) occurred too late for consideration in the preparation of this piece.

4. Marcus Tullius Cicero *De inventione*, trans. H. M. Hubbell, Loeb Classical Library (Cambridge: Harvard Univ. Press, 1968).

5. Marcus Tullius Cicero *Ad Herennium*, trans. H. Caplan, Loeb Classical Library (Cambridge: Harvard Univ. Press, 1968).

6. The "fool's speech" and its function here have been noted by others. Cf. Furnish's references to it (*2 Corinthians*, 490, 496, 498) and his mention of Plutarch's *On Praising Oneself Inoffensively*.

7. William Baird, "Visions, Revelation, and Ministry: Reflections on 2 Cor. 12:1–5 and Gal 1:11–17," *Journal of Biblical Literature* 104 (1985): 651–62, esp. 654. Cf. Ernst Käsemann, "Die Legitimät des Apostels," *Zeitschrift für die neutestamentliche Wissenschaft* 41 (1942): 33–71.

8. Though Paul reflects his opponents' charges, he refrains from repeating their proofs—and thereby also proceeds in accord with the handbooks. Quintilian says it most directly: "But we must never under any circumstances repeat our opponent's charges together with their proofs" (5.13.27).

9. There is a fourth course that one may follow. "He who neither denies nor defends his act nor asserts that it was of a different nature from that alleged, must take his stand on some point of law that tells in his favour, a form of defence which generally turns on the legality of the action brought against him" (Quint. 7.5.1).

10. Another slight variation appears in *Ad Herennium*: "Orestes killed his mother; on that I agree with my opponents. But did he have the right to commit the deed, and was he justified in committing it? That is in dispute" (1.10.7).

11. See my treatment of Paul's agents as his doubles in *Pauline Partnership in Christ: Christian Community and Commitment in Light of Roman Law* (Philadelphia: Fortress Press, 1980), 87–91.

12. C. K. Barrett, *A Commentary on the Second Epistle to the Corinthians*, 2d ed. (London: A. & C. Black, 1973), 279: "*Unskilled* is not an adjective but a noun . . . depicting one who stands outside a particular activity or office . . . and therefore is untrained in the skills proper to that activity or office. Paul disclaims ability in the art of speaking. . . . More probably Paul is admitting (and in the admission continues his ironical vein) a judgement of his eloquence based upon presuppositions he did not himself share" (emphasis his). E. A. Judge, "Paul's Boasting," 37: In 2 Cor. 11:6, Paul "may himself in that very phrase have been exhibiting one of the recognized *tropoi* of the rhetorical profession."

13. Contrast the RSV ("my needs were supplied by the brethren who came from Macedonia") which shifts the emphasis in a way that gives credence to Paul's opponents!

14. Furnish, *2 Corinthians*, 532–33: "Paul is not really matching the claims of his rivals, although he appears to start out this way." Following Hans-Dieter Betz and E. A. Judge, Furnish says, "Paul ends up parodying the claims of his rivals." But our study shows that the matter may be more complex and that *Paul and his rivals*, in an appeal to the emotions, seem to recount past and present difficulties encountered while working in behalf of the Corinthians. Even Judge ("Paul's Boasting," 47) backs off a bit from his earlier labeling of Paul's rhetoric as a "parody of conventional norms" and declares it not "merely a mockery."

15. *Ad Herennium* presents the same general points but with slightly different nuances: "From the discussion of the person of our adversaries we shall secure goodwill by bringing them into hatred, unpopularity, or contempt. We shall force hatred upon them by adducing some base, high-handed, treacherous, cruel, impudent, malicious, or shameful act of theirs. We shall make our adversaries unpopular by setting forth their violent behaviour, their dominance, factiousness, wealth, lack of self-restraint, high birth, clients, hospitality, club allegiance, or marriage alliances, and by making clear that they rely more upon these supports than upon the truth. We shall bring our adversaries into contempt by presenting their idleness, cowardice, sloth, and luxurious habits" (1.5.8).

16. Cf. the same root word in the accusation against Paul in 12:16.

17. See H. D. Betz, "Der Apostel Paulus und die socratische Tradition," *Beiträge zur historischen Theologie* 45 (1972): 100–117; G. Theissen, *The Social Setting of*

Pauline Christianity: Essays on Corinth (Philadelphia: Fortress Press, 1982), 39–40; and Sampley, *Pauline Partnership,* 81–87.

18. In his earlier correspondence with these Corinthians, Paul has discounted human judgment as a "small thing that I should be judged by you or by any human court" (1 Cor. 4:3).

19. A. J. Malherbe, "Antisthenes and Odysseus, and Paul at War," *Harvard Theological Review* 76 (1983): 143–73.

20. Furnish (*2 Corinthians,* 533) evaluates this reported vision as providing "no useful religious knowledge," but that is not the function of Paul's mention of it.

21. C. K. Barrett ("Paul's Opponents in II Corinthians," *New Testament Studies* 17 [1971]: 246) may overdo it slightly when he says that Paul was not "defending himself, his integrity and also his position and authority." Yes, "his objectives are theological," but one errs if too sharp a line is drawn between theological and practical matters in Paul.

Paul, God, and Israel:
Romans 9—11 in Recent Research

HEIKKI RÄISÄNEN
University of Helsinki

Romans 9—11 has long been a test case in Pauline exegesis.[1] Decisions made concerning the internal consistency or inconsistency of these chapters, or concerning the place of the thoughts expressed in them in Paul's theology at large, will deeply influence—or quickly reveal—one's understanding of many central issues of New Testament interpretation. Past generations were stimulated by this section in Romans to ponder theological problems that had loomed large in the history of Christian dogmatics: predestination, free will, theodicy. Later on, the question of "salvation history" came to occupy the minds of expositors. All these topics represent aspects of Paul's message in Romans 9—11, but it is now generally agreed that his real concern is the question of the *trustworthiness of God* as regards his promises to Israel.[2]

Paul affirms that God will keep his promises. The salvation of "all Israel" will be the final solution in the problem now posed by Israel's enmity to the church and its message (11:25–32). But here problems arise, concerning both the nature of the salvation envisaged and the relation of Romans 11 to Paul's other treatments of the problem of "Israel"—including Romans 9.

Does the "mystery" of 11:25–26 imply that Paul recognized two different ways to salvation? For some interpreters, such a possibility means no more than that unbelieving Israel will find faith in Christ in a way different from Gentiles.[3] Others, however, advocate the thesis that Israel will be saved apart from faith in Christ: that, in fact, Jesus was not for Paul the Messiah of Israel but only the Savior of the Gentiles who now offers for them that righteousness which had so long been available to Israel through the torah, as it still is.[4]

Whether or not Paul conceived of a special way to salvation for Israel, the relation of Rom. 11:25–27 to Paul's evaluations of Israel elsewhere presents a problem. How does this passage relate to 1 Thess. 2:15-16 or to Gal. 4:21-31? Some try to read even Galatians 4 in pro-Israel terms.[5] More often, a development is posited in Paul's theology from Galatians to Romans.[6]

But if Paul's thought developed from the time of Galatians so that he could write Romans 11, what about Romans 9? Many interpreters who do not hold the view that Paul developed regard Romans 9—11 as self-contradictory.[7] Advocates of this position mostly tend to emphasize the critical view of Israel they find in chapter 9, playing down the positive view found in chapter 11. Conversely, those who think that Romans 11 represents Paul's final or "real" view play down chapter 9 in one way or another, putting all emphasis on 11:11-36.

There is a growing awareness among recent interpreters of Romans 9—11 that earlier research has focused excessively on Paul's theoretical theological ideas.[8] It is felt that the social context and function of Paul's writings has to be taken much more seriously. Practical problems caused by the coexistence of Jews and Gentiles in Christian congregations are reflected throughout the section.

No one can study Paul today without being aware of the challenge of the Holocaust to biblical interpretation. It has to be kept in mind, however, that there is no straightforward correlation between a scholar's attitude toward Judaism and his or her answer to the question whether Paul is "positive" or "negative" toward Israel. The scholar may find Paul "negative" and nevertheless take a "positive" attitude.[9] It is imperative to insist that historical scholarship cannot produce normative results. What it can do is give impulses for constructive thinking in new situations.

In what follows, then, I will approach Romans 9—11 and its recent interpretations with the following questions in mind: What do the chapters tell of Paul's attitude toward Israel? Is Paul consistent? How do his statements relate to his statements in other letters? What do the chapters reveal of Paul's personal and social situation? What is their concrete significance for him and his cause?

THE LINE OF THOUGHT IN
ROMANS 9—11

Romans 9:1-5: The Privileges of the Accursed

Romans 9:1 seems to mark a fresh start. The lack of any immediately obvious connection with chapter 8 prompted earlier expositors to treat chapters 9—11 as a self-contained unit "which can be read quite satisfactorily without reference to the rest of the epistle."[10] At the other extreme, some interpreters now take the section as the goal and climax of the whole epistle, to which chapters 1—8 form a "preface."[11] It seems safest to start from a less pronounced view of the place of the chapters in the letter.

Although 9:1 clearly opens up the discussion of a new topic, the discussion is not unrelated to what precedes, as terminological connections with chapter 8 indicate (e.g., $\upsilon\iota o\theta\epsilon\sigma\iota a$ in 8:15, 23; 9:4; $\pi\rho\delta\theta\epsilon\sigma\iota s$ in 8:28; 9:11).[12] The treatment of the certitude of salvation (chap. 8) evokes the question of Israel's destiny.[13] But central themes of Romans 9—11 have also made their appearance earlier in the letter. A portrait of the true Jew was sketched in 2:25–29; a provisional discussion of the advantages of the Jew in view of the actual $\dot a\pi\iota\sigma\tau\iota a$ of "some" followed in 3:1–8. Abraham and his seed figured in chapter 4. Thus Paul has given several hints that he is deeply concerned with the problems to which he turns in 9:1. Whether it is a question of problems that have become acute in the Roman congregation(s) or of problems that worried Paul for other reasons (because of past conflicts or the impending visit to Jerusalem) is best not decided before a discussion of the chapters.

Paul introduces the depiction of his sorrow with a surprisingly strong threefold assurance that he does indeed tell the truth. Apparently he has to dispel suspicions that he is hostile or indifferent to Israel.[14] Who needs this information—Jewish Christians whose concern Paul is affirming or gentile Christians who may take indifference to Israel as a matter of course and need to be corrected in their views? An answer is possible after the reason for Paul's sorrow has been determined.

All commentators note that Paul does not explicitly mention the unbelief of Israel with regard to the gospel as the reason for his sorrow and anguish. Lloyd Gaston lays great weight on Paul's silence.[15] Nevertheless, no other reason makes sense.[16] If Israel merely lacks understanding or faithfulness "with respect to the Gentile mission,"[17] why should Paul have such deep sorrow in his heart?[18] Paul goes even further. In v. 3 he expresses the unreal wish that he could be "accursed [$\dot a\nu\dot a\theta\epsilon\mu a$] and cut off from Christ" for the sake of his kinsmen. This implies that they must be "in a plight as serious as the one he is willing to enter for their sake."[19] They are anathema. This can only be due to their unbelief when faced with the gospel. Israel's $\dot a\pi\iota\sigma\tau\iota a$ is in fact mentioned in 3:3 and 11:20, 23, and her disobedience with respect to Christ is described in 9:30—10:21. In 10:1, Paul refers to his prayers for the salvation of Israel. This presupposes that his kinsmen are for the moment outside the sphere of salvation. Paul's pathos shows that very much is at stake.

In v. 6a, Paul undertakes to refute the claim that God's word should have failed. Such an allegation must somehow result from what Paul says in vv. 1–5. What else could have caused it, except the fact that Israel has rejected the gospel and thus forfeited salvation? Israel's being anathema raises the question of the dependability of God. What sort of God does not see to it that his promises to Israel come true?[20] A personal difficulty was involved for Paul, moreover. Some hearers of his might have fallen on the idea that "either the truth of the divine promise is questionable or Jesus whom Paul preaches is not the Messiah of the Lord."[21] No wonder Paul abstains from spelling out such an alternative, being content with "emotion-laden intimations."[22]

It should be clear by now whom Paul is addressing in chapter 9. He has to face the worries of Jewish Christians about the implications of his gospel. Roman gentile Christians would not have cared, at least not if they had to be warned against a boasting attitude toward Jews (11:18, 20). Paul addresses those who felt the plight of Israel to be a calamity rather than a matter of course.[23]

That Israelites should be anathema is all the more startling, since they have a great number of advantages over against Gentiles, as Paul shows in vv. 4-5. In the opinion of many, this list alone provides decisive evidence against the view that Paul had in effect broken with Judaism.[24] We will see that the issue is more complex, however.

Interpreters disagree over whether Paul speaks of past or present "privileges" of the Jews.[25] His wording would seem to point to the present. The list opens with catchwords from chapter 8—$vio\theta\epsilon\sigma ia$ and $\delta\delta\xi a$. In chapter 8 both were applied to Christians, laden with eschatological connotations.[26] Throughout the list, suggestive words are used.[27]

And yet if the privileges listed are really meant to denote present salvific possession, it is striking that these very privileges are *denied* to Israel "according to the flesh" in what follows. Sonship is denied to the "children of the flesh" in 9:6-13[28] and glory in 9:22-23. This is comparable to the treatment of the glory, the Mosaic covenant, and the lawgiving[29] in 2 Corinthians 3 and to the ejaculation that Paul regards his circumcision and Jewish birth as $\sigma\kappa\iota\beta a\lambda a$, in Philippians 3. Romans 9:6-13 shows that Paul had not when dictating Romans left behind the view expressed shortly before in 2 Corinthians. Philippians too is nowadays often dated in the time before Romans; should it nevertheless be later,[30] Philippians 3 alone would disprove the view that Paul had developed a new, positive attitude toward Israel at the time of Romans (unless, of course, he returned to the old attitude in Philippians!).

In the light of his other letters and of the very next verses after 9:1-5, it would seem that Paul pays lip service to Israel's privileges in 9:4-5. It remains to be seen whether chapter 11 will necessitate a revision of this picture.

Romans 9:6-13: All Israel Was Never Elected

Paul answers the worrisome question whether God's promise has failed by denying that all those who are $\dot{\epsilon}\xi$ 'I$\sigma\rho a\dot{\eta}\lambda$ really belong to "Israel." He distinguishes between "empirical" and "eschatological" Israel.³¹ The criterion is not that those are the true Israel who behave like true Jews.³² The point is that God has in the course of Israel's history made perfectly free choices. He called Isaac to be a "son."³³ His election depends on nothing but his own ever-new sovereign decision. This is made perfectly clear in the section about Jacob and Esau (vv. 10–13). Thus, Paul diverges in v. 11 from his normal usage by contrasting ἐξ ἔργων not with ἐκ πίστεως³⁴ but rather with ἐκ τοῦ καλοῦντος. The issue is not justification by faith.³⁵ On the contrary, any emphasis on human faith would spoil Paul's line of argument here. God elects simply whom he wills. He has, in the past of Israel, called some and not others without any regard to who and what these people were, "in order that God's purpose of election would stand firm."

The implication is clear. *The majority of Israel*—the litotes οὐ πάντες notwithstanding³⁶ (cf. 10:16 and τινες in 3:3; 11:17)—*have never been elected.*³⁷ This is so because God is free to love some and hate others (v. 13). The present tense (εἰσίν) in v. 7 indicates that Paul is thinking of his own generation. More important, this interpretation is required by the logic of 9:1–13.³⁸ The issue is, does not the unbelief of God's chosen people falsify either the trustworthiness of God's promise or the message proclaimed by Paul? Paul meets the question by suggesting that it is falsely put. The gospel is not being rejected by the elect of God. Because the majority of Israel never belonged to the elect, God's promise is not affected by the unbelief of empirical Israel.

From the Jewish point of view, Paul's argument is curious. It implies that empirical Israel—the unbelieving majority—should be identified with Ishmael and Esau.³⁹ But what seems bewildering in terms of common sense is possible in Pauline theology. After all, the same thing had happened in Gal. 4:21–31.⁴⁰ One wonders whether it was not the nemesis of religious history that took revenge when Paul came to be identified with Simon Magus in the Jewish Christian Pseudo-Clementines.

Romans 9:14–18: Israel Hardened by God

A real Jewish opponent might have replied that Paul's inferences from Ishmael and Esau are nonsense. Paul's imaginary discussion partner, however, starts from immanent Pauline problems. He asks whether God is not morally unjust if he acts in the way described.⁴¹ Paul answers by introducing more examples of God's sovereign conduct. He has mercy on whom he has mercy (v. 15) so that nothing depends on human "willing or running" (v. 16) but all depends on the merciful God alone.

Although vv. 15–16 stress God's mercy, in the next verses a different point is made.⁴² An instance of God's sovereignty is his treatment of the Pharaoh. Astonishingly, this classical enemy of Israel here stands for the

Jews of Paul's time.[43] Paul at first mentions a positive purpose for God's "raising up" of Pharaoh. This is important for him, for he has sought a quotation (Exod. 9:16) that states God's purpose with Pharaoh rather than citing any of the well-known hardening passages of Exodus. God raised up Pharaoh in order to show in him his power all over the earth. The purpose clause ὅπως ἐνδείξωμαι ἐν σοὶ τὴν δύναμίν μου has a parallel in v. 22: θέλων . . . ἐνδείξασθαι τὴν ὀργὴν καὶ γνωρίσαι τὸ δυνατὸν αὐτοῦ. This verse, in turn, seems to anticipate 11:11–12.[44] Thus the idea that the obduracy of Israel has a God-given purpose, developed in chapter 11, is perhaps hinted at here already.[45] Is it far-fetched to think that Paul had the gentile mission in mind when he quoted the clause ὅπως διαγγέλη τὸ ὄνομα μου ἐν πάσῃ τῇ γῇ from Exodus?

The positive purpose notwithstanding, the lesson is drawn from the case of Pharaoh that God "hardens whom he wills." Even human reprobation depends, according to this passage, on God's sovereign decision.[46]

Romans 9:19-23: The Potter and His Vessels

Verse 19 confirms that Paul senses that a moral problem is involved in his argument. How can human beings be held responsible for their doings if everything is effected by God? All Paul can do to meet the objection is to reject it on the ground that creatures are not in a position to talk back to the Creator. The Great Potter has the right to create vessels for menial as well as worthy use.[47] He can make "vessels of mercy" or "vessels of wrath" just as he pleases. There are indeed "vessels of wrath," which have been prepared (κατηρτισμένα) for destruction. Verse 22 implies predestination in damnation.[48] The unbelieving Jews of Paul's time are to be seen as such vessels of wrath. Still, in vv. 22–23 Paul's attention turns more to the "vessels of mercy," predestined (προητοίμασεν) for glory. Paul dictates a sentence that implies double predestination. He is not quite at rest with the notion, however, and it is probably no coincidence that the sentence ends as an anacoluthon.[49] The way of strict predestination on which Paul has here begun leads to a dead end.

Romans 9:24-29: The Inclusion of Gentiles

When Paul's thought proceeds forward, he stresses the positive state of the elect, whether Jews or Gentiles by birth. In two citations, Paul shows from Scripture that God will call also Gentiles to be his sons (υἱοὶ θεοῦ, v. 26; cf. υἱοθεσία, v. 4, and τέκνα, v. 8). It now seems as if inclusion of the Gentiles were the point of the whole chapter, the thing in need of justification; and such a view is indeed taken by some interpreters.[50] But this was not the starting point of chapter 9. It is not the inclusion of Gentiles that could have aroused the suspicion that Paul's God does not keep his promises. Such an allegation is due to the apparent *exclusion of the majority of Israel*.[51] Had the inclusion of Gentiles been the point of the whole chapter, this might account for the emphasis on God's having mercy on whomever he wills. It would not, however, explain the stress placed on the notion that God hardens whom he wills as well, nor the idea that God has in his sovereign freedom prepared vessels of wrath for destruction. It is the *negative* traits in God's dealings that according to Romans 9 cry for an explanation; the salvation of Gentiles is not a sufficient one. Paul's thought has taken on a new turn in v. 24.

To some extent, this seems also true of vv. 27-29, where the idea of a remnant appears. Paul argues from Scripture that not all Israel will be saved but only such seed as God has *left* in Israel. The idea is not entirely in keeping with the notion implicit in the earlier part of the chapter that not all Israel has been elected in the first place. The notion that not all Israel in the ethnic sense will be saved is consistent throughout the chapter, however.

As a whole, 9:6–29 is a fairly coherent, self-contained unit.[52] It gives a coherent answer to the question, Has God's word failed? The answer is no, for God never promised anything for ethnic Israel. His promises are meant for those whom he chooses to call to be his people, such as Isaac, Jacob, or the Christians, whether of Jewish or gentile birth. Paul goes to great lengths in defending this solution. He presents a "justification of God" (J. Piper), contending that nothing the Creator does to his creatures can be wrong. The Christians participate in salvation; most Jews remain outside it. This is so because God has mercy on whomever he wills and hardens whomever he wills. There was never a promise for those whom God has hardened. Double predestination is not the main issue of the section, but that idea is there. It seems clear that the majority of the Jews will be damned at the judgment.[53]

At this point the reader hardly feels that the treatise should go on. Nothing seems to be lacking; there is no need for a continuation.[54] Paul's way of justifying God's dealings with human beings may not convince very many readers,[55] much less his identification of Israel with her classical enemies, but it seems reasonably clear what Paul's answer to his burning question is.

But here we meet a problem, for Paul does not leave the issue at that. There are more answers to come.

Romans 9:30—10:21: Israel's Resistance
to God's Eschatological Action

Romans 9:30—10:21 will be dealt with extremely briefly. This is not the place to probe into an examination of Paul's view of righteousness or of the law, or of his use of Scripture, although the section offers important material from all these points of view. Our only concern is the flow of Paul's argument about Israel's plight and future.

The Jew-Gentile dichotomy remains in focus. Paul explains why Israel, now spoken of as an ethnic entity, has failed to attain righteousness whereas Gentiles have found it. Non-Christian Israel has come to a fall, for it has stumbled over Christ, the stumbling stone (9:32b–33; cf. 10:11).[56]

In 9:6–29, divine predestination loomed large. On the contrary, in the entire section 9:30—10:21 we hear nothing about God's sovereign decision.[57] Instead, false decisions and attitudes on the part of Israel are envisaged. Clinging to works, Israel has refused to obey God and accept his eschatological action in Christ with faith.

Romans 10:1 recalls 9:1–3. Paul prays for the salvation of Israel—who, therefore, must be outside salvation at the present time. Israel has zeal for God but lacks understanding. This failure is not attributed to a divine closing of minds, as it is again in 11:7–10.[58] The fault lies with the stubbornness of Israel. Wishing to establish their own righteousness, the Jews do not admit that Christ has brought the true righteousness and made it available to all who believe in him, Jew and Greek alike. There is no difference between them, for all have the same Lord who "bestows his riches upon all who call upon him."[59]

Romans 10:14–21 emphasizes the importance of proclaiming and hearing the kerygma. It is not quite clear about whom Paul is talking in vv. 14–18.[60] Although vv. 14–15 and 17 would suit Jews as well as Gentiles, v. 16 surely refers to Jews.[61] The phrase οὐ πάντες recalls 9:6,[62] and οὐ . . . ὑπήκουσαν τῷ εὐαγγελίῳ parallels τῇ δικαιοσύνῃ τοῦ θεοῦ οὐχ ὑπετάγησαν, of 10:3. In itself, v. 18 would seem to suit Gentiles better. But if Jews are envisaged before and after (v. 19) the verse, they must be in focus in v. 18 as well. And why should Paul be concerned to stress that Gentiles have heard—though not always accepted—the message? Verses 16–18 only make sense in the overall context, if seen as an attempt to grapple with the unbelief of Israel.

Has Israel not understood what the gospel of Christ is all about (v. 19)? Surely it has, for Deut. 32:21 says that God will provoke Israel to jealousy (παραζηλώσω) through a nation which is none. The quotation seems strange, but its meaning will become clear in 11:14. There is thus a connection between chapters 10 and 11. Paul intimates that God has a purpose with Israel. But then he goes on to state that God has let himself be found by Gentiles. He has also held out his hands toward disobedient and stubborn Israel all day long (v. 21). The people, it is implied, has persisted in its stubbornness. The assessment of Israel parallels that in 1 Thess. 2:14–15, although the language is less biting.

God's way of dealing with Gentiles is justified from Scripture. Israel's fate is this time not described as a result of God's inscrutable πρόθεσις, as in chapter 9. Israel's own refusal to accept God's offer has played a crucial part. Gentiles have found God, for they have responded with faith. The difference between 9:6 and 10:16 is typical. Both times a negative statement is made about οὐ πάντες. But in chapter 9 Paul stresses that "not all" belong to the true Israel—in effect, not all have been elected. In chapter 10, on the contrary, he says that "not all" have heeded the gospel. The fault now lies with the hearer.

Logically 9:30—10:21 is in disagreement with the predestination section 9:6-29. The disharmony between divine predestination and human responsibility is no Pauline peculiarity, however. It appears in the Old Testament, in Qumran, and in the Gospels. It later looms large in the Koran.[63] The talk of predestination has probably always a social function, or a set of functions.[64] Predestination is never preached to would-be converts. The idea crops up in conflict settings where the religious majority does not accept the message preached by a minority group. The notion of a sovereign divine initiative explains to the minority why they (alone) are elected and saved.[65] It consoles them when the efforts to convert the rest of the people fail. The tension between divine hardening and the human ability to make decisions—which is presupposed in preaching—is seldom felt.[66] It is typical of Paul's environment and should not cause much astonishment.[67]

It should be noted that Paul can occasionally attribute the supernatural blinding of the unbelievers to the "god of this aeon" as well (2 Cor. 4:4). This shows how far he is from possessing a "systematic" doctrine of hardening. The problem—Israel's unbelief—remains the same. The solutions diverge (the introduction of the devil into Romans 9 would have utterly destroyed the argument based on God's sovereignty).

At the close of the section 9:30—10:21 one again gets the impression that Paul could well have ended his treatise here.[68] But he does go on!

Romans 11:1-10: The Chosen Remnant

In 11:1, Paul continues to talk of Israel in the ethnic sense of the word. He now asserts that God cannot possibly have rejected his chosen people.[69] This is rather surprising after chapter 9[70] but continues Paul's way of speaking from 9:27 onward.[71] Paul takes up and develops the concept of remnant which he introduced in 9:27. Paul himself, one of the few believing Israelites, is a living testimony to the fact that Israel has not been rejected.[72] In Paul's time, as in Elijah's (vv. 2-4), a "remnant according to the election of grace" (v. 5) exists. In v. 6, Paul contrasts grace with works, thus suggesting that God's grace reigns among the elect Christians only. Empirical Israel has split into two parts: the elect remnant and the hardened rest (v. 7). Verse 8 makes clear that it is God who has given those hardened a "spirit of stupor" and thus prevented them from seeing and hearing.[73]

Romans 11:1–10 is in keeping with 9:6–29 insofar as the contrast between divine election and divine hardening is the decisive thing.[74] There is also a difference. Romans 9:6–23 seemed to imply that not all Israel was ever chosen. In chapter 11 it is the empirical people that is chosen and cannot be rejected. That is, it cannot be *totally* rejected. There will always be *some* who are "left," the remnant. Thus Paul is precisely where he started: some believe, the great majority do not. No happy end is envisaged for God's people as a whole.[75]

It is the next section that introduces a different tone.

Romans 11:11–24: God's Purpose with
the Hardening of Israel

In 11:11, Paul suggests that the hardening of Israel has a positive purpose in God's plans. The stumbling of Israel does not amount to a definitive fall but serves to bring salvation to the Gentiles. For if Israel had accepted the gospel right away, the mission to Gentiles would never have started.[76] This view parallels the idea that Pharaoh was hardened by God for a specific purpose (9:17). The ἥττημα of Israel will not be God's last word but will be followed by their πλήρωμα (v. 12). These terms are to be understood in the light of v. 15, so that ἥττημα equals ἀποβολή, and πλήρωμα corresponds to πρόσλημψις. On the other hand, πλήρωμα should probably be understood in the light of its use in v. 25: it signifies the completion of the remnant to the full number of Israel. The word ἥττημα then means the previous reduction of this number.[77] In vv. 12 and 15, Paul clearly hints at a change in the state of ethnic Israel, which is something quite unexpected after 9:6—11:10.

In v. 14 the "apostle to the Gentiles" (v. 13) gives a strange account of his motives.[78] The real purpose of his mission is to aid the salvation of *Israelites* by making them "jealous" of gentile Christians (v. 14). Still, it is only some (τινας) that Paul hopes to win in this way. That the idea of "salvation through jealousy" cannot in reality have been the driving force behind Paul's missionary effort is beyond doubt. When Paul speaks of his call, he speaks of a task among Gentiles and alludes to Isa. 49:1, a passage concerned with the nations (Gal. 1:15–16). He cannot have *grounded* his mission on an idiosyncratic reading of Deut. 32:21. His use of that verse in Romans 10—11, where it figures no less than three times (10:19; 11:11b, 14) shows that he desperately needed something that would make of him a missionary to Israel as well, Galatians 2 notwithstanding. Even a most unlikely verse would do, when Paul searched through the Scriptures in order to find a clue. It is hard to avoid the suspicion that the notion of "jealousy" is designed to serve an apologetic purpose with regard to Jewish Christians. It reinforces Paul's concern for his kinsmen expressed in 9:2-3; 10:1. But whatever Paul's own role, v. 15 shows how great are the hopes he connects with the πρόσλημψις of Israel: it will be followed by the eschatological fulfillment (ζωὴ ἐκ νεκρῶν).

Verse 16 is not especially clear. It seems to say that Israel as a whole is "holy" because the ἀπαρχή and the ῥίζα are holy. Most commentators think that the "first fruits" and the "root" refer to the patriarchs (cf. 11:28).[79] The verse forms a bridge to the olive-tree allegory that plays such a role in many recent interpretations of Paul's attitude to Israel. In this allegory, ethnic Israel is seen as God's people, and the Gentiles viewed as proselytes. The rest of Romans notwithstanding, there is, then, a difference between Jew and Gentile.[80]

Israel is likened to a cultivated olive tree. "Some" branches have been broken off, and branches of a wild olive tree have been grafted into their place. In this way, gentile Christians have come to share the "rich root." Most interpreters identify the ῥίζα with Israel.[81] Logically, it should perhaps refer to something else,[82] since Israel seems to consist rather of the branches. Paul, however, is not famous for keeping his comparisons always strictly in order,[83] and in any case there is no great difference between the alternatives. Gentiles are proselytes, Israel is the people. Gentiles are not to boast, for they do not support the root, they are supported by it.

Debating with an imaginary gentile Christian who may or may not represent the attitudes of some in Rome, Paul states that some branches have been broken off because of their *unbelief* (v. 20). This is in line with 9:30—10:21: human failure, rather than divine predestination, has caused the present state of things. In the course of a parenetic exhortation to gentile Christians this is most natural. Gentiles are admonished to remain in faith so that they will not be broken off too. In such a context the idea of divine hardening—or even divine protection—would be out of place. God has the power to graft in again those fallen, provided they will not persist in their unbelief (vv. 22-23). This recalls the statement about unbelieving Jews in 2 Cor. 3:16: "When a man returns to the Lord, the veil is removed."

In this section one no longer receives the impression that unbelieving Israelites are doomed to destruction by a divine decree. They have fallen away but can be accepted again as soon as they abandon their unbelief. The olive tree is, after all, their "own" (v. 24).

Romans 11:25-36: All Israel Will Be Saved

Paul discloses to his readers a "mystery": the divine hardening of Israel is of a temporary nature. When the πλήρωμα of the Gentiles has "come in," all

Israel will be saved.[84] Isaiah 59:20–21 and Isa. 27:9 are cited in support. A Deliverer (ῥυόμενος) will come from Zion and banish ungodliness from Jacob.

It is no longer a mere remnant that will be saved. *All* Israel will be forgiven and restored.[85] The reason is that God loves Israel because of the fathers (v. 28), and his gifts and call are irrevocable (v. 29). Verse 28 seems to say that God has caused the Israelites to become "enemies" of the Christians for a *purpose:* in order to aid Gentiles to salvation (δὶ ὑμᾶς probably refers to 11:11–12). This is but a temporary arrangement. As regards the election, Israel remains beloved.

God has not rejected his people (11:1–2). Instead, Paul has rejected the thrust of his argument begun in 9:6. The sovereignty of God is a theme common to chapters 9 and 11, but in the latter chapter all emphasis has moved on to God's overwhelming mercy. God has consigned all people to disobedience that he may have mercy upon all (v. 32). The "treatise" thus ends with proclaiming God's triumph over human disobedience.[86]

Does Israel Have a Special Way to Salvation?

But how will the salvation of Israel take place and what is involved in it? The nature of Israel's salvation has recently been the object of intense discussion. It will be convenient to join the debate by evaluating the interpretation recently put forward by John Gager, who acknowledges his debt to Gaston. The page numbers in the following paragraphs refer to Gager's *The Origins of Anti-Semitism.*[87]

According to Gager, the salvation of Israel does not consist in its conversion to Christianity (261, 263). Paul does not even regard Jesus as the Messiah of the Jews. Jesus was not the climax of God's dealings with Israel (239, 241). Instead, Christ now offers to *Gentiles* righteousness and knowledge of God (214). The significance of the torah for Israel "has now been replicated for Gentiles through Christ" (214). For Jews, justification is still "through the Torah" (218).

This thesis, though vigorously argued, is simply insupportable. Why did Paul call Jesus "[the] Christ" in the first place (even in Rom. 9:5) if he did not regard him as the Messiah of Israel? The question is not even asked by Gager.

Still in Rom. 10:12–13, Paul repeats the main thesis of the letter: there is no difference between Jew and Greek as regards salvation. Both have the same κύριος (10:12). Romans 10:8–13 specifies the conditions of salvation (σώζεσθαι, vv. 9, 13; σωτηρία, v. 10) for Jew and Greek (v. 12). Christ is the Lord of all and sundry. Gager never mentions in his book Rom. 1:16, the motto of the epistle: the gospel is "the power of God for *salvation* to every one who has faith, *to the Jew* first . . ."

Assuming that the gospel was not meant to be proclaimed to the Jews at all, Gager plays down σῴζειν in Rom. 11:14, takes no notice of ᾿Ιουδαίους κερδαίνειν in 1 Cor. 9:20,[88] and is unable to come to grips with Peter's *gospel to the circumcision* (Gal. 2:7).[89] But Paul's argument in Rome. 11:11–12, 19, 28a, 31a makes no sense at all if the gospel about Jesus Christ was not meant to be proclaimed to Jews. If it was not, how could the "disobedience" of the Jews (v. 31) become the chance for the Gentiles to receive salvation? If the gospel was meant for Gentiles only, why was it not preached to them right away? Why does Paul suggest that Israel's "fall" had to occur first?

According to Gager, Paul's problem in Romans 9—11 is "Israel's refusal to recognize and to accept the obvious continuity between God's promise to Abraham and his act of redemption in Christ" (223), its "failure to recognize Paul's gospel to and about the Gentiles as fully at one with God's righteousness" (250). This is why they stumbled, failing to see that righteousness rests on faith (252), both for the circumcised and for the uncircumcised.[90] But why should this cognitive failure have to occur first, before Paul's gospel could reach the Gentiles, its only intended addressees? Just how does the "disobedience of the Jews" provide the "divinely ordained opportunity for God to show mercy on the Gentiles" (254–55)? Gager is quite vague on these issues.

If Israel was not supposed to believe in Jesus as the Messiah at all, it becomes unclear why Paul should speak of its ἀπιστία, as in Rom. 11:20–23, or of its disobedience (Rom. 11:31). And why does Paul resort to even much stronger language about divine *hardening* and double predestination (not mentioned by Gager)? Why was Israel "cut off" (260)? Why should the rejection of Paul's mission to Gentiles (not rejection of Christ!) count as so enormous a problem that the apology of God put forward in chapter 9 is needed? And *what* should Israel be made jealous of (11:11ff.) if Gentiles do not possess anything that is not available to Israel as well?[91] Why the *deep sorrow* expressed by Paul in 9:1–2; 10:1? A lot of Paul's statements make little sense if it was not Israel's failure to *believe in Jesus as the Christ* that was his problem.

Gager puts forward a forced exegesis of a number of crucial passages.[92] Paul's negative comments on the torah[93] are eliminated through the interpretation that they apply to the torah *if imposed on Gentiles*. But it is impossible to read, for example, all ὑπὸ νόμον passages, including those in Galatians 3—4, from such a point of view. On the other hand, Gager does admit that *Paul himself had given up the law and Israel's covenant* (234). This is indeed the only feasible way to interpret Gal. 2:18–21 or Phil. 3:7–8. Gager even speaks of Paul's "apostolic apostasy" (244). But no one else was, in his opinion, supposed to emulate the apostle in this regard (247). The rejection of the law was Paul's personal decision, made necessary by his special mission among Gentiles.

This, however, is not the case. Paul was not the only Jewish Christian to neglect parts of the torah. The same position was taken—before Paul—by the "Hellenists" and by the congregation in Antioch. How could not only Barnabas but even Peter "live like Gentiles" in Antioch (Gal. 2:14) if "tearing down" the ritual law (Gal. 2:18) was a Pauline idiosyncrasy?

If Paul was an apostate and he knew it, how could he still put himself forward as an instance of those faithful Jews who constitute the remnant (Rom. 11:1-2)?

Gager lays great stress on the fact that Paul's treatment of the torah and of justification is part of a debate with fellow Christians, not with Jews (202, etc.).[94] But this is not very important, for precisely the Jewish identity of those opposed to Paul was at stake.[95]

In view of all this—and many more observations could be added[96]—it is quite incredible that Paul should have heeded the notion that Israel could be saved apart from Christ. Should such a notion be there in Rom. 11:25–26, then that statement would be unique in Paul's letters. In view of the overwhelming evidence, still present in Romans 10, it is not advisable to posit such a unique meaning in Romans 11.

A more plausible interpretation of Israel's "special way" to salvation is given by scholars who allow that *solus Christus* consistently remains the center of Paul's soteriology and that Jesus is also the Messiah of the Jews.[97] Israel's special way consists in its having "a special eschatological destiny."[98] Israel's conversion is not the result of Christian mission.[99]

Even on this understanding, 11:25-27 is a completely singular passage in Paul.[100] In 11:14, Paul expressed his hope that he could save "some" of his kinsmen. Perhaps one should not take the modest $\tau\iota\nu\alpha\varsigma$ literally any more than $\tau\iota\nu\epsilon\varsigma$ in 3:3 or 11:17. Romans 11:14 is immediately followed by v. 15, in which Paul makes a connection between his bringing—indirectly, through "jealousy"—Jews to salvation and the eschatological $\pi\rho\dot{o}\sigma\lambda\eta\mu\psi\iota\varsigma$ of Israel, which amounts to "life from the dead."[101] If 11:25-26 is interpreted in the light of v. 12 ($\tau\dot{o}$ $\pi\lambda\dot{\eta}\rho\omega\mu\alpha$ $\alpha\dot{\upsilon}\tau\hat{\omega}\nu$ corresponds to $\tau\dot{o}$ $\pi\lambda\dot{\eta}\rho\omega\mu\alpha$ $\tau\hat{\omega}\nu$ $\dot{\epsilon}\theta\nu\hat{\omega}\nu$) and vv. 14-15, it seems quite possible that Paul expected the final conversion of Israel to take place in the course of his—and others'—proclamation of the gospel. While a miracle is necessary, it is perhaps not worked through a deus ex machina but is worked through the agency of God's apostles.[102]

Although the decision on this issue is important to one's understanding of the nature of Paul's mission, it is not vital for the main concern of the present essay. In any case, Paul expresses his assurance that a miracle at the imminent eschaton will convert Israel to faith in Christ. In effect, Paul thus assures the "ultimate vindication of the Church."[103]

The Meaning of μυστήριον

The initial formula "I want you to understand" (v. 25a) normally introduces something new.[104] The word μυστήριον belongs to the standard apocalyptic vocabulary and denotes a special revelation, whether to Paul himself[105] or to another prophet.[106] The choice of word suggests supernatural knowledge.

This is contested by some interpreters who assume that Paul is putting forward a personal *dream* or a hope, and that he knows it.[107] In the subsequent doxology Paul confesses that God's ways are inscrutable: human beings cannot know them (vv. 33–34). This seems to stand in some tension with Paul's actual knowledge of the divine plans a few verses before; therefore some scholars understand the doxology as a conscious mitigation of the "mystery" statement.[108] Paul knew that he had not solved the problem of squaring the circle![109] Yet the doxology is an expression of *praise*.[110] The genre traditionally has a place in an apocalyptic setting such as this,[111] so that it is hardly advisable to look for hidden mental reservations in it. Whatever his thoughts and feelings, Paul at least conveys to his readers the impression that he is in possession of a divinely imparted secret.

THE QUESTION OF CONSISTENCY IN ROMANS 9—11

On the basis of this analysis, it would seem that there are considerable internal contradictions in Romans 9—11. For the topic of this essay, the relationship between divine hardening and man's disobedience is of less interest (see above, p. 186). The crucial question is the treatment of Israel, and for this question there are two sharply diverging solutions[112] (the remnant idea standing in the middle): that empirical Israel is not elected but hardened and damned in advance to reprobation (9:6–29), and that empirical Israel—or most of it—will be saved because of God's loyalty to his promises and to the election of the people (11:11–36). It is necessary now to review different attempts to resolve the tension or to account for its existence.

Successive Phases in the Sovereign Plan?

John Piper, in the course of a lengthy critique of E. Dinkler's position, denies the contradiction by stressing God's right to show his sovereignty in bringing the end-time generation of Israel to faith and to membership in the "eschatological Israel."[113] But this is an anachronistic standpoint; for Paul, the Israel hardened and the Israel to be saved were one and the same generation. In chapter 9, Paul denies to God any "juridical" responsibility to act in a certain way. He goes to great lengths to show that God does just what he pleases. In 11:29–30, however, he presupposes that God has *bound* himself to Israel through his promises. He is, so to speak, under a juridical constraint.[114] But sovereignty entails that God's action is incalculable—that he can either save *or condemn* "all Israel." As this is not the case in chapter 11, God does not, according to that chapter, act "sovereignly." His action is calculable, except for its mode and time. The result is known to humanity in advance.

Rejection of Romans 11

Some of those who perceive the existence of a contradiction are content to declare that chapter 11 is in disagreement with Paul's other statements, including Romans 9. In itself, this is correct. But it does not take us very far simply to discard Romans 11.[115] Why, then, did Paul write that chapter? This question becomes all the more urgent.

Romans 9 a Necessary Preparation?

Several interpreters emphasize that chapter 9 is of only a propaedeutic nature. It is a "necessary first step,"[116] for "the disillusionment is the presupposition of the declaration of salvation."[117] The dramatic structure of the three chapters becomes evident.[118]

These interpreters often try to have their cake and eat it. Thus H. Hübner speaks not only of a dramatic effect but also of a contradiction that cannot be solved in terms of our logic.[119] For good measure, he also assumes a theological development from Galatians, which is entirely negative with regard to Israel, to Romans, which displays a positive attitude. Yet, on Hübner's own showing, the positive attitude crops up only in Romans 11, whereas Romans 9 is just as negative as Galatians 4![120] Ulrich Wilckens senses indeed such a difference between chapters 9 and 11 that he reckons with a turn in Paul's thought after the composition of Romans 9![121] This will be discussed in our next section. For the moment, the point is that Romans 9 can hardly represent a *necessary* first step if Paul soon turns *away* from the solution given in that chapter. As for the disillusionment, chapter 10 would have sufficed for that purpose. Chapter 9, with its talk of pre-destination and hardening, goes to quite unnecessary lengths from that point of view.

A Development from Earlier Letters to Romans?

A few exegetes explain Paul's positive attitude to Israel in chapter 11 in terms of a development theory, without paying due attention to the fact that the "older" position is also present in Romans.[122] Mention of this was made in the previous section: Romans 9 is no less negative than is Galatians.[123] It is of no help, then, to posit a shift between Galatians and Romans.[124] The shift should, rather, be placed between Romans 9 and Romans 10, or more precisely, between Romans 11:10 and Romans 11:11! Or are we to suppose that Paul gave up the negative view as present in Galatians but still put it forward in Romans 9 for the sake of dramatic effect, until he finally replaced it by the positive view in Romans 11?[125]

A Change during the Composition of Romans?

More logically, some scholars assume indeed that Paul hit upon the ideas set forth in 11:11ff. during the process of dictating Romans.[126] When he expressed his deep sorrow in 9:1-3, he did not yet know what he would say in chapter 11.

U. Müller assumes that 11:25-26 represents a divine response to Paul's prayer contained in 10:1.[127] But why, then, did Paul continue the old line of thought until 11:10? If there really is a change in Paul's thought, it should be placed after 11:10. This is the position of B. Noack, who maintains that the mystery was revealed to Paul "at the very moment of his dictating the second part of ch. xi, vv. 13-36."[128] One might reply that there seem to be some slight points of anticipation already in chapter 9 (the final clauses in 9:17, 22-23 *may* point to 11:11ff.),[129] and 10:19 sets the stage for 11:14.[130] Romans 3:1-8, a passage saturated with parallels to chapters 9—11,[131] anticipates in v. 4 ("Let God be true, but every man a liar") both chapters 9 and (in the teleological quotation in v. 4b) 11:32, in a way that *may* indicate that Paul has the positive solution of 11:25-26 in mind already.[132] Yet this is only a possibility. More important, perhaps, is the observation that 2 Corinthians 3, a chapter extremely critical of the Mosaic covenant, contains both the idea of divine hardening or veiling (v. 14) *and* the prospect that the veil will be taken away "whenever a man returns to the Lord" (v. 16). This indicates that Paul could think of divine hardening as temporary and conditional even before composing Romans 9. It is very hard to trace a straightforward development from one position to another; different lines of thought cross one another in Paul's mind.

In any case, why did Paul not care to cancel his earlier reflections if he had changed his mind and felt that he now knew better?

Different Strategies?

F. Watson makes no secret of Paul's self-contradictions and concludes, "If one is not satisfied with the view that Paul was capable of thinking coherently only for very short periods of time and if one rejects an artificial harmonizing exegesis, the only possible solution seems to be to examine the social context and function of Romans."[133] Considered from this standpoint, "Romans is a highly coherent piece of writing," virtually every part of which contributes to "Paul's attempt to persuade the Jewish Christian congregation in Rome to separate themselves from the Jewish community, to accept the legitimacy of the Pauline Gentile congregation in which the law is not observed."[134]

The contradiction between chapters 9 and 11 is traced back simply to different *strategies* to reach the same goal. In Romans 4 and 9 in particular, Paul is asking the Jewish Christians to "make a considerable sacrifice," in abandoning their old self-understanding. In Romans 11, Paul "adopts a different strategy," seeking to "make his own view more attractive and more persuasive by presenting it as far as possible in the contexts of Jewish Christian beliefs and hopes."[135]

This view tends to convert Paul to a coolly calculating tactician. Watson does not take Paul's anguish and sorrow (9:1-3; 10:1) seriously enough. Moreover, he denies that the unbelief of the Jews is the theme of Romans 9—11, regarding 9:24ff. as the real purpose of the section.[136] We have seen above that this is hardly a correct assessment of the situation.[137]

It seems wiser to explain Romans 9—11 in terms of Paul's own experience rather than on some strong hypothesis about the situation in Rome. Romans is a multipurpose writing. Conflicts in the immediate past, new travel plans (Jerusalem, Rome, Spain), the wish to create confidential relations with the Roman Christians, and also the wish to intervene in some local problems (chaps. 14—15) are intermingled and form together the background of the letter. In our section, direct references to local circumstances are sparse and appear late (not until 11:13).[138]

Paul does say that gentile Christians should not grow boastful, but his real concern seems to be with Jewish Christian queries (see above, "Romans 9:1-5: The Privileges of the Accursed") that touch the heart of his existence as a missionary of the gospel. And Paul has not ceased to be a Jewish Christian himself. Inconvenient questions surface in his own mind too, the more so as time goes on and the Parousia should draw near.

Anguish Caused by a Dilemma

For E. P. Sanders, the feelings that chapters 9—11 of Romans convey—concern, anguish, and triumphant expectation—are "far more important than the ideas which they contain."[139] The anguish of the chapters is caused by a dilemma about God. Paul worried about the constancy of God's will. His solution in chapter 11 is a "somewhat desperate expedient." Paul had a "problem of conflicting convictions which can be better asserted than explained," and therefore he "desperately sought for a formula which would keep God's promises to Israel intact, while insisting on faith in Jesus Christ."[140] "What is interesting is how far Paul was from denying anything that he held deeply, even when he could not maintain all his convictions at once without both anguish and finally a lack of logic."[141]

Conclusion

To me, this last solution is the most persuasive one. The revelation vocabulary of 11:25–26 notwithstanding, Paul is wrestling with a burning personal problem,[142] attempting to "square the circle,"[143] trying different solutions.[144]

A side glance at the chronologically not too remote passage 2 Cor. 3:4—4:6 confirms that this is so. While 3:14–16 refers to divine hardening and veiling of the gospel, 4:4 attributes the incomprehensible blindness of the unbelievers to a ruse of the devil.

Paul's wrestling points to an insoluble *heilsgeschichtlich* dilemma in his theology. He presupposes (*a*) that God has acted in a decisive way in the past and given his people promises that cannot change or vanish, and (*b*) that God has acted in a decisive way in Christ and that there can be no salvation apart from Christ. Paul is grappling with a perennial theological problem: the conflict between sacred tradition and new experience. Paul experienced new things and tried to reinterpret his tradition in the light of his experience. In his case, this could only result in violence against the tradition. It was not possible to invest Jesus Christ with exclusive soteriological significance without at the same time in effect breaking with the classical covenantal nomism.[145] Paul will have it both ways, and this brings him into an insoluble self-contradiction as regards Israel.

Thus, in view of Paul's actual practice, the olive-tree allegory is in some ways misleading. Even a Jew had to become part of the "new creation" (Gal. 6:15) in order to have a share in God's salvation.[146] Sanders has shown that Paul in effect expects that Jews will be *converted* (Gal. 2:16). They have to *enter* a new community socially distinct from the synagogue; they have to undergo a new initiation rite; they have to give up their loyalty to God's law, the order of the Mosaic covenant, whenever it interferes with the intercourse with gentile Christians.[147] To retain Paul's image, his position actually entails a third tree, as it were, to which both Jew and Gentile are grafted.

The issue in Romans 9—11, then, is not merely the "justification of God." Paul is in effect concerned to justify his own activity as a preacher of the gospel. He is not constructing abstract theology. He is struggling to find peace and consolation in view of the nagging problem of Israel's rejection of his message. The answers found by him diverge on the theoretical level. Each of them, however, serves to give him consolation and reassurance— and, he must have hoped, his audience confidence in him and his task. Things are not the way they are by chance. God is in control.

NOTES

1. P. Stuhlmacher, "Zur Interpretation von Römer 11.25-32," in *Probleme biblischer Theologie*, Festschrift G. von Rad, ed. H. W. Wolff (Munich, 1971), 555; W. G. Kümmel, "Die Probleme von Römer 9—11 in der gegenwärtigen Forschungslage," in *Heilsgeschehen und Geschichte*, vol. 2 (Marburg, 1978), 245-46.

2. E.g., C. Müller, *Gottes Gerechtigkeit und Gottes Volk: Eine Untersuchung zu Römer 9—11*, Forschungen zur Religion und Literatur des Alten und Neuen Testaments 85 (Göttingen, 1964), 54-55; U. Luz, *Das Geschichtsverständnis des Paulus*, Beiträge zur evangelischen Theologie 49 (Munich, 1968), 27-28; J. Piper, *The Justification of God: An Exegetical and Theological Study of Romans 9:1-23* (Grand Rapids: Baker Book House, 1983), 5; and H. Hübner, *Gottes Ich und Israel: Zum Schriftgebrauch des Paulus in Römer 9—11*, Forschungen zur Religion und Literatur des Alten und Neuen Testaments 136 (Göttingen, 1984), 16.

3. E.g., F. Mussner, *Traktat über die Juden* (Munich, 1979), 59-60.

4. L. Gaston, "Paul and the Torah," in *Antisemitism and the Foundations of Christianity*, ed. A. T. Davies (New York: Paulist Press, 1979), 66; and J. G. Gager, *The Origins of Anti-Semitism: Attitudes Toward Judaism in Pagan and Christian Antiquity* (New York: Oxford Univ. Press, 1983), 239, 241. Gager, praising the work of Gaston, speaks of a potential "paradigm shift" in the study of Paul (*Origins*, 198); cf. R. Jewett, "The Law and the Coexistence of Jews and Gentiles in Romans," *Interpretation* 39 (1985): 341.

5. L. Gaston, "Israel's Enemies in Pauline Theology," *New Testament Studies* 28 (1982): 402-11; cf. Gager, *Origins*, 241-43.

6. U. Wilckens, *Der Brief an die Römer*, vol. 2, Evangelisch-katholischer Kommentar zum Neuen Testament 6/2 (Neukirchen, 1980), 185; G. Lüdemann, *Paulus und das Judentum*, Theologische Existenz heute 215 (Munich, 1983), 41; Hübner, *Gottes Ich*, 127-35; and Jewett, "Law and the Coexistence," 342.

7. R. Bultmann, "Geschichte und Eschatologie im Neuen Testament," in *Glauben und Verstehen*, vol. 3 (Tübingen, 1960) 101; E. Dinkler, "Prädestination bei Paulus," in *Signum Crucis: Aufsätze zum Neuen Testament und zur christlichen Archäologie* (Tübingen, 1967), 252-53; and E. Güttgemanns, "Heilsgeschichte bei Paulus oder Dynamik des Evangeliums? Zur strukturellen Relevanz von Röm 9—11 für die Theologie des Römerbriefs," in *Studia linguistica neotestamentica: Gesammelte Aufsätze zur linguistischen Grundlage einer neutestamentlichen Theologie* (Munich, 1971), 51.

8. This emphasis is still obvious in the works of Luz and Piper and in E. Käsemann's *Commentary on Romans* (Grand Rapids: Wm. B. Eerdmans, 1980). Käsemann states (p. 261) that Rom. 9:6ff. contains "theological reflection" rather than apologetics or controversy with specific opponents.

9. Thus R. Ruether (*Faith and Fratricide: The Theological Roots of Anti-Semitism* [New York: Crossroad, 1974], 106-7) attributes to Paul an inherently "anti-Judaic" position even in Romans 11, without thereby exposing herself to the charge of anti-Judaism.

10. Thus C. H. Dodd, *The Epistle of Paul to the Romans*, Moffatt New Testament Commentary (London, 1932), 148. Dodd assumes that the chapters were originally a separate treatise.

11. K. Stendahl, *Paul among Jews and Gentiles* (Philadelphia: Fortress Press,

1976), 29. Similarly J. C. Beker, *Paul the Apostle: The Triumph of God in Life and Thought* (Philadelphia: Fortress Press, 1980), 87.

12. See B. Byrne, *"Sons of God"—"Seed of Abraham": A Study of the Idea of Sonship of God of All Christians in Paul against the Jewish Background,* Analecta biblica (Rome, 1979), 127–30.

13. See H.-J. Schoeps, *Paulus: Die Theologie des Apostels im Lichte der jüdischen Religionsgeschichte* (Tübingen, 1959), 249.

14. Cf. Käsemann, *Commentary,* 257; Wilckens, *Der Brief an die Römer* 2:189–90. Apart from Rom. 9:1, οὐ ψεύδομαι occurs in Paul only in 2 Cor. 11:31; Gal. 1:20. In both cases, Paul is refuting existing rumors.

15. Gaston, "Israel's Enemies," 411.

16. G. Eichholz (*Die Theologie des Paulus im Umriss* [Neukirchen, 1972], 290–91) does not refer to the unbelief of Israel in connection with Rom. 9:1-5 either but defines the topic of the passage as "Paul's yes to Israel." But whence Paul's sorrow? Eichholz's assertion that Romans 9—11 is *kirchenkritisch* rather than *israelkritisch* is taken over by Gaston.

17. Gaston, "Israel's Enemies," 418. According to Gaston, Paul does not in Romans 9—11 or elsewhere "charge Israel with a lack of faith," although he does refer to "Israel's lack of understanding (10:3, 19), to Israel's disobedience (10:21; 11:11-12, 31), and to Israel's lack of faithfulness (3:3; 11:20), all with respect to the Gentile mission." But can we seriously assume that Paul wished himself to be anathema for the sake of his kinsmen merely because they failed to undertake gentile mission and to recognize Paul's mission to Gentiles?

18. An impressive account of Paul's pathos is given by H. Schlier in *Der Römerbrief,* Herders theologischer Kommentar zum Neuen Testament 6 (Freiburg/Basel/Wien, 1977), 284-86. Cf. F. Siegert, *Argumentation bei Paulus gezeigt an Röm 9—11,* Wissenschaftliche Untersuchungen zum Neuen Testament 34 (Tübingen, 1985), 120-21.

19. Piper, *Justification,* 29.

20. See ibid., 4; Hübner, *Gottes Ich,* 15.

21. Calvin, cited by Siegert in *Argumentation,* 121.

22. Siegert, *Argumentation,* 121.

23. Against Eichholz (*Die Theologie,* 291), for whom "der einzig denkbare Addressat ist die junge Kirche von Rom, die Paulus in der Gefahr begriffen sieht, Israel—abzuschreiben, Israels Erwählung als gegenwärtig nicht mehr gültig anzusehen." This may be the case in 11:17ff., but 9:1ff. points in another direction.

24. Thus, e.g., Jewett, "Coexistence," 343.

25. Present: Piper, *Justification,* 8; Mussner, *Traktat,* 46-47; and B. Klappert, "Traktat für Israel (Römer 9—11)," in *Jüdische Existenz und die Erneuerung der christlichen Theologie,* ed. M. Stöhr (Munich, 1981), 73. Past: J. Munck, *Christus und Israel: Eine Auslegung von Röm 9—11,* Acta Jutlandica, Teologisk Serie 7 (Copenhagen, 1966), 28.

26. This connection indicates that, contrary to Byrne (*Sons,* 82-83), the list of privileges is a creation of Paul rather than of Hellenistic Judaism. Comparable lists are not available, and υἱοθεσία used in a religious sense is a typically Pauline word. See Luz, *Das Geschichtsverständnis,* 270-71; and Piper, *Justification,* 7. As for the individual parts of the list, perhaps structure and rhyme have had a share in their

formulation so that the total impact is more important than the analysis of every individual member (thus Piper, *Justification*, 6).

27. Piper (*Justification*, 25) states, with some exaggeration, that each privilege mentioned "is laden with saving implications and eschatological promise." This is certainly not true of the νομοθεσία. Only a forced exegesis can claim that "in the law itself God expressed his saving purpose for Israel" (p. 22). Piper (pp. 21–22) shares the mistaken view that what Paul opposes in his letters is not the law itself but only its legalistic misunderstanding. See on this H. Räisänen, *Paul and the Law* (Philadelphia: Fortress Press, 1986), 42–50.

28. As opposed to the "children of promise," Gager (*Origins*, 250) arbitrarily complements v. 8: "It is not the children of flesh who are the *only* (!) children of God, but the children of the promise are (*also*) reckoned as descendants" (emphasis added). Only thus can he assert that Paul "never speaks of Israel as rejected by God."

29. Note that the killing γράμμα is engraved in the stone tablets—a reference to the Decalogue itself!

30. An attempt to date Philippians after Romans is undertaken by H.-H. Schade in *Apokalyptische Christologie bei Paulus: Studien zum Zusammenhang von Christologie und Eschatologie in den Paulusbriefen*, Göttinger theologische Arbeiten 18 (Göttingen, 1981), 181–89.

31. Dinkler, "Prädestination," 249. Hübner, *Gottes Ich*, 17: Paul "juggles with the concept 'Israel.'" Gaston ("Israel's Enemies," 413) finds that Paul "emphatically affirms" in 9:6–13 the "common Jewish concept of election and that by grace alone." I fail to see the force of the observation that v. 6b contains a γάρ rather than ἀλλά. The passage provides an explanation why God's word should not be deemed to have failed despite the behavior of Israel. Gaston seems to understand ἐξ ᾽Ισραήλ in a very special way, comprising even Gentiles as "Abraham's other children." If I understand him correctly, he takes v. 6b to mean that not all descendants of Abraham, i.e., Gentiles (gentile believers?), belong to the empirical (ethnic) Israel.

32. Against Schoeps, *Paulus*, 251. That is the point made in 2:25–29 but not here. Still less does Paul indicate that God's call must be proclaimed and accepted time and again (thus Käsemann, *Commentary*, 262, 266).

33. Hübner, *Gottes Ich*, 18; and Wilckens, *Der Brief an die Römer*, 192.

34. Paul is not involved here in an attack against "works righteousness," as he will be later, in 9:30ff. In fact, in 9:6ff. he is attacking an emphatic Jewish theology of grace! Cf. F. Watson, *Paul, Judaism, and the Gentiles: A Sociological Approach*, Society for New Testament Studies Monograph Series (Cambridge, 1986), 162–63.

35. Notwithstanding those commentators who read the "doctrine" of justification of faith into this passage as well—notably, Käsemann (*Commentary*, 254–55, 256). Cf. Güttgemanns, "Heilsgeschichte," 41; and Eichholz, *Die Theologie des Paulus*, 287. Correctly Hübner (*Gottes Ich*, 24–25) also points out that the passage is in disagreement with Romans 2. He further notes (p. 34) that 9:6–13 does not fit easily with the descriptions of the role of *sin* in 1:18—3:20 and 5:12–21 either.

36. The problem consists for Paul in the very fact that the great *majority* of the Jews refuse to believe. This is blurred by many who mitigate the difference between chap. 9 and chap. 11 (e.g., Piper [*Justification*, 33]: God's purpose never included the salvation of every individual Israelite). But a small minority of unbelievers

would have posed no problem at all. Eichholz (*Die Theologie des Paulus*, 292) takes τινες in 3:3 and οὐ πάντες in 10:16 literally!

37. This is elaborated by Hübner in *Gottes Ich*, 15–24. Cf. Watson, *Paul, Judaism, and the Gentiles*, 227 n.9; and Piper, *Justification*, 54. This is against C. E. B. Cranfield (*The Epistle to the Romans*, vol. 2 [Greenwood, S.C.: Attic Press, 1979], 471), who sees here a "distinction between different levels or forms of election, not between election and non-election."

38. Convincingly shown by Hübner in *Gottes Ich*, 19–21.

39. Gaston ("Israel's Enemies," 413, 416) flatly denies that Ishmael and Esau stand for Jews.

40. This time too Gaston (ibid., 408–11) denies that the reference is to Jews. Gager (*Origins*, 242) also claims that "Jews are absent from the entire passage" of Gal. 4:21–31.

41. Piper (*Justification*, 70–79) argues that the problem is not a moral one for Paul. The statement that there is no ἀδικία in God means that "God cannot be faulted with a disposition or conduct that contradicts the truth of who he is" (p. 73). "God's righteousness consists in his unswerving commitment always to act for the glory of his name" (p. 78). But often enough ἀδικία carries clear moral overtones (e.g., Rom. 6:13 [contrasted with ἁμαρτία]; 2 Cor. 12:13; 1 Cor. 6:1, 9).

42. Against Cranfield (*Epistle to the Romans* 2:472), according to whom v. 15 governs v. 18 so that the section as a whole bears witness to the freedom of God's mercy—and to no other freedom.

43. Correctly Hübner, *Gottes Ich*, 45.

44. See Güttgemanns, "Heilsgeschichte," 44.

45. See C. K. Barrett, *A Commentary on the Epistle to the Romans*, Black's New Testament Commentaries (London, 1957), 187; and H. Räisänen, *The Idea of Divine Hardening: A Comparative Study of the Notion of Divine Hardening, Leading Astray, and Inciting to Evil in the Bible and in the Qur'ān*, Pubs. of the Finnish Exegetical Soc. 25 (Helsinki, 1976), 81, 84.

46. Correctly Piper, *Justification*, 156–60; and G. Maier, *Mensch und freier Wille nach den jüdischen Religionsparteien zwischen Ben Sira und Paulus*, Wissenschaftliche Untersuchungen zum Neuen Testament 12 (Tübingen, 1971), 368–71.

47. Müller (*Gottes Gerechtigkeit*, 28–29) projects the notion of creation, indubitably present in vv. 19–21, back to vv. 6b–13 as well. The notion of the right of the Creator with his creatures then looms large in Käsemann's interpretation of Romans 9—11.

48. Correctly Maier, *Mensch und freier Wille*, 381; Wilckens, *Der Brief an die Römer*, 205; Piper, *Justification*, 192–96; and Watson, *Paul, Judaism, and the Gentiles*, 164. "Ripe for destruction" (Cranfield, *Epistle to the Romans* 2:495–96) is too weak. The parallelism between κατηρτισμένα and προητοίμασεν should be noted.

49. This is not the place to discuss syntactical and other problems of these vv. I join those who take θέλων in a causal sense.

50. Thus Gaston, "Israel's Enemies," 413; Klappert, "Traktat," 74–75; and Watson, *Paul, Judaism, and the Gentiles*, 162. More correctly, D. Zeller, *Juden und Heiden in der Mission des Paulus: Studien zum Römerbrief*, Forschungen zur Bibel (Stuttgart, 1973), 116: "Dass nun die Berufung der Heiden so breiten Raum erhält, war vielleicht 9, 6ff. noch gar nicht beabsichtigt."

51. If the "point of the whole chapter" is that "Roman Gentiles must understand that Israel's election depends solely on God's mercy because their own election depends on that same mercy" (Gaston, "Israel's Enemies," 416), why did Paul have to tell it to them so emphatically? Why did he emphasize his great sorrow (9:1–3)?

52. Cf. Watson, *Paul, Judaism, and the Gentiles,* 164: "By Pauline standards a relatively clear and coherent argument."

53. Hübner, *Gottes Ich,* 57.

54. See ibid., 59.

55. Dodd was sharply critical: vv. 17–18 are a "false step," and vv. 19–21—the "weakest point in the whole epistle"—make God a "non-moral despot" (*Epistle,* 157, 159). Likewise J. C. O'Neill: "However important it might be for God's power to be made known [v. 17], the achievement of that end cannot turn unjust power into just power." Verse 18 contains a "thoroughly immoral doctrine," and the objection in v. 19 "is entirely warranted, and the reply does nothing to answer it" (*Paul's Letter to the Romans* [London: Penguin Books, 1975], 157–58). O'Neill denies that Paul was the author of these vv. The opposite evaluation is given by Piper (*Justification,* ix): "If there is a God, he must be the God of Romans 9."

56. For my exegesis of 9:30–33, see *Paul and the Law,* 174–75; for 10:1ff., see pp. 53–55.

57. Müller (*Gottes Gerechtigkeit,* 36) finds the idea of predestination in τίθημι (v. 33a). Yet v. 33b refers to the possibility of faith without restrictions; the reappearance of the latter quotation in 10:11 in a universalistic and evangelistic context confirms this interpretation.

58. Maier (*Mensch und freier Wille,* 388–92), concerned to interpret chaps. 9—11 in a unitary way, finds divine prevention of understanding in the words οὐ κατ' ἐπίγνωσιν and ἀγνοεῖν. But this is far-fetched.

59. πλουτῶν εἰς πάντας τοὺς ἐπικαλουμένους αὐτόν recalls 9:23: ἵνα γνωρίσῃ τὸν πλοῦτον τῆς δόξης αὐτοῦ ἐπὶ σκεύη ἐλέους. The differences are characteristic: predestined "vessels," on the one hand, and man's turning to God on the other.

60. Watson (*Paul, Judaism, and the Gentiles,* 166–67) thinks that the passage 10:14–21 speaks of gentile mission only. Verse 16 would point out that not all Gentiles have believed.

61. Hübner (*Gottes Ich,* 95) thinks that the reference is to Jews from v. 14 onwards. Wilckens (*Der Brief an die Römer,* 229) thinks that Paul turns to Jews in v. 16. It is indeed difficult to imagine why Paul should have dwelt on the rejection of the gospel by many *Gentiles* in this connection.

62. See Munck, *Christus,* 72; and Hübner, *Gottes Ich,* 95.

63. See Räisänen, *Idea of Divine Hardening.*

64. For a summary, see ibid., 96–98.

65. See E. P. Sanders, *Paul and Palestinian Judaism: A Comparison of Patterns of Religion* (Philadelphia: Fortress Press, 1977), 266–70, where there is a discussion of predestination in Qumran.

66. For instances in which it *has* been felt, however, see Räisänen, *Idea of Divine Hardening,* 97.

67. Many of those who sense a contradiction between Romans 9 and Romans 11 deny that any exists between chaps. 9 and 10: e.g., Dinkler, "Prädestination," 255; and Hübner, *Gottes Ich,* 98.

68. See Hübner, *Gottes Ich,* 99.

69. προέγνω in 11:2 recalls 8:28–29, with the chain προέγνω, προώρισεν, ἐκάλεσεν, etc. Cf. D. G. Johnson, "The Structure and Meaning of Romans 11," *Catholic Biblical Quarterly* 45 (1984): 95.

70. Dinkler, "Prädestination," 251: The presupposition of the question and the answer (vv. 1–2)—that the promise was given to the historical people—"stands in a clear contradiction to the passage 9.6ff." Watson (*Paul, Judaism, and the Gentiles,* 168) finds 11:1–2 "diametrically opposed to 9.6ff."

71. See Güttgemanns, "Heilsgeschichte," 47.

72. This, of course, is a weak argument, if the unbelief of the *majority* is the problem. Johnson ("Structure and Meaning," 94) therefore proposes a different interpretation: "I, an Israelite, . . . would never have held to such an idea [vis., that Israel has been rejected]." But Paul's subjective views are not the issue he tries to cope with.

73. Käsemann (*Commentary*, 302) strangely sees here a "demonic depth which resists the Spirit of God who expresses himself in the Christian message." This amounts to turning the text upside down.

74. Lüdemann (*Paulus und das Judentum*, 32–33) finds that 11:1–10 does not contradict chap. 9 (although 11:11ff. does).

75. Johnson ("Structure and Meaning," 96) takes the "remnant" in chap. 11 as a "sign of hope that all Israel will be saved." This would mean that Paul uses the concept of the remnant in a way different from 9:27, where it serves as a "sign of judgment." But even 11:4 only signifies that the remnant is not quite insignificant quantitatively, and in v. 7 the remnant is called ἡ ἐκλογή as distinct from Israel at large. Johnson takes 11:1–16 as a unit and v. 16 as a reference to the remnant (rather than, say, to the patriarchs).

76. Watson (*Paul, Judaism, and the Gentiles,* 31–32, 169) assumes that Rom. 11:11ff. reflects Paul's personal experience. At first he preached to Jews alone; it was only at a relatively late stage that, disillusioned at the hardening of his hearers, he turned to Gentiles. Though a good deal can be said for this unorthodox view, it also faces some grave difficulties; see H. Räisänen, "The 'Hellenists'—a Bridge between Jesus and Paul?" in *The Torah and Christ: Essays in German and English on the Problem of the Law in Early Christianity,* Pubs. of the Finnish Exegetical Soc. 45 (Helsinki, 1986), 251 n.1. For instance, Watson has to deny the existence of the 'Hellenists' around Stephen as a separate group. Perhaps we may modify his reading of Rom. 11:11ff. a bit: Individual Gentiles were accepted into Christian congregations (without circumcision) very early by the "Hellenists"; this, indeed was the reason Paul persecuted them (see Räisänen, "The 'Hellenists,'" 282). Thus, when Paul was converted, he already knew that his relation to the Gentiles was at stake. But *purposeful* mission to Gentiles *on a larger scale* started only later, in Antioch— quite possibly accelerated through the unreceptiveness of local Jews.

77. Wilckens, *Der Brief an die Römer,* 243.

78. See Dinkler, "Prädestination," 259–60; and Güttgemanns, "Heilsgeschichte," 55.

79. Käsemann, *Commentary,* 308; and Wilckens, *Der Brief an die Römer,* 246. Beker (*Paul the Apostle,* 90) and Johnson ("Structure and Meaning," 98–99) think, however, of the Jewish Christian remnant.

80. Watson, *Paul, Judaism, and the Gentiles,* 169.

81. E.g., Wilckens, *Der Brief an die Römer,* 247; Mussner, *Traktat,* 70; Käsemann, *Commentary,* 299–300 (adding the comment that this is not the main line in Paul's ecclesiology, however); and Klappert, "Traktat," 92.

82. N. Walter, "Zur Interpretation von Römer 9—11," *Zeitschrift für Theologie und Kirche* 81 (1984): 182–83: God's dealings with Israel. Luz, *Das Geschichtsverständnis,* 276: the patriarchs. Siegert, *Argumentation,* 186–87: the faith of Abraham.

83. See Rom. 7:1–6, and Räisänen, *Paul and the Law,* 61–62.

84. It is also disputed how καὶ οὕτως should be understood. It probably refers to what precedes, indicating the mode of Israel's salvation, which will occur unexpectedly, in the midst of Israel's hardening. See Luz, *Das Geschichtsverständnis,* 249; and Wilckens, *Der Brief an die Römer,* 255.

85. This is occasionally denied—e.g., by H. Ponsot in "Et ainsi tout Israel sera sauvé: Rom., XI, 26a: Salut et conversion," *Revue biblique* 89 (1982): 406–17. He takes πᾶς ᾿Ισραήλ to mean the *spiritual* Israel only. On this reading, ᾿Ισραήλ changes its meaning after v. 25, where it does mean the people. But there is too clear a correlation between ἀπὸ μέρους in v. 25 and πᾶς in v. 26 for such an interpretation to carry conviction. Moreover, in what sense would the salvation of the spiritual Israel (in the sense of 9:6ff.) be a "mystery" at all? And what would the significance of vv. 26b–27 be? What is the ungodliness of the spiritual Israel that still needs to be taken away? πώρωσις ἀπὸ μέρους ἄχρι οὗ . . . implies that the πώρωσις will *disappear,* when the moment indicated by ἄχρι οὗ is there. The word πᾶς need not mean "every individual," but it must include "many, many more."

86. Käsemann (*Commentary,* 314–18) proclaims with much rhetorical vigor that the Pauline doctrine of justification is the climax of Romans 9—11 as well as of the whole letter. The passage shows that Paul understands grace as a power that finally overcomes unbelief (p. 311). But again, it should be noted that words typical of "justification" passages are *lacking* in 11:32, just as they are lacking in 9:6ff. Characteristically different is the roughly parallel statement in Gal. 3:22 that contains ἐκ πίστεως and οἱ πιστεύοντες. In Rom. 11:32—in a context stressing God's call, election, and mercy alone—works and faith are absent, and this is not so by chance. The logical outcome of the thrust of this passage would no doubt be the idea of ἀποκατάστασις πάντων (found here by some older interpreters). Yet what happens to non-Christian Gentiles is outside Paul's sphere of interest.

87. Gaston's view is summarized by Gager in *Origins,* 200–201.

88. On the significance of the phrase, see G. Klein, "'Christlicher Antijudaismus': Bemerkungen zu einem semantischen Einschüchterungsversuch," *Zeitschrift für Theologie und Kirche* 79 (1982): 443; and E. P. Sanders, *Paul, the Law, and the Jewish People* (Philadelphia: Fortress Press, 1983), 177.

89. According to Gager (*Origins,* 262), Paul first assented to the legitimacy of Peter's gospel but then never mentioned it except in Galatians 2; it may have become "increasingly irrelevant."

90. Gager (ibid., 251) defines πίστις so that it includes both Jews and Christians if they respond faithfully to God. The word πίστις can mean, for instance, that sonship lies in doing the torah rather than merely hearing it!

91. See E. Grässer, "Zwei Heilswege? Zum theologischen Verhältnis von Israel und Kirche," in *Kontinuitet und Einheit,* Festschrift F. Mussner (Freiburg/Basel/Wien, 1981), 427 n.54.

92. These include Rom. 3:21 (χωρὶς νόμου is taken to mean alongside and in conformity with the law; see Gager, *Origins,* 251–52); Rom. 9:8 (p. 250; see above, n. 28); Rom. 9:32 (Israel stumbled over the *Gentiles* [p. 250], although the stumbling stone is characterized as the object of πιστεύειν in both 9:32 and 10:11).

93. Jewett ("Law and the Coexistence," 353–54) thinks that Paul does not repudiate the torah, if it can be shown that τέλος means goal rather than termination in Rom. 10:4. But in whatever way one interprets *that* particular v., a number of other passages (also in Romans, cf. 7:1–6) suggest that Paul *had* repudiated the law. In the light of Rom. 9:6ff.; 8:2 (the "law of sin"); 5:20; etc., Romans may not be of so much help in the dialogue between Christians and Jews as Jewett hopes.

94. This is also stressed by Mussner in *Traktat,* 228, and by others.

95. See K. Haacker, "Paulus und das Judentum," *Judaica* 33 (1977): 162–63; and Klein, "'Christlicher Antijudaismus,'" 431. Haacker points out that the opponents of Paul understood themselves to be not Jewish Christians but Christian Jews. Gager (*Origins,* 231) has adopted J. Munck's implausible thesis that Paul's Judaizing opponents were Gentiles.

96. E.g., in Phil. 3:2–3, circumcision is claimed exclusively for Christianity (Gager [*Origins,* 244] stresses that the adjective "true" is absent, but he misses the force of the definitive article). Cf. Klein, "'Christlicher Antijudaismus,'" 435–36. In 1 Cor. 10:32, Paul could think of the "congregation of God" as a *tertium genus* over against Jews and Gentiles (Klein, "'Christlicher Antijudaismus,'" 439. Moreover, 1 Cor. 10:1–13 militates against a *character indelebilis* of Israel on the ground of the promise to the fathers; see Güttgemanns, "Heilsgeschichte," 56). For a thorough discussion of the whole soteriological issue (with the German discussion in view), see Klein, "'Christlicher Antijudaismus'"; cf. Grässer, "Zwei Heilswege?" 423–28.

97. Thus Mussner, *Traktat,* 59–60.

98. Beker, *Paul the Apostle,* 335. That Paul makes use of traditions about the eschatological pilgrimage to Jerusalem, which he reinterprets, is generally recognized.

99. Ibid., 334. Others, e.g., Mussner, refuse to speak of a "conversion" of Israel. According to Mussner, God's sovereign initiative leads the Israelites to an act of faith (*aemuna*). It is very hard to see what the difference would be between this and a conversion.

100. The tension between vv. 11:25–27 (if applied to the Parousia) and the preceding section is acutely observed by C. Plag (*Israels Wege zum Heil: Eine Untersuchung zu Römer 9 bis 11,* Arbeiten zur Theologie 1/40 [Stuttgart, 1969], 61 [summary]). Plag distinguishes between the "way through conversion" and the "way through the Deliverer." His solution—that 11:25–27 is a fragment from another letter—does not carry conviction, however. A number of interpreters think that Gal. 6:16 ("the Israel of God") anticipates Rom. 11:25–26. It is quite likely, however, that that phrase refers to the church; see Lüdemann, *Paulus und das Judentum,* 27–30. Should it, however, refer to unbelieving Israel, then Galatians would contain an enormous contradiction. On Israel elsewhere in Galatians see below, n. 123.

101. Cf. Klein, "'Christlicher Antijudaismus,'" 432.

102. Sanders, *Paul, the Law, and the Jewish People,* 196. Cf. Schoeps, *Paulus,* 257 n. 6; and Käsemann, *Commentary,* 306–7.

103. Ruether, *Faith and Fratricide,* 107.

104. Lüdemann, *Paulus und das Judentum,* 34.

105. Zeller, *Juden und Heiden,* 252-53. Hübner (*Gottes Ich,* 121) thinks that Paul received his insight when studying Scripture (Isa. 45:25).

106. Müller, *Gottes Gerechtigkeit,* 38.

107. Dinkler, "Prädestination," 259; cf. Schoeps, *Paulus,* 258.

108. Dinkler, "Prädestination," 260; and Walter, "Zur Interpretation," 176-77.

109. Walter, "Zur Interpretation," 177.

110. Zeller, *Juden und Heiden,* 267-68.

111. See ibid., 267, n. 111.

112. See Dinkler, "Prädestination," 251-52; Grässer, "Zwei Heilswege?" 428; Güttgemanns, "Heilsgeschichte," 51; Lüdemann, *Paulus und Judentum,* 33; Walter, "Zur Interpretation," 176-77; and Watson, *Paul, Judaism, and the Gentiles,* 168.

113. Piper, *Justification,* 9-15.

114. Schoeps, *Paulus,* 256 n. 1.

115. Thus Klein, "'Christlicher Antijudaismus'"; and Grässer, "Zwei Heilswege?"

116. Wilckens, *Der Brief an die Römer,* 197.

117. Käsemann, *Commentary,* 298; cf. Luz, *Das Geschichtsverständnis,* 401-2; and Müller, *Gottes Gerechtigkeit,* 46-49. For Käsemann, Romans 9—11 contains a "thoroughly logical, systematic course of thought" (p. 257).

118. Hübner, *Gottes Ich,* 105.

119. Ibid., 122.

120. Ibid., 20.

121. Wilckens, *Der Brief an die Römer,* 185. Wilckens states (p. 209) that Romans 9 fulfills in its context a function similar to that of Rom. 2:17ff. But this is hardly the case. The solution to the human plight given in 3:21ff. does not do away with the description of the plight in 2:17ff. in Paul's mind.

122. See above, n. 6

123. On the "absence of Israel in Galatians," see Luz, *Das Geschichtsverständnis,* 279-86.

124. Plag's view (*Israels Wege zum Heil,* 60-61, 65-66) that Rom. 11:25-27 stems from another letter of Paul's is, though implausible, more logical.

125. Hübner, *Gottes Ich,* 105.

126. B. Noack, "Current and Backwater in the Epistle to the Romans," *Studia theologica* 19 (1965): 165-66; and Walter, "Zur Interpretation," 176.

127. U. Müller, *Prophetie und Predigt im Neuen Testament,* Studien zum Neuen Testament 10 (Gütersloh, 1975), 177-78. Müller assumes that Paul's sorrow and his prayer were caused by another prophecy, that found, according to Müller, in 1 Thess. 2:15-16. Wilckens (*Der Brief an die Römer,* 254) finds Müller's thesis fascinating and is inclined to accept it (see also p. 219).

128. Noack, "Current and Backwater," 165.

129. See above, "Romans 9:14-18: Israel Hardened by God."

130. Romans 4 also presupposes Israel's special status (vv. 9, 16; cf. 3:29). In this regard, Gager (*Origins,* 218, 220) is quite correct.

131. See H. Räisänen, "Zum Verständnis von Röm 3,1-8," in *Torah,* 185-205.

132. See ibid., 194.

133. Watson, *Paul, Judaism, and the Gentiles,* 170.

134. Ibid., 173. Watson assumes that Jewish Christians and gentile Christians lived in separate congregations in Rome; Paul's aim is to make these congregations unite for worship (whereby Jewish Christians ought to give up their observance of the law).

135. Ibid., 172–73.

136. Ibid., 162.

137. See above, "Romans 9:24–29: The Inclusion of Gentiles."

138. Cf. Walter, "Zur Interpretation," 175.

139. Sanders, *Paul, the Law, and the Jewish People*, 193.

140. Ibid., 197–99. More existentially oriented interpreters resort here to talk of dialectic and of a duality in Paul's view of God (or in God himself); see Dinkler, "Prädestination," 253, 261; and Luz, *Das Geschichtsverständnis*, 296–97. But the duality is rooted in divergent experiences of what are believed to be actions of one and the same God. When absolute authority is required for particular events or traditions, insoluble logical contradictions are bound to appear in the thought of people who—like Paul—stand with one foot in each "symbolic world."

141. Sanders, *Paul, the Law, and the Jewish People*, 199.

142. Noack, "Current and Backwater," 165–66. Noack regards Romans 9—11 as "almost the opposite of a treatise," namely, "Paul's vexed monologue written down immediately, with questions and answers, complaint and comfort, objections and assertions, prayers and thanksgiving." But this is an oversimplification, for 9:6–23 looks rather cool in tone. In fact, chaps. 9—11 consist of several "treatises," with emotional exclamations inserted in between.

143. Walter, "Zur Interpretation," 173, 176.

144. Ruether, *Faith and Fratricide*, 105.

145. See H. Räisänen, "Galatians 2.16 and Paul's Break with Judaism," *New Testament Studies* 31 (1985): 543–53, esp. 549–50; reprinted in *Torah*, 168–84.

146. On the significance of "new creation" in Galatians, see J. L. Martyn, "Apocalyptic Antinomies in Paul's Letter to the Galatians," *New Testament Studies* 31 (1985), 410–24.

147. Sanders, *Paul, the Law, and the Jewish People*, 172, 176–78.

13

Honor, Shame, and the Outside World in Paul's Letter to the Romans

HALVOR MOXNES
University of Oslo

Words and phrases in the Bible not only have a "theological" meaning but they have a social meaning as well: they function in a social context. This insight has characterized much of Howard Clark Kee's work, and it is therefore appropriate here to try to apply it to a theological text, Paul's Letter to the Romans.

When Paul said, "I am not ashamed of the Gospel" (Rom. 1:16), what did he actually mean? I shall not enter into the discussion of this phrase at large[1] but focus only on the use of the word "ashamed." C. K. Barrett has argued against one traditional way of explaining these words in a psychological sense. He concludes that "not being ashamed is an antecedent, Christian, rather than a social condition; its cause lies not in Paul's relation to his environment but in the nature of the Gospel."[2] Here Barrett makes an unfortunate distinction between a "social" and a "Christian" condition and between "Paul's relation to his environment" and the "nature of the Gospel." Although the ground for Paul's confidence is found in the gospel, the fact that he is not ashamed expresses his relations to his environment. Even in their most theological use, "shame" and "not to be ashamed" do not relinquish their everyday meaning, in which a person stands within a relationship not only to God but to other people within a community.

What is the social meaning of shame? To answer this question, a model is needed that will provide a framework within which concepts and symbols function within a cultural system. Traditional interpretation of Romans has often focused on "faith" and "justification" as concepts related to the individual in a strictly theological way. Thus, the model for interpreting Romans has been an individualistic one with the individual's religious belief as the controlling concept. To focus on "shame" and its related concept "honor," however, means more than just adding concepts to this traditional model. It means questioning the model itself and suggesting an interpretation based on a model of an honor-and-shame society.

In anthropological studies, shame and honor have usually been closely linked. The modern study of honor and shame is above all associated with J. Pitt-Rivers and the studies of traditional values in Mediterranean societies which he initiated.[3] These societies experienced less drastic changes in social structure since the classical period than many Northern European societies.[4] Therefore, this is an area of study in which social anthropology and classical studies have exercised a mutual influence. In his seminal study *The World of Odysseus*,[5] Moses Finley shows how Homerian society was characterized by the quest for honor. That quest continued to play a prominent role in the later Greek and Hellenistic periods,[6] as well as in Roman society during both the period of the republic and that of the empire.[7] In biblical studies, however, the perspective of honor and shame has been neglected.[8] Only recently, Bruce J. Malina has pointed out how honor and shame were pivotal values in the world of the early Christians.[9]

What are the main characteristics of an honor-and-shame society? In the Greco-Roman world the group was more important than the individual. The individual received status from the group. Therefore, recognition and approval from others were important. Interaction between people was characterized by the competition for recognition and the defense of one's own status and honor. To refuse a person's claim for honor was to put the person to shame. The basic notion in all studies of honor and shame is that they represent the value of a person in her or his own eyes but also in the eyes of his or her society.

Pitt-Rivers has given a summary of the multifaceted concept of honor:

> It is a sentiment, a manifestation of this sentiment in conduct, and the evaluation of this conduct by others, that is to say, reputation. . . . It stands as a mediator between individual aspirations and the judgment of society. It can, therefore, be seen to reflect the values of a group with which a person identifies himself. But honor as a fact, rather than a sentiment, refers not merely to the judgment of others but to their behavior. The facets of honor may be viewed as related in the following way: honor felt becomes honor claimed, and honor claimed becomes honor paid.
>
> The same principles that govern the transactions of honor are present in those of dishonor though in reverse: the withdrawal of respect dishonors, since it implies a rejection of the claim to honor and this inspires the sentiment of shame. To be put to shame is to be denied honor, and it follows that this can only be done to those who have some pretension to it. . . . Honor and dishonor, therefore, provide the currency in which people compete for a reputation and the means whereby their appraisal of themselves can be validated and integrated into the social system—or rejected, thus obliging them to revise it.[10]

This premise that honor and shame are binary concepts has been questioned, however. Unni Wikan has pointed out that in some present-day societies in the Mediterranean region and the Middle East, shame rather than honor is the predominant concern.[11] Moreover, there are also differences between the genders: "Honour is bound up with male ideology and is not on a par with shame."[12] Wikan also suggests that shame is an "experience-near" concept, whereas honor is "experience-distant." In short, Wikan argues that rather than going by the "illusionary generality and abstraction which the anthropologist's concept of 'honor' and 'shame' provide," one should attempt a substantive characterization of the "ethos" of a cultural area.[13]

Wikan suggests a three-level approach. (1) The larger sets of concepts employed to judge or to express value must be discovered and mapped. (2) Not only the concepts but also their use in interaction and behavior must be studied. For example, do these concepts focus on specific acts or do they define the substance of a person? (3) The society in whose eyes value is sought and judged must be established. Who are the relevant persons in terms of position and gender?

Before attempting to apply this approach to Paul's Letter to the Romans, a cautionary remark is necessary. It was Wikan's fieldwork among women in Cairo and Oman that made her realize that the predominant interest in honor was bound up with male ideology. Not unexpectedly, material from Greco-Roman society is primarily interested in honor as a male value. Thus, honor is intimately related to power and might, that is, the power to assert one's honor in public. Within this context, women are subordinate, with a small public role, and slaves even more so, since they have no autonomy over their own lives.[14]

Who are the significant others in whose eyes value is sought in connection with Paul's Letter to the Romans? The question of the identity of one's significant others is particularly critical if one's group is not well defined, or if one has conflicting loyalties. This seems to be the situation that Paul faces in Romans. In his letter, Paul is concerned about how groups of Christians can establish their identity within Roman society at large and, in particular, vis-à-vis the Jewish synagogue. Paul's mission, breaking the barriers between Jews and non-Jews, created conflicts with the synagogues and brought about the need to forge a separate identity. At the same time the young Christian groups needed to find a way to function within Greco-Roman society, both in their local milieus and in relation to the authorities. Within the context of this search for a new identity, the issue of honor and shame played an important role in relation to Roman society, in relation to the synagogue, and within the Christian groups themselves. In this brief article, some observations will be offered on the first of these aspects—on the role of honor and shame in relation to Greco-Roman society.

That honor and shame play an important role in Romans is partly conveyed by Paul's vocabulary, with words for "honor," "to honor," "to boast" ("to claim honor"), "shame," "to put to shame."[15] These terms are found in all sections of the letter and are thus more evenly distributed than the terminology of justification. It is not only a matter of individual words, however, but also of the general tenor of Paul's argument. His discussion of justification by faith is closely linked to questions of honor. He adds a disclaimer to the Jewish demands for honor made on the basis of their "special status" (2:17–24). He is concerned, however, with the same question of honor: Who is the righteous man? Who are the sons of Abraham and heirs to the promises (4:1–25; 9:6–13)? Who are the people of God, the sons of God (8:14–17; 9:25–29; 11:1–6)? One of his most moving pictures of what it is like to become a Christian is the image of moving from slavery into sonship.[16] And it is not God's *dikaiosynē* that is Paul's main theme in Romans but rather the *power* of God which has been revealed in God's *dikaiosynē* outside the law.[17]

Did Paul share the values of honor and shame that were at large in Roman society? To what extent was the urban society at large the "significant other" in whose eyes approval was sought? Two areas were of great importance in this regard: power structures and sex roles.[18]

In chapter 13, Paul addresses the issue of the Christians and their attitude to the authorities of Greco-Roman society. This chapter has been interpreted in a number of ways in the history of the church. Most prominently, and dangerously, it has been read as Paul's theory of the state.[19] This is not, however, a theoretical, systematic statement of the nature of the state. Rather, it is an excellent description of a society that holds honor as its most prominent value. Thus, Paul gives his advice on how Christians ought to live within the political structures of the Greco-Roman world. A. Strobel has collected convincing evidence to demonstrate that Paul here describes the Greek ideals of the just and honorable man and that the vocabulary he uses is that of Hellenistic administration.[20]

Against this background, it is evident that Paul describes a society based on honor, and many of the connotations of honor in the definition given by Pitt-Rivers are present. First of all, honor is linked to *power*. The frequent occurrence of the term *exousia* (13:1, 2, 3) and other words related to "might" and "power" (*krima*, 13:2; *machaira, orgē*, 13:4) is significant. The terminology that Paul employs here designates representatives of Hellenistic administration, Roman officials or municipal authorities (*exousia*, 13:1; *leitourgos*, 13:6; *archōn*, 13:3). In order to avoid interpreting this chapter within the framework of our own political and bureaucratic system, it is important to notice that Paul does not speak of "institutions" or "systems." Rather, he speaks in terms of personal relationships. Furthermore, the officials he speaks of do not correspond to our notion of civil servants, who perform their duties on behalf of the citizenry and are thus, so to speak, our "servants." Paul speaks of them as the "bearers of power with whom the common man may come in contact" and behind which he sees the regional or central administration.[21]

Paul presupposes a society with a given order, and he demands that individual Christians recognize that order. The society he describes is stratified, and he is clearly addressing the subordinates. The primary thrust of his argument is that they shall be subject (*hypotassesthō*, 13:1, 5; cf. *tetagmenai*, 13:1; *antitassomenos*, 13:2; *diatagē*, 13:2), thus emphasizing the dependent and subordinate position of his addressees. The relationship between the officials and Paul's addressees, therefore, is best understood in terms of a patron-client relationship,[22] that is, a relationship between unequals but with a common bond in the quest for honor. This quest is implied in the admonition to the addressees to accept their role as subjects: "Pay all of them their dues, taxes to whom taxes are due, revenue to whom revenue is due, respect to whom respect is due, honor to whom honor is due" (13:7). The phrase "Pay all . . . their dues [*opheilas*]" was widely used to describe the relations between rulers and subjects, patrons and clients.[23] Likewise, to "give honor [*timēn*]" was the obligation of subjects, who thereby accepted their position.[24] Taxes and dues, beyond their economic importance, had a symbolic significance by granting precedence and honor. In fact, honor was more important than economy.[25] Thus, the economic, ritual, and social aspects came together to form a symbolic and practical reality, a world order.

Equally significant for the upholding of the social order was the praise the subordinate received from the superior: "For rulers are not a terror to good conduct, but to bad. Would you have no fear of him who is in authority? Then do what is good and you will receive his approval [*epainon*]" (13:3). Strobel and van Unnik have convincingly shown that Paul is here speaking in terms well known in Greek society.[26] The "good acts" refer to the ideal of the good man (*anēr kalos kai agathos*) who knew his place and who acted accordingly. The reward for such behavior was praise (*epainos*, a technical term referring to specific forms of recognition granted by rulers to clients, cities, or citizens who had contributed to the common good). This recognition was public and could take the form of letters or inscriptions. To lead a life that was honored and made memorable through such praise was an important goal in the ancient world.[27] Greek as well as early Christian literature testifies that it belonged to the very nature of authority not only to punish the wicked but also to praise the good.[28]

Thus, this was a mutually reinforcing system. Persons who wielded power were accorded respect and honor. In return they distributed praise and approval as favors to obedient subjects. The main characteristic of this stratified society with rulers and subordinates was that this order was kept together by a common quest for honor and praise. Paul does not seem to qualify this. Rather, he emphasizes "civic" virtues by stressing that the power of the authorities comes from God. It is possible that Paul's main goal in this passage was to warn Christian enthusiasts who wanted their Christian freedom to spill over into civic life.[29] Paul makes a strong case that Christians ought to accept the obligations of their society. He recognizes the traditional societal values of "good" and "bad" as well as the mutually reinforcing system of giving honor and receiving praise. Considering that Paul's addressees are "subjects," his references to God can only serve to strengthen his case that Christians should not break with this structure. They should be obedient in order to avoid criticism and to be recognized as good citizens. Paul's exhortation served to strengthen an integration of Christians into the Hellenistic symbolic universe, visualized in inscriptions, memorials, temples, and altars in the cities.

"Shame" is not an issue in this context. There was no possibility that subjects could put the authorities to shame by refusing to give them their due honor: the status difference was too great to pose such a challenge. Thus, the subjects were faced with only one alternative: either praise for the good deed, or punishment for the bad. The lines of authority were clear. This was the public sphere, that is, the men's world, in which the quest for honor and praise reigned.

Paul uses shame language, however, in connection with honor language when he speaks of the fallenness of all creation (1:18–32) and the former life of the Christians (6:12–23). These passages are descriptions of the outside world in contrast to the present position of the Christians, and they serve to set Christians apart from that world. Thus there is a strong contrast between the acceptance of the world of civic obligations in Romans 13 and the total rejection of the life style of the outside world in Romans 1 and 6.

In Romans 1, Paul works with a broad canvas. Society, with its stratifications and various authorities, does not play a part. Honor here is not a civic virtue but is reserved exclusively for God. Paul uses *doxa* (1:23; cf. 1:21) to signify both "honor" and "glory, radiance,"[30] and this is linked to God's power and divinity (1:20). Thus, Paul's perspective in this chapter is humanity in relation to God, and here too there is an order to be observed: it is the duty of humanity to recognize God, to render the honor due to God (1:21).

Humanity, however, refused to grant God this honor. Since a contest for honor can take place only among equals, this refusal did not represent a real challenge. But the challenge was escalated: mere human beings substituted images of self and of animals (1:23) for the glory of God! Moreover, they made claim to be wise; that is, they boasted of a wisdom they did not possess (1:22). This was the ultimate sin: mere humans not only refused to give due honor to God but even claimed this honor for themselves. Such *hybris* not only was typical of human beings vis-à-vis God but also characterized them in their social life, as Paul points out at the end of the chapter.[31]

This challenge God could not let go unaddressed. Refusing to grant humanity this honor which it claimed, God instead put them to shame: "Therefore, God gave them up in the lusts of their hearts to impurity, to the dishonoring [*atimazesthai*] of their bodies among themselves" (1:24). Paul goes on to describe this impurity as "unnatural" use of sexuality. Instead of turning to the opposite sex, men and women turned to their own sex and committed shameless acts (*tēn aschēmosynēn*, 1:27). Paul speaks here of a break with the order of the world that becomes visible in social life.

Paul does not here discuss homosexuality as an ethical issue in our sense of the term when we discuss same-sex relationships. To Paul the issue was much more basic: it was one of sex roles and borders between genders. In most honor-and-shame cultures there is a strong emphasis upon clearly defined sex roles. A blurring of such roles is perceived as a threat.[32] Within Judaism there was a strong emphasis on such distinctions, with heavy sanctions against all forms of deviance.

In a significant departure from the almost complete silence on female homosexuality in antiquity, Paul also speaks of women breaking with sex roles (1:26). It is for men, however, that he reserves his harshest indictment, speaking of their "shameless acts" (1:27). Paul uses a similar argument, based on gender roles, in 1 Cor. 11:2–16. In that passage differences in hairstyles between men and women are seen as integral to their given gender roles.[33] A break with these roles, if only with hairstyles, incurred shame (11:4–5).

In light of Wikan's characterization of shame as an "experience-near concept," it is worth noting that Paul here takes his example from private life, and not from public life as in chapter 13. Apparently, it is within the area of "life style" that Paul wants to establish the distinctive characterizations of a specific Christian identity. It is in this area of common, everyday experience, including the experience of women and slaves, that Paul speaks of shame, as the more "experience-near" concept.

In Romans 13 the authorities were the judges of honor, who granted recognition and praise. The operation of shame in Romans 1 presents a different situation. It is God who gives human beings over to shameful acts, and there is no need for judges to give the verdict. What is shameful is common knowledge that needs no elaboration or supporting argument. Paul is assured of consent by his readers; their experience will confirm his argument. We may say that Paul presupposes that the verdict is rendered by "people's talk,"[34] analogously to the way it is in a modern shame culture such as Egypt. Paul's examples were meant to show the utter depravity of the godless, the total break with God's order for the world, and thus to mark the absolute difference between Christians and their surroundings.

When Paul speaks of the former life of Christians in Romans 6, within the soteriological contrast pattern of "once—but now,"[35] the description of the "once" is very similar to that in 1:23–30: "For just as you once yielded your members to impurity [akatharsiq] and to greater and greater iniquity [anomiq], so now yield your members to righteousness for sanctification [hagiasmon]" (6:19). What were the results of their former life? "You must now be ashamed of it [epaischynesthe]. For death was its result" (6:21). Epaischynomai does not only imply a sentiment, "feeling ashamed," but also implies an objective situation of "being shamed."[36] Shame is here the mark of non-Christian life and of the Christians' former life. Its opposite is not honor but holiness (hagiasmos, 6:19, 22, a word which signifies distinction and separateness from the world). Thus, the warning not to incur shame functions as a border against the outside world. The hyperbolic character of the descriptions in chapters 1 and 6 suggests that the symbolic importance was more important than the practical warnings.

Why did Paul single out as examples breaks with God's order for the world in the area of sex roles and sexual behavior? His accusations are polemical and do not give a correct description of the Hellenistic world. Moreover, his recommendations for a Christian life style were not exclusively or even originally Christian. Rather, both Jewish and Hellenistic teachers would concur with Paul. Thus, Wayne Meeks remarks, "On the whole, though, the sexual purity for which Pauline Christians strive in an impure world is defined mostly in terms of values that are widely affirmed by the larger society."[37] That is, even in this area, Paul could have chosen a similar path to that in Romans 13 and urged his readers to follow what was regarded as good and honorable in society at large.

That Paul did not do so can only partially be explained by the situation in his communities or by his own social position. His accusations are stock language, a topos frequently used in writings of the Jewish Diaspora.[38] These writings also emphasize the distinctiveness of the Jewish people over against other nations, on the ground that they did not practice incest and homosexual acts. Thus, it is the distinctiveness of the Christians that is the real goal of Paul's argument.

Therefore, the focal point of his argument in chapter 6 is the way he contrasts former "shame" with present "holiness." In a passage on marriage in 1 Thess. 4:3–8, with a vocabulary similar to that of Rom. 1:24–26 and Rom. 6:19–21, this emphasis on holiness is even stronger. Here the holiness of the Christians is explicitly contrasted with the lust of the Gentiles "who do not know God."[39] Similarly, in Rom. 12:1–2 the parenesis to present themselves as a holy sacrifice is combined with a warning not to be like "this world." That the Christians are to be holy is a recurrent theme in Romans (1:7; 8:27; 12:13) as well as in Paul's other letters.

This emphasis on holiness served an important need: it helped create a separate universe for the Christians which distinguished them from others. The area in which Paul chose to do that was the area of sex roles and sexual behavior. It was here that the "holy" was contrasted with the "shameful." That Paul follows a tradition from the Jewish Diaspora still does not quite explain why he chose to use this topos, why it was sexual behavior he branded as shameful and impure. This was not the only option for a preacher attempting to establish a separate identity for Christians in the Hellenistic world. One generation later, Luke emphasized the break with God's order for the world in the social and economic sphere but paid scant attention to sexual matters.

That Paul accepts the system of honor operating in the public arena of Hellenistic society but rejects this society as shameful in the area of sex roles and sexual life may reflect the position of Christians as an "outside group." Thus, in Paul's usage, "honor" is related to the more distant area of power in society, "shame" to the nearer one of gender roles and sexual relations. Paul's "urban Christians" had to live within the given power structures and to conform to the civic virtues of honor and praise. Paul called the Christians to live honorable lives by these standards. Thus, the concept of honor was related to the public world.

The private world concerned with relationships between the sexes, on the other hand, was the shame area. Sexuality and sex roles were close to home; they represented an area the Christians themselves could influence and control, whereas the public world was outside their control. This had significant implications for the symbolic universe they created. It was God's universe, and the Christians were heirs to the world. Thus, they were expecting honor and a share in the glory of God (Rom. 8:18–39). But there was a big gap between that expectation and their actual situation as a small minority group. When they wanted to speak of their separate identity, they could not apply any of the larger structures of society to themselves. They were thrown back to their private lives. There, issues that might not loom large in society could receive special emphasis in the minority group.

In this area of life they could distance themselves from their neighbors. True to facts or not, they characterized the nonbelieving world and their own past as shameful, full of sexual deviance and gender blurring. In this context, the opposite of shameful was not honorable but "holy." This concept expressed not the commonality but the separateness of Christian life; it was used of the group, not of society at large. It was this private area of life that was the specifically Christian domain. To Paul, to uphold a traditional role pattern was not part of civic honor but a distinctive mark of Christian holiness.

Both Romans 13 and 1 are important to understand the position of the first Christians within Greco-Roman society. Both passages served basic needs for communities in the process of forging a distinctive identity. There was a need for acceptance and integration in society at large as well as for border making. To see how Paul attempted to meet both needs, Wikan's suggestion that honor and shame were not always binary concepts but might be related to different areas of life proved helpful.

Still, this is only one aspect of Paul's use of these concepts in Romans. A study of their use in Paul's polemics with the Jews and in his regulations of the Christian community will show other aspects.[40] In many passages dealing with these issues, "shame" and "to be ashamed" take on a different meaning from the meaning they have in Romans 1 and 6, and function in tandem with honor. The main asset of this honor-and-shame perspective on Romans is that it gives a unified perspective to the letter. It gives a model for the interaction between human beings, as well as between God and humanity. Here only a few general remarks can be offered.

Since God is the ultimate source of honor, God is the "significant other" who can grant or withhold honor and praise. Thus, human beings cannot make claim to honor, cannot boast of their prerogatives. This understanding of honor as accorded by God provides a background against which to read Paul's teaching of righteousness, that is, of being in an honorable situation, as granted by God. Furthermore, it is against the model of a society based on a quest for honor that the focus of Paul's vision of the Christian community becomes clear. Within the group, he urges a break with the competition for honor. Across differences in status, tasks, and power, everybody shall receive equal honor (12:1-12).

Finally, Paul's discussion of the suffering that Christians experienced must be understood in an honor-and-shame context. In a context of competition for honor, rejection of a claim to honor implied shame. Believing that they were "sons of God," Christians considered themselves to be in an honored position (8:14-17). This honor was invisible to others, however, and it was contradicted by their sufferings, which inflicted shame upon them in the eyes of outsiders. Their claim to a position of honor that was visible for all to see could only be confirmed by God at his judgment of the world (8:18-30). Thus, Paul considers it the ultimate promise to the Christians that they shall not be put to shame in front of their adversaries (9:33; 10:11). And it was his trust in the power of God to fulfill this promise that made Paul proclaim that he was not ashamed of the gospel. Thus, his social condition of being without fear of shame was determined by his faith in the power of God.

NOTES

1. See C. K. Barrett, "I Am Not Ashamed of the Gospel," in *Foi et salut selon S. Paul,* colloquium proceedings, Analecta biblica 42 (Rome, 1970), 19–50.

2. Ibid., 20.

3. J. Pitt-Rivers, *The People of the Sierra* (London: Weidenfeld & Nicolson, 1954); idem, "Honor," in *Encyclopedia of the Social Sciences,* 2d ed. (New York: Macmillan Co., 1968), 503–11. See the representative collection of essays, *Honour and Shame: The Values of Mediterranean Society,* ed. J. D. Peristiany (London: Weidenfeld & Nicolson, 1965).

4. For the continuation of patron-client relationships with their emphasis on honor, see S. N. Eisenstadt and L. Roniger, *Patrons, Clients, and Friends* (Cambridge: Cambridge Univ. Press, 1984), 50–52.

5. Moses Finley, *The World of Odysseus* (London: Penguin Books, 1962).

6. A. W. Adkins, *Merit and Responsibility: A Study in Greek Values* (Oxford: Oxford Univ. Press, 1960).

7. H. Oppermann, ed., *Römische Wertbegriffe* (Darmstadt: Wissenschaftliche Buchgesellschaft, 1983), esp. U. Knoche, "Der römische Ruhmesgedanke," 420–45 (reprinted from *Philologus* 89 [1934]: 102–24).

8. The article "Shame" in *Interpreter's Dictionary of the Bible* 4:305–6 has no bibliography; "Honor" in *IDB* 2:639–40 lists only two books, the most recent from 1926! Even in a recent Old Testament study of "shame" (M. A. Klofenstein, *Scham und Schande nach dem Alten Testament,* Abhandlungen zur Theologie des Alten und Neuen Testaments 62 [Zurich, 1972]), awareness of the social context is absent.

9. Bruce J. Malina, *The New Testament World: Insights from Cultural Anthropology* (Atlanta: John Knox Press, 1981), 25–50.

10. Pitt-Rivers, "Honor," 503–4.

11. Unni Wikan, "Shame and Honour: A Contestable Pair," *Man* 19 (1984): 635–52.

12. Ibid., 638.

13. Ibid., 648.

14. O. Patterson, *Slavery and Social Death* (Cambridge: Harvard Univ. Press, 1982), 86–92.

15. *timē:* 2:7, 10; 9:21; 12:10; 13:7. *doxa:* 1:23; 2:7, 10; 3:7, 23; 4:20; 5:2; 6:4; 8:18, 21; 9:4, 23; 11:36; 15:7; 16:27. *doxazō:* 1:21; 8:30; 11:30; 15:6, 9. *epainos:* 2:29; 13:3. *epaineō:* 15:11. *kauchēma:* 4:2. *kauchēsis:* 3:27; 15:17. *kauchaomai:* 2:17, 23; 5:2, 3, 11. *aschēmosynē:* 1:27. *atimia:* 1:26; 9:21. *atimazō:* 1:24; 2:23. *epaischynomai:* 1:16; 6:21. *kataischynō:* 5:5; 9:33; 10:11.

16. Rom. 8:15–17. But Paul can also describe the Christian situation by means of slavery imagery, as a transition from a bad master to a good master (6:12–23).

17. Rom. 1:17; 4:21; 11:23. Cf. N. A. Dahl, *Studies in Paul* (Minneapolis: Augsburg Pub. House, 1977), 78.

18. Malina (*New Testament World*, 26–27) points out how honor in the Mediterranean world is located at the intersection of power, sex roles, and religion.

19. See E. Käsemann, "Grundsätzliches zur Interpretation von Römer 13," *Exegetische Versuche und Besinnungen 2* (Göttingen: Vandenhoeck & Ruprecht, 1964), 204–22.

20. A. Strobel, "Zum Verständnis von Röm 13," *Zeitschrift für die neutestamentliche Wissenschaft* 47 (1956): 67–93; idem, "Furcht, wem Furcht gebührt: Zum profangriechischen Hintergrund von Röm 13:7," ibid. 55 (1964): 58–62. See also W. C. van Unnik, "Lob und Strafe durch die Obrigkeit: Hellenistisches zu Röm 13,3–4," in *Jesus und Paulus*, Festschrift W. G. Kümmel, ed. E. E. Ellis et al. (Göttingen: Vandenhoeck & Ruprecht, 1975), 334–43.

21. E. Käsemann, *Commentary on Romans* (Grand Rapids: Wm. B. Eerdmans, 1980), 354.

22. Eisenstadt and Roniger, *Patrons, Clients, and Friends*, 43–50.

23. Strobel, "Zum Verständnis," 88.

24. Ibid., 84.

25. See the excellent discussion of the relation between the ritual and the practical aspects of the Roman administration which is in S. R. F. Price's *Rituals and Power: The Roman Imperial Cult in Asia Minor* (Cambridge: Cambridge Univ. Press, 1984), esp. 239–48.

26. Strobel, "Zum Verständnis," esp. 82–85; and van Unnik, "Lob," 334–43.

27. H. Preisker, "epainos," in *Theological Dictionary of the New Testament* 2:586.

28. Van Unnik, "Lob," 336–43. Cf. 1 Pet. 2:14, of the ruler; and Paul of himself, 1 Cor. 11:2, 17, 22.

29. Käsemann, *Commentary*, 357.

30. Ibid., 45.

31. Rom. 1:30: *hybristas, hyperēfanous, alazonas;* see C. Forbes, "Comparison, Self-Praise, and Irony: Paul's Boasting and the Conventions of Hellenistic Rhetoric," *New Testament Studies* 32 (1986): 1–30, esp. 13.

32. Malina, *New Testament World*, 42–44.

33. J. Murphy-O'Connor, "Sex and Logic in 1 Corinthians 11:2–16," *Catholic Biblical Quarterly* 42 (1980): 482–500.

34. Wikan, "Shame and Honour," 636.

35. N. A. Dahl, "Form-Critical Observations on Early Christian Preaching," in *Jesus in the Memory of the Early Church* (Minneapolis: Augsburg Pub. House, 1976), 33–34.

36. Käsemann, *Commentary*, 185.

37. Wayne Meeks, *The First Urban Christians* (New Haven: Yale Univ. Press, 1983), 101.

38. See O. Larry Yarbrough, *Not Like the Gentiles: Marriage Rules in the Letters of Paul*, Dissertation Series (Atlanta: Scholars Press, 1985), 7–29.

39. In 1 Thess. 4:4, however, *hagiasmos* and *timē* are combined. For the text as a whole, see Yarbrough, *Not Like the Gentiles*, 65–87.

40. H. Moxnes, "Paulus og den norske värematen: 'Skam' og 'äre' i Romerbrevet," *Norsk teologisk tidsskrift* 86 (1985): 129–40.

14

Some Unorthodox Thoughts on the "Household-Code Form"

L. HARTMAN
University of Uppsala

When professors of New Testament exegesis teach their students about form criticism and approach New Testament texts outside the Gospels, they discuss confessions, hymns, catalogues of vices and virtues, and the like. If they should be so fortunate as to use Howard Clark Kee's collection *The Origins of Christianity,* they would refer to the lists on pp. 232ff. (Diogenes Laertius, Zeno). Among the parenetic lists, one normally also cites the so-called household codes. Depending on the religious stands of the teachers and on the character of the institutions at which they teach, they may or may not wrestle with questions of the lists' application today, and in such a context would refer to the handbooks that tell that the codes in question are taken over from or inspired by some non-Christian milieus or other.

To the early form critics the sociological perspective of the texts and the implications of this were natural. Such features still play a decisive role when scholars today grapple with the household codes. One sees some relationships between their literary form and certain literary forms to be found in antiquity, and this leads to assumptions concerning the thinking, the life, and the development of the early church.

In this study a little closer look will be taken into the form-critical aspects of the New Testament household codes, concentrating on the oldest one, namely, Col. 3:18—4:1. I will conclude with some pessimism as to the strength of some of the positions in this case which are allegedly based on form criticism. Perhaps they are not sufficiently critical.

It will be necessary to begin with a brief report of some features in the previous scholarly discussion concerning these household codes, paying particular attention to the form-critical assessments and the terminology used in this connection. Then I will apply to Col. 3:18—4:1 some analytical tools provided by scholars in text linguistics who have dealt with problems of genres and forms. This will be done in a rather unsophisticated way, but I hope the analysis will suffice to explain the pessimism I just mentioned.

First of all, some features of the scholarly debate concerning the household codes.[1] One of the fathers of form criticism, Martin Dibelius, devoted a few pages in his commentary on Colossians, Ephesians, and Philemon (1st ed., 1913)[2] to dealing with the *Haustafeln*. He suggested that the early church had taken over a "schema" that was originally Stoic. This meant that one organized one's discussion of ethical rules according to a certain pattern. Such rules concerned what was fitting (*kathēkon*) "towards the gods, one's parents, brothers, country, and towards foreigners." The quotation is from Epictetus (2.17.31) and is the example Dibelius takes as a point of departure. The Christians took over this scheme, possibly via "Hellenistic Judaism,"[3] and the *anēken* of Col. 3:18 was understood as a variant of the Stoic *kathēkon*. The adoption meant that "the early church had started to try to come to grips with the world" and to forget about the imminent end.

Karl Weidinger followed up Dibelius's thesis.[4] He reaffirmed the opinion that the household-code schema had its origin in Stoic-Cynic philosophy. It was used also in Hellenistic Judaism. Colossians 3:18—4:1 not only represented the schema taken over, but also the text itself had been borrowed after having been only slightly revised: one had, for example, added the phrase "in the Lord" to the rule "you wives, be submissive to your husbands, as it is fitting."

Some forty-five years after Weidinger, J. E. Crouch published a study of the Colossian household code.[5] Like Dibelius and Weidinger, he believed that its origin was Hellenistic, but he stressed the influence of Hellenistic Judaism and pointed to a formal feature that Jewish material shared with the New Testament *Haustafeln*, that of reciprocity: people were summoned to fulfill their duties toward one another, wives toward husband and vice versa, children toward parents, etc.[6] Crouch also claimed that Weidinger had been careless in his assessment of the tradition history of the schema: there were differences between "typically Stoic codes and many of the Hellenistic Jewish codes" (p. 23). He had also, according to Crouch, failed "to note the significance of the variations among the Christian *Haustafeln* themselves" (ibid.).

In his article in the *Interpreter's Dictionary of the Bible* supplement of 1976, David Schroeder apparently tried to harmonize several of the opinions advanced, including those which assumed a Christian origin of the code.[7] He noted that "formally" the codes were indebted to Old Testament apodictic law (address, imperative, motivation) but that "stating the ethic in terms of stations in life is typically Hellenistic, especially Stoic." "The content is drawn basically from the Old Testament, Judaic tradition, although with the addition of certain Greek (what is fitting) and Christian (*agape*) concepts." Furthermore, the "Judaic tradition" represents formal differences from the Stoic lists in two respects: First, "Hellenistic Judaism," especially Philo, mentions the groups in the same order as do the household codes of Colossians and Ephesians—wives, children, slaves. Second, the duties are presented in pairs—wives and husbands, children and parents, slaves and husbands.[8]

After some preliminary moves, new suggestions were advanced around 1980 concerning the issue of the relevant background material behind the household codes in terms of both their "form" and their content. It seems that the men behind them had worked independently, but they all pointed to the *oikonomia* tradition, that is, that of philosophical discussions of how one should manage one's "house." Texts from this tradition appeared to be closer to the household codes than the Stoic-Cynic duty lists.[9] As a matter of fact, some of the passages that had been quoted as examples of the Stoic-Cynic schema belonged to this very tradition, which was represented by texts from Plato and Aristotle and down through the first centuries C.E. The house was, of course, the kernel of society, largely independent, and of fundamental importance to the life of the members of the household and to the community as a whole.

When Klaus Berger in 1984[10] discussed the origin of the household-code form, he combined the two suggestions of the past: certainly the *oikonomia Gattung* must be taken into account when one wants to explain the *Gattung Haustafel*, but the connection with behavior toward the state and the catalogue form are, he wrote, a remaining heritage from the Stoic catalogues (p. 1081). In addition, he claims, one should not underestimate the influence that the popular gnomic traditions have had on the form (*Gestalt*) of the New Testament household codes (p. 1085).

The scholars who follow the *oikonomia* track have drawn different conclusions from this for the sociolinguistic function of the household codes. Thus, D. Lührmann advanced the thought that this new comparative material indicated that the early church made a latent (not more, though) claim that the Christian house was a model for larger circles of the society (p. 86). D. L. Balch and K. Müller suggest that when the church promoted the morality of the household codes against this sort of background, this meant that it chose a middle course, turning down certain more extreme, "liberal" tendencies.[11]

So much for a review of some features of the scholarly discussion of the household codes. Terms like "schema," "form," "formulas," "typical codes" recur in it. In the latest contribution to the topic that I have come across, one by Karlheinz Müller, a similar swarm of terms clouds the discussion;

thus we hear of "die traditionsgeschichtliche Zuordnung der Haustafeln . . . zum antiken Schrifttum 'Uber die Ökonomie,'" which is commented upon in a footnote as being a *Gattungsbestimmung* (p. 285); in that literature, we are told, there is also to be found "ein Dreier bzw. Zweierschema" and certain *Leitmotive* (pp. 285–86). We also learn that knowledge of the *Literaturgattung peri oikōn*, etc., liberates the modern exegete from the old feeling of moral obligation to defend the Christian character of Col. 3:18— 4:1, a *Literaturgattung* that is also referred to as the "zeitgenössische Textsorte zur Ökonomie" (p. 290).

Thus, in the literature on the household codes one finds a considerable number of analytical terms and classifications that, furthermore, play a role both when the same authors assess features of the history of the early church and its ways of thinking and when they approach the hermeneutics of the household codes.

This means, however, that they are posing the sort of questions to these texts that scholars of linguistics and of literature have treated with considerable refinement. Even to somebody who, like the present writer, has only a shallow acquaintance with these areas, it seems desirable that one try to take advantage of such studies in order to be as fair as possible to the object of our research.[12] I will dare to make a first move, and if there is anything worthwhile in my deliberations, others who are more competent may correct or refine my tentative results.

For my purpose, I will apply the approach of Egon Werlich in his *Typologie der Texte*.[13] I will, however, make more explicit the semiotic differentiation between the syntactic, the semantic, and the pragmatic aspects. (The terms will be explained in due course.)

Let me begin with a short description of Werlich's analytical system. After distinguishing the fictional group of texts (*Textgruppe*) from the nonfictional one, he identifies five text types (*Texttypen*), namely, description, narration, exposition, argumentation, and instruction. Speaking of text types means moving on a rather high level of abstraction. Werlich defines them as "ideally typical norms for text structuring, available to the adult speaker as cognitively determined matrices of text-forming elements in linguistic communication concerning things and circumstances."[14]

On a lower level of abstraction we encounter text forms (*Textformen*),[15] defined as "realizations of groups of text constituents, which speakers choose when producing texts according to text-typical invariants on the one hand, and comformably to certain conventions for textual utterances ensuing from history on the other."[16]

As examples of constituents that may be characteristic of a text form, Werlich mentions particular points of view (*Sprecherperspektive*): Is a text personal or impersonal, subjectively or objectively presented? Are present or past tenses used? Other constituents include idiom, style, kind of communication (dialogue, letter, etc.).

A text form can be represented in text-form variants (*Textformvarianten*, pp. 70ff.). Thus, for example, the subjective text form of narrative can cover such text-form variants as anecdote, children's story, and detective novel, all representing different conventions.

Within text-form variants one can use different compositional patterns (*Kompositionsmuster*, pp. 73ff.), which may be established by literary tradition (e.g., the haiku or the tanka) or by a particular social-rule system (e.g., an abstract, a bibliography, a doctoral thesis). Already the examples just mentioned indicate that one can go on and subdivide the compositional patterns into variants of them (pp. 76–77).

Let us now try to apply this classification to the household code of Colossians and, in so doing, approach the task from the syntactic, semantic, and pragmatic angles.

To consider texts as well as text types[17] in their *syntactic* dimension means assessing the texts and text types from a literal point of view. It means taking into account the ways in which their signs (words, phrases, clauses, etc.) are related to one another. The *semantic* dimension has to do with the same signs, and their relationships, as related to that which they designate (the contents, to use a less technical term). The *pragmatic* dimension regards the signs and the contents of the texts in relation to the receiver and the receiver's situation, not least as in some sense shared by the sender and, quite often, as the object of the sender's aims, argument, etc.

There is no doubt that our text[18] belongs to the text type of instruction. According to Werlich, instruction is characterized by an enumerative construction, and, seen from a syntactic angle, the Colossians passage follows that rule. The text types have different typical "textual bases," that is, real or reconstructed headlines or text openings, out of which the following text is developed. The typically instructive textual basis is a verb in the imperative that forms a predicate to be performed by a subject person.[19] Also in this respect Col. 3:18—4:1 presents itself as belonging to the instructive text type, since a reconstructed textual basis could be "Behave in a Christian way in the house."

Regarding our text from the semantic perspective, we can easily see that it displays contents that list certain required attitudes. Thus, also from the semantic perspective, the text qualifies as an exponent of the instructive text type.

With regard to the pragmatic dimension, a discussion on this level of abstraction asks for *typical* communicative external functions of a text type.

It is to be expected that texts of the instructive type address human beings in some sort of social situation in order that certain moral and practical goals be achieved. With Col. 3:18—4:1 this is certainly true.

Already on this very high level of abstraction we may ask ourselves what happens if we try to pour the parallel material that one normally adduces into these very wide molds, those of the text types. I dare to try to answer the question by testing a single but frequently adduced text, namely, the Stoic Hierocles' fragments of the second century C.E., which were of primary importance for Weidinger's investigation. As far as I can see, they represent the expository text type. This also holds true of the sanctions on household management and marriage. It is characteristic of texts belonging to this text type that statements are related to one another by adverbs such as "namely, for example, in other words" or "similarly, also, not . . . either."[20] Their textual basis is a subject (a nominal phrase) followed by a form of "be" or "have" in the present tense as a predicate, and a complement (a nominal phrase). Thus a passage of Hierocles' treatment of marriage is introduced in such a way that the textual basis can be expressed in this way: "Married life is something beautiful" (*Stob.* 4.22.24, 4.505, 5–22 Hense).

As "expositions," texts of this type can have contents (we are using the semantic perspective now) that may be anything that can be explained or that one thinks should be explained. When seen under a pragmatic aspect, Hierocles' treatises may be said to communicate certain concepts of the sender, which are formed through observations in space and time.[21]

Now for the text form, beginning from a syntactic point of view. Our Colossians passage has a personal perspective that is visible in the second-person address and in the letter context. Accordingly, its text form is more a set of directions than a series of statutory rules. A text form is often also characterized by a certain idiom. The instructive text idiom can be seen as an application of the textual basis, and accordingly it takes the form of a series of imperatives. The communication is, of course, written—although the written message is to be read out and listened to, the letter replacing the sender—and it takes the form of a monologue.

In a way I have already intimated the semantic and pragmatic dimensions of this text form: it contains directions presented in a personal manner by an authority, and they should be respected by all the receivers.

What about the text form of Hierocles' fragments dealing with household management and marriage? Its exposition is personal, but it has a mixture of subjective and objective presentation and it is held in the present tense. Its text idiom is colored by the expository textual basis we reconstructed above. The communication is a monologue but receives a seemingly dia-logical flavor through rhetorical questions that belong to the conventions of the philosophical treatise of those days. In terms of semantics and pragmatics there is not much to add: the contents exposed should be accepted by the audience.

Continuing down the abstraction staircase we arrive at the text-form variants. I suggest that Col. 3:18—4:1, having the text form of a "set of directions" with the characteristics mentioned above, represents a text-form variant of "set of directions concerning ethical conduct." The contents, then, concern ethics and, pragmatically seen, the ethics of the addressees in their present situation.

Hierocles' fragments can be referred to the text-form variant of the expository philosophical treatise. The presentation of such texts had to do with several aspects of human life, often ethics. They addressed those people who could attend the lectures of the philosophers, and should as treatises presumably be held apart from the speeches of the popular philosophers in the street. The latter can hardly be regarded as equal to treatises, even though the contents may have been partly similar in the two cases.

The next step leads to the *compositional patterns*. Syntactically seen, Col. 3:18—4:1 is structured according to the diverse stations in life. We may immediately proceed to state that this compositional pattern appears in a variant because of a social convention of the epoch, the "house" pattern (cf. Werlich's *Epochenvariante des Kompositionsmusters*, 76). Not surprisingly, this sort of compositional pattern is concomitant with that which one finds when regarding the text's semantic dimension, namely, the way of thinking of the house and its structure of authority and responsibilities. This thought pattern is the "schema" that has played such an important and puzzling role in the form-critical assessments of the household codes from Dibelius on. We should be aware of the fact that it existed independently of household codes and, for that matter, also independently of texts of any sort, because it presented a social structure. As such, it would appear to be as natural as biologically conditioned thought structures, such as those in which one combines hunger and thirst, or eyes, ears, nose, and mouth, or such human behaviors as sitting, standing, walking, and lying down (e.g., Ps. 139:2–3). In the case of the house pattern, this is also a role pattern of the type that children learn not only by being part of it but also by reenacting it in their play.[22]

Within this semantic structure an instructive text, having the characteristics we have noted when descending the abstraction steps, gives directions on the ethical conduct of the people of the house. It is also natural that the contents of these rules are structured according to the relevant persons' relationships as defined by the social system inherent in the thought pattern.

It is not totally impossible that the code existed in a literary convention before Col. 3:18—4:1. In that case we can safely state that, as to the pragmatic dimension, the function of the compositional pattern in its household-code variant was to instruct people to relate in a moral way to the common social system of the time. If, on the other hand, the first household code to appear was that of Col. 3:18—4:1, we can assume with some certainty that it introduced a convention of a pragmatic dimension like the one just sketched.

If we ask for the compositional pattern of Hierocles' treatises on *oiko-nomia* and marriage, it seems that the former was structured according to the duties to be performed by husband and wife. In the marriage treatise it is not surprising to find traces of the schema in summarizing statements like this one: "We have summarily shown how we ought to conduct ourselves towards our kindred, having before taught how we should act towards ourselves, our parents, and brothers, and, besides these, towards our wife and children" (*Stob.* 4.27.23, 4.672, 11.14 Hense; from Balch, *Let Wives be Submissive,* 4). But it is hardly correct to say that the schema has a syntactically structuring function in the same way it had in the case of Col. 3:18—4:1. The pattern can work on several levels: on the one hand, in the case of the philosophical treatise, it organizes the chapters in a certain order; on the other, in the household code, there is not only a short set of instructions structured according to it but the instructions also directly address people who represent the different roles in the pattern.

In terms of semantics and pragmatics, it seems that Hierocles' treatises present conventional teaching on social behavior with the expected effect that a mildly Stoic view on the established society be adopted and carried out.

Above, I expressed a hint of doubt as to whether we could assume that before Col. 3:18—4:1 there had existed an instructive text form with a variant following a subdivision of a compositional pattern, namely, the "household code." In other words, did the literary convention "household code" exist? So far nothing of the sort is known—only thought patterns that reappear in different text types, text forms, text-form variants, etc.

On the other hand—and this observation also belongs to the syntactic aspect—Col. 3:18—4:1 has a style of its own as compared with the surrounding text: the sentences are built in a more straightforward manner than not only the argumentative parts of the letter but also the preceding parenetic section. But even if Col. 3:18—4:1 is a text that, more or less in its present shape, existed before the writing of Colossians, this does not indicate per se that it represented a literary convention, namely, that of the household code. In other words, to pursue the discussion to one or two further levels of abstraction becomes a rather hypothetical undertaking. Instead, I now wish to take the step down to the level of our text itself, from *langue* to *parole,* to use the famous distinction of Saussure. First, we note that it represents some particular features as seen in its syntactic dimension, namely, the composition according to pairs and reciprocity. As mentioned above, Crouch argued that this had counterparts in Jewish but not in Stoic-Cynic material. Balch, however, pointed to the fact that household-man-agement tradition from Plato and Aristotle through Dionysius of Hali-carnassus reflected it.[23] Another syntactic particularity is the construction of the individual directions: address, imperative, plus motivation. These compositional structures, of course, also exist outside Col. 3:18—4:1. Thus, the last-mentioned construction is that of Jewish apodictic law and of certain sayings in the wisdom tradition: for example, "You children, listen to me, your father, and act in this way in order that you may be saved" (Sir. 3:1).[24]

Turning to the semantic dimension of Col. 3:18—4:1, we need not worry too much about it. The author remains within the framework of the estab-lished social system, although placed under a certain modification through the "in the Lord" theme struck previously in 3:17 and returned to in the repeated references to "the Lord" in 3:18—4:1. This should not conceal the fact that it is possible to find counterparts for the individual directions in other texts in antiquity, both Stoic-Cynic and Jewish. The structure of reciprocity is not least a structure of contents: the duties are mutual.

The pragmatic aspect of Col. 3:18—4:1 need not occupy us very much either, since our task is not an exegesis of a text. When one assesses this task, however, one should primarily take into account the context, that is, both the literary one, the letter, and the situational one, which can be imagined behind and around the text. The fact that the passage on the slaves is longer and more detailed has to be accounted for in such an assessment. But one should not discuss the pair structures or the "apodictic law" construction of the directions only as though they were the result of a *Formzwang*—as if the author just slipped into that way of expressing himself because there was a literary setup of conventions that drove him to it. It seems to me that my discussion above and the comparative material brought forward in the scholarly debate indicate that there were no such conventions in terms of the reciprocity and the address-imperative-moti-vation structures; or more precisely, those syntactic features existed but not as characteristics of a text-form variant following a particular compositional pattern similar to that of a household code. Rather, they can be taken as apt for the situation: the duties *were* regarded as mutual, in the Lord; the subordinates, wives, children, and slaves were regarded as worthy of being directly addressed and having a moral responsibility, although, of course, one in submission.

The stylistic properties of Col. 3:18—4:1 which I touched upon above can suggest that even if there was no wider convention, there were traditions. The parenetic context and its rather close relationships to the preceding argument on the Christian status of the addressees can indicate that the code represents traditional instruction of the Christian community, possibly baptismal instruction (but only possibly).[25] This would, then, mean that one regards the pragmatics of Col. 3:18—4:1 from a diachronic point of view.

The considerations above are a rough sketch. In addition, they are mostly made on a synchronic basis. But as we saw in the beginning, most scholars who have discussed the household codes have done so diachronically, explaining the *Gattung,* form, schema, etc. of the different codes as the result of taking over, inheriting, being influenced, etc., from particular literary or cultural circles. Furthermore, those suggestions have led to conclusions of what the adaptation of the form, schema, etc., had to say about the social, religious, or theological situation of the Christian circle in which the form, schema, etc., were taken up.

It seems to me, however, that applying Werlich's analytical model to our material can open our eyes a little to what exegetes have been doing when they have compared the household codes with other literature and drawn conclusions in terms of dependence and interpretation. (I am persuaded that any linguistic analysis dealing with the genre problems would give a similar result; Werlich is not *the* linguist to me.)

The characteristics of a given text can be said to belong to it on different levels of classification. That, for example, an apocalypse normally belongs to the text type of narration is something it shares with a detective story. Both can also be said to represent the story text form, as distinguished from that of a report, but after that they separate. Furthermore, the differentiation between the three semiotic dimensions should receive careful attention. On the one hand, certain syntactic, semantic, or pragmatic characteristics may belong to a piece of text or to a text-form variant, etc.; on the other, those properties may be found in other texts or text-form variants, etc., that are quite different from the first one. In the Book of Susanna, for instance, Daniel demonstrates the innocence of the beautiful and virtuous Susanna in that he examines the two elders and makes them contradict each other. This example of cunning examination has made some people label the book the first detective story. Of course, this is wrong; the similarity consists of the semantic detail of the intelligent examiner who ensnares the guilty person so as to solve the mystery. But this detail has different functions in the Book of Susanna from those in Dorothy Sayers's *Gaudy Night.* There is a difference both in terms of the function of the motif within the plot and in terms of its role within the different sociolinguistic functions of the stories,[26] that is, the stories regarded from the pragmatic aspect. The first one is admonishing in some way or other,[27] whereas the other is meant to function as entertainment.

With these observations in mind we turn to Col. 3:18—4:1 again. Thus, the Stoic *kathēkon* lists do not actually belong to the instructive text type but summarize or structure the contents of ethical treatises, which can best be referred to in the expository text type. Furthermore, the examples adduced often list on an abstraction level not what is "fitting" but the relationships for which the contents of the treatise discuss what is "fitting" for the loyal citizen. The pragmatic aspect is, thus, different from the one we can surmise behind Col. 3:18—4:1. Regarded from the syntactic aspect there is a certain similarity between the Stoic lists and Col. 3:18—4:1 in that both have an enumerative style. Epictetus (2.17, 31) says he is dealing with "what is fitting towards the gods, one's parents, one's brothers, one's country, and towards foreigners." Enumeration is a widespread phenomenon, however, to be found both in shopping lists and in menus. As the shopping list and the menu are closer to each other than the shopping list and an inventory list of a laboratory—both list food!—so are the Epictetus quotation and Col. 3:18—4:1, because both deal with social duties. Note, however, that here we are moving into the area of the semantic aspect. I have already noted that the schema that has played such a role in the scholarly treatment of the household codes is a semantic structure that is not bound to any particular text form or text-form variant, etc. The same thing holds true of the syntactic and semantic characterizations which come into view when one focuses on the "pairs" and on the "apodictic law."

In sum, I think it would be wise to take as wide a perspective as possible when posing form-critical questions to the household codes, to pay attention to the level of abstraction on which one moves, and to remember that it may be fatal not to take all three of the semiotic dimensions into account.

What I have said so far must not be understood as intimating any desire on my part to deny that the early church was influenced by its contemporary world. Nor am I out to defend New Testament authors against the suspicion of being too indulgent to contemporary social conventions. I do, however, suggest that we cease confusing a socially given thought pattern with conventionally established literary forms, and furthermore, that we cease drawing hasty conclusions in terms of implied content and situation from literary form or literary shape (the former being supraindividual, the latter the formal characteristics of a given text). In brief, the Christians behind the household codes were certainly influenced by their social environment in the normal human way. This influence is also seen in the household codes, but not so much in the fact that they should represent a particular literary convention—a form or *Gattung*—as in their contents. What matters is more *what* is said than *how* it is said because the how in this

L. HARTMAN

case is not so well established as a communicative convention that it can be of any real help when assessing the what. (Cf., e.g., the literary convention of the minutes, which already as such indicates that a text that is shaped according to these conventions has normally sprung from a particular kind of situation.)

Thus, even if Col. 3:18—4:1 is taken into the letter from elsewhere, the material that should enable us to conjecture the existence of the literary form "household code" is very fragile, and when it comes to drawing conclusions about the history and thinking of the early church from this presumed literary form, the case must be even more fragile. The other Christian passages that are usually labeled household codes hardly corroborate the assumptions. *If* Col. 3:18—4:1 could be regarded as bringing a literary form to birth in the church—that of the household code—one would immediately have to conclude that in such a case this form disintegrated very quickly, so quickly, indeed, that one should be reticent in drawing any conclusions from the literary form as such, when appearing in later texts.

Thus, it is my unorthodox contention that New Testament scholars should approach the form-critical problem of the early Christian household codes by applying sharper tools and a stricter analysis. I doubt the validity of the conclusions about early Christian life and thinking which they have drawn from their alleged form-critical analyses. I may be something of a heretic, but is it not true that several heretics have drawn attention to things that have been forgotten or fallen into misuse in orthodox circles?

NOTES

1. These discussions are summarized in J. E. Crouch's *The Origin and Intention of the Colossian Haustafel*, Forschungen zur Religion und Literatur des Alten und Neuen Testaments 109 (Göttingen: Vandenhoeck & Ruprecht, 1972), 13–36; D. L. Balch, *Let Wives Be Submissive: The Domestic Code in 1 Peter*, SBLM 26 (Chico, Calif.: Scholars Press, 1981), 2–20; K. Müller, "Die Haustafel des Kolosserbriefes und das antike Frauenthema," in *Die Frau im Urchristentum*, by G. Dautzenberg, H. Merklein, K. Müller, Quaestiones disputatae 95 (Freiburg/Basel/Vienna: Herder & Herder, 1983), 263–319.

2. M. Dibelius, *An die Kolosser, Epheser, an Philemon*, Handbuch zum Neuen Testament 3d ed., ed. H. Greeven, 12 (Tübingen: J. C. B. Mohr [Paul Siebeck], 1953), 48–50.

3. I put the expression within quotation marks since, in a way, all Judaism of the time was Hellenistic. Here it stands for Greek-speaking, largely non-Palestinian Judaism.

4. K. Weidinger, *Die Haustafeln: Ein Stück urchristlicher Paränese*, Untersuchungen zum Neuen Testament 14 (Leipzig: J. C. Hinrichs, 1928).

5. Crouch, *Origin and Intention.*

230

6. Ibid., 5 and 7.1.

7. D. Schroeder, "Lists, Ethical," in *Interpreter's Dictionary of the Bible*, sup. vol. (1976), 546–47. His unpublished Hamburg dissertation from 1959 dealt with the household codes, their origin, and their theological meaning. It has not been available to me. The contributions of E. Lohmeyer and K. H. Rengstorf may be said to deal with the form-critical aspect only indirectly. See Lohmeyer's *Die Briefe an die Philipper, an die Kolosser und an Philemon*, 9th ed., ed. W. Schmauch, Kritisch-exegetischer Kommentar über das Neue Testament, ed. H. A. W. Meyer, no. 9 (Göttingen: Vandenhoeck & Ruprecht, 1953; the 8th ed., which was the first to be written by Lohmeyer, appeared in 1930). Lohmeyer held that Col. 3:18—4:1 was a pre-Colossian unit of Jewish origin, but he did not ask so much for the "schema," etc., as for the root system of ideas expressed in the code. See also Rengstorf, "Die neutestamentliche Mahnungen an die Frau, sich dem Manne unterzuordnen," in *Verbum Dei Manet in Aeternum*, Festschrift Otto Schmitz, ed. W. Foerster (Wittenberg: Luther Verlag, 1953), 131–45. Rengstorf claimed the household codes were a purely Christian creation that owed to interest in the *oikos* (cf. the more recent adducing of the *oikonomia* treatises as a background).

8. The two formal issues mentioned last are not in Schroeder's "Lists, Ethical" but are in his thesis (according to Balch [*Let Wives Be Submissive*, 6] and Crouch [*Origin*, 102]). The last item is the same as the one Crouch calls reciprocity. D. C. Verner (*The Household of God: The Social World of the Pastoral Epistles*, SBLMS 71 [Chico, Calif.: Scholars Press, 1983], 83–91) distinguishes between the topos of the household management employed in the *Haustafeln*, and their schema, namely, their literary characteristics.

9. D. Lührmann, "Wo man nicht mehr Sklave oder Freier ist," *Wort und Dienst* n.s. 13 (1975): 53–83; idem, "Neutestamentliche Haustafeln und antike Öko-nomie," *New Testament Studies* 27 (1980–81): 83–97; K. Thraede, "Ärger mit der Freiheit," in *Freunde in Christus werden . . .*, by G. Scharffenorth and K. Thraede (Gelmhausen and Berlin: Burkhardtshaus, 1977), 31–182; idem, "Zum historischen Hintergrund der 'Haustafeln' des Neuen Testament," in *Pietas*, Festschrift B. Kötting, ed. E. Dassmann and K. G. Frank, Jahrbuch für Antike und Christentum supp. vol. 8 (Münster: Aschendorff, 1980), 359–68; and Balch, *Let Wives Be Submissive* (after a Yale diss. of 1974); and Müller, "Haustafel."

10. K. Berger, "Hellenistische Gattungen im Neuen Testament," in *Aufstieg und Niedergang der römischen Welt* 2.25.2 (New York and Berlin: Walter de Gruyter, 1984), 1031–1432.

11. Balch, *Let Wives Be Submissive*, 109; Müller, "Haustafel," 290.

12. More specialized studies in my scholarly surroundings approach the form-critical issues with linguistics: D. Hellholm, *Das Visionenbuch des Hermas als Apokalypse: Formgeschichtliche und texttheoretische Studien zu einer literarischen Gattung*, vol. 1, Coniectanea biblica—New Testament series 13/1 (Lund: C. W. K. Gleerup, 1980); idem, "The Problem of Apocalyptic Genre and the Apocalypse of John," Society of Biblical Literature Abstracts and Seminar Papers, ed. K. H. Richards (Chico, Calif.: Scholars Press, 1982), 157–98; and B. Johanson, *To All the Brethren: A Textlinguistic and Rhetorical Approach to 1 Thessalonians*, Coniectanea biblica—New Testament series 16 (Stockholm: Almqvist & Wiksell International, 1987).

13. E. Werlich, *Typologie der Texte: Entwurf eines textlinguistischen Modells zur*

Grundlegung einer Textgrammatik, 2d ed., Uni-Taschenbücher 450 (Heidelberg: Quelle & Meyer, 1979). For a wider discussion, see also K. W. Hempfer, *Gattungstheorie: Information und Synthese,* Uni-Taschenbücher 133 (Munich: Fink, 1973), 150–91.

14. "Idealtypische Normen für Textstrukturierung . . . , die der erwachsene Sprecher als kognitiv determinierte Matrices textformender Elemente in der sprachlichen Kommunikation über Gegenstände und Sachverhalte generell verfügbar hat" (Werlich, *Typologie,* 44).

15. Werlich prefers this expression to "Textsorte" (ibid., 116 n. 42).

16. "Aktualisierungen von Gruppen von Textkonstituenten . . . , die Sprecher einerseits in Übereinstimmung mit texttypischen Invarianten und andererseits gemäss bestimmten historisch ausgebildeter Konventionen für textliche Äusserungen in der Textproduktion auswählen" (ibid., 44).

17. See further D. Hellholm, "The Problem of Apocalyptic Genre and the Apocalypse of John," part 3, *Dispersa membra,* forthcoming in Coniectanea biblica—New Testament series.

18. I take the risk of not discussing any "text" definition, nor the delimitation of Col. 3:18—4:1.

19. Werlich, *Typologie,* 33.

20. Ibid., 36.

21. Ibid., 38. Since we have only fragments of the texts, it is difficult to be positive about the text type: possibly it is argumentative.

22. Cf. L. Grasberger, *Erziehung und Unterricht im klassischen Altertum,* vol. 1/1 (Würzburg: Stahel, 1864), 53, 227–35; and S. Oppermann, "Spiele," in *Der kleine Pauly* 5 (1975): 310–11. See also Plato *Laws* 1.643C; Aristotle *Politics* 7.15.5 (the play prepares the child for the adult life).

23. Balch, *Let Wives Be Submissive,* 53ff.

24. Cf. E. Gerstenberger, *Wesen und Herkunft des "apodiktischen Rechts,"* Wissenschaftliche Monographien zum Alten und Neuen Testament 20 (Neukirchen-Vluyn: Neukirchener Verlag, 1965), 121; and J. Gnilka, *Der Kolosserbrief,* Herders theologischer Kommentar zum Neuen Testament 10/1 (Freiburg/Basel/Vienna: Herder & Herder, 1980), 214–15. But note that the one addressed in Sirach, in 3:1 as so often elsewhere, is the "son," i.e., the student.

25. E.g., G. E. Cannon, *The Use of Traditional Materials in Colossians* (Macon, Ga.: Mercer Univ. Press, 1983), chap. 4.

26. Hellholm ("Problem," 3.3.3) prefers distinguishing between text-internal and text-external functions.

27. Cf. R. A. F. MacKenzie, "The Meaning of the Susanna Story," *Canadian Journal of Theology* 3 (1957): 211–18.

PART THREE

LITERARY STUDIES:
JESUS AND THE GOSPELS

15

Parables and the
Search for a New Community

JOHN RICHES
University of Glasgow

Students of the Gospel parables have rarely paid much attention to the social dynamics of early Christianity; equally, students of the social dynamics of early Christianity have rarely looked to the parables as clues to the processes whereby the new communities emerged. Indeed, much of the attraction of the parables has been their apparent accessibility to people of all ages, their apparent transcendence of particular issues and interests, and their ability to express compellingly timeless, universal truths. Here we have texts that can speak for themselves from one generation to another. But even those, like Adolf Jülicher, who have argued thus have been only too aware of the vagaries of parable interpretation over the centuries; and those who have followed in his steps, notably Dodd and Jeremias, have attempted to get as firm a control as possible on the sense of the parables by relating them to their original situation and context.[1] In this they have not wanted to abandon in any way the belief that the parables are able to speak with particular force to people of all ages. The parables, says Dodd, "have an imaginative and poetic quality. They are works of art, and any serious work of art has significance beyond its original occasion." Their teaching may be reapplied, but "a just understanding of their original import in relation to a particular situation in the past will put us on right lines in applying them to our own new situations."[2] And recent work on the parables, both in the United States and in Germany, has tended to concentrate attention more on the abiding character of the parables as works of literature than on any attempt to read their significance out of the situation to which they are addressed.[3]

It might then seem perverse and certainly against the tide of recent New Testament studies to argue as I would like to do in this paper that we shall learn more about the parables if we focus our attention not so much on their aesthetic and literary character and abiding theological significance as on the extent to which in them Jesus was reaching out for a new life world for his community, attempting to delineate the characteristics of the new age that he expected so vividly. I hope, however, to be able to show that there is in fact an important sense in which such an inquiry can be seen to lead on quite logically from the recent introduction of perspectives from literary theory into New Testament studies.

My contention then very simply is this: In the parables Jesus attempted to express what the coming kingdom would be like, what kind of society it would involve, and how such developments were consistent with God's nature and actions as so far revealed to Jews. All this involved attempting to describe what was significantly new and beyond the experience of those in his own community. As employed by Jesus, the parable form was an important instrument for achieving this end, because it enabled him to express theological and anthropological perceptions that stretched the normal linguistic means of his own community to the breaking point. This in turn opened the way for others after him whose linguistic conventions were different—either because of different cultural milieus or because of the impact Jesus' teaching had had on their language—to develop these initial insights into the quite complex social, some would say symbolic, world of the New Testament. As such, they have contributed to the shaping of cultural webs whose strength today is still not to be underestimated.

Such a thesis, it will readily appear, will involve discussing the literary form of parables. But it will be a discussion that does not attempt to detach that form from its contemporary setting but that rather will see such a literary form as a form of *linguistic communication.* That is to say, it will conceive of such forms as forms that operate within particular natural-language communities at particular times and that therefore, despite their obvious general intelligibility at one level to people of different times and places, may be in other respects so closely tied to the linguistic exigencies of the particular community that they become extremely difficult to interpret once removed from their original context. Setting them back into that context may not only help to get some control on their original sense but may also help to bring out something of the processes by which the Christian social world was formed. It goes without saying that in a paper such as this we can only indicate the kind of detailed exegetical work required to sustain such a thesis.

This might suggest that what I have to offer will be closest to debates about the literary character of the parables, and that is certainly where I shall start. But I do not want to suggest that because I am concerned with social dynamics, I am not interested in the theological content of the parables. Quite the contrary; insofar as this is an essay in the sociology of knowledge of early Christianity, its subject is of course principally the formation of those theological beliefs which would give legitimacy and coherence to the life world of early Christians. And this means that *within such a project* attention will focus principally on the significant shifts in theological understanding which enabled the emergence of new social worlds. This, though it is not always appreciated, is to be carefully distinguished from the attempt to extract from the texts a contemporary meaning as they are read from within the very different horizons of expectation of our various twentieth-century natural-language communities.

Perhaps it will help to locate the kind of approach I wish to advocate if I compare and contrast it first with the quite early work of D. O. Via in *The Parables*. This is an important and intellectually vigorous book that develops the kinds of claims about the aesthetic quality of the parables which Dodd made somewhat *en passant*. What Via suggests is that we should take something of a lead from the New Criticism and give more weight in our interpretation to the aesthetic integrity of the New Testament "texts"— which in the case of the parables means the parables as reconstructed by traditiohistorical means. I say, "something of a lead," because Via is quite rightly reluctant to follow the New Critics all the way in their denunciation of the "intentional fallacy" (identifying the goal of interpretation with the author's intention) or indeed of the "affective fallacy" (offering interpretations in terms of the emotions aroused by the text in the reader). Via—and I gloss somewhat—wants to insist that texts are acts of communication between an author and the author's readers and as such do indeed involve both sides. But he equally wants to insist with the New Critics that it is the *texts* which communicate and which therefore have an organic unity of their own and a certain measure of autonomy even over against their author. What the author communicates *is* what he has written—as it is understood by his readers.

Via was writing twenty years ago, before the full force of the attack on the New Criticism by semiotics and recent literary theory was felt. In that context his reservations anticipate important criticisms that were to come, and show a proper caution against a simple divorce of the text from its communicative context. In other respects, however, his work pays its tribute to what was most distinctive in that movement—the belief that works of literature do speak for themselves of certain basic human values, goals, and attitudes[4]—and this fits very well with his interpretive project. What he hopes to show is that these texts do have a basic existential sense: they illuminate aspects of human existence and, from there, as parabolic comparisons, go on to point to a theological understanding of existence. What is compared, that is to say, is a particular understanding of existence as portrayed in the story, with a particular kind of human relation to God: the *tertium comparationis* is variously the willingness to risk one's life, the desire to have strict canons of reward for merit, the desire for security, and the like.

Even this brief list suggests that despite the considerable elegance of the argument there are in the end few surprises. What comes out of such an existential analysis of Jesus' parables is much the same Lutheran perspective as dominated Bultmann's interpretation of Paul, and by contrast of Judaism, and which has been the subject of such vigorous attack recently by E. P. Sanders.

Now by contrast I would like to suggest that we need to attach even greater importance to the sense in which texts—whether spoken or written—are acts of communication between author and reader/hearer. This means generally that such texts are addressed to people with certain "horizons of expectation."[5] Such horizons of expectation may be literary; they will embrace the commonplace beliefs of a particular culture, and they will, significantly, include expectations of linguistic use. The author will successfully communicate only insofar as he addresses himself to such expectations.

Now, of course, some recent critics[6] have argued that just because texts are part of a process of communication where the readers' horizons of expectation will be quite diverse, we cannot properly speak of *a* particular meaning of a text at all. But this fails to do justice precisely to the skill a writer may employ in playing with the literary expectations of his readers.[7] I therefore prefer to follow writers, like Hans Jauss, who are concerned to plot the literary history of a text from its original moment of interaction with its readers' expectations through its subsequent readings and, indeed, reproductions in literary form as those expectations change, not least perhaps as a result of the impact of the text itself. Texts do indeed have literary histories—which is to say that unless they die, they live on in a literary (or indeed religious) tradition that spawns new works and interpretations as the corporate consciousness of the society and culture changes and adapts. Thus a text is not simply like a monument of which each generation may view perhaps different aspects; it is more like a musical score that must be performed to have life at all and whose performances will differ perhaps quite dramatically from generation to generation.[8] The understanding of this varied history of interpretation is, to Jauss, an essential part of the understanding of the text.

Via's approach, it will be seen, cheerfully abstracts from this historical perspective: he assumes that those aspects of human experience which a modern interpreter finds illuminated in a text are a sufficient guide to its interpretation, and thereby he is in danger of reducing a text's meaning and richness to one particular kind of performance. What I propose promises at least to open up the richness and complexity of such texts by showing something of their very early history in the development of the Christian community's social world. But Via's lasting contribution to the debate is that he has drawn New Testament scholars' attention to the textual character of the New Testament documents, that is to say, to the fact that they are texts with an autonomy and integrity of their own which cannot be simply reduced to an account in terms of their origins and the original intentions of their authors. That is an insight to which New Testament scholars will need to give continued attention.

An interestingly different approach to the parables is offered by Hans Weder in his *Die Gleichnisse Jesu als Metaphern*. Here the approach is, in the first place, rhetorical—concerned, that is, to analyze the nature of the speech forms employed in the parabolic literature, less concerned with questions of the autonomy of texts as such. Beyond this, however, Weder's principal concern is with the theological interpretation of texts, and here he shows himself in his own way equally indebted to the Lutheran tradition. Yet, different as it is from Via's work, Weder's book raises similar questions about the need to incorporate within its perspective considerations relating to the social, conventional nature of language.

Weder, taking his lead from work inspired by recent American literary criticism, is critical of Jülicher's view that parables should be understood as forms of simile. He argues that they should be more properly seen as forms of metaphor. Similes link two entities by virtue of a shared characteristic or shared characteristics, a *tertium comparationis*. "Jack is like a tree" may mean that Jack is physically sturdy; it may mean that he cannot easily be moved. "A tree is like a straw" may refer to the way trees can draw up water through their roots and trunk. Metaphors, to Weder, are essentially propositions (as opposed to terms) of the form subject-copula-predicate where two *Sinnhorizonte* (horizons of meaning) are combined and where the copula "is" (as in the example "Achilles is a lion") signifies both "is" and "is not." Weder, however, wants to insist that we should speak of parables as metaphors only in an analogous sense. "By contrast with metaphors, whose semantic tension occurs on the level of the *sentence* as a tension between the *words*, parabolic speech is effective on the level of *composition*."[9] For this reason he believes that there is also a distinction to be made as regards the greater length of life of parabolic stories. And he further notes that whereas in normal metaphors two different horizons of meaning are brought together, in the case of Jesus' parables it is two horizons that are different *in principle* which are brought together, namely, God and the world.

There are many aspects of Weder's thesis that it would be helpful to discuss. Here I must limit myself to two. In the first instance, he wants to insist on the untranslatability of metaphor.[10] Precisely because metaphor brings together two concepts that are properly incompatible, its metaphorical sense cannot be translated into literal speech. For this reason metaphorical speech can be creative, producing new meanings, bringing to expression new areas of experience and reality. The second point is that we must abandon Jülicher's distinction of *comparandum* and *comparatum:* of the thing which is to be compared and the image with which it is compared. "The parable does not merely find a new, figurative way of expressing old truths; the truth which is expressed in it cannot be expressed in any other way than figuratively." Thus he maintains that the form of the parable cannot be detached from its content and that this therefore fatally undermines any theory "which seeks to understand Jesus' parables on the basis of their effects."[11]

It is clear from what follows where Weder is heading. He wants to argue that Jesus' parables do bring to expression a unique understanding of God and do so in a way that alone is adequate to the purpose. At the same time he wishes to insist that the form of the parables is not in any way conditioned by the circumstances in which they came to be: it is the truth itself that comes to expression in the parables "which demands this form. The parables are not a justification or defense of the good news, they are *themselves gospel.*"[12] In what follows I would like to suggest that what is original to Jesus' teaching is something that could only be worked out in a process of interaction with his contemporaries and their understanding of God and reality; that the metaphorical form of parables is indeed well suited to explore those areas of reality and experience which lie at the bounds of a particular community's world; and that parables and metaphors, far from being somehow specially related to the expression of a particular kind of theological truth, are particularly suited to the exploration of a wide range of experience. This is not in any way to deny that they may be well suited to the task of expressing Jesus' own theological vision; it is to insist that we should see that task as continuous with other forms of searching for the truth.

One way in which it may be helpful to discuss the notion of metaphor is in terms of its cognitive content. There is here a vigorous debate in progress among philosophers which may cast light on the issues raised by Weder. In what sense, or to what extent, if we utter the sentence "You are the salt of the earth," are we *saying* something about "you" as opposed, for example, to *enjoining* the hearers to have some thoughts of their own on the subject? In what sense is this a declarative sentence as opposed to a performative of some kind? Some, like Donald Davidson, would deny that in any but a fairly trivial sense it is *saying* anything about "you." The only *sense* to be attached to such a sentence is its literal one, and that is plainly false. The point about such statements is to make us think what we are, to prompt and suggest. Like the Delphic oracle, "it does not say and it does not hide, it intimates."[13] Others—Max Black, I. A. Richards—would not deny that a metaphor might, does indeed, prompt us to think on, but would assert that it does so in virtue of some special *insight* it communicates. This, of course, involves them in giving an account of the metaphorical, as opposed to the literal, sense of sentences. They argue that metaphorical expressions are not just rhetorical adornments of literal statements but that sentences with a metaphorical focus make their point—*say* what they say—in a particular way. Specifically, they say what they say by virtue of the interaction of two ideas (Richards), by implying statements about the principal subject that normally apply to the subsidiary subject: "The metaphor selects, emphasizes, suppresses, and organizes features of the principal subject by *implying* statements about it that normally apply to the subsidiary subject."[14]

Thus, if we say, "Man is a wolf," we evoke, in any given culture, a system of associated commonplaces: "If the man is a wolf, he preys upon other animals, is fierce, hungry, engaged in constant struggle, a scavenger and so on. Each of these implied assertions has now to be made to fit the principal subject (man) *either in normal or abnormal senses.*" What is happening is that the normal implications of "man" are being revised, "screened," "filtered" by those provided by the term "wolf." This leads to a recasting of the ways in which we think about man; it also leads to an extension of the sense of "wolf": "The metaphor makes the wolf seem more human than he otherwise would."[15]

Now, one of the interesting features of this account of metaphor is that it shows how metaphors may challenge the commonplace beliefs of a particular group by using language in a creative, nonconventional sense. To use a sentence literally is to use it in its standard conventional sense, invoking, as it were, its commonly accepted implications. To use it metaphorically is to invoke its commonly accepted implications and then to juxtapose alongside those a term or terms with a discordant set of implications. Thus if Jesus told parables about the *basileia theou,* he used a term that carried a fairly well established set of implications about God's rule and the manner of his exercise of it, and then set alongside it stories of people behaving in ways that were strikingly or puzzlingly different. In this way Jesus' hearers were invited to revise their standard understanding of God's rule and to entertain a rather different view of contemporary values and practice in the sphere of life related in his stories.

Such pointed use of metaphor may thus challenge the associations of ideas and experiences that are standard in a particular group at a particular time. Not merely does it challenge such associations but by the substitutions and deletions which it makes in the accepted patterns of association it in fact opens the way for people to form new networks of sentences and experiences in terms of which to make sense of their worlds. Just as Jauss wants to speak of the way in which texts may interact with and challenge the "horizons of expectation" of their readers, thus transforming the literary tradition, so we may say metaphors may challenge the accepted patterns of association and pave the way for significant linguistic and conceptual change in a particular society.

It is now time to consider the implications of this discussion for our understanding of the Gospel parables. Jesus uttered both short parabolic sayings and more extended parables that may consist largely in extended narratives. Sometimes the principal subject is expressed formally, sometimes it is not. Sometimes the subsidiary subject or predicate is expressed by means of a single sentence or term, sometimes it is expressed by a considerable number of sentences in a complex narrative. That is to say, sometimes Jesus takes fairly simple, straightforward metaphors, availing himself of the existing associated commonplaces of a particular term; at others he may construct for himself a metaphor of a more complex kind. "Metaphors," as Max Black says, "can be supported by specially constructed systems of implications, as well as by accepted commonplaces; they can be made to measure and need not be reach-me-downs."[16] The task for the interpreter is, first, to discover what the associated commonplaces of particular terms were then and there; second, to see to what extent Jesus adapted such terms to suit his own purposes; and third, to discover what was being said when he applied such metaphorical terms and metaphors to the primary subject of his parables. That may then allow us to see the extent to which Jesus was attempting to refashion the lineaments of his world.

Let me consider each of these in turn:

1. This forms part of a general injunction for interpreters of ancient texts. In order to know what is being *said* on a particular occasion, it is first necessary to know what the commonly accepted implications of a particular sentence were at that time. To discover that, we need to know what other sentences the hearer who accepted any given sentence in a text would also have accepted because he accepted that sentence. Not only that, we also need to know what other expectations the acceptance of such and such a sentence would have aroused in a particular hearer, expectations, that is, about what kinds of experiences and practices were linked to the particular states of affairs referred to. In this connection, then, we shall not only need to be apprised of the network of particular terms and sentences that pertains to the specific terms used within parabolic utterance but we shall also need

to be apprised as fully as possible of contemporary expectations concerning, for example, legal practice and custom, and agricultural methods.[17]

This is of primary importance, of greater importance than knowing what other analogous occurrences of such sentences there may have been in other, noncontemporary contexts.

There is a point here, however, that relates specifically to the question of parables. It may be that within the specific context of parable telling, certain motifs have gained specific associations. Thus the frequently recurring themes of meals, feasts, and work would have been widely taken to refer to human beings' relationship to God, in terms of duties owed to him, of the proper and appropriate behavior of men and women in relation to God.[18] What is being said here is that within the tradition of parable telling, certain keys may be given as to the nature of the primary subject to which the parable, the metaphor, applies. It is not that the literal sense and associations of a particular term have been substantially changed but that we are being given hints as to how to read the parable, how to interpret it. And this is no more than to say that within a particular tradition such motifs within the context of storytelling have come to arouse certain expectations. More of this anon.

2. The second task is to determine how far Jesus simply used existing terms in their standard senses (invoking, that is, the conventional system of implications pertaining at the time), how far he adapted them to his own needs. The question is, to what extent did Jesus, when he uttered parables and parabolic sayings simply take over the existing range of associations of a particular term, theme, and so on, and to what extent did he adapt it for his own metaphorical ends? As Max Black has written, "In a poem or a piece of sustained prose, the writer can establish a novel pattern of implications for the literal uses of key expressions, prior to using them as vehicles for his metaphors."[19]

One simple rule here might be that the simpler, the shorter the saying, the less the likelihood of there being any serious modification of its conventional implications. Consider: "You are the salt of the earth." Salt has, of course, a range of associations; among its properties are not only its ability to bring out the flavor of food but also its preservative, purifying, and corrosive properties. Its value in ancient society was great and arguably much greater than in ours. The saying therefore is not unambiguously clear, and it is thus the role of the associated question both to call out the intended association (salt as savor) and to fill out the hearers' (the downcast, "savorless" disciples) understanding of themselves. The same is true of the linked saying "You are the light of the world." But it is not just parabolic sayings that thus stick close to their standard sense.

In some of the short parables—for example, the parable of the lost coin—

the actions described seem to contain little that is unexpected. Things of value are things that normally we expect people to grieve for, to search for when lost. Nevertheless, the image of the poor woman searching for her lost coin is itself an evocative image that brings out something not only about the value of the coin to her but about her own indigence, and this again, with the contrast between her determined searching and her rejoicing with her friends, is illuminative of God's dealings with men and women. So much in this kind of extended metaphor is a matter of fine touches. But equally important is the substitution of this kind of image for others—for example, the more common images of masters and workers, kings and servants.

It is when we come to the more elaborate parables that we may expect to find the clearest examples of what Max Black calls "tailoring." Here we may distinguish various kinds. You may tell a story more or less straight, doing no more than to highlight or draw out certain aspects of events and ideas that in themselves are much as expected. Or you may tell a story or develop an image in a way that is very different from contemporary expectations and that challenges the hearers to rethink their attitudes to and beliefs about the matter that forms the literal subject of the story. Thus in the first instance you may tell a story about a father forgiving his wayward son and the jealousy of his elder brother. There may be nothing deeply surprising or out of character here, nothing that seriously runs counter to a contemporary understanding of expected behavioral patterns of fathers and elder brothers. What may be thought-provoking and innovative is that we should bring this story to bear on our understanding of how God deals with his wayward people.

In a rather different way, contemporary practice may be used as a foil for a denouement that surprises the hearers (e.g., the parables of the laborers in the vineyard and of the wedding feast). Here the contemporary sense of expressions is assumed, but equally the behavior of the main characters flouts the conventional expectations: the *oikodespotēs* rewards not, as might be expected, according to the laborers' deserts; the king invites the dishonorable to his feast. There is nothing unconventional about the use of the terms "rewarding," "inviting"; but a challenge is given to the hearers to rethink their understanding of what is deserving, who is honorable and worthy to be invited to a feast, what is goodness, justice, generosity, hospitality. And then they are further invited to rethink the implications of this for their understanding of God.

Somewhere in between these two poles, stories may be told emphasizing and contrasting familiar aspects of contemporary experience in such a way that the hearers are encouraged to look more closely at one aspect than at another (e.g., at yield rather than failure, in the parable of the sower). In this respect a certain amount of poetic license may be permissible within what is otherwise a realistic description of the state of affairs. Again a story may have a framework that bears on contemporary experience, but its detail and action may be determined by analogues in the subject (e.g., the wicked vineyarders). (There is a question here as to whether all these four types of parabolic utterance are original to Jesus, but at least there is nothing to lead us to suppose initially that any of the four types belongs to an altogether different genre.)

The more obvious cases of "tailoring," however, come in parables where a deliberate contrast is engineered between contemporary practice and expectations and the outcome of the story. Let us take a rather closer look at one of these. In the parable of the laborers in the vineyard, the repetitive account of the hiring of laborers emphasizes the contractual relationship between the master and the laborers. *Symphōneo, misthos, apodidōmi,* and the expressions employed using the *dik* root certainly do all that, and on a first hearing, at least, it might seem that, as others have suggested, this is "merely a foil for the denouement which emphasizes that God's mercy knows no bounds."[20] This is clearly true—up to a point. The language is there; and the reactions of the first-hired show that they at least expect there to be some kind of pro rata reward for services rendered, that they should therefore receive more, have some kind of preeminence. A closer look confirms however what the master says: *ouk adikō se,* he has not broken the agreement with anyone; he gives to the first what is theirs by right, *ho ean ēi dikaion,* and to the last what *he* of his goodness thinks fit. The general point still stands: the master is good, merciful; he will give generously even where he is not bound by contract. But there is more in the story: there is an *argument* that also indemnifies the master against the charge of *injustice* against those who receive less when their work is costed on a pro rata basis. Now here *dikaios, adikō* are being used in interestingly different senses: partly they are being used in the context of adhering to the terms of an agreement, partly in a more extended sense as doing what is right, appropriate to someone, *ho ean ēi dikaion dōsō humin.* The former sense is not entirely that which informs the first-hireds' objections. They equate *adikein* with not rewarding according to a fixed scale of so much work, so much reward. The second sense of *dikaios*—what is appropriate, right—does not, of course, as it stands conflict with the first-hireds' sense of what is right. But it requires further definition: What is appropriate, right? Is it a living wage or pro rata payments? The final remarks of the master prompt further reflection on the sense of the phrase *ho ean ēi dikaion dōsō humin* by introducing the terms *ponēros* and *agathos.* It is not so much contracts and fair apportionment that determine the nature of the *misthos* as the goodness of the master's intentions toward the people he is dealing with. What is

245

JOHN RICHES

given is still a *misthos* but is certainly not one where what is given is simply
apportioned to the work of the recipient, though in every case their willingness to work is a condition. For the master's relation to the laborers is not
exhausted by his contractual obligations, though these are not overlooked.
It is also determined by more general considerations of good and evil which
are related to fundamental questions of human need (cf. Matt. 7:12!). Thus
here we have a case where a good deal of modification has been made to
some of the contemporary accepted senses of terms and phrases used in the
parable. Terms like *misthos* are being prized away from their associations
with notions of pro rata payment, as expressed through certain usages of
others like *dikaios,* and made to stand alongside terms like *ponēros, agathos*—but again also *dikaios.* There is, that is to say, already in the story—as
distinct from the metaphorical predication of the story of the kingdom—a
reworking of contemporary commonplace beliefs about justice and reward.

3. Once we have seen how far the terms of a story are being used
conventionally, how far in the modified sense, we need to see what happens
when the parabolic saying or story is applied to the primary subject. The
first question must be, what precisely is the primary subject? This is by no
means such an obvious question as might appear. Even in such simple
sayings as "You are the salt of the earth" (Matt. 5:13) the question needs to
be asked, though in practice it rarely is. What is the primary subject of the
Greek sentence *humeis este to halas tēs gēs?* If, by contrast with the standard
rendering above, we translate, "The salt of the earth are you!"—taking "salt
of the earth" as primary subject and "you" as the qualifying predicate—then
the matter looks quite different. The primary subject is not just "salt" with
its many obvious properties of which perhaps only some are relevant; it is
rather the religious notion of salt *of the earth,* that which brings savor to the
world, to life. And the surprising thing is that this is now associated with the
dispirited or doubting disciples: they are the ones who are to bring life and
light to the world. And this certainly says a lot both about them and about
the notion of the salt of the earth, of salvation and the ways of God with his
people. So the apparently straightforward application of the notion of salt to
the disciples turns out to be more creative; and much the same could be said
of the linked saying about the light of the world. There is, that is to say, a
very real *interaction* between the hearers' expectations and self-understanding and what is being said in this saying. The "horizons of expectation" are
being redrawn.[21]

Identifying the primary subject is even more complicated in the case of
the laborers in the vineyard. In Matthew's version the subject is, it is true,
explicitly stated as the kingdom of heaven. That is, of course, an expression
whose exact significance was—is—less than wholly clear but which is

certainly firmly linked to notions of God's rule and dealings with his people. Do we have any further pointers to how this parable is to be read? Certainly if it is true that in the parable tradition certain themes would have been widely understood to refer to specific aspects of God's dealings with human beings, we could go a little further. We might then say that the ruler refers to God and the work in the vineyard refers to the duty owed to God and that this is specifically a parable about the way God rules the world, about the way he orders its affairs in accordance both with people's efforts and his own good will for them.[22]

The frequency of the linkage of work and its wages with fulfillment of the law and divine recompense has, of course, been noted by many commentators.[23] What we need to be cautious about is assuming too readily that there was a clear view about the matter which was agreed to by all except Jesus. We need to press much more firmly the question how far in employing parables to speak about such matters, Jews—both Jesus and those who laid the foundations of other significant developments in ancient Judaism—were exploring and probing *popular* understandings of human obligations to God and of divine rewards and thereby, variously, paving the way for the construction of new social worlds.

It is of course not enough just to suggest that the thematic material of the parable indicates that it is concerned with the *theological* question of rewards and punishments. Such questions have their setting in a wider theological framework, and it is hard to see how a story that details different agreements made between the *oikodespotēs* and different groups of laborers would not also have raised questions about *the* covenant (i.e., the Mosaic covenant) and other covenants that God had or would make with people. The covenant for Jews was that pact between God and human beings which *grounded* and regulated their existence and was therefore as such of central theological importance. This point has been amply demonstrated by Sanders.[24] But although it may indeed be accepted that, despite the relative paucity of discussion of the topic in the rabbinic material, belief in the covenant was basic to first-century Judaism, there is still an interesting question to be pursued as to how such belief was further spelled out—for example, in relation to beliefs about other covenants, about the Gentiles, about God's dealings with sinners. Of particular interest is Sanders's discussion of the Mekilta on Exod. 18:27, which distinguishes different types of divine covenant: unconditional and conditional.[25] What is particularly interesting here is that this discussion occurs in the context of the loss to Israel of the temple, which with the law and the kingdom is said to be given conditionally.[26] That is to say, changes in Israel's circumstances, insofar as they substantially affect the expectations that have been traditionally associated with certain terms and beliefs, may prompt reflection on the nature of God's dealings with his people, in an attempt to reconstruct a model of reality in which expectations and beliefs may more nearly coincide.

The question then arises, if such a story would have raised such general issues for Jesus' first-century listeners, what specific problem or puzzle was Jesus addressing, attempting to illuminate, in his parable? In a Matthean context it would be easy to see this as addressed to the question, how can God reward the Gentiles—as late entries—in a way equal to the Jews? And this, as Matt. 20:16 and 19:30 show, would then have interesting points of comparison and contrast with Paul's concern to preserve a priority of some kind for the Jews. But what of Jesus' use, if the parable is original to him? It would seem that it must have referred to those whose work was seen as a kind of last-minute, eleventh-hour minimum. God will out of his goodness also "reward" these with what is good and fitting if they respond to his call.

This is not the place to speculate on the precise identification of such people, interesting and profitable though that would be. The extent to which Jesus is addressing himself to the condition of those "sinners" whom he called into the kingdom,[27] the extent to which he is speaking here to a more general condition of social anomie which beset contemporary Jews who found themselves unable to maintain their traditional norms through force of social, economic, and cultural pressures[28]—to cast the question in these terms is to be made aware of a difficulty that besets a great deal of this kind of historical discussion. It may be that we know quite clearly what the technical definition of a "sinner" was in first-century Judaism. But that is not quite the same as knowing how particular Jews, or indeed whole groups of Jews, from time to time may have seen themselves. Theological definitions of sin and of individual or group consciousness of sin may be two very different things and may, *pace* Sanders, be influenced from time to time by groups whose official standing is relatively weak. In this context it is perhaps more enlightening to consider those groups who appear to have had a strong consciousness of their own "sinfulness." Those who flocked to hear John's preaching of "baptism of repentance for the forgiveness of sins" were, Mark at least tells us, baptized "confessing their sins." Such behavior is clearly less indicative of a personal awareness of having as an individual overstepped group boundaries than of a group's awareness of a general collapse of group norms. Moreover, where such behavior is also accompanied by the vivid expectation of the coming of a new age or of some redeemer figure, it is reasonable to suggest that the group's awareness of the collapse of its norms is also accompanied by a lively sense of the need for their fundamental renewal—and not just for a redoubling of group efforts to sustain them. Whether such a sense of need is always accompanied by an equally lively hope that it will be effectively met is, however, a different question. Without pressing the case further, I would suggest that there is much to be said in favor of the view that it was to those with a lively awareness of the breakdown of group norms—but with no clear sense of how to respond—that Jesus addressed himself. We should have enough historical imagination to ask what kinds of insecurity were engendered among those who had been baptized "confessing their sins" but in the enthusiastic hope of a coming deliverance, when their hopes were dashed by the execution of John.

We may now perhaps see how aspects of the parable we had not previously noticed serve to illuminate the particular question of how God deals with his people through the covenant and the law. There are certain somewhat artificial aspects of the story: the master's repeated going in search of laborers seems at least less than realistic; certainly it is not explained, even if explanations could be found. It is more likely that such traits, while they are clearly necessary for the structure of the story, insofar as they make possible the various agreements that the householder strikes with those he hires, are designed to bring out something germane to the main point of the parabolic statement, namely, about God's initiative in calling people into his "vineyard." Again the obviously stylized repetition of the master's visits, with its emphasis on the particular *times* of the visits, serves to highlight the increasing urgency of the call—in a way that goes beyond simple realism and suggests something of the urgency of the last days. Whether or not that is something that can be insisted on, certainly the frequent references to the times of day may be taken as an indication of the concern with history. The central point of the story is that the householder has called workers into his vineyard throughout the course of the day and yet wishes to deal with them all equally. The argument is concerned precisely with the question how it is possible for someone to have acted in such a way and still to have acted justly—and that is an argument which it may be necessary to conduct both with those who feel that they, as the first-hired, have been treated unjustly, and with those who cannot believe that there can be a future for them in the divine scheme of things.[29]

The question of the worth of the last-hired is also raised by the question the householder addressed to them: "Why do you stand here idle all day?" It is important to see that the term *argos* is used quite neutrally throughout the parable to mean simply "unemployed," and that therefore it would be mistaken to read into this a simplistically negative sense of "idle" or "lazy."[30] But that does not quite do justice to the tone of the householder's remark, which more naturally carries a tone of reproof than of polite inquiry. Indeed, whatever the tone, the question still brings home and underlines their basic predicament: that they have been without work all day, that they stand outside the vineyard. In terms of the dominant metaphor of work as applied to men and women's relationship to God their lack of work signifies their being outside any significant relationship of obedience to God. And their reply indicates equally clearly their sense that it is in no way of their choosing but something imposed. Only the householder's charge can resolve their predicament—and yet the question must remain whether it is not already too late for them to earn an adequate reward. And that is a question that can be answered only in terms of a fundamental discussion of the questions of justice and goodness which, as we saw earlier, form the central core of the story.

Thus, the central discussion of God's justice and mercy can be seen to be directed toward a resolution of certain quite specific questions in the development of the community's self-understanding. That is to say, *pace* Via, the questions of self-understanding that the parable undoubtedly raises are *in the first instance* neither to be divorced from the context of their utterance nor simply to be taken as of universal validity relating both to human beings' need to live out of the pure grace of God and to the sense in which people "may be too calculating to accept the risks in such dealings."[31] Via stresses the potentially tragic element in the story which is located in the fate of the first-hired, who at the end are dismissed from the presence of the householder: "Take what is yours and go!" This is well observed, but the reason for their dismissal is not that they were hired according to a set system of so much work for so much pay (merit) but rather that they were unable to accept that God might deal with others on another basis. Thus their dismissal in the story is hardly a reason for discounting the view that the parable teaches "that God deals with some on the basis of merit,"[32] nor is it immediately obvious that their reactions are well characterized by the next sentence: "Because of their impenetrable legalistic understanding of existence, grounded in the effort to effect their own security, they exclude themselves from the source of grace." Is the belief that justice requires some sense of proportionality "impenetrably legalistic"? The questions of self-understanding raised in this foundational parable are ones that are specific to the cultural situation of Jesus' hearers. But their resolution—or at least partial resolution—in the parable opens up the way for setting broad cultural conditions that may enable possibilities of self-understanding for centuries to come. We should neither underestimate the extent to which certain utterances are culturally specific nor overestimate the range of cultural diversity we encounter in history.

Such an exegesis runs counter to the view that says that what is happening here is that Jesus is replacing *human* ideas of reward and deserts with divine (evangelical) ones of grace. "In the *basileia*, conditions are determined by the goodness of God. Because of this, the *basileia* comes into sharp conflict with our conditions, in which the human 'concepts of justice, rewards, and achievement' are normative."[33] Weder, however, sees that it is itself an act of the goodness of God that his nearness is manifest in the form of a parable that takes our concepts and uses them to lead us into a new way of looking at things. He thus readily acknowledges that, as indeed Born-kamm asserts, the notion of rewards is not to be abandoned altogether, in that it preserves an awareness of the sense in which God takes human work seriously—though he is careful to deny that this is relevant to any human claims. Certainly there is a reworking of the notion of rewards and, in particular, of pro rata rewards, and this leads to a reworking of the language of giving and of good and evil which suggests that a *strictly* contractual relationship is by no means the only one available to God in his dealings with his people. But there is no suggestion that God has not, should not have, established such a relationship or that it could not have worked. We are however encouraged to look at other ways in which God regulates his dealing with his people, encouraged indeed to imagine a world in which such ways would be the norm rather than the surprising exception.

We have so far been discussing the ways in which parables considered as sometimes quite complex metaphors may have *informed* their lis-teners/readers, may have *said* things about God and his dealings with his creatures. This is not to deny that they may also have had a *function or functions* alongside or related to the particular *sense* they contained and were intended to communicate. I want now briefly to consider specifically the sociological function of metaphors such as the parables.

We should at this point recall earlier discussion of Jauss's important essay *Literaturgeschichte als Provokation*. There Jauss argues, against the clas-sical view, that literature is *weltbildend* rather than *weltabbildend*, "world-building" rather than "world-imitating." Those who tell stories do create a "story world"; but, we might say, the function of that world is not to imitate the actual world but to tease us into discovering new ones. And the teasing occurs as the teller takes our common beliefs and expectations and plays with them. He argues with us by encouraging us to take sides with one group and then giving them their comeuppance. In particular, he takes our commonplace views and scrutinizes them, parodying, distorting, or lending them new senses half-perceived, yet to be fully discovered. There is, that is to say, an *interaction* between the existing world of the reader/listener and the teller by means of which, it may be, new worlds are shaped. And metaphorical predication, I have been arguing, is particularly suited to encouraging this transformation of worlds, because it is essentially an interactive form of communication, bringing into relation two systems of thought that are not wholly compatible and allowing each to influence the other.

251

What this means in terms of our understanding of the parables is, at least, this. The established view that the parable form is essentially a realistic form will have to be abandoned if by that is meant that parables are to be seen as an accurate reflection of contemporary life and practice. We may indeed expect to find much in the stories that reflects contemporary practice and belief quite accurately, but if we suppose that the story *in its entirety* is an accurate reflection, we shall miss precisely the point lying in the teller's challenge of the normal—the way the parable may involve a deliberate reshaping of contemporary practice and accepted beliefs as different sets of commonplace beliefs are brought into interaction with one another. Consider the parable in question. It would seem reasonable to assume that it reflects accurately enough the practice of hiring laborers on a daily basis in the Palestine of Jesus' time. It may provide some evidence for contemporary wage levels, though of course we cannot be sure whether such details have been accurately transmitted. But will it tell us much that is really reliable about contemporary levels of unemployment? At least, perhaps, that unemployment was not unknown; but probably no more, for the fact that there are still men waiting to be hired "at the eleventh hour" is more related to points Jesus (or Matthew) wanted to make about "rewards" in the kingdom of heaven than it is to any existing social conditions or to the practice of masters going to scour the labor market even at the end of the day.

Where Jesus' contemporary social situation is reflected in the parables is in the leading questions behind his preaching: How is God's rule realized, manifested in such a world? How does a Jew remain faithful? Where does a subject's duty lie? When will all be fulfilled? What hope is there for those who are or feel themselves to be beyond the pale, outside the group? These are questions that arose directly out of the Jews' experience of alienation from the means of redemption in Jewish society, an experience that led them in turn to question traditional ways of understanding God's rule and power. How then do parables assist in the birth of new worlds?

There is a view quite widely held among social anthropologists that although prophetic figures do not develop programs of political action as such, they do contribute significantly to the articulation of new assumptions about power which may lay the basis for major political and social change.[34] More specifically, there has recently been a considerable discussion of the way in which such figures may use metaphors to articulate such new assumptions.

Metaphors, it is argued, if they are sufficiently fecund, have the power to organize anew our understanding of large areas of experience both in the sphere of scientific inquiry[35] and more generally in that of our conduct and ordering of human society and affairs. Here remarks of Victor Turner are of interest. Metaphors, he believes, share with symbols a "certain kind of polarization of meaning in which the subsidiary subject is really a depth world of prophetic, half-glimpsed images, and the principal subject, the visible, fully known (or thought to be fully known) component at the opposite pole to it, acquires new and surprising contours and valences from its dark companion";[36] and he believes that we can expect the key or fundamental metaphors of this type "to appear in the work of exceptionally liminal thinkers—poets, writers, religious prophets, 'the unacknowledged legislators of mankind'—just before outstanding limina of history, major crises of societal change, since such shamanistic figures are possessed by spirits of change before changes become visible in public arenas."[37]

These words seem to me remarkably applicable to Jesus and his parables. We should not always expect the political consequences of prophetic utterances to be immediate or, indeed, always explicitly envisaged: prophets give voice to an imaginative vision of a new world; they do not, often, consider very closely how such a world is to be achieved or, indeed, give much attention to how it will be ordered and regulated. None of that is to deny that the articulation of such a vision may not have deep and long-lasting political consequences. It is not "idealistic" to dwell on the ideational content of prophets' teaching, because it is this which, refined and schematized (and thereby possibly distorted), provides the basis of new attempts to transform existing social worlds.

The point that Turner makes is that—by contrast with the "acknowledged legislators" of society—prophets and poets, in working with metaphor rather than literal prose, are producing something that can prompt people to see their daily reality in novel ways: "The unknown is brought just a little more into the light by the known." Full grasp is to be left to those who work in terms of "imageless thought, conceptualization at various degrees of abstractness." I have tried to argue, without denying in any way the distinction between metaphor and abstract-literal ways of expressing sense contents, that there is or can be an exactness about metaphorical thought which subsequently we may only with difficulty succeed in repeating; that it is often indeed the *only* way in which certain senses can be communicated in a particular natural language to a community, because of the conventional constraints on language when used in its standard literal sense. I should also like to go on to argue that the fecundity of metaphor is thus concerned with the way in which it challenges established chains of implication and therefore sets tasks for rational reconstruction, rather than in its half-glimpsedness. But this clearly is only a generalization. How sharply a particular metaphor is grasped will depend on its author in any given case.

That is to say, prophets who use metaphors initiate processes of societal

253

change (from their position of liminality) which, certainly, may proceed to stages of more explicit political and legislative activity.

Let me try to put some flesh on this by considering the way in which this relates to the parable we have been considering. The parable is, we have said, essentially a parable about the relationship between God and his people, about the way he rules over them in history, about the obligations of his subjects to him, and about the rewards that God gives—ultimately about the very nature of God's justice and goodness. That is to say, it is a parable that raises issues which were of central concern to Jesus and his contemporaries as they sought a way out of the erosion of Jewish norms, of the social anomie that beset them. The parable tells the story of, essentially, two groups of people, those who are hired first and have a firm agreement that guarantees them a wage for the day and those who are hired on an open ticket and who can only depend on the goodness and good will of the householder for what might come to them. It is a contrast between those with an agreed pattern of employment and reward and those who have to rely on the householder's good grace; and that at least evokes images of an Israel that lived securely under the covenant and a people that now sees its institutions undermined and looks for some resolution of the problem by the direct intervention of God.[38]

Now what the parable does is, on the one hand, promise just the help that is hoped for—the last hired are indeed rewarded and blessed—and on the other, reassure those who hope in this way that this is indeed God's way and not some inferior mode of salvation, some counterfeit. And the reassurance is given by tackling the problem at its roots, by exposing the notions of justice and reward that underlie their unease and insecurity. Their "horizon of expectations," which certainly includes notions of distributive justice, is being stretched and redrawn in such a way that the contours of a new social world can begin to emerge. That is to say, those who long for salvation to come in this way are also being taught to perceive the world in a new way that will give due significance to that longing. One might say then that important elements in their experience are being allowed to bear on the basic theological beliefs of their society in such a way that a new sacred universe can emerge.

Now, it would be important to trace this development further in the history of the texts themselves. Wirkungsgeschichte *is not just a useful adjunct of the central exegetical task of explicating* the *meaning of a text but the tracing-out of the fruitfulness of particular texts in their various realizations, which is an essential part of understanding both their function and their sense.* Clearly that task lies beyond the scope of this essay, but a couple of indications may be given. In the first place, it is interesting to note the fact that this parable occurs only in Matthew's Gospel. Of course, not much can be read off that fact with any confidence, but it is, I think, at least a lively option that the reason for its restriction to Matthew is precisely its closeness to the conventions and narrative traditions of Jesus' day. Its real originality lies in the way in which it takes and remakes the commonplace beliefs of Jesus and his hearers. Outside that context it is apt to confuse and become obscure. Indeed we might suggest that whoever was responsible for Mark 4:11-12 and for the interpretation of the parable of the sower in Mark was expressing just such a sense of puzzlement about parables in general—though he was clearly wanting to make other assertions as well. Thus in Mark the real continuing history of the parables, with their exploration of notions of goodness and justice, may be thought to reside more in analogous or even in quite different forms of literary production, notably in his development of sayings of Jesus' about the nature of power and authority in terms of suffering and service.[39] And similarly we may see this process continued in Paul's exploration of notions like the justification of the ungodly, and in Luke's exemplary tales that explore the ethical implications of this kind of recasting of notions of goodness and justice. The parables play a vital part in the initiation of this process; their part in its continuation is far more ambiguous, as indeed Jülicher showed.

But Matthew does of course use the parable. And this is not surprising in itself, for Matthew of all the evangelists stands closest to the cultural traditions with which Jesus interacted. How Matthew uses it, however, is less clear and by no means widely agreed among commentators. It is easy enough to suppose that when Matthew uses it he is applying it to the situation of the Gentiles in relation to the Jews; and Matt. 22:1-14 suggests that this is at least a concern of Matthew's.[40] On the other hand, the context in the Gospel and the link between the final verse of the parable and the final verse of chapter 19 suggest that Matthew's interest is concentrated much more closely on the theme of reversal both as it applies to the rich young man in chapter 19 and as it is applied to the sons of Zebedee who wish to sit at Jesus' right and left hand in chapter 20. This concentration on the import of the parable for the church comes out in the note of warning sounded in the conclusion of the parable.[41] Thus the parable now must be seen as addressed to Matthew's community as he attempts to draw together its beliefs into a coherent whole that can shape and guide its life.

There are, of course, major problems about the interpretation of Matthew's understanding of the parable. He has chosen to set it in a Markan context, which he leaves virtually unaltered with the significant exception of the insertion of the saying—of which a variant is also found in Luke—about the disciples sitting on the twelve thrones judging the twelve tribes in the *paliggenesia*, and of the toning-down of Mark's saying about rewards for discipleship in this life. At one simple level the connection between the Markan context and Matthew's parable is given by the connection between Mark 10:31 and the stage direction in Matt. 20:8: *arxamenos apo tōn eschatōn heōs tōn prōtōn*. But whether or not that is Matthean redaction, Matthew underscores the point in his own conclusion to the parable, which almost has the effect of turning the saying in Mark 10:31 into a general rule.

The effect of setting the parable in this context is, of course, to underscore the themes of reward and reversal. The disciples who are promised the reward of sitting in judgment over the tribes of Israel are refused particular places of power in Jesus' kingdom and instead offered Jesus' cup to drink. And this is followed by a further warning against striving for preeminence and the injunction to seek the way of serving. In this way the emphasis is being laid on the reversal in the parable of the fortunes of the first- and the last-hired rather than on the question how a just man can reward different groups according to different standards. And if therefore the emphasis in the original version of the parable is on the nature of God and his justice, generosity, and goodness, here it has been thrown more sharply onto the reversal of values. What is to be rewarded is leaving all and following Jesus, rather than the—albeit righteous—accumulation of wealth. And even here care is required, for those who leave all must not in the end be concerned with position and power but must be prepared to suffer and to serve. In this they are indeed reflecting the nature of God and his Son Jesus.

That is to say, there is an interesting discontinuity and continuity between the original parable and Matthew's treatment of it. If both Jesus and Matthew rework the notion of rewards, there is nevertheless an interesting difference. For Jesus the question is what the fact that God rewards in different ways tells us about the nature of his rule and the consequences of this for those who feel outside his dispensation. In Matthew there is no question of two different parallel systems; rather, he seeks to inculcate what he sees as the essence of the law and the prophets which has been revealed and "fulfilled" by Jesus (Matt. 7:12). Indeed, the interesting thing is that Matthew, in constructing a new world for his community, is using as essential building blocks the notions of law, of commands which those who are called into the service of the kingdom are to obey, and of obedience that will be duly rewarded in the age to come. These are all notions taken over, albeit with a specific christological emphasis, from the Jewish tradition in order to provide a framework for Matthew's community with its own distinctive set of values. Interestingly, in Matthew 19—20 it is less the argument about the nature of God's justice that provides the key to the new values of the community than the surrounding Markan discussion of the notions of power and authority. The parable serves rather to reinforce the notions of obedience and rewards, which are indeed reworked by their inclusion in this context.

In this the parable and the surrounding teaching are directed not solely against Jews but also against the ways of the gentile world. There is, of course, no doubt about the fierceness of the polemic against the scribes and Pharisees in Matthew 23, but even here the polemic is directed against what Matthew sees as a misuse of the scribes' and Pharisees' position as interpreters of the Mosaic tradition.[42] Nor should the promise to the disciples that they will judge the twelve tribes be taken in a purely polemical sense, even with the saying in Matt. 19:30. The very inclusion by Matthew here of the reference to the twelve tribes shows the extent to which Matthew thinks in Jewish terms. However much Matthew may distance himself from the Pharisees and "their synagogues," he himself still understands himself as standing in full continuity with the Mosaic tradition.

All this of course requires much fuller discussion. My point here has to be a more general one—namely, to raise the question how far in the process of world building that follows on the preaching and death and resurrection of Jesus the new wine of Jesus almost inevitably has to be put into old skins for want of anything else. Matthew constructs a sacred universe of great attraction to the subsequent church, which will almost forget Mark in consequence. And yet much of the internal dynamic of this passage of Matthew comes directly from Mark, with Matthew providing a framework that is more traditional and that in the end obscures some of the more radical theological claims expressed, albeit elusively and metaphorically, in Jesus' parable. The strength of Matthew's Gospel is in linking the Christian community firmly with the religious traditions and aspirations of Judaism at the same time as reaffirming central aspects of Jesus' teaching about power and about forgiveness. But this linkage is achieved at the cost of blunting something of the radicalness of Jesus' perceptions of the graciousness and freedom of God. That is to say, the process of world building initiated by the parables and evidenced in their interpretation in the Gospels contains within itself that which is opposed to the very forces that set it in motion. But equally the literary history of the parables—their literary preservation, interpretation, and reproduction, by means of which the new worlds of Christianity were created—itself preserves those forces that can again set in motion the processes of reconstruction, if one has the key.

NOTES

1. Dodd's position is not altogether clear and certainly not always clearly reproduced. In principle, he would like to know exactly what the occasion of

utterance of a particular parable was; this is often taken to mean that he would like to know what was the particular *Sitz im Leben*—i.e., the type of social setting of the parable—but Dodd has more in mind the historical setting of the parables in Jesus' ministry. He concedes, however, that it is only rarely that we can have such detailed information, and in practice he has to be content with setting the parables in the context of Jesus' preaching of the kingdom. See C. H. Dodd, *The Parables of the Kingdom*, rev. ed. (London, 1936), 26–33, esp. 27: "It is only where something in the parable itself seems to link it with some special phase of the ministry that we dare press the precise connection. More often we shall have to be content with relating it to the situation as a whole."

2. Ibid., 195.

3. Of the works that could be mentioned here, two must stand for many: D. O. Via, *The Parables: Their Literary and Existential Dimension* (Philadelphia: Fortress Press, 1967), here quoted from the 1974 ed.; and Hans Weder, *Die Gleichnisse Jesu als Metaphern: Traditions- und redaktionsgeschichtliche Analysen und Interpretationen* Forschungen zur Religion und Literatur des Alten und Neuen Testaments (Göttingen: Vandenhoeck & Ruprecht, 1978). Weder, however, remains firmly committed to the attempt to place the parables and their senses in the history of the Christian tradition.

4. Cf. R. S. Crane's list: "life and death, good and evil, love and hate, harmony and strife, order and disorder, eternity and time, reality and appearance, truth and falsity, . . . emotion and reason, simplicity and complexity, nature and art" (*The Languages of Criticism and the Structure of Poetry* [Toronto, 1953], 123–24; quoted by J. Culler in *The Pursuit of Signs* [Ithaca, N.Y.: Cornell Univ. Press], 5).

5. The term, which is used by Karl Mannheim and Karl Popper, has been introduced into literary theory by Hans Robert Jauss; see his *Literaturgeschichte als Provokation* (Frankfurt, 1970), esp. 171ff. Jauss believes that the history of literature must attempt to describe the process of interaction between the readers' horizons of expectation and the text in such a way that the world-building (*weltbildend*, "world-forming," as opposed to *weltabbildend*, "world-imagining") function of the work becomes clear. This means *both* the abandonment of a historical objectivism that identifies the meaning of a work solely with its bringing to expression of the spirit of a particular age *and* the dismantling of purely mimetic understandings of literature. Such a process of interaction within a particular tradition extends, of course, beyond the immediate historical setting of the work; equally it will not be possible to understand the history of that process without an understanding of the initial context of communication, nor without relating it as a particular history to general history.

6. E.g., Culler, *Pursuit of Signs,* 47–79.

7. Cf. here Jauss's excellent discussion of the reception of *Madame Bovary* (*Literaturgeschichte*, 203ff.) and M. Riffaterre's discussion of Baudelaire's "Spleen" (*The Semiotics of Poetry* [Bloomington: Indiana Univ. Press, 1978], 63ff.).

8. Jauss, *Literaturgeschichte*, 171–72: "Das literarische Werk ist kein für sich bestehendes Objekt, das jedem Betrachter zu jeder Zeit den gleichen Augenblick darbietet. Es ist kein Monument, das monologisch sein zeitloses Wesen offenbart. Es ist vielmehr wie eine Partitur auf die immer erneuerte Resonanz der Lektüre angelegt, die den Text aus der Materie der Worte erlöst und ihn zu aktuellem

Dasein bringt: 'parôle qui doit, en même temps qu'elle lui parle, créer un inter-locuteur capable de l'entendre.'"

9. Weder, *Die Gleichnisse,* 62.

10. Ibid., 63.

11. Ibid., 64.

12. Ibid., 65.

13. Donald Davidson, "What Metaphors Mean," in *On Metaphor,* ed. S. Sacks (Chicago: Univ. of Chicago Press, 1979), 44.

14. Max Black, "Metaphor," *Proceedings of the Aristotelian Society* 55 (1954–55): 273–94, esp. 291ff. See the references there (285 n. 17) to I. A. Richards's work.

15. This interaction of the two ideas is strikingly missed by Weder, who writes, "The 'lion' receives a new sense by his appearing in Achilles' horizon; he is taken to describe *Achilles,* not Achilles to describe the lion." It is clear that Weder wants to deny such interaction because of his insistence (*Die Gleichnisse,* 68–69) that Jesus' concern is to understand man and the world in God's horizon, not to make God a function of human existence. But it seems hard to imagine how it is possible to explore or expound the nature of God without engaging in some kind of dialogue with contemporary understanding of human existence. Clearly, in any case, for Jesus' contemporaries such understanding would have been theological, and it is important to attempt to gain a fuller understanding of how such contemporary "horizons of expectation" are transformed in such parabolic utterance, without thereby denying the originality and freshness of Jesus' own theological perspective.

16. Black, "Metaphor," 290. This rather undercuts Weder's point (*Die Gleichnisse,* 62) that there is a difference in kind between the parables and metaphor such that we should speak only of an analogy between the two because in metaphors the semantic tension occurs within the framework of a sentence whereas in a parable it occurs within a more extended composition. It is perhaps true that more extended metaphors have a longer life, but this is likely to be a function more of their success as stories than of their difference in kind. Weder's further suggestion (n. 18) that the Gospel parables have lasted longer because the tension in them between *God's* rule and *worldly* experience is not so easily absorbed may have some force. But should we not speak of the tension as being not so much between God's rule and worldly experience as between different human conceptions of God's rule—that implicit in the standard sense of the primary subject and that conveyed by the metaphorical predication of the subsidiary subject?

17. For a fuller discussion of the manner in which conventional implications are determined by sentence-to-sentence and sentence-to-experience links, see A. M. Millar and J. K. Riches, "Interpretation: A Theoretical Perspective and Some Applications," *Numen* 28 (1981): 29–53; idem, "Conceptual Change in the Synoptic Tradition," in *Alternative Approaches to New Testament Study,* ed. A. E. Harvey (London, 1985), 37–60. To say that the interpreter needs to know as much as possible about contemporary practice and expectations does not mean that we are therefore committed to a view of the parables as realistic literature, such as has been vigorously advocated by Dodd and Jeremias. As we shall see immediately, the teller of parables may choose to modify contemporary practice in the course of his storytelling in order to make the metaphorical point he wishes to make. But he still does so against the background of contemporary expectations.

18. D. Flusser (*Die rabbinischen Gleichnisse und der Gleichniserzähler Jesus*, part 1, *Das Wesen der Gleichnisse* [Bern, 1981]) argues that the parables as a genre are closely similar to European fables, both in respect of the employment in the tradition of well-tried motifs with clearly understood references and in respect of the artificiality of the treatment of such themes. He suggests, moreover (p. 21), that the tradition of Jewish parable telling to which Jesus and the rabbinic parables belong was essentially concerned with religious interpretation of human life, of human behavior in the sight of God. After 120 c.e. there was a partial change in the tradition: the parables were used to illustrate biblical verses. Flusser points to two main themes that occur frequently in the rabbinic parables and that are common to Jesus' parables: the invited meal and work (p. 37; see the useful list of rabbinic texts on pp. 332–35). Flusser's linking of the parables with fables has been severely criticized by Hans Weder in a review in *Theologische Literaturzeitung* 109 (1984): 195–98, but his points about the use of traditional themes and his suggestions about the history of the rabbinic parables deserve more serious attention. By contrast, J. H. Drury's discussion of the antecedents of the Gospel parables (*The Parables in the Gospels: History and Allegory* [London, 1985]) concentrates too narrowly on the tradition of Ezekiel, *1 Enoch*, and 2 Esdras, with their strong tendency toward allegorization of the parables, though Drury does show again the correspondence of thematic material between the parables he cites and those in the Gospels. Of particular interest here are the "seed parables" Drury refers to in 2 Esdras 4:26–32; 8:41; 9:31 (pp. 26–28). Drury can argue so strongly for the connection between the Gospel parables and this tradition because he assumes that the background to the Gospel parables—and he is, of course, concerned hardly at all with what Jesus might have produced—was an entirely literary one. This seems odd when they contain so much obviously—originally at least—oral material. But here Drury's skepticism about scholars' ability to reconstruct the oral material behind the Gospels seems to encourage him to neglect even the possibility of its existence.

19. Black, "Metaphor," 290.

20. Cf. G. Bornkamm, "Der Lohngedanke im Neuen Testament," in *Studien zur Antike und Urchristentum: Gesammelte Aufsätze*, vol. 2 (Munich, 1963), 82.

21. This is, of course, very similar to what I perceive to be distinctive about Jesus' use of the term "kingdom of God"; see my *Jesus and the Transformation of Judaism* (New York: Seabury Press, 1982), esp. chap. 5. By announcing the kingdom in the context of his meals with tax collectors and sinners, Jesus is substantially revising the commonplace beliefs many of his contemporaries associated with that term and is introducing others. That is to say, the understanding of the term is changed by the new range of associations with which it is linked; at the same time the self-understanding of those to whom such an invitation is made is also being substantially challenged.

22. For Flusser's discussion, see *Die rabbinischen Gleichnisse*, 141ff., where he argues that the saying of Rabbi Tarphon (*m. Abot* 2.15–16) is evidence for a traditional rabbinic saying which underlies both the saying in *Abot* and Jesus' similar saying in Matt. 9:37–38//Luke 10:2. The saying in *Abot* reads, "Rabbi Tarphon says, 'The day is short and the work is great, the workers are slothful and the wages are rich and the administrator presses.' He used also to say, 'It is not for you to complete the work and you are not free to be idle. If you have learnt much

instruction, your task-master (the lord of your work) is faithful and will pay you the reward of your labor.'" We need not follow Flusser's detailed analysis all the way, though it is interesting to note that he suspects behind this saying the well-known Hippocratic saying "Life is short, art is long," as he generally argues for the influence of Hellenistic popular ethics on the rabbinic sayings and parables. In outline what he argues for is (a) that the tradition originally made a quite broad identification between work and "man's activity before and for God," as is also suggested by the earliest rabbinic parabolic saying attributed to Antigonus of Socho (1st half of 2d cent. B.C.E.) "Do not be like servants who serve their master on condition that they receive their wage. Rather be like servants who serve their master without insisting on being paid their wages"; (b) that the identification between work and learning or doing torah occurred in the tradition before Rabbi Tarphon; and (c) that therefore both Jesus, with his emphasis on the urgency of the harvest, that is, of the need for missionary work, and Rabbi Tarphon, with his application of the saying to (probably) doing torah, were producing variations on a common theme. The prevalence of this after all rather obvious equation is also shown by the address given by Rabbi Zeera on the death of Rabbi Bun (325 C.E.), where Rabbi Bun's early death is explained by the story of the king who, having hired a large crowd of laborers, goes out at the second hour and finds one whose work is of such quality that he calls him out and spends the rest of the day in conversation with him, for he had done more in two hours than the others in the whole day. This, of course, means that we must be cautious in comparing such parables to see just where the lines of similarity and dissimilarity lie.

23. E.g., Weder, *Die Gleichnisse*, 223 n.70, citing *Abot* 2:15–16; *Exod. Rab.* 30 (90d); *Lev. Rab.* 24 (123a); *p. Ber.* 2.5c, 15; *S. Lev.* 26.9 (450a); *Tanch* ביתסא 19b; *Abot* 1.3.

24. E. P. Sanders, *Paul and Palestinian Judaism* (Philadelphia: Fortress Press, 1977), passim.

25. Ibid., 94–95.

26. Cf. J. D. M. Derrett, "Workers in the Vineyard: A Parable of Jesus," *Journal of Jewish Studies* 25 (1974): 64–91.

27. Cf. E. P. Sanders, "Jesus and the Sinners," *Journal for the Study of the New Testament* 19 (1983): 5–36—and the interestingly revised version of that essay in *Jesus and Judaism* (Philadelphia: Fortress Press, 1985), 174–211—for a discussion of what constituted a "sinner" in 1st-cent. Judaism. Sanders reminds scholars that *reshachim* referred to those in flagrant breach of the law and castigates scholars he believes to have overemphasized the importance of the *haberim*'s influence on 1st-cent. Judaism. On this latter point, however, his own views have changed not uninterestingly between the two versions of the paper (see esp. *Jesus and Judaism*, 180–88), reflecting perhaps the general difficulty about making confident judgments in this area.

28. Cf. G Theissen, *The First Followers of Jesus* (London, 1978), esp. 33–95; idem, "'Wir haben alles verlassen' (Mc. X, 28): Nachfolge und soziale Entwurzelung in der jüdisch-palästinischen Gesellschaft des I. Jahrhunderts n. Chr.," *Novum Testamentum* 19 (1976): 144–58.

29. The point is made by Hans Weder (*Die Gleichnisse*, 227–28), though without much consideration of the actual identity of the "sinners and tax collectors," whom

he simply refers to as the "weak" as opposed to the "strong," namely, the Pharisees. "Are not the weak, the tax collectors and sinners, just as much subject to that notion of achievement [*Leistung*], though in a negative sense, insofar as they take over the dominant scale of values of strong and weak and determine their own place within it? The admired can never do without their admirers. *In the end everyone is subject* to the 'network of works' [*Werkzusammenhang*] that the parable is attacking" (p. 228, my trans., his emphasis). If such identification of the strong with the Pharisees is to be taken to refer to Jesus' situation in Galilee, then it raises serious questions about the strength of the Pharisaic presence there at the time, as well as about the precise nature of the Pharisees' teaching. In any case, the simple opposition between strong Pharisees and weak sinners is altogether too undifferentiated. Jesus' hearers may have had doubts about their entitlement to enter the kingdom, but these may have been motivated less by their admiration for the Pharisees than by the fact that their longing for a new age was linked with an acute sense of their own sinfulness, that they had betrayed their group's traditional norms—with an inability, that is, to come to terms with their particular tradition and heritage. The fact that the Pharisees advocated a renewal of the traditional norms by a redoubling of the group's efforts to keep the law certainly means that the two groups would sooner or later have been likely to come into conflict with each other; it does not mean that the parable's hearers originally defined themselves in terms of the Pharisees' self-understanding.

30. So rightly Weder, *Die Gleichnisse*, 221 n.54, agreeing with Derrett against Jeremias.

31. Against Via, *Parables*, 155.

32. Ibid., 154.

33. Weder, *Die Gleichnisse*, 226, quoting Bornkamm in "Der Lohngedanke," 88.

34. There are important discussions of this in P. Worsley's *The Trumpet Shall Sound: A Study of Cargo Cults in Melanesia* (New York: Schocken Books, 1968) and in Y. Talmon's "The Pursuit of the Millennium: The Relation between Religious and Social Change," in *Reader in Comparative Religion: An Anthropological Approach*, ed. W. Lessa and E. Vogt, 2d ed. (New York: Harper & Row, 1965), 522–37.

35. Cf. the important essay by Mary Hesse, *Science and the Human Imagination* (New York: Philosophical Library, 1955), where she argues that certain key analogies have dominated each period of scientific discovery, enabling scientists to schematize and make sense of their observations and experience.

36. Victor Turner, *Drama, Fields, and Metaphors: Symbolic Action in Human Society* (Ithaca, N.Y.: Cornell Univ. Press, 1974), 51.

37. Ibid., 28.

38. Cf. Theissen (*First Followers*, 34–35), who identifies various patterns of response to social anomie: evasive, aggressive, and subsiditive. In his terms, this is clearly a subsiditive response; but whereas many of the prophetic responses, as reported by Josephus, do no more than call up images from Israel's past history of deliverance, what Jesus' parable does is explore the theological implications of such patterns of response. It is this which may account for its power to suggest new worlds.

39. Jauss (*Literaturgeschichte*, 173–77) makes the important point that a literary tradition may be continued either by the continued reading and interpretation of

texts or by the production of new works of literature within that tradition. One of the advantages that students of the synoptic tradition possess in this respect is that they have evidence for the process of reception both in terms of continuing acts of interpretation and in terms of the production of new literary works and forms.

40. Cf. A. Kretzer, *Die Herrschaft der Himmel und die Söhne des Reiches* (Stuttgart, 1971), 288; and J. Dupont, "La parabole des ouvriers de la vigne (Matthieu, XX, 1–16)," *Nouvelle revue théologique* 89 (1957): 790.

41. Weder, *Die Gleichnisse,* 230.

42. There are those who believe that even here we should see "Pharisees" as a coded term for Matthew's Christian opponents; see the discussion by R. Garland in *The Intention of Matthew 23* (Leiden, 1979), 159–62. Though I find this ultimately unconvincing, it would, of course, only serve to underline the point.

16

Pharisees, Sinners, and Jesus

JAMES D. G. DUNN
University of Durham

One of the most striking features of the study of Christianity's beginnings in the past ten years or so has been the reassessment of Jesus' relationship with his native faith, particularly with the Pharisees, and the increasing impact of that reassessment. It is, of course, part of a much larger reappraisal of the relationship between Christianity and Judaism, a central element of which has been a growing realization that Christian attitudes toward Judaism have been deeply tainted and indeed warped by centuries of misunderstanding and prejudice. Already before the Second World War individual voices had been raised in protest on the non-Jewish side.[1] But the horror of the Holocaust forced a much wider circle of Christians to reexamine the nature and roots of anti-Semitism and to face up to the stark issue of whether, and if so to what extent, anti-Semitism is endemic to Christianity and rooted in its own sacred scriptures.[2] Since the Pharisees are the most immediate predecessors of rabbinic Judaism, which became Judaism's enduring form (and so the object of anti-Semitism through the centuries), it was inevitable that Christian perception of the Pharisees, not least in the Gospels, would have to come under particularly close scrutiny. And since Jesus is the founder of Christianity, which came to display such regrettable antagonism towards its founder's ancestral faith, it was equally inevitable that Jesus' relationship to the Pharisees should be a crucial issue within the larger debate.

As the reassessment of Jesus' relationship with the Pharisees has gathered strength a number of important claims have been staked out:

1. The Pharisees, the contemporaries of Jesus, have been misrepresented in at least some degree in the Gospels, particularly in Matthew and John, which reflect the growing antagonism between Christianity

and rabbinic Judaism after 70 C.E. This judgment would now command a widespread consensus within New Testament as well as Jewish scholarship.[3]

2. The Pharisees were not responsible for and had no part in the death of Jesus—a view long championed by Jewish scholars (H. Maccoby: the "Jewish view of Jesus".)[4]

3. Pharisees would not have been hostile to Jesus. Indeed, on the Jewish side the claim is quite often made that Jesus, far from being an opponent of the Pharisees, was himself a Pharisee.[5]

The high-water mark, so far, in this tide of reevaluation is the work of E. P. Sanders. In his *Jesus and Judaism*[6] he reexpresses all the claims so far outlined in his own terms and develops especially the last. In Sanders's judgment there was no substantive point of disagreement between Jesus and the Pharisees. In particular, the Pharisees would not have regarded the ordinary people (*'am ha-aretz*) as "sinners" beyond the pale of the law and would not have criticized Jesus for associating with them. The Pharisees did not have the power to exclude others from the social and religious life of Judaism. And the depiction of the Pharisees as superbigots attacking Jesus for offering forgiveness to the common people is ridiculous and offensive.[7]

All this can be summed up under the head of Jewish-Christian rapprochement: on the one hand, the Jewish attempt to reclaim Jesus; on the other, the Christian attempt to demonstrate the Jewishness of Jesus.[8] The proponents on both sides are usually well aware of the corollary: that the "blame" for any anti-Jewish element within the Christian Scriptures is to be shifted well beyond Jesus to a later stage—to Paul (as in Maccoby), or beyond 70 C.E. (as in Sanders).[9] The problem and consequences of thus separating Jesus from subsequent Christianity, however, have not been fully worked out. Nor has it been sufficiently appreciated that to replace the wedge between Jesus and Judaism with a wedge between Jesus and gentile Christianity has an unnerving echo of the equivalent attempts at the turn of the last century to isolate Jesus as a purveyor of a purer and less offensive gospel from the "Hellenization" begun by Paul and his successors.[10] Before the echos of the last Jesus-v.-Paul debate have died away there seems to be a growing need for a rematch.

Obviously there are too many issues caught up in the whole affair to be dealt with in a single essay. Here we can look at only one: the question of Jesus' relationship with the Pharisees as posed most recently and most challengingly by Sanders. In particular, is it the case that opposition between Jesus and the Pharisees as portrayed in the Gospels is all a retrojection of later controversies, without historical foundation within the ministry of Jesus? And is it the case that the "sinners" Jesus was criticized for befriending were the "truly wicked"?[11] These are only two of the many issues raised by Sanders's important work, but they provide a sizable enough agenda for the moment.

PHARISEES . . .

Despite repeated studies of the Pharisees there are still an astonishing number of disputed claims and unresolved questions on the subject. Here we confine ourselves to the single issue of the Pharisees' character and influence in the period prior to 70 C.E., with the years of Jesus' ministry particularly in mind. Only if we can gain a reasonably clear picture here will we be in any position to answer our question as to whether the opposition between Jesus and the Pharisees as portrayed in the Gospels reflects the historical realities of Jesus' ministry. We have in fact *four* potential sources from which to glean the relevant information: the rabbinic traditions themselves, Josephus, Paul, and the Gospels.

The Pharisees from the Perspective of
the Rabbinic Traditions

Here we are bound to start with the work of Jacob Neusner. Whatever issues he has left unresolved and however one may dispute particular findings, it cannot be denied that he has made a decisive beginning in the too long delayed task of providing a tradition-historical analysis of the amazingly rich and diverse traditions of the rabbis.[12] In particular, we must refer to his careful study of the traditions regarding the Pharisees before 70 C.E.[13] These traditions naturally have a first call on our attention, if only for the important fact that they provide *a picture of the Pharisees as the later rabbis chose to remember them.*

Neusner's findings are very striking. The traditions about the Pharisees before 70 C.E. specifically attributed to individuals or houses (the houses of Hillel and Shammai) consist of approximately 371 separate items. "Approximately 67% of all legal pericopae deal with dietary laws: ritual purity for meals and agricultural rules governing the fitness of food for Pharisaic consumption."[14] In his numerous subsequent writings, Neusner has continued to maintain the same point: this much-repeated concern with rules on agricultural tithes and ritual purity all focuses on table fellowship; the attempt to maintain in everyday life the purity laws designed for the temple was most at risk at the meal table.[15] The pre-70 strata of the Mishnaic law bear witness to a group where food taboos were the chief mode of social differentiation by which they maintained their continued existence as a group: "The Mishnah before the wars begins its life among a group of people who are joined by a common conviction about the eating of food under ordinary circumstances in accord with cultic rules to begin with applicable . . . to the Temple alone. This group, moreover, had other rules which affected who might join and who might not . . . [which] formed a protective boundary, keeping in those who were in, keeping out those who were not."[16]

Sanders however finds Neusner's analysis of the rabbinic texts "unpersuasive" and "made especially dubious by the evidence from Josephus." In more detail, Sanders's objection is that Neusner's conclusions are drawn only from the traditions explicitly assigned to individuals or to houses. "The summary does not reflect the numerous anonymous laws which probably represent *common* belief and practice, including large bodies of law on civil matters, worship, feasts and the temple cult." And Josephus shows the Pharisees to be simply lay experts in the law and says nothing about their having peculiar food and purity laws.[17]

There is some force in both points. But Neusner is by no means so vulnerable to the criticism as might at first appear. In his original treatment of the tradition attributed to the houses he had allowed the possibility that they were "relatively small and constituted only one part of the Pharisaic group in Jerusalem, a still smaller segment of Pharisaism as a whole."[18] And in *Judaism* he is scrupulously careful not to identify this early stage of the Mishnaic tradition with a particular named group. In the face of Josephus's silence regarding any concern on the part of the Pharisees for the purity of the meal table, he had made the important observation that on this point the Pharisaic group were different from the Qumran covenanters (not to mention the Christians latterly). For they "evidently did not conduct table-fellowship meals *as rituals*. The table-fellowship laws pertained not merely to group life, but to daily life quite apart from a sectarian setting and ritual occasion."[19] Consequently, they would be less distinctive for a readership looking at Judaism from outside, for whom the Jewish food laws would be striking enough,[20] so that the refinements of subgroups within Judaism would be lost on them (cf. Mark 7:3: ". . . the Pharisees and *all* the Jews . . ."). Besides this, Josephus with his strong Roman contacts would be well aware of Roman suspicion that special dietary laws were an indication of strange cults[21] and would not be anxious to highlight this aspect of Pharisaism in writings that take such pains to conceal the less acceptable (in Roman eyes) features of Pharisaism (see below).[22]

As for Sanders's former criticism, no doubt many of the unattributed traditions do go back to the pre-70 period. But even so, that should not be allowed to detract so much from Neusner's findings. It may simply mean that there was a strand of Pharisaism which, among other things, emphasized dietary rules at the daily meal table. But in fact the evidence calls for a stronger conclusion. For despite Sanders, it must be significant that such a high percentage of the attributed traditions focus upon one main aspect of practical piety. It strongly suggests that these rulings were sensitive matters or matters of dispute among the predecessors of the rabbis, so that relevant rulings were remembered by the post-70 dominant party by their attribution to leading figures of the past or as part of the houses disputes. The clear implication is that the purity of table fellowship was thus remembered as a matter of great importance within pre-70 Pharisaic circles or by a group or faction of Pharisees.[23] And whatever their numerical size in that period, they were strong enough not only to survive the catastrophe of 70 C.E. but also to stamp their authority on the tradition preserved by the rabbis.

In short, the evidence of the rabbinic traditions points clearly to the conclusion that *the purity of the meal table was an important concern among many of the Pharisees of Jesus' time* or at least within a significant faction of the Pharisees.

The Pharisees in Josephus

Here the main question is twofold: how to account for the differences in the pictures of the Pharisees which emerge from Josephus and from the rabbinic traditions; and what weight to give to the different emphases present in the various accounts of the Pharisees provided by Josephus himself.

The answer to the first is probably fairly straightforward, as we have already suggested. Josephus writes of the Pharisees, as on other matters, with an eye to his wider readership in sophisticated Greek-speaking society. This is particularly clear in what is his most consistent emphasis when he makes a point of describing the Pharisees: they are a "philosophy" (*War* 2.119, 166; *Ant.* 18.11); their beliefs are described in philosophical terms (*War* 2.163; *Ant.* 13.172); they resemble quite closely ($\pi\alpha\rho\alpha\pi\lambda\eta\sigma\iotaos$) the Stoic school or sect (*Life* 12). Clearly evident here is a deliberate and sustained strategy of commending the Pharisees as a philosophical school. Josephus was hardly likely to put that strategy in jeopardy by also presenting the Pharisees in the contrasting and much less appealing terms of a foreign superstition.[24]

When we consider the internal tensions between Josephus's various references to the Pharisees, particularly as between the *War* and *Antiquities,* the issue that comes to the fore is whether and, if so, to what extent the Pharisees were a significant influence on the religious and political life of the nation. The issue is posed by M. Smith:

> In the *War* [Josephus] says nothing of the Pharisees having any influence with the people. . . . In the *Antiquities,* however, written twenty years later, the picture is quite different. Here whenever Josephus discusses the Jewish sects, the Pharisees take first place, and every time he mentions them he emphasizes their popularity. . . .[25]

From this Neusner concludes, "We must discount all of [Josephus's] references to the influence and power of the Pharisees [in the Herodian period]."[26] They *had* been deeply involved in politics during the Hasmonean period, but at the time of Jesus they were a relatively small sect concerned primarily with matters of ritual purity.

This position must, however, be regarded as something of an overstatement. For one thing, the contrast between *War* and *Antiquities* is not so marked as Smith argues. *Whenever* Josephus mentions the three sects of the Jews, he always names the Pharisees "first," with Sadducees "second" and Essenes "third," in *War* as much as in *Antiquities,* as also in his *Life* (*War* 2.119, 162, 164; *Ant.* 13.171; 18.11; *Life* 10). On this point Josephus is again consistent: the Pharisees were the leading or most important of the different factions within first-century Judaism.

As to the difference in emphasis between *War* and *Antiquities* on the matter of the Pharisees' popularity and influence, an obvious explanation lies near to hand here too. In the immediate aftermath of the Jewish revolt (assuming the consensus view that *War* was published in the 70s), it would hardly be wise for Josephus to highlight the political influence of the Pharisees in the period leading up to the revolt. In fact he does note that "distinguished Pharisees" were consulted as the crisis deepened (*War* 2.411). And in his later writings it is not only the Pharisees' popularity with the people on religious matters of which he speaks (as in *Ant.* 18.15, 17) but also Pharisaic involvement in the revolt against Rome (*Ant.* 18.4; *Life* 21, 191, 197; note also *Ant.* 18.23). It would be unwise therefore wholly to discount the *Antiquities'* picture of Pharisaic influence and popularity: it is as likely that such an emphasis has been suppressed in *War* as that it has been exaggerated in *Antiquities;* apologetic considerations would play an important role in both cases. The truth probably lies somewhere in between.[27]

In short, the strong impression given by Josephus is that the Pharisees were the most important of the three or four main factions in Jewish social and religious life, outside the temple, of this period, and that the Pharisees were divided among themselves on the question of active involvement in the growing political crisis, with some leading Pharisees having influence in the highest Jewish councils and others active in the developing resistance. Even if the depiction of Pharisaic influence in *Antiquities* is exaggerated, therefore, the Pharisees cannot be discounted as a merely quietistic, purity sect without significant influence beyond their own circles. On the contrary, if we can speak of them as a coherent sect (as not only Josephus consistently does but also Acts 15:5, 26:5), we have to recognize *the likelihood that their influence reached well beyond their own ranks.*[28]

In addition, we should note the point made by A. I. Baumgarten: that when Josephus speaks of the Pharisees he regularly describes them as the party of ἀκρίβεια (*War* 1.110; 2.162; *Ant.* 17.41; *Life* 191; cf. *Ant.* 20.201 and note again the striking correlation in Acts 22:3, 26:5). The word denotes "exactness or precision," and when used in connection with "law" is most naturally taken in a sense like "strictness or severity" (*Greek-English Lexicon,* ed. H. Liddell and R. Scott). So when we read, for example, in *War* 2.162, that the Pharisees interpreted the laws or customs μετ᾽ ἀκριβείας, the implication is clear that *they were well known as those who interpreted the law with scrupulous exactness and strictness in detail.*[29] This strongly suggests that the Pharisees also saw themselves in an important sense as *guardians of the law and of the ancestral customs* (*Ant.* 13.297, 408; 17.41; *Life* 198). Moreover, if Josephus, the self-confessed Pharisee, is any guide, they naturally wished to commend such "strictness" to others (*Ant.* 1.14; 4.309; 5.132; 8.21; 18.345; *Ap.* 2.149, 187, 227–8). The implications of this for their relationship to a movement like that of Jesus are potentially important, but the picture is too incomplete to say more at this stage.

Paul the Pharisee

It is very surprising that in such discussions the potential evidence of Paul is rarely taken into account.[30] For Paul is the only first-century Pharisee apart from Josephus from whom we have any first-hand evidence. And Paul is the only Pharisee who speaks to us with his own voice from the period under scrutiny. Of course, Paul's testimony has to be discounted to some extent at least, since he can be regarded as a "hostile witness." But the testimony should certainly not be ignored or disparaged out of hand.[31]

The passages which obviously call for consideration are the two where he speaks of his own pre-Christian past: Gal. 1:13–14; Phil. 3:5–6. In addition, however, there are one or two passages where he speaks of his fellow Jews and where the most obvious interpretation is that he is thinking of the Judaism he knew best: especially Rom. 10:2–3, but also Rom. 2:17ff. In Gal. 1:13–14 he briefly describes his "way of life when he was in Judaism" in three clauses: he persecuted the church of God καθ᾽ ὑπερβολήν; he progressed in Judaism beyond many of those of his own age among his people; he was much more of a zealot (ζηλωτής) for the traditions handed down from the fathers. In Phil. 3:5–6 the most relevant part again has three elements: in terms of the law, a Pharisee; in terms of zeal (ζῆλος), a persecutor of the church; in terms of righteousness which is in the law, blameless (ἄμεμπτος). In Rom. 10:2–3, Paul bears personal testimony (no doubt on the basis of his own experience) to Israel's zeal for God (ζῆλον θεοῦ) and concern "to establish their own righteousness."

There are two features which recur in each description and which are worthy of special note. One characteristic of Judaism which Paul recalls and most naturally thinks of as typical of Judaism is "zeal"—zeal for God, zeal for the traditions of the fathers. In Jewish circles the classic examples of such zeal were well known: Simeon and Levi (Genesis 34; Jth. 9:4; *Jub.* 30.5–20), Phinehas (Num. 25:10–13; Sir. 45:23–24; 1 Macc. 2:54; 4 Macc. 18:12), Elijah (Sir. 48:2; 1 Macc. 2:58), and the Maccabees (1 Macc. 2:19–27, 50, 58; 2 Macc. 4:2; Josephus *Ant.* 12.271). It is notable that in each case this zeal led to taking the sword to maintain Israel's distinctiveness as God's covenant people. It is certainly just such zeal which motivated the Zealots, and it was also such zeal which Paul had in mind in Phil. 3:6 ("in terms of zeal a persecutor") when he recalled his own past.[32] But Gal. 1:14 indicates that "zeal for God," "zeal for the law," could be a relative thing ("much more a zealot") and could therefore presumably express itself in dedication to observing and maintaining the law as the mark of Israel's distinctiveness without necessarily resorting to the sword (cf. 1QS 4.4; 9.23; 1QH 14.14; *T. Ash.* 4.5). The implication is that Paul was comparing himself with his fellow students or younger Pharisees as all "zealous," but he much the more so because he resorted to the sword.

The other feature of these Pauline passages is the strong conviction of a secure status sustained not least by such zeal—of a progress beyond others (Gal. 1:14), of a righteousness sustained without reproach (Phil. 3:6), of a confidence of possessing light and knowledge to higher advantage than others by virtue of having the law (Rom. 2:17–20, 23). All this is most naturally understood as tied into and as a corollary to the "strictness" which, according to Josephus, characterized the Pharisees. The point seems to be confirmed beyond reasonable dispute by the corroborative evidence of two other witnesses: Acts 22:3 confirms that "zeal for God" and "strictness" in observing the ancestral law are closely synonymous concepts in the description of a Pharisee; and in *Ant.* 17.41, Josephus provides the nearest parallel to what Paul implies in the passages cited—that the Pharisees were a group of Jews who prided themselves on the strict observance (ἐξακριβώσει) of their ancestral law(s).

The picture which emerges from Paul, therefore, is what one might fairly call a Pharisee's view of Judaism. Or to be more precise, in such passages Paul recalls his self-understanding as a Pharisee and uses language and sentiments which must have been characteristic of the Pharisees as a "sect" (and which, of course, Paul now regards as mistaken). This should *not* be taken as evidence for the old interpretation of Pharisaism as boastful of self-achievement and consumed with meritorious point scoring. In speaking of his life as a Pharisee as "blameless" (Phil. 3:6), Paul most likely meant that he had lived to the full in the terms laid down for members of the covenant people (κατὰ δικαιοσύνην τὴν ἐν νόμῳ), including the law's provision for atonement and forgiveness.[33] And in talking of Israel's "seeking to establish its own righteousness" (Rom. 10:3), the thought is of *Israel's* righteousness—not available to those outside the covenant people—not of a righteousness achieved by Paul (τὴν ἰδίαν δικαιοσύνην).[34] Nor does it follow that Paul speaks in these passages for all Pharisees, or for Pharisees alone. But he probably does speak as a Pharisee and express views typical of Pharisees of his own day. From such evidence, therefore, we may fairly conclude that *in the middle decades of the first century, Pharisees were characterized by zeal for the law and concern to practice that pattern of life which maintained the righteousness of the covenant and Israel's status as the people of God.*

The Pharisees in the Synoptic Gospels

On this issue, Sanders is at his most confrontational: "It is incorrect to make purity the issue between Jesus and his critics." "Jesus' eating with the sinners probably did not involve him in a dispute with a superscrupulous group (whether called *haberim* or Pharisees)." "It is very probable that the issues of food and Sabbath are so prominent in the Gospels because of the importance which they assumed in the church." "There was no substantial conflict between Jesus and the Pharisees with regard to Sabbath, food, and purity laws."[35] A repeated claim is that the stories of such conflict are "obviously unrealistic":

> The extraordinarily unrealistic settings of many of the conflict stories should be realized: Pharisees did not organize themselves into groups to spend their Sabbaths in Galilean cornfields in the hope of catching someone transgressing (Mark 2:23–4), nor is it credible that scribes and Pharisees made a special trip to Galilee from Jerusalem to inspect Jesus' disciples' hands (Mark 7:1f). Surely stories such as these should not be read as describing actual debates between Jesus and others.[36]

There are a number of issues here to which we must come in due course (particularly the identity of the "sinners" and the likelihood of Pharisees seeking to influence religious practice in Galilee). For the moment, however, we will confine ourselves to the issue of whether the Synoptic testimony, and if so how much of it, can be admitted as evidence for Pharisaic attitudes in the period before 70 C.E., and particularly in regard to Jesus.

There is no question that many of the references to "Pharisees" in the Synoptic accounts are redactional: we need think only of such passages as Matt. 3:7; 5:20; 9:34; 12:24; 21:45; Luke 5:17, 21; 7:30; 19:39; not to mention the strong sequence of references found only in one of the evangelists (particularly Matthew 23 passim; Luke 14:1, 3; 15:2; 16:14; 18:10–11). Few would dispute that at least a considerable portion of this testimony has to be read in the light of the increasing conflict between Christianity and rabbinic Judaism in the 80s of the first century, and that traditions have been shaped and particularized to make them more serviceable for congregations (usually Jewish Christian congregations) who felt themselves under threat from the successors of the Pharisees. But that still leaves a core of references strongly attested in the triple tradition, that is, including Mark—particularly Mark 2:16, 18, 24 pars.; 7:1 pars. And it is a good deal more difficult to treat these as the product of disputes of the post-70 period.

1. It is of course arguable that Mark was written after 70 C.E.,[37] though most scholars find the late 60s more compelling.[38] But even if a post-70 date for Mark should be accepted, that may still be inadequate for the case. In the aftermath of the destruction of Jerusalem the rabbinic school at Jabneh did not immediately leap into prominence. The probability is that they took time to find their feet and that their influence took some years to spread.[39] The hypothesis that rabbinic pressure on the Christian congregations of the post-70 period left its imprint on the Jesus tradition used by Mark probably requires a date for Mark into the early 80s before it becomes realistic. Such a date is not impossible, but the later Mark has to be dated the weaker the hypothesis becomes.

2. Few would want to argue that the material in Mark 2:15–28 and 7:1–5 was created de novo at the final stage of the Gospel. Apart from anything else, there are too many indications of editorial work on a preformed tradition: in particular, Mark 2:20 as a qualification added in the light not least of the Christian congregations' continuation (or resumption) of the practice of fasting some time after Jesus' death; and Mark 7:3–4 as added to explain Pharisaic practice to a gentile readership, making it necessary for 7:5a to recapitulate the introduction (7:1–2). There is clear evidence in these chapters of Mark's having taken over an *earlier* tradition in which Christian congregations in the period before 70 C.E. felt it necessary to defend themselves from criticism particularly on matters of table fellowship, ritual purity, and Sabbath observance, and in which the criticism is explicitly attributed to Pharisees.[40]

3. Looked at from a slightly different angle, the same evidence also indicates that at the pre-Markan level of the tradition it is *internal Jewish* disputes which are in view: a dispute over *how* the Sabbath should be observed, not yet *whether* it should be observed (Mark: 2:27–28; contrast Rom. 14:5), and a dispute where the indisputably Jewish use of κοινός in the sense of "impure, defiled" has also to be explained to Gentiles (7:2). The indication again is of *Jewish* Christian congregations, who from within Judaism or as part of Judaism felt the need to explain and defend themselves to other Jews.

4. This evidence accords well with other indicators of intra-Jewish concerns in the period prior to 70 C.E. (apart from those already reviewed above). On the one hand there is evidence of both *Jub.* 2.29–30, 50.6–13

and CD 10.14—11.18 that concern to protect the Sabbath by means of particular halakoth was already well developed before the time of Jesus.[41] On the other there is the strong testimony of Gal. 2:11-14 that pressure was exerted on the Antioch congregation from within the Jerusalem leadership anxious to maintain the traditional dietary laws. Mark's portrayal of Pharisees concerned about issues of Sabbath observance and ritual purity fits much more closely into the period of Jesus' ministry than Sanders allows,[42] as does Mark's depiction of Pharisees' high regard for ancestral traditions (Mark 7:3, 5; cf. Gal. 1:14; Josephus *Ant.* 13.297, 408; 17.41; *Life* 198).

To sum up, when the four strands of testimony regarding the Pharisees examined above are put together, a remarkably coherent picture emerges of Pharisees as a sufficiently clearly defined group to be described as a "sect," αἵρεσις, whose most characteristic concern was to observe the law and ancestral traditions with scrupulous care, with a deep desire to maintain Israel's identity as the people of the law, as expressed not least in developing halakoth regarding the Sabbath and particularly ritual purity. To attempt to undermine this picture by setting Neusner's findings aside, by failing to follow through the logic of Josephus's description of the Pharisees as ἀκρίβεις, by ignoring the testimony of Paul, or by banishing all the evidence of the Synoptics to as late a date as possible must be counted a policy of desperation. It is not necessary to argue that the picture applies equally to all Pharisees ("the Pharisees"). Nor does the precise relation of the *haberim* in particular to the Pharisees in general (or of Pharisees/*perushim* to sages, or of scribes to Pharisees) need to be resolved.[43] But *that there were at the time of Jesus a number of Pharisees, and probably a significant body of Pharisees, who felt passionately concerned to preserve, maintain, and defend Israel's status as the people of the covenant and the righteousness of the law, as understood in the already developed halakoth, must be regarded as virtually certain.*

... SINNERS ...

The thrust of Sanders's attack on older positions, however, is that the Pharisees would not have been critical of those who did not observe the law in the way and to the degree they accepted as their own obligation. In particular, they would not have condemned the ordinary people as "sinners" because they failed to observe all the halakoth they took upon themselves. The "sinners" with whom Jesus consorted were genuinely "wicked" and "traitors."[44] And contraction of impurity did not constitute one a "sinner" or exclude from the covenant; it simply prevented participation in the temple cult for the period of impurity, and lack of concern about impurity outside the temple simply made one a non-*haber*.[45] Here again Sanders is justified in reacting against overstatements by too many New

Testament scholars about Pharisaic hostility to the ordinary people.[46] But here too the question has to be asked whether Sanders in turn has *over-reacted* and tried to push the pendulum too far in the opposite direction.

The Role of Social Conflict in Group Self-Definition

We may consider, first of all, the insights of sociology and social anthropology into the nature of groups and their self-definition. Once we realize that the social identity of a group depends to a large extent on the distinctiveness of its practices and beliefs, it also becomes evident that the corollary of "identity" is "boundary," that self-definition involves self-differentiation.[47] In all this, ritual as a visible expression of social relationships usually plays a particularly important role.[48] Moreover, wherever there are other groups whose distinctives differ, each group is liable to be particularly protective of its identity and react strongly to any perceived threat to its boundaries.[49] Indeed, group conflict can play an important role in binding a group more closely together[50] and will often cause it to put still greater emphasis on the distinctiveness of its rituals. And particularly where groups are close to one another in origin or character or distinctives, the conflict is liable to be all the more intense:[51] it is the brother who threatens identity most ("sibling rivalry"); it is the party most like your own which threatens to draw away your support and undermine your reason for existence as a distinct entity.

Such generalized observations provide a remarkably close fit with the data we have already gleaned: the Pharisees as a distinct "sect" whose distinctives included particularly their zeal for scrupulous interpretation and observance of the law and, for at least a large proportion of their number, concern to maintain temple purity at the meal table (the "separated ones").[52] It is inherently likely that such zeal would cause friction with other groups, not least with the other main "sects" of the time—Sadducees and Essenes. And so the evidence indicates, as we shall see. But it would also be unsurprising if at least some Pharisees refused to settle quietly behind their boundaries or opt merely for self-defense but sought to maintain their identity by taking the offensive. This was all the more true when there was any sense or conviction that what Pharisee or *ḥaber* practiced was what God required of Israel as a whole.[53] Certainly wherever the zeal of a Phinehas or a Mattathias was lauded and the concern of such heroes to preserve Israel's integrity as the people of God was taken as an ideal, a highly likely corollary would be a sharp criticism of any who seemed to threaten Israel's birthright or to deny Israel's obligation under the covenant—if not outright persecution of the offenders. None of this goes beyond the evidence already examined. On the contrary, the portrayal of the Pharisees in Mark 2 and 7 is shown to have considerable plausibility, and Paul's persecuting zeal to be not necessarily exceptional. The alternative of a quietistic group wholly absorbed in their own affairs and completely uncritical of others becomes increasingly unrealistic.[54]

Finally we should note that Sanders's argument is in danger of rebounding on him. For the effect of arguing that Jesus was very close to the Pharisees, not least on matters of the law, is to *increase* the likelihood of tension between Jesus and the Pharisees, not to lessen it. A Jesus who sat wholly loose to the law would pose little threat: he was self-condemned. But a successful Jesus who was observant of the law and yet not a Pharisee or *ḥaber* was bound to be regarded as some sort of competitor and to cause some friction and conflict.[55] And a Jesus who was as loyal to the covenant but who had different ideas of what covenant loyalty involved would almost certainly pose a threat to Pharisaic self-understanding and identity. In particular, where issues such as Sabbath or purity halakoth were put in question by Jesus' conduct, critical and defensive questions were bound to arise for those who prized such halakoth.

In short, given the data we have regarding the Pharisees in the period prior to 70 C.E., it would be very surprising had they *not* been critical of Jesus and his disciples.

Who Were the Sinners?

But what about the "sinners"? Was the "offense" of Jesus at this point that he consorted with the wicked and promised them the kingdom even though they remained unrepentant of their wickedness?[56] Certainly Sanders is on good ground when he questions the too simplistic equation of "sinners" and "people of the land." In the Old Testament the word (ἁμαρτωλός) occurs most frequently in the Psalms, almost always translating רָשָׁע, and the rendering "wicked" is wholly appropriate. Similarly, with the word's most common use in the apocryphal writings (Sirach). But Sanders ignores the fact that the word is also used in a *factional* context to denote those outside the boundary of the group who use it, where wickedness, by definition, is conduct outside the boundary, conduct unacceptable to those inside.[57]

The most obvious example of this is where "sinner" is used more or less as a synonym for "Gentile": Ps. 9:17; Tobit 13:8 (6); *Jub.* 23.23–24; *Pss. Sol.* 1.1; 2.1–2; Luke 6:33 = Matt. 5:47; Mark 14:41 pars.; Gal. 2:15. In such passages the unifying concept is not that Gentiles are by definition murderers and robbers. Rather it is that their conduct lay outside the boundary of the law. They were literally lawless: they did not have the law because they did not belong to the covenant people, the people of the law. And so, not knowing the torah, naturally they did not keep it.

More to the present point, however, is the fact that boundaries could also be drawn *within* the people of Israel, with "sinners" used to describe those of whom a particular faction disapproved. So in the case of 1 Maccabees, where the "sinners and lawless men" (1:34; 2:44, 48) certainly at least include those whom the Maccabeans regarded as apostate Jews, as Israelites who had abandoned the law.[58] Of course, what is in view here is no mere breach of Sabbath or purity halakoth but full-scale apostasy, conduct no longer contained within the bounds of the covenant. Nevertheless, the fact remains that this is a factional viewpoint: "sinners" is language used by one group of Israelites to describe another.

What is at issue here is the definition of what conduct proper to the covenant actually involves and who determines it. In the case of 1 Maccabees the issue was fairly clear cut, at least for the Maccabeans: the Syrian sympathizers among the Jews had departed too far from the torah. But in the subsequent period the issue became more blurred as different heirs of the first wave of Maccabean resistance sought to define in their own terms what walking in the ways of the torah meant. For example, *Jubilees* shows that the calendar became an important bone of contention. The implication is clear: that observance of festival or ordinance whose date had been wrongly computed was regarded (by those for whom *Jubilees* speaks) as *non*observance, as failure to maintain the covenant, as walking in the errors of the Gentiles (particularly *Jub.* 6.32–35; also 23.16, 26).[59] *Jubilees* does not use the pejorative "sinner" in this context, but the connotation is the same: those Jews who disagreed on the calendar showed disregard for the law of festivals and so put themselves outside the covenant, made themselves like gentile sinners.

A similar attitude is evident in the earliest parts of the *Enoch* corpus and provides further evidence of a bitter calendrical dispute which divided Judaism probably in the second century B.C.E. "The righteous," "who walk in the ways of righteousness," clearly marked themselves off from those who "sin like the sinners" in wrongly reckoning the months and the feasts and the years (82.4–7).[60] Less specific is the accusation of *1 Enoch* 1–5, where again a clear line of distinction is drawn between the "righteous/chosen" and the "sinners/impious" (1.1, 7–9; 5.6–7). But here too an internal Jewish factional dispute is clearly in view: the sinners are addressed directly and roundly rebuked ("You have not persevered, nor observed the law of the Lord," 5.4). "Sinners" here are Jews who practiced their Judaism differently from the "righteous."[61]

A more virulent usage of the same kind occurs regularly, as we might have expected, in the Dead Sea Scrolls. Again and again the political and religious opponents of the sectarians are attacked as the wicked, the men of the lot of Belial, who have departed from the paths of righteousness, transgressed the covenant, and suchlike (e.g., CD 1.13-21; 1QS 2.4-5; 1QH 2.8-19; 1QpHab 2.1-4; 5.3-8). And again and again it is clear that the touchstone which divides "righteous" from "sinner" was not what the typical non-Essene would regard as blatant wickedness but the torah as interpreted within the community (e.g., CD 4.8; 1QS 5.7-11; 1QH 7.12)— that is, a sectarian interpretation which would doubtless have been disputed at many points by the nonsectarians, who were categorized in turn as "those who seek smooth things" and "deceivers" (1QH 2.14-16; 4.6-8; 4QpNah 2.7-10). If we follow the usual view of these opponents, such denunciations were directed particularly against the Pharisees:[62] in this case it is the Pharisees themselves who are the "sinners"! The point, however, is that once again we have clear evidence that in the period leading up to the time of Jesus, and in a community in existence during Jesus' ministry and beyond, "sinner" was used as a sectarian word to denounce those outside the bounds of the sect itself.[63]

A further example is the *Psalms of Solomon,* written less than a century before Jesus' ministry. They too clearly have been composed by those who regarded themselves as the "righteous," the "devout" (e.g., 3.3-7; 4.1, 8; 9.3; 10.6; 13.6-12; 15.6-7). But the "righteous" are not the covenant people as a whole; the usage is again clearly factional and amounts to a claim that only this faction properly "live in the righteousness of [the Lord's] commandments" (14.2). Similarly with the obverse in the repeated attacks on "sinners." Once again "sinners" are not synonymous with Gentiles or the blatantly wicked. On the contrary, "sinners" often refers to the Jewish opponents of the "devout," probably the Hasmonean Sadducees who had usurped the monarchy and defiled the sanctuary (1.8; 2.3; 7.2; 8.12-13; 17.5-8; 23).[64] According to 4.1-8 they sit in the Sanhedrin, they live in hypocrisy, they try to impress the people, they deceitfully quote the law. They do not maintain proper standards of ritual purity (8.12).[65] In the reckoning of the devout, such sinners have no part in Israel's inheritance: the promise was not made to them (17.5, 23). Here then is another case where "sinners" was used by Jews for other Jews who did not live by the standards of righteousness which the devout held before themselves.

A similar internal Jewish polemic is evident in the document which of all the "intertestamental" literature is usually dated (in its present form) closest to the time of Jesus: the *Testament* (or *Assumption*) *of Moses.* In *T. Mos.* 7 (set in the final author's own time) there is a forthright attack on "godless men, who represent themselves as being righteous"; "with hand and mind" they "touch unclean things" even though they themselves say, "Do not touch me, lest you pollute me" (7.3, 9-10). In view of our earlier findings we may well have to recognize here another attack on the Pharisees themselves, where different interpretations of ritual purity requirements were at the heart of the dispute.[66]

It should not escape notice that we have just reviewed a sequence of documents which include those having the strongest claim to represent attitudes of Jewish groups in Palestine contemporaneous with Jesus. And a common feature of them all is a factional conflict within the Judaism of their time. In view of this evidence we may well have to conclude that no period of ancient Judaism was so riven with factional dispute as the time of Jesus. Nor should we regard those labeled "sinners" simply as "apostates"[67]—those who in the eyes of all Jews had abandoned the covenant. That they *had* done so is certainly the view of the various authors; but that is simply to underline the factional character of these documents. From the perspective of those with a narrower definition of what covenant righteousness required it was natural to accuse those who disagreed with that definition of having abandoned the covenant. Such has been the attitude of rigorists and traditionalists throughout the ages. But those (i.e., sinners) who viewed things from *outside* the circle of the "righteous" would doubtless have a different understanding of the matter.

Against this background it has to be said that the Gospel usage of "sinners" makes perfect sense. It is wholly plausible to see "sinner" functioning in the Gospels as a *factional term*, describing those whose conduct was regarded as unacceptable to a sectarian mentality—that is, not just the blatantly wicked but those who did not accept the sect's interpretation of the law or live in sufficient accord with that interpretation. This fits too well with what we have learned of the Pharisees to be easily ignored. It is precisely those who were "scrupulous" in their adherence to the law and the ancestral customs who would be most liable to criticize others whose observance was, in their eyes, significantly less scrupulous (= *un*scrupulous). It is precisely those who were earnest in their practice of ritual purity who would be most likely to count others as sinners who did not share that zeal or who blatantly disregarded matters of purity. The fact that "tax collectors" are linked with "sinners" in the Synoptic testimony (Mark 2:15–16 pars.; Matt. 11:19//Luke 7:34) should not be counted as evidence that "sinners" meant blatant lawbreakers: tax collectors were despised more for national and political than religious reasons; only the Zealots would have regarded the job of tax collecting for the Romans as antithetical per se to a life lived in accordance with the law. More relevant is Mark 2:16 pars.: "sinners" as the antithesis of the "righteous." This is precisely the language of sectarianism reviewed above: the sin of the "sinners" is that they stand outside the boundaries of righteousness as defined by the "righteous." We need not assume that the Pharisees were as rigid on this matter as the

Essenes: they did not necessarily regard all non-Pharisees as sinners—perhaps only those who made light of Pharisaic concerns.[68] Nevertheless, the conclusion presses upon us: *The more that members of the Jewish community departed from the standards which the Pharisees as a rule saw to be necessary to maintain covenant righteousness, the more likely these Pharisees would be to dub them "sinners".*

Pharisees in Galilee?

One other issue cannot be ignored: whether the Gospel's portrayal of Jesus coming under attack from Pharisees *in Galilee* is credible. Sanders questions it, following the conclusion of Smith: "There is strong evidence that there were practically no Pharisees in Galilee during Jesus' lifetime."[69] But Smith's reading of the evidence is at least open to question and may have to be discounted as tendentious.[70]

1. It is certainly the case that the only Pharisees Josephus speaks of in Galilee had been sent from Jerusalem (*War* 2.569; *Life* 189–98). But in these accounts Josephus was not attempting to describe social or religious life in Galilee; he was writing a military history, and the Pharisees in question are mentioned because they served as emissaries from Jerusalem. For the same reason he speaks of synagogues only in the context of narrating factional disputes (*Life* 276–80, 293–303) and mentions the Sabbath only when it inhibited military action (*Life* 159, 275–79; *War* 2.634). A more accurate description of Josephus's testimony on this matter therefore would be that the only Pharisees Josephus had *cause* to mention in these passages were from Jerusalem. Since the matter of whether there were or were not Pharisees in Galilee is irrelevant to his purpose, his silence on the score means nothing.

2. Smith plays down the significance of the fact that the great Pharisee Yohanan ben Zakkai lived in Galilee—in a village called 'Arav—for eighteen years (probably between 20 and 40 C.E.), during which time only two cases of halakah were brought to him.[71] But as Neusner has noted, the explanation for this may simply be that Yohanan was not yet well known and that the Galileans preferred to seek halakic rulings elsewhere.[72] We may note in addition that Hanina ben Dosa, who is once described as Yohanan's pupil (*b. Ber.* 34b), also came from 'Arav.[73] Yohanan's period of residence in Galilee may not therefore be read as evidence for Pharisaic disengagement from Galilee. On the contrary, it may be evidence of a deliberate Pharisaic strategy to station some of the most promising younger Pharisees in different parts of the country to ensure that halakic rulings were readily available.[74] Indeed, if part of Pharisaic motivation in practicing temple purity outside the temple was to demonstrate and maintain covenant righteousness throughout Israel, a natural corollary would be for

some at least to follow the Pharisaic halakoth in different population centers throughout the promised land.

3. Smith has overlooked a further piece of evidence of potential importance. In *Ant.* 20.38–48, Josephus narrates the conversion of Izates, king of Adiabene, who initially had been told that circumcision would not be necessary. But then another Jew arrived, one Eleazar, who came from Galilee and who had a reputation for being very strict (πάνυ ἀκριβής) concerning the ancestral laws (20.43). When he learned of the situation he sternly warned Izates against committing the impiety of offending against the law and thereby against God (20.44). Since ἀκριβής is Josephus's characteristic description of the Pharisees (see above, "The Pharisees in Josephus"), the most obvious conclusion is that Eleazar was a Pharisee. And even if he was not so designated he clearly shared the typical Pharisaic concern to maintain the law and the traditions with scrupulous care. Either way, Eleazar confirms that at the time of Jesus Galilee was by no means devoid of those who observed the law with Pharisaic strictness. Moreover, the episode provides some confirmation that such a one would also and naturally be concerned that others who yoked themselves to Israel should be properly observant of the law. The issue here, of course, is that of circumcision, but in the perspective of the devout, proper observance of food laws and Sabbath were equally obligatory for the member of the covenant people.[75] And the readiness to find fault with others who failed to maintain that observance would likely be equally vocal.

4. Finally, we may simply repeat the point already made: that the evidence of the Gospels themselves cannot *all* be dismissed or postponed to a post-70 context. Passages like Mark 2 and 7 in particular must be allowed as testimony at least for the presence of *some* Pharisees on *some* occasions in Galilee in the period before 70 C.E. No more than that is needed.[76] It is not even necessary to argue for many Pharisees having residence in Galilee. As Mark 7:1 indicates, Pharisees may have been sent or have come down from Jerusalem to view the new phenomenon which Jesus represented.[77] In short, the relative lack of reference to Pharisees in Galilee constitutes very little of a case for rejecting the Gospels' own testimony on the point. There is evidence that some Pharisees, or equally strict devotees to the law and the customs, did live in or come from Galilee. And the likelihood that such a popular movement as the one represented by Jesus would attract attention from the larger grouping of Pharisees in Jerusalem must be considered rather high, and certainly much higher than either Smith or Sanders allows.

We may conclude, therefore, that Pharisees were liable to be critical of conduct and teaching which called into some question the priorities they regarded as covenant imperatives. Those who sat light to this righteousness they would regard as unrighteous, or "sinners." If Jesus was seen to encourage such attitudes they would be likely to criticize him too. All the more so if on other points Jesus and the Pharisees shared similar concerns: the closer Jesus was to the Pharisees, the more he would actually constitute a threat to their identity and boundaries, and the more hostile they would be to him. There is no good reason to doubt that Jesus came under such criticism already during his period of success and popularity in Galilee. The Gospel pictures offered in Mark 2 and 7 are at this point wholly plausible and should not be lightly discarded. There is no need to exaggerate Pharisaic influence on religious attitudes and practices of the day,[78] or Pharisaic hostility to non-Pharisees or to "people of the land" in particular. But neither is it helpful to resort to caricature, as though the Gospels' portrayal depended on the assumption that the Pharisees were "supersnoopers" who spent their time looking for infringements of Sabbath or purity halakoth. All that the data require is that there were Pharisees in Galilee at some points during Jesus' ministry who were critical of his conduct, in respect of Sabbath, ritual purity, and table fellowship with those whom the Pharisees regarded as "sinners." That portrayal fits too well with all the available data to be set aside.

... AND JESUS

Despite the objections raised most recently by Sanders, the earliest portrayal of Jesus in relation to Pharisees and sinners is remarkably consistent with what we know of his Pharisaic contemporaries. The degree to which the evidence is mutually supportive has not been given sufficient weight.

1. The Pharisees were scrupulous in their interpretation of the law and maintenance of the customs handed down (so Josephus; and Paul and the Gospels agree).

2. One very important aspect of that strictness in relation to law and tradition was a concern to maintain temple purity at the daily meal table (so rabbinic tradition, which is strongly supported by the Gospels and consistent with a view which Paul had abandoned [contrast Gal. 1:13–14; Rom. 14:14]).

3. Such zeal for the law as expressed not least in ritual was probably one of the chief identity markers of the "sect" of the Pharisees, which marked them off from other Jews at least in the degree of their devotion. Where any threat to that identity and boundary was perceived, Pharisees were liable to react against that threat; the more zealous they were, the more violent the reaction (as Paul himself confirms; and again the Gospels cohere).

4. As a sect with clear ideas of what character of life and conduct was required to maintain the covenant righteousness of the people of God,

Pharisees were highly likely to regard as "sinners" those who disagreed with them and who lived in open disregard of this righteousness—as had the groups behind the early *Enoch* writings, the *Psalms of Solomon,* and the Dead Sea Scrolls (so again the Gospels).

5. Other scattered evidence refutes the notion that the Pharisees would have avoided Galilee, and suggests rather that at least some Pharisees would have been concerned enough about a movement in Galilee like that around Jesus to inquire more closely into it and to criticize it for failure on sensitive points where they saw their interpretation of Israel's heritage being disregarded or threatened (as, once again, the Gospels narrate).

In short, it is very likely, after all, that the portrayal of Pharisees, sinners, and Jesus in passages like Mark 2 and 7 accords very closely with the historical realities of Jesus' ministry and may not be discounted as a retrojection of later controversies into the period of Jesus' ministry.

Indeed, far from being left with an uncomfortable wedge between Jesus and gentile Christianity, the overall perspective we have gained from our study enables us to recognize an important line of continuity between Jesus and his successors. For behind the particular objections and charges leveled against Jesus was the central fact that Jesus was ignoring and abolishing boundaries which more sectarian attitudes had erected *within* Israel. This is in no way an anti-Semitic conclusion, nor should it be regarded as a blanket criticism of all Pharisees. It simply attempts to reckon seriously with what was an *internal* Jewish dispute, a confrontation between Jewish factions. Nor does it necessarily implicate the Pharisees in Jesus' crucifixion: that is a further question requiring further discussion. Nor does it solve all problems regarding the transition from Jesus to Paul: that too requires more careful delineation. But at least it does help us see how a Christianity which broke through the boundaries of Israel's own distinctiveness sprang from a Jesus who posed such a challenge to the boundary between Pharisee and sinner. In other words, the recognition of the Jewishness of Jesus need not separate Jesus from the Christianity he founded, just as the recognition of the Christian significance of Jesus need not separate him from the faith of his own people.

NOTES

1. Particularly G. F. Moore, "Christian Writers on Judaism," *Harvard Theological Review* 14 (1921): 197–254; R. T. Herford, *The Pharisees* (London: George Allen & Unwin, 1924; Boston: Beacon Press, 1962); and J. Parkes, *The Conflict of the Church and the Synagogue* (1934; New York: Atheneum, 1969).

2. See esp. the debate occasioned by R. Ruether's *Faith and Fratricide: The Theological Roots of Anti-Semitism* (New York: Seabury Press, 1974); A. T. Davies,

ed., *AntiSemitism and the Foundations of Christianity* (New York: Paulist Press, 1979); and J. G. Gager, *The Origins of Anti-Semitism* (New York: Oxford University Press, 1983). Note also C. Klein, *Anti-Judaism in Christian Theology* (Philadelphia: Fortress Press, 1978); note from the Jewish side S. Sandmel, *Anti-Semitism in the New Testament* (Philadelphia: Fortress Press, 1978).

3. See, e.g., W. D. Davies, *The Setting of the Sermon on the Mount* (New York and Cambridge: Cambridge Univ. Press, 1964), 256–315, esp. 290–92; J. Koenig, *Jews and Christians in Dialogue* (Philadelphia: Westminster Press, 1979), chaps. 4 and 6; and F. Mussner, *Tractate on the Jews* (London: SPCK, 1984), 164–76.

4. The most recent proponents are H. Maccoby (*The Mythmaker: Paul and the Invention of Christianity* [London: Weidenfeld & Nicolson, 1986], 45–49 [the phrase is used on pp. 208–10]) and E. Rivkin (*What Crucified Jesus?* [Nashville: Abingdon Press, 1984]). For earlier literature, see esp. D. R. Catchpole, *The Trial of Jesus* (Leiden: E. J. Brill, 1971).

5. Most recently by H. Falk (*Jesus the Pharisee* [New York: Paulist Press, 1985]) and Maccoby (*Mythmaker*, 29–44). So also J. T. Pawlikowski (*Christ in the Light of Christian-Jewish Dialogue* [New York: Paulist Press, 102]). The claim is usually firmly denied on the Christian side; see, e.g., S. Westerholm, *Jesus and Scribal Authority*, Coniectanea biblica, New Testament (Lund: C. W. K. Gleerup, 1978), 128.

6. E. P. Sanders, *Jesus and Judaism* (Philadelphia: Fortress Press, 1985).

7. See ibid., esp. chap. 7, "The Sinners," which is a reworking of "Jesus and the Sinners," *Journal for the Study of the New Testament* 19 (1983): 5–36.

8. For other literature, see D. A. Hagner, *The Jewish Reclamation of Jesus* (Grand Rapids: Zondervan, 1984), 23–39; and Mussner, *Tractate*, 109–14.

9. Though some Jewish scholars are willing to shift "blame" for the hostility to Jesus from one group within 1st-cent. Judaism to another: from Pharisees to high priests (Rivkin, *What Crucified Jesus?*) or to Pharisees over against charismatics (G. Vermes, *Jesus the Jew* [London: William Collins Sons, 1973], 80–82), or from Pharisees in general to the house of Shammai in particular (A. Finkel, *The Pharisees and the Teacher of Nazareth* [Leiden: E. J. Brill, 1964], 134–43; Falk, *Jesus*). Cf. J. Bowker, *Jesus and the Pharisees* (New York and Cambridge: Cambridge Univ. Press, 1973): Pharisees/*perushim* as a more extreme wing of the Hakamim (sages). For older discussion, see, e.g., J. Jocz, *The Jewish People and Jesus Christ* (London: SPCK, 1954), 17–42.

10. See, e.g., A. Harnack, *What is Christianity?* (London: Williams & Norgate, 1901); and W. Wrede, *Paul* (London: Green, 1907), 177–80.

11. Sanders, *Jesus*, 210.

12. For questions of methodology, see, e.g., J. Neusner, "The Use of the Later Rabbinic Evidence for the Study of First-Century Pharisaism," in *Approaches to Ancient Judaism: Theory and Practice*, Brown Judaic Studies 1 (Missoula, Mont.: Scholars Press, 1978), 215–28. But P. S. Alexander's protest ("Rabbinic Judaism and the New Testament," *Zeitschrift für die neutestamentliche Wissenschaft* 74 [1983]: 237–46) is evidently still necessary.

13. J. Neusner, *The Rabbinic Traditions about the Pharisees before 70*, 3 vols. (Leiden: E. J. Brill, 1971).

14. Ibid., 3:303–4.

15. J. Neusner, *From Politics to Piety: The Emergence of Pharisaic Judaism* (Englewood Cliffs, N.J.: Prentice-Hall, 1973), 81–96.

16. J. Neusner, *Judaism: The Evidence of the Mishnah* (Chicago: Univ. of Chicago Press, 1981), 69–70.

17. Sanders, *Jesus*, 188, n. 59.

18. Neusner, *Rabbinic Traditions* 3:279. See also idem, "The Fellowship (חבורה) in the Second Jewish Commonwealth," *Harvard Theological Review* 53 (1960): 125, 128.

19. Neusner, *From Politics to Piety*, 87–88.

20. See, e.g., Philo *Leg.* 361; Plutarch *Quaest. Conviv.* 4.5; Tacitus *Hist.* 5.4.2.

21. Seneca *Ep. Mor.* 108.22: "Abstinence from certain kinds of animal food was set down as a proof of interest in the strange cult." Cicero *Pro Flacco* 28.67: "barbarous superstition." Tacitus *Ann.* 2.85.4: ". . . Jewish rites . . . that superstition."

22. Josephus, on the other hand, can given an extensive account of the Essenes (*War* 2.119–261) since he had distinguished them from the Pharisees and since they were no longer a factor within Judaism in the post-70 period.

23. Note also that the very name "Pharisees" (the "separated") points to their having a characteristic practice that set them apart from their fellow Jews. See esp. E. Schürer, *The History of the Jewish People in the Age of Jesus Christ*, rev. and ed. G. Vermes et al., vol. 2 (Edinburgh: T. & T. Clark, 1979), 396–98: "A separation from uncleanness is always a simultaneous separation from unclean persons." "The Pharisees must have obtained their name from a separation in which the main body of the people did not participate, in other words, from having set themselves apart, by virtue of their stricter understanding of the concept of purity . . . from that uncleanness which, in their opinion, adhered to a great part of the people itself." See also below, nn. 29, 53.

24. See again n. 21 above.

25. M. Smith, "Palestinian Judaism in the First Century," in *Israel: Its Role in Civilization*, ed. M. Davies (New York: Jewish Theological Seminary of America, 1956), 75–76.

26. Neusner, *From Politics to Piety*, 65.

27. Cf. Schürer, *History*, 395: "However indifferent to politics Pharisaism was to begin with, the revolutionary trend which gained increasing ground among the Jews in the first century C.E. is to be attributed, indirectly at least, to its influence."

28. According to Neusner (*Judaism in the Beginning of Christianity* [London: SPCK, 1984], 53), the Pharisees "claimed the right to rule all the Jews by virtue of their possessing the 'Oral Torah' of Moses"; so also Schürer, *History*, 389–91; and Rivkin, *What Crucified Jesus?* 41, 44–47. Sanders (*Jesus*, 188) thinks that Josephus has exaggerated the success of the Pharisees but accepts that "there is every reason to think that the Pharisees tried to have their views of the law carry the day."

29. A. I. Baumgarten, "The Name of the Pharisees," *Journal of Biblical Literature* 102 (1983): 413–17. Baumgarten goes on to argue that the name "Pharisees" probably also involved a play on the sense *parosim*, "specifiers," during our period (pp. 422–28).

30. Regrettably Maccoby chooses to ignore or to discount Paul's own testimony in Rom. 11:1; Gal. 1:13–14; Phil. 3:4–6; and to argue the fanciful thesis that Paul

was a Greek/Gentile on the basis of a reference in Epiphanius (*Pan.* 30.16.6–9), whose tendentiousness is not hard to detect. Since Paul's role as persecutor would require political sanction, it must certainly have enjoyed high priestly backing, and cooperation between high priest and Pharisee on such a matter is entirely plausible (cf. *Ant.* 2.411, 4.159–60; *Life* 21, 191–94).

31. So, e.g., Neusner (*Judaism in the Beginning*, 45–61; and "Three Pictures of the Pharisees: A Reprise," in *Formative Judaism: Religious, Historical, and Literary Studies*, 5th ser., Brown Judaic Studies 91 [Chico, Calif.: Scholars Press, 1985], 51–77) still confines his discussion of the Pharisees to our other three sources. E. Rivkin (*A Hidden Revolution* [Nashville: Abingdon Press, 1978]) recognizes the importance of Paul's testimony but devotes only a little over two pages to it.

32. See further J. D. G. Dunn, "'Righteousness from the Law' and 'Righteousness from Faith': Paul's Interpretation of Scripture in Romans 10:1–10," in *Tradition and Interpretation in the New Testament* (E. E. Ellis festschrift), ed. G. F. Hawthorne (Grand Rapids: Wm. B. Eerdmans, 1987), 216–28. See also my *Romans*, Word Biblical Commentary 38 (Waco: Word, Inc., 1988).

33. For the importance of atonement and forgiveness within Judaism, see esp. E. P. Sanders, *Paul and Palestinian Judaism: A Comparison of Patterns of Religion* (Philadelphia: Fortress Press, 1977), index under "atonement" and "forgiveness."

34. See ἴδιος, in *Greek-English Lexicon of the New Testament*, ed. W. Bauer, W. F. Arndt, and F. W. Gingrich. Cf. E. P. Sanders, *Paul, the Law, and the Jewish People* (Philadelphia: Fortress Press, 1983), 38: "'Their own' righteousness, then, is not characterized as being self-righteous, but rather as being the righteousness which is limited to followers of the law" (further literature in n.107).

35. Sanders, *Jesus*, 199, 209, 264.

36. Ibid., 178, 265.

37. So Sanders would maintain; for others, see W. G. Kümmel, *Introduction to the New Testament* (London: SCM Press, 1975), 98 n.65.

38. Kümmel, *Introduction*, 98; and see now esp. M. Hengel, *Studies in the Gospel of Mark* (Philadelphia: Fortress Press, 1985), 1–30, nn.

39. See esp. G. Alon, *The Jews in Their Land in the Talmudic Age*, vol. 1 (Jerusalem: Magnes Press, 1980).

40. See the much fuller tradition-history analysis in J. D. G. Dunn's "Mark 2:1—3:6: A Bridge between Jesus and Paul on the Question of the Law," *New Testament Studies* 30 (1984): 395–414. See also idem, "Jesus and Ritual Purity: A Study of the Tradition History of Mark 7:15," in *A cause de l'Evangile*, Festschrift J. Dupont, Lectio Divina 123 (Paris: Editions du Cerf, 1985), 251–76. Among other literature, see, e.g., H. Merkel, "Jesus und die Pharisäer," *New Testament Studies* 14 (1967–68): 194–208, esp. 202–6; H. F. Weiss, φαρισαῖος, in *Theological Dictionary of the New Testament* 9:41; Westerholm, *Jesus*, 71–75, 96–103; and Mussner, *Tractate*, 176–79.

41. In his various studies (see above, nn.13, 15, 16, 28), Neusner notes that in the pre-70 rabbinic traditions, concern for observances of Sabbaths and festivals follows rulings on ritual purity and agricultural matters in frequency.

42. C. Thoma (*A Christian Theology of Judaism* [New York: Paulist Press, 1980], 113) summarizes the position fairly: "Not only the final, redacted parts of the New

Testament but even the earlier ones indicate opposition as well as affinity between Jesus and the Pharisees."

43. Sanders questions whether *haberim* and Pharisees were identical but accepts that "before 70 there was probably an appreciable overlap between Pharisees and *haberim*" (*Jesus*, 187). Bowker (*Jesus*, 35) expresses the point neatly: "There is no indication that all Pharisees were members of a fellowship, although all members were Pharisees and accepted their views on Jewish law." See also A. Oppenheimer, *The 'Am Ha-aretz* (Leiden: E. J. Brill, 1977), 118–19; and Westerholm, *Jesus*, 13–15. It is worth noting that the more one discounts Josephus's picture of the Pharisees as widely influential (as Sanders does; see above, n. 28), the more closely they will tend to approximate to the *haberim*—whereas the less significant the *haberim* were within the important Pharisee sect, the more difficult it is to account for the strong influence they had on subsequent rabbinic ideals. In fact *haberim* and "Pharisee" are usually regarded as to all intents and purposes synonymous terms (see esp. Schürer, *History*, 398–99). On Pharisees and sages, scribes and Pharisees, see Bowker, *Jesus*, esp. 13–15, 21–23. Rivkin (*Hidden Revolution*) sees "scribes" and "Pharisees" as synonymous terms; contrast J. Jeremias, *Jerusalem in the Time of Jesus* (Philadelphia: Fortress Press, 1969), 254–56.

44. Sanders, *Jesus*, esp. 177–80; see below, n. 68.

45. Ibid., esp. 180–87.

46. Sanders's criticism is directed particularly against J. Jeremias, *New Testament Theology*, vol. 1, *The Proclamation of Jesus* (London: SCM Press, 1971), 108–13; see Sanders, *Jesus*, esp. 385 n. 14. But see also below, n. 68.

47. See esp. H. Mol, *Identity and the Sacred* (Oxford: Basil Blackwell, 1976), 57–58: "It is precisely the boundary . . . which provides the sense of identity."

48. Mol, *Identity*, 233; and M. Douglas, *Purity and Danger* (London: Routledge & Kegan Paul, 1966), 62–65, 128.

49. Douglas, *Purity*, 124. Cf. P. L. Berger and T. Luckman, *The Social Construction of Reality* (Baltimore: Penguin Books, 1967), 126: "The appearance of an alternative symbolic universe poses a threat because its very existence demonstrates empirically that one's own universe is less than inevitable."

50. See esp. L. A. Coser, *The Foundations of Social Conflict* (London: Routledge & Kegan Paul, 1956).

51. Coser, *Foundations*, 67–72.

52. See above, n. 23. As J. Neusner ("The Pharisees in the Light of the Historical Sources of Judaism," in *Formative Judaism*, Brown Judaic Studies 37 [Chico, Calif.: Scholars Press, 1982], 71–83) notes, since Pharisees lived among their fellow Jews (contrast the Qumran covenanters), "this made the actual purity-rules and food-restrictions all the more important, for only they set the Pharisee apart from the people among whom he constantly lived." Jeremias (*Jerusalem* 259–62), however, makes the surprising assumption that the regulations regarding the Qumran community can be used to build up a picture of "Pharisaic communities." But see Oppenheimer, *'Am Ha-aretz*, 147–51.

53. Bowker, *Jesus*, 21: "In *theory* the extent of the Ḥakamic movement was coterminous with the Jewish people. . . . The movement was not intended to be a party within Israel. It was intended to be Israel itself." There is all the difference, however, between such a self-perception or ideal and the social reality of such a

movement. Bowker also notes that "Pharisees/*perushim*" probably first appeared as a description of the Ḥakamic movement used by *others* (p. 15). See also below, n. 63.

54. Neusner shows keen awareness of the sociological dimensions of his discussion; see, e.g., *Judaism*, 69–75.

55. For the possibility of quite serious conflict among the Pharisees themselves, see above, n. 9. That Pharisees would also differ in their attitudes to Jesus (cf. esp. Luke 13:31) is also inherently probable.

56. Sanders, *Jesus*, 206.

57. In one place, Sanders does define "sinners" quite properly as "those beyond the pale and outside the common religion by virtue of their implicit or explicit rejection of the commandments of the God of Israel" (ibid., 210). But the question is, What counted as implicit rejection of the commandments? And in whose eyes?

58. J. A. Goldstein, *1 Maccabees*, Anchor Bible 41 (New York: Doubleday & Co., 1976), 123–24.

59. We need not presuppose that a clear rupture had already taken place within Israel at this time such as the establishment of the Qumran community involved (see, e.g., Sanders, *Paul*, 367–74; and J. C. Vanderkam, *Textual and Historical Studies in the Book of Jubilees* [Missoula, Mont.: Scholars Press, 1977], 281–83), but a factional attitude is clearly evident.

60. Sanders, *Paul*, 360; and G. W. E. Nickelsburg, *Jewish Literature between the Bible and the Mishnah* (Philadelphia: Fortress Press, 1981), 48.

61. Cf. L. Hartman, *Asking for a Meaning: A Study of 1 Enoch 1–5*, Coniectanea biblica, New Testament (Lund: C. W. K. Gleerup, 1979), 132.

62. See, e.g., M. Black, *The Scrolls and Christian Origins* (London: Thomas Nelson & Sons, 1961), 23–24; G. Vermes, *The Dead Sea Scrolls* (London: William Collins & Co., 1977), 152; and Nickelsburg, *Jewish Literature*, 131.

63. See further M. Newton, *The Concept of Purity at Qumran and in the Letters of Paul*, Society for New Testament Studies Monograph Series 53 (Cambridge: Cambridge Univ. Press, 1985), esp. 15–19. We need not attempt any further clarification on the very difficult question of whether the Qumran covenanters regarded themselves as the people of the covenant in toto, and so Pharisees, etc., as those outside the covenant ("sinners"); or as representative of the eschatological people of the covenant whose boundaries at least in principle stretched beyond the membership of the sect (see Sanders, *Paul*, 240–57). Either way the point remains the same: they regarded others as sinners who saw themselves as full, law-abiding members of the covenant people and who were so regarded by the bulk of their fellow Jews.

64. R. B. Wright, "Psalms of Solomon," in *The Old Testament Pseudepigrapha*, ed. J. Charlesworth, vol. 2 (New York: Doubleday & Co., 1985), 642. Sanders warns against a simple lumping-together of Sadducees with Hasmoneans (*Paul*, 403–4). A straightforward equation of the psalmist(s) with the Pharisees should also be avoided, although of the Jewish sects known to us "it is the Pharisees whom they most closely approximate" (Nickelsburg, *Jewish Literature*, 212).

65. The accusations of a passage like 8:11–13 should not be read as an impartial and objective testimony. This is factional propaganda and polemic, with a fair degree of exaggeration, reflecting the priority which the "righteous" placed on the correct observance of rituals laid down in the torah.

66. Where opponents are identified, the usual assumption is that Pharisees are in

view. See, e.g., D. Flusser, *Jesus* (New York: Herder & Herder, 1969), 47; and Jeremias, *Jerusalem*, 250.

67. As Sanders (*Paul*) tends to do—though, of course, he is treating the texts on their own terms.

68. The antagonism between Pharisees (or *ḥaberim*) and the people of the land should not be exaggerated; see Oppenheimer, *'Am Ha-aretz*, 156–69; and Sanders, *Jesus,* esp. 177–80. We should note also the references in Luke 7:36; 11:37; 14:1, which speak of Pharisaic hospitality. But Jeremias has not overstated the position as much as Sanders claims (see above, n. 46.).

69. M. Smith, *Jesus the Magician* (New York: Harper & Row, 1978), 157; cited by Sanders, *Jesus,* 292, 390 n. 90. Josephus (*Ant.* 18.15) does imply that the Pharisees' influence was greatest in the cities, though in the same context he refers to their influence on the people, the multitude (18.15, 17).

70. I owe several observations in what follows to a working paper prepared by my research student Paul Trebilco.

71. Smith, *Jesus,* 157.

72. J. Neusner, *A Life of Rabban Yohanan ben Zakkai,* 2d ed. (Leiden: E. J. Brill, 1970), 47.

73. Ibid., 47, 51.

74. Ibid., 48; and Sean Freyne, *Galilee from Alexander the Great to Hadrian, 323* B.C.E. *to 135* B.C.E.: *A Study of Second Temple Judaism* (Wilmington, Del.: Michael Glazier, n.d.), 317, 321–23, 341 n. 78. I. Abrahams (*Studies in Pharisaism and the Gospels,* ser. 1 [1917; New York: Ktav, 1967]) refers to Buchler's conjecture that Shammai was a Galilean. See further Freyne, *Galilee,* 341 n. 74.

75. Circumcision: esp. Gen. 17:9–14. Food laws: esp. Leviticus 11; Deuteronomy 14; 1 Macc. 1:62–63; cf. Acts 10:14; 11:3. Sabbath: esp. Exod. 31:12–17; Isa. 56:6–8.

76. Smith's talk of "the synoptics' picture of a Galilee swarming with Pharisees" (*Jesus,* 157) is an unnecessary exaggeration.

77. Apart from Josephus's accounts of Pharisees being sent to Galilee (*War* 2.569; *Life* 189–98), there is a rabbinic tradition that one of Johanan's pupils was sent to investigate a *ḥasid* living at Beth Rama (probably Galilee) who is said to have been strangely ignorant of purity regulations (Freyne, *Galilee,* 316). See also Vermes, *Jesus,* 56–57.

78. See again above, n. 28.

17

Jesus: Aspects of the Question of His Authority

HUGH ANDERSON
Florida Southern College

Howard Clark Kee occupies a prominent place in the recent movement among biblical scholars, especially in North America, toward full and explicit treatment of the social dimension in ancient history.[1] "Both sociology of knowledge and sociology of religion are now seen to be essential to the analysis of the shared world views that provide the coherence and rallying-point for the rise of religious movements and for their subsequent development."[2]

My particular interest is in the way Professor Kee applies this type of sociological analysis to the subject of authority models in the early church. Referring to Max Weber's classic discussion of charismatic authority,[3] he distinguishes between two kinds of authority reflected in the New Testament: the first spirit-bestowed, and the second by contrast official or delegated, or in some cases hereditary, authority. In the scenario that emerges with the Q layer of materials in the Synoptic Gospels, and to some extent in Mark, Jesus and his followers appear as charismatic leaders: their authority derives not from any professional training or qualification but from a personal dynamism stemming from above, from the divine. At another level, charisma becomes domesticated when the spirit's power is channeled and controlled institutionally, and is replaced by an organizational structure the right of entry to which is governed by rules and regulations. The authority to admit to membership, to include or to exclude, is then imposed by duly appointed "officers." This model of authority is beginning to appear in the pastoral epistles, where developing ecclesiastical polity is on the way toward the later monarchical episcopacy.[4]

Lacking Professor Kee's competence and experience in sociological method and research, I am nevertheless prompted to take up the much-controverted issue of the authority of Jesus, in the light of recent interest in the "functional" (i.e., charismatic) model of authority. In general the whole authority problem within the fabric of our societies and cultures is of great existential urgency for us. In whose hands lies the destiny of multitudes of ordinary human beings? We find it extraordinarily difficult to divorce the question from ideas of power. We identify authority with external or formal authority and normally associate it with the exercise of power, coercion, and constraint. The crisis of authority that has been a feature of our time is usually connected with rebellion against, and an active desire for, emancipation from dominative forces of one kind or another, whether institutions or individuals or objects—like the Bible, lately described as America's "iconic book."[5]

It is therefore important to notice at the outset that in the New Testament context the word ἐξουσία is primarily focused upon a quite different idea or set of ideas. Basically it generally signifies that one is of moral right or qualified or permitted to act, or sanctioned by another morally accredited source or person. "It does not have the connotation of jurisdiction over others, much less the power to impose force on other persons, but rather the holder's rightful freedom to act."[6] If we bear this in mind, we should at least be saved from the uncritical conceit that what overwhelmed those around Jesus was the sheer unprecedented *sovereignty* of his presence and being.[7]

Despite the recent tendency to play down the significance of the redaction-critical method in the study of the Gospels,[8] it is, in my view, imperative that in dealing with the matter of Jesus' authority we should try to keep apart as rigorously as possible historical inquiry into the *Sitz im Leben Jesu* of the evangelical traditions and inquiry into the intention and perspective of the redactor(s) responsible for the Gospels in the form in which they have come down to us. The confusion that results from running these two types of inquiry together, as if diverse Gospel materials could be laid alongside one another in an undifferentiated way for the purpose of historical reconstruction, may best be exemplified by brief consideration of E. G. Selwyn's essay "The Authority of Christ."[9] Selwyn maintains that Mark 1:22 could well be paraphrased, "He [Jesus] taught them like a sovereign and not as the rabbis." Jesus' sovereignty resides for Selwyn in the messianic authority he claims and exercises, mainly by going far beyond the Jewish scribes in superseding the plain sense of the law "by one that lay far deeper and had wider range, and belonged not to the Jewish Church but to the Kingdom of God." At the close of his article, on the other hand, Selwyn holds that the Emmaus story (Luke 24:13–35) testifies to Christ's own method of teaching "by the appeal to Scripture and Tradition": "Beginning with Moses and all the prophets he interpreted to them in all the scriptures the things concerning himself" (Luke 24:27). The Jesus who supersedes scribal interpretation is thus finally brought back into line with the scribal style.

The obvious inconsistency in Selwyn's presentation could be avoided by observing that the editorial or redactional hand of Luke is much in evidence in his Easter witness. The Emmaus story reveals Luke's artistry and embodies one of his most prominent redactional motifs, the "fulfillment of prophecy."[10] The motif appears already in Luke 4:20, when in the synagogue at Nazareth, Jesus crowns the marvelous prophecy of Isa. 62:1–2 with the words "Today this scripture has been fulfilled in your hearing." Accordingly, Luke 4:20; 24:26–27; 24:44ff. are best understood not as descriptive of Jesus' own mode of teaching but as indicators of Luke's redactional standpoint from which he views Christ as the fulfillment of the entire Scripture and as *the mediator of its meaning as a whole.*[11]

Redaction criticism has concerned itself mainly with the overall purpose, intention, and theology of each evangelist. Our interest here is to investigate briefly the evangelists' individual attitudes to our specific issue, the authority of Jesus.[12] Luke's account of the healing of the man with the unclean spirit on the Sabbath day (Luke 4:31–37) corresponds fairly closely with Mark's (Mark 1:21–27). Both link Jesus' authority with his teaching ministry, though Mark alone characterizes his teaching as new ("What is this? A new teaching!" 1:27) and differentiates it from the scribal manner of teaching. Whereas the scribes depended on the sanction of a carefully transmitted chain of tradition, which by their exegetical expertise they traced back to the Scripture or, more particularly, the Pentateuch, Jesus is presented in Mark especially as claiming a remarkable freedom to say his own say without founding himself upon the old texts, as in the Beelzebub controversy story (Mark 3:21–30), for instance. Is this emphasis, we might ask, part of Mark's understanding of the event of Jesus Christ as a *novum?*

Mark, followed less emphatically by Matthew (10:1) and Luke (10:19), couples Jesus' teaching activity with his exorcism or healing, his healing power being directly related to his authority (Mark 3:15; 6:7). That Jesus was in fact both exorcist and teacher is highly probable. D. Daube remarks that a great rabbi was expected to be prominent in both teaching and healing, and cites the case of Johanan ben Zakkai (died around 80 C.E.), a pupil of Hillel. But the talmudic passage he refers to is a rather generalized description of how the rabbi should be versed in the subtleties of torah as well as in astronomy and geometry, the conversations of angels and those of evil spirits.[13] By comparison, what Jesus was versed in as teacher, Mark is simply not interested in. From the redactional point of view, his account diverts attention from *what* Jesus taught, to the healing power of his person as the source of his authority. This is not negated by Mark's stress on *Jesus' teaching in parables* in chapter 4, for there the focus is not on Jesus' words as easily grasped holy words but on the mysterious relation between Jesus' own person and the presence of the kingdom of God.

What of the so-called conflict stories in Mark 2:1—3:6? Here once again Mark divulges virtually nothing of the content of Jesus' teaching. In the prominent stories of 2:15-17, and 2:23-28, the searchlight is turned on a presumably "floating" saying of Jesus, which in the process of its trans-mission has become encased in a brief narrative framework. Now, it has to be conceded that the narrative setting of each of these five stories (con-cerning, respectively, the forgiveness of sin, table fellowship with sinners, fasting, plucking ears of grain, and healing on the Sabbath) is implausible and artificial. The scribes and Pharisees appear as if from nowhere in Mark's Gospel, in the most unlikely places. Nevertheless, eminent modern critics have not been deterred from finding in these five reports the real ground for the radical split and bitter hostility between Jesus and the Jewish religion, Jesus' apparent disregard for the law, and his attack on Jewish or pharisaical legalism.[14]

In my view, E. P. Sanders is correct in holding that there is no direct violation of the law on Jesus' part. Certainly in Mark 2:1—3:5 there is nothing so outrageously offensive to Jewish religious susceptibilities as to culminate in the conspiracy of the Pharisees and Herodians to destroy Jesus (Mark 3:6). The centerpiece of the account of the healing of the paralytic (Mark 2:1-12; cf. Matt. 9:2-8; Luke 5:18-26) is actually Jesus' disputation with the scribes (Mark 2:5b-10a) interposed somewhat awkwardly within the report of the miracle. Accordingly, though Mark's report does close with the usual amazement of the crowd at the miracle, the reader is turned away from the miracle itself to what appears to be decisive for Mark, namely, Jesus' authoritative affirmation to the paralytic: "My son, your sins are forgiven" (Mark 2:5b).

The pericope does not justify the common view that Jesus *places himself in God's stead* by forgiving sins.[15] Sanders rightly observes that the scribes' charge of blasphemy against Jesus and their question "Who can forgive sins but God alone?" are incompatible with Jesus' statement "Your sins are forgiven." The passive is significant and, as frequently in the New Testa-ment, points to God as the one who forgives—and this neither the scribes nor Jesus himself would have denied. At most, then, Jesus appears here as a divinely authorized spokesman for God, which would have been an irritant to the scribes but certainly not tantamount to blasphemy.[16] The Markan record of 2:1-12 has probably been shaped up in light of the later church's conviction that sin could be forgiven *by and in the name of Jesus.*

Jesus' table fellowship with "tax collectors and sinners" must have scan-dalized the Pharisees, extremely scrupulous as they were about purity and dietary laws.[17] But once again his call to such people to repent of their sins, far from causing vexation to Jewish religious leaders, would have been lauded by them.[18]

The debates in Mark 2:23–28 and 3:1–5 are really about the interpretation of the law, and though Jesus' interpretation may have irked the Pharisees, they could hardly have wanted to kill him for doing what they habitually did among themselves: venture a different opinion. Since for Mark, Jesus is primarily the teacher in parables par excellence, it is quite unlikely that he believes his authority lies in his superior and magisterial unfolding of the law's true intent. In fact, in the concluding conflict story (3:1–6) he reverts to the theme of Jesus' healing power, connected by the evangelist with the forgiveness of sins (2:5ff.).

When we turn to Matthew's account of the healing of the paralytic (9:1–8), we find explicit support for our previous contention that the story has been influenced by the later church's practice of absolution. "When the crowds saw it, they were afraid, and they glorified God, who had given such authority to men" (Matt. 9:8). It is inconceivable, especially in the light of the commissioning of Peter in Matthew 16:18–19 and the more general commissioning of the disciples in 19:18, that by the word "men" here Matthew means just "anyone and everyone." He surely has in view the ministers of Christ's church, whose derived power to "bind and loose" is awesome.[19]

Earlier in his Gospel, however, Matthew reveals his own individual emphasis. He takes up verbatim the sentence of Mark 1:22, "The crowd was amazed at the way he taught," and locates it quite differently at the close of the Sermon on the Mount (7:28). For Mark the awed response of the crowd occurs before they ever hear a word of Jesus' teaching. For Matthew the actual content of Jesus' teaching establishes his authority. For Mark, Jesus' authority resides in his Person, in his power to heal and declare the forgiveness of sins. On the other hand, "Matthew is skeptical about any post-Easter proclamation that God entered the world in Jesus which does not also contain the substance of Jesus' teaching—for Matthew to believe that God came in Jesus necessitates that you will do his teaching, otherwise it is not belief" (see Matt. 28:18–20).[20]

It would be a mistake to suppose, however, that these different redactional nuances are carried through consistently by Mark and Matthew. The depiction of the scene in the temple (Mark 11:27—12:44; Matt. 21:23—23:39) is broadly similar in the two Gospels. In both, Jesus undertakes the so-called cleansing of the temple and engages in lengthy dialogue with various Jewish groups. The setting and content of the dialogue are, it has to be said, improbable and far-fetched. Would Jesus have been able to walk and teach unimpeded in the temple area,[21] especially if, with Sanders, we interpret his overthrowing the tables of the money-changers not as a cleansing, the initiation of a movement for the reform of the temple cultus and worship, but as a prophetic symbolic act signifying the imminent destruction of the temple revered by all Jews?[22] Would not members of the Great Sanhedrin of Jerusalem, who had jurisdiction over the temple, have known full well that Jesus possessed no authority in their territory? Would they have dallied to question him instead of merely calling the temple guard?

The temple episode is scarcely plausible historically. But it does serve the evangelists' redactional intention or purpose rather well. It is highly significant that Jesus appears to have taken over leading occupancy of the temple precincts (Mark 11:27; Matt. 21:23): *he* it is who is visited by the main representative cross sections of Jewish life, chief priests and elders (Mark 11:27; Matt. 21:23), scribes (Mark 12:28; Matt. 21:23), Pharisees (Matt. 21:15) and even some of the Herodians (Mark 12:13), and Sadducees (Mark 12:18). In debate with these groups, who appear on the scene in random fashion, Jesus holds the upper hand, and that too at the very heart and center of the ancestral religion, the temple in Jerusalem. It is not hard to detect what Matthew and Mark are about: they really are affirming that in word as well as deed Jesus Christ has completely superseded the old dispensation of Judaism. Only Matthew does so with much greater dramatic intensity by extending Mark's relatively mild strictures against the exhibitionism of the scribes (Mark 12:38–40) into a long, impassioned, and vituperative outburst against the scribes and the Pharisees—"hypocrites" (Matt. 23:13, 15, 23, 25, 27, 29), "blind guides" (Matt. 23:16), "sons of those who shed the blood of the prophets" (Matt. 23:30–31).

Luke, for his part, shares these same redactional motifs with Mark and Matthew (e.g., Luke 5:17–39; 20). But for Luke, Jesus' authority has another dimension: in his person and presence, he sums up and fulfills within himself the whole meaning of the whole of the old Scriptures. This is brought out, as noted earlier, by the placement of the appearances of Jesus in the synagogue at Nazareth at the very beginning of his public ministry: having read from the Isaiah Scroll the prophecy of 61:1–2, Jesus announces, "Today this scripture has been fulfilled in your hearing" (Luke 4:16ff.). Even more explicit is the declaration of the risen Christ in the Emmaus story (as we suggested previously): "And beginning with Moses and all the prophets, he interpreted to them in *all* the scriptures the things concerning himself" (Luke 24:27; cf. 24:44ff.).[23]

In the Fourth Gospel, the word ἐξουσία occurs three times in contexts relevant to the subject of Christ's authority (5:27; 10:18; 17:2), and there are numerous echoes of the Synoptic conflict stories (e.g., John 5:1–18; 9:1–41). But everything is now transposed into a very different key. In the Synoptics the debate with the Jewish leaders revolves around the law, and the freedom Jesus claims over against it, his power of exorcism and healing, and his offer of forgiveness in God's name: the neutrality of his person and presence is still preserved, since his relatives can accuse him of "being beside himself" (Mark 3:21), and the scribes of casting out demons by "Beelzebub, the prince of demons" (Mark 3:22). In John's Gospel, conflict about the law has really become marginal to the larger issue of the heavenly, divine status of Christ's own Person. This is evident from the close of the account of the healing of the lame or paralyzed man at the pool of Bethesda: "This was why the Jews sought all the more to kill him, because he not only broke the sabbath but also called God his father, making himself equal with God" (John 5:18). And immediately thereafter, in fact, the healing story provides the opportunity for Christ to enter into a lengthy discourse on his "oneness" with the Father, and specifically on his divine authorization to be Judge of the world: "For as the Father has life in himself, so he has granted the Son also to have life in himself, and has given him authority to execute judgment, because he is the Son of man" (John 5:26-27). Similarly, the healing of the blind man leads into the statement "Jesus said, 'For judgment I came into this world, that those who do not see may see, and that those who see may become blind'" (John 9:39). In the high-priestly prayer of chapter 17 the focus is on the God-given power (ἐξουσία) of Christ to bestow eternal life (John 17:1-2).

As we have seen, the idea of Christ's supremacy over Moses, and by implication the church's supremacy over the synagogue, is by no means wanting in the Synoptics. But in the Fourth Gospel the idea of Christian "supersessionism" is pervasive. In the Johannine context, Christ is the One sent by God into the world to carry on God's work in all its fullness (see, e.g., 10:37-38): he is the absolute master of his own destiny (John 10:18): and suffers no constraint of external force or circumstance (cf. John 2:4; 7:10; 13:27; etc.). As recipient of the "full revelation of the Messianic glory of Jesus,"[24] the Johannine community can regard Judaism as passé, its own separate and independent identity as thoroughly established, and its mission to the world inspired by the authoritative rulership of its Christ, stamped as that is by the divine imprimatur.

In all four Gospels, in spite of the difference of emphasis between the Synoptics and John, allusions to the authority of Jesus in his earthly ministry are undoubtedly highly colored by the retrojection into that ministry of the post-Easter church's faith in the divine legitimation of Christ as King-Messiah and of his heavenly status. Similarly the honorific titles ascribed to Christ in the Gospel tradition are signposts to the ways in which the crucified, risen, and exalted Christ functioned authoritatively in the life and worship of the believing communities.

The time is or should be past when we could assume, as many undoubtedly did, a straight genetic relationship between the "messianic conscious-ness" or self-interpretation of Jesus and the titles of Christ, with all that they meant in the Christology or rather Christologies of the early church.[25] Writing on the subject of Jesus and Christian origins in the early 1960s, I suggested that

> no single name or title, whether it be *Christos* (Messiah) or *Kyrios*, continues to bear in Christian testimony and confession simply the significance it had for Judaism or Hellenism. The person and history of Jesus of Nazareth have, in fact, introduced into the titles a paradoxical meaning and content. For the Church's *Christos* is not the mighty leader of Jewish expectation but the one who goes the way of the Cross. Similarly the Church's *Kyrios*—and this is contrary to what the Hellenist could have believed—is the one who became flesh (cf. Jn. 1:14; Heb. 4:14; Phil. 2:6f.; I Tim. 3:16). It follows, therefore, that such titles as *Christos* and *Kyrios*, and whatever meaning for them we can draw out of our knowledge of Judaism or Hellenism, are not so much constitutive for the person and history of Jesus, as his person and history are constitutive for the titles. "What the Messianic titles imply in their application to him cannot be appreciated from the titles themselves, but only from Jesus himself."[26]

In a recent article, arguing persuasively that the study of New Testament Christology must be liberated from the tyranny of titles, L. E. Keck makes the same point: "The Jesus event interprets the titles. This is obvious in John (e.g., 7:40–43), but is no less true elsewhere as well (e.g., Mark 9:30–32), but the customary focus on titles will not disclose it."[27] Those scholars who have held that Jesus' self-consciousness or self-interpretation was shaped up by the application to himself of titles and led directly to the church's christological formulations (both of which in our view are ex-tremely unlikely) unwittingly acknowledge how constitutive Jesus' own person and history were for the titles when they maintain that he "simul-taneously reinterpreted, 'spiritualized' or 'transformed' such titles."[28] I find myself in agreement, then, with Keck's statement:

> Neither the effort to understand a christology, nor to discern its capacity, nor to assess its validity depends on a historian's success in tracing it to the mind of Jesus. Nor, conversely may a christology be disallowed because it did not occur to Jesus to avow it. In other words, the christology of the critically-reconstructed historical Jesus is not part of the christology of the New Testament.[29]

Neither does it follow, of course, that the historical question of the authority and significance of Jesus for his contemporaries during the course of his ministry in Galilee and finally in Jerusalem is of no account. Only, our concern has been to suggest that we should not "read off" the sig-nificance or authority of Jesus from his own self-consciousness or self-interpretation by means of the arrogation to himself of christological titles. The fabric of history does not consist of what or who human beings inwardly think they are but is woven out of impact and response, the impact that persons or a person, in particular Jesus of Nazareth, makes upon others, and the response these others make in turn to him. In short, in investigating Jesus' own authority, we must focus not on his "christological self-perception" but on the impressions he conveyed to and that were appropriated by those around him, through his acts and through his words concerning God and world and humanity.

A good many scholars, perhaps most notably J. Jeremias,[30] have traced one essential element in the authority of Jesus to the christological claim implicit in his linguistic usage, especially his address to God as Abba and his placing of "amen" as a solemn asseveration at the beginning of a sentence. But to name God by the intimate term "abba," however unusual that may have been in the Judaism of Jesus' time, is certainly not the same as calling attention to *oneself* as the Son of God. Likewise the formula *Amen lego hymin,* which occurs some seventy-five times in the Gospels on the lips of Jesus and is particularly prominent in the Sermon on the Mount in Matthew, probably does no more than demarcate Jesus as *prophet*—the one title, incidentally, that may well have proved acceptable to Jesus himself but that stands very much on the margin of the "high" christological confessions of the early church.

It is scarcely likely therefore that Jesus' use of either "abba" or the formulary "amen" would have rendered those around him spellbound by his unique or even extraordinary authority. We have to turn elsewhere.

Some time ago David Daube attempted a rather imaginative historical reconstruction of what constituted Jesus' authority during his earthly ministry. His authority was in fact a much more practical-institutional and mundane phenomenon than the lordly dignity the term "authority" signified for the church after his death. The background to the encounter between Jesus and the contemporary scribes was the matter of the rights and privileges belonging to the proper rabbi (his *reshuth*) through his ordination (*semikhah,* literally "leaning on" of hands).

In Mark 1:22, 27, a "new teaching with authority" is accordingly quite specific. The text distinguishes not between "teaching with authority" and the teaching of the proper or venerable rabbis. Rather, the contrast is between "teaching with the authority of an ordained Rabbi who had the power to introduce novel doctrines and lay down some decisions of binding force" and the "teaching of those not ordained."[31] Whereas in the New Testament the "scribes" are normally the learned theologians, in the context of Mark 1:21–28 they must belong to another category denoted by the term, namely, the somewhat humdrum elementary Bible teachers "of whom there were certainly more than enough in any Palestinian village."[32] In comparison with the everyday instruction of the school-teacher scribes,

Jesus' teaching would have seemed exceptional and exciting, all the more so since, on the one hand, not being ordained, he should speak and act like one ordained, and on the other hand, "the general standard of learning in Galilee was low."[33]

Interesting and ingenious though it is, Daube's argument has serious flaws. The rabbinic sources on which we have largely to depend for knowledge of the pre-70 C.E. scribes and Pharisees consistently project back into the earlier period the well-established institutions of their own day. Consequently, it is notoriously difficult to determine scribal-Pharisaic attitudes, teaching and training methods, and practices and procedures in the time of Jesus and the early Christian movement.[34] In particular, there is no clear-cut evidence that ordination was required for admission to a full and proper rabbinate. Probably the only prerequisites for becoming a scholar of the Pharisees were attachment to a master and the expertise in the tradition acquired from that attachment.[35]

It is sometimes supposed that ordination in the early church through the laying-on of hands was derived from the prior rabbinic practice of *semikhah*. But this is doubtful. The New Testament texts that may be cited in support (e.g., Acts 6:6; 13:3; 1 Tim. 4:14; 5:22; 2 Tim. 1:6) do not suggest an act of authorization on the part of a person already possessed of official status. The laying-on of hands—frequent enough in the New Testament—is associated with the channeling of the divine healing (e.g., Mark 10:16) or the gift of the Holy Spirit (e.g., Acts 8:17–19; 19:6). In the pastoral epistles, it is true, the laying-on of hands is connected with teaching and is performed by someone in authority (1 Tim. 4:11–16; 2 Tim. 1:6), but even here what is bestowed is a charisma. Even if the Pastorals should reflect ordination to a venerable order of scholar-teacher in a late first-century Christian milieu, that would certainly not prove the practice of rabbinic ordination in the time of Jesus.[36]

It is therefore quite improbable that the authority question affecting Jesus in his ministry had anything to do with rabbinic ordination versus nonordination. In any case, the word ἐξουσία, like the Hebrew *reshuth*, has a wider range of meaning than rabbinic authorization, as Daube himself is prepared to concede.[37]

At the outset we took note of Professor Kee's interest in the authority issue in the New Testament—in particular, Max Weber's analysis of charismatic authority:

> Charisma lacks any abstract code and any formal means of adjudication. Its principles emanate concretely from the highly personal experience of heavenly grace and from the personal power of the leader, which derives from the gods. It rejects ties to external order, transvalues everything, calls for a break with traditional norms, and settles disputes by prophetic revelation or oracle.[38]

Now that statement provides a useful summary of the nature of the authority attributed to Jesus in leading scholarly works of the present century, most prominently those by J. Klausner, Geza Vermes, and M. Hengel. Klausner thought of the Galilee of Jesus' ministry as peopled only by Zealot revolutionaries or, on the other hand, by the "meek." As belonging to the company of the meek in the hotbed of insurrectionist zeal that was Galilee, Jesus sought to turn the eyes of his contemporaries away from worldly political aims and goals toward a higher messianic idea or ideal and a new life of the future rooted in the noble ethical teaching of the prophets.[39] Vermes characterized Jesus as a holy man or charismatic bearing a certain resemblance to such "odd" personalities on the Galilean religious fringe as Rabbis Hanina ben Dosa and Honi, the circle drawer and the rainmaker, and like them conscious of possessing a God-given power that was at variance with the powers of, and in fact offended, those who acquired their authority from official channels.[40]

Hengel's treatment of Jesus' charismatic authority in certain respects follows a similar line to that of Vermes and Klausner, but it is both more detailed and more extensively developed. Accordingly, in the remainder of the essay we shall concentrate on discussing Hengel's views. His thesis is in effect that Jesus' authority or the secret of that authority lay not in the teacher-pupil context but in the leader-follower or disciple relationship. The foundational text on which he builds up a sizable edifice is Matt. 8:21–22: "Another of the disciples said to him, 'Lord, let me first go and bury my father.' But Jesus said to him, 'Follow me and leave the dead to bury their own dead.'"

Hengel finds his point of departure in the statements of two earlier scholars. First, C. G. Montefiore: "Discipleship such as Jesus demanded and inspired (a following not for *study* but for service—to help the Master in his mission, to carry out his instructions and so on) was apparently a new thing, at all events something which did not fit in, was not on all fours with usual Rabbinic custom or with customary Rabbinic phenomena."[41] Second, A. Schlatter: "That *pietas* could be denied at this point, and the duty of a son overridden, was completely unthinkable to Jewish sensitivities. It was a purely sacrilegious act of impiety. Such sayings could easily suggest the thought that Jesus was abolishing the law."[42]

Hengel wholeheartedly endorses Schlatter's view of the extreme harshness of the saying of Jesus in Matt. 8:22, as an open breach of the filial obligation imposed by God in the Torah.[43] Not only so, in his exploration of other religiocultural contexts—Old Testament prophetic, apocalyptic, Zealot, the Hellenistic world, the Pythagorean tradition, the early Academy, and the Cynics—he discovers certain affinities with the Jesus movement but no real parallel to the absolute stringency of Jesus' "call to follow."[44] Neither "rabbi" nor "prophet" therefore is a term adequately covering the activity of Jesus: his charisma defies categorization in terms of the phenomenology of religion: his call to individuals to "follow after him" to the abandonment of all human ties and considerations is an expression of his underivable "messianic authority."

Sanders goes even further than Hengel in stressing the *negative* implications of Matt. 8:22, which as he observes, have "not been widely recognized." "Disobedience of the requirement to care for one's dead parents is actually disobedience to God."[45] Both Hengel and Sanders, of course, in agreement with the majority of scholars, assume the authenticity of the *logion.* Sanders in fact holds that the criterion of dissimilarity applies here rather well: the saying is entirely un-Jewish and "is not comprehensible as a creation of the early community."[46]

We should not, however, accept the foregoing interpretation unquestioningly or without reservation. It is not that we would advocate removing the sting from the difficult words of Matt. 8:22 by taking the verse as a broadly generalizing proverb about the priority of discipleship over domestic responsibilities. (The absence of parallels in Judaism and the Greco-Roman world militate against this.) Nor should we shrug it off as probably meaning no more than an innocuous "Let that matter take care of itself."[47] But questions there are about the genuineness of the *logion* as *verba ipsissima* of Jesus.

1. Whereas Bultmann thinks of the saying of Luke 9:60a as authentic, he regards the settings of the two *logia* of Matt. 8:19–22 and the three *logia* of Luke 9:57–62 as imaginary.[48] And in the Jewish-Christian milieu of Matthew's Gospel, it is not so incredible "that the request to go and bury one's father first was created as a frame for the saying to let the dead bury their dead."[49] The particularization enhances the prophetic character of the saying (with Christ transcending Moses and the Mosaic torah).

2. The various pericopes on calling to discipleship in the Gospels reflect facets of the early church's understanding of the nature of call to discipleship in the light of its own broader missionary experience. In Mark 1:16–20, for instance, the call is sudden, mysterious: there is not the slightest hint of any prior conditioning or preparation of those called. The impression we have is that the report is suffused with the light of the later church's standpoint: everything decisive has *already* happened here; the hour of God's grace has struck; the One appointed by him has fully come; and in response to the church's mission the world can only say yes or no. Hengel for his part hovers between acknowledgment of the redactional element in these stories and of their actual historicity. Of the call to follow in Mark he says, "With Mark, the call to follow (Mk. 2:14; cf. 1:17, 20) acquires in Jesus' mouth a potency which is quite simply miraculous and

which abruptly detaches those called from their previous obligations."[50] But we are not clearly told whether the "miraculous" call to follow is due to Markan redaction or really represents the *Sitz im Leben Jesu* at the beginning of the Galilean ministry.

Similarly, linking together Jesus' call to follow him with the commissioning of the disciples for mission in Matt. 9:37—10:42, Hengel at one and the same time expresses his awareness of the church's own "multi-layered and rich missionary experience" and invites us to accept its historicity "in principle."[51] Hengel's tendency to deemphasize the redactional features in these reports and his strong advocacy of the genuineness of Matt. 8:22 have a lot to do, we may suppose, with his eagerness to locate the developed Christology of the post-Easter church in the uniquely authoritative messianic status of Jesus enshrined in his magisterial call to follow him.

3. The word νεκροί, which occurs twice in the saying "Leave the dead to bury their own dead" is very problematic, and a wide range of meanings has been assigned to it: for example, "physically dead" in both cases (on the face of it a nonsensical suggestion!); "dying" in the first case (presumably, "on the way to spiritual death"); "waverers" or "people who prevaricate" in the first case (on the ground that the underlying Aramaic term, which is very close etymologically to the term מתים, denoted just that); and "spiritually dead" in the first case and "physically dead" in the second case[52] (this last described by F. W. Beare as an extravagant interpretation).[53]

It does seem best to think of both uses as signifying the same thing: and since it is manifestly absurd to suppose that νεκροί in both instances means literal corpses, it is most natural to take both as metaphorical, indicating death in the religious or spiritual sense. We may then render it, "Let the religiously or spiritually dead conduct their own obsequies." Accordingly, it is not inconceivable that we are here dealing with an early church formulation, in which Judaism is declared obsolete and superseded by the gospel and by discipleship to the Christ whom it proclaims. There may be some support for this in the Lukan version of Matt. 8:22, where the person called is told to go and proclaim the kingdom of God (Luke 9:60); that is, the old dispensation gives way to the new, in which discipleship to Christ is now equated with the promulgation of the good news.

If, however, these considerations fail to persuade and we abide by the consensus that both the setting and the saying of Matt. 8:22 are authentic, we need not read into them nearly so much as Hengel does. Neither in its Matthean nor in its Lukan form (9:60) does Jesus' saying deny outright that the follower has a filial obligation, although what is only implied in Matthew becomes explicit in Luke's version, namely, that another commitment comes into view and is in order: heralding the kingdom. The harshness, cruelty, and impiety of the *logion* have probably been overstressed.[54]

Possibly appropriate to the saying is the aphorism that the most difficult of choices is not between good and evil but between the good and the best.

We turn next to those Synoptic sayings which connect discipleship with crossbearing (Mark 8:34; Matt. 10:38; Luke 14:27). Jesus' summons to his followers to "accept" (Matthew) or "carry" (Luke) the cross Hengel regards as authentic—and so as support for his casting of Jesus in the type of an "eschatological charismatic" whose authority is founded on his call to people to follow in the service of the dawning kingdom. It is of course true that by Jesus' day, crucifixion had a long history behind it, and it is quite possible that more than one "messianic prophet" was executed on the cross. Josephus furnishes evidence for mass crucifixions of Pharisees by Alexander Jannaeus, and of Jews by Varus, before the time of Christ, as well as of individual revolutionaries.[55] But that Jesus picked up and used the image of crossbearing from a Zealot source is extremely unlikely. Prior to Jesus' own death on the cross, with all that it implied for the life and faith of the first Christians, the cross would surely have functioned for Jews either as a hated symbol of Roman oppression or as a gesture of defiance against Rome and a sign of Jewish readiness to accept martyrdom for the revolutionary cause. Would not Jesus, by speaking of crossbearing discipleship, have in effect been fanning the very flames of political messianic agitation among the masses which the main weight of Synoptic evidence suggests he wanted to avoid?[56]

Crossbearing as symbolizing world-renouncing discipleship, with total commitment to the Master, and as echoing the Pauline affirmations about "suffering with Christ" or "being crucified with Christ" (e.g., 2 Cor. 4:10–11; Gal. 2:20; Rom. 6:6; 8:17), belongs not to the setting and circumstances of Jesus' Galilean ministry but rather to those of the early church and its mission.[57]

Finally, we revert to our earlier remark that Hengel finds the secret of Jesus' authority not in the teacher-pupil but in the leader-follower relationship. He does in fact point out that Jesus' call to service of the coming kingdom is not incompatible with his role as wisdom or ethical teacher.[58] Nevertheless, so strenuously does Hengel emphasize the eschatological charisma of Jesus, and so painstakingly does he seek to remove Jesus with his disciples from the rabbi-pupil model, that whether he means to or not he seriously subordinates the wisdom and ethical teaching. Yet a call to follow in the light of the dawning kingdom becomes arid and arbitrary when the implications of such following are not filled out by appeal to the wisdom sayings and ethical precepts of Jesus.

Our discussion leads to a meager enough conclusion. Gospel pericopes relating to the authority issue are not unnaturally colored to a lesser or greater extent by the christological perspectives of the early church. We are all too frequently tempted to take redactional statements as factual accounts. The temptation arises from the desire to trace the roots of the later church's christological confessions back into the person and event we name Jesus. Theological or christological judgments are allowed to become determinants of what happened or how things were on the historical plane.[59] Only an a priori conviction about Jesus' underivable status claim would lead one to suppose any *necessary* connection between his call to discipleship in service of the dawning kingdom and his authoritative "messianic consciousness." Jesus was not, after all, the only one in that period of Jewish history to gather followers and ask them to share in his task: we know of Judas the Galilean, Theudas, and the person called the Egyptian, among others.[60] How the authority they exercised in collecting followers around them differed from that of Jesus is very difficult to gauge.

Whereas it is debatable whether Jesus actually called the Twelve, that he did invite disciples to join him (albeit not all Israel in a universal movement of repentance or reform) is incontrovertible fact. Presumably they were attracted by something other or more in him than his abrupt and mysterious call to follow. If the itinerant ministry initiated by Jesus differentiates him from the rabbis (Hengel), to hold that the title of rabbi or teacher *does not fit him at all* is nevertheless, to go too far.[61] His prophetic teaching on the kingdom of God and his pronouncements on God's providential care of his creation (Matt. 6:25–34, reminiscent of the sages of Israel) must inter alia have carried their own appeal. It is, of course, easy to see how in time terms like "rabbi" or "teacher" or "prophet" seemed inadequate and gave way to the church's use of more elevated christological titles. But the category of prophet or teacher extraordinary is applicable to Jesus himself, and its significance should not be underrated. The category of charismatic leader hardly embraces the whole of Jesus' being or of his authority.[62]

NOTES

1. H. C. Kee, *Christian Origins in Sociological Perspective* (Philadelphia: Westminster Press, 1980). All references to Scripture in what follows are to the RSV.

2. H. C. Kee, *Understanding the New Testament,* 4th ed. (Englewood Cliffs, N.J.: Prentice-Hall, 1983), 395.

3. Max Weber, "The Sociology of Charismatic Authority," in *From Max Weber: Essays in Sociology,* trans. and ed. H. H. Garth and C. Wright Mills (New York: Oxford Univ. Press, 1977), 245–48.

4. Kee, *Understanding,* 396–99.

5. M. Marty, "America's Iconic Book," in *Humanizing America's Iconic Book,* ed. G. M. Tucker and D. A. Knight, SBL Centennial Addresses 1980 (Chico, Calif.: Scholars Press, 1981).

6. R. Murray, "Authority and the Spirit in the New Testament," in *Authority in a*

Changing Church (New York and London: Sheed & Ward, 1968), 32–33. Cf. N. Lash, *Voices of Authority* (New York and London: Sheed & Ward, 1976), 20.

7. In the interpretation of Luke's account of the amazing escape of Jesus from the crowd attempting to execute him ("But passing through the midst of them he went away," Luke 4:30), earlier commentators like F. L. Godet (*Commentary on the Gospel of Saint Luke* [1870; Edinburgh: T. & T. Clark]) suggested that, faced with the unique and indeed miraculous majesty of Jesus' person, the throng quite simply melted away. Such an understanding surely savors more of the highly legendary embellishments of Christ's exalted power in the apocryphal *Gospel of Peter* than of any real intention of the canonical evangelists. If in John's Gospel, Christ is a figure of supreme authority, it consists not of sovereignty but of the power of love.

8. Advocates of canonical criticism uphold as a primary hermeneutical principle the need to view each book of the Bible *in its relation to the dynamic reality of the whole canon of Scripture.* Not unnaturally therefore they deemphasize the role of redaction criticism, since it is preoccupied with each document or each author as an individual or independent entity. See e.g., Brevard Childs, *Introduction to the Old Testament as Scripture* (Philadelphia: Fortress Press, 1979), esp. 74–77; and J. A. Sanders, *Canon and Community: A Guide to Canonical Criticism* (Philadelphia: Fortress Press, 1984). Both Childs and Sanders continue, of course, to employ redaction criticism—*inevitably,* one might claim especially for Childs, whose chief concern is with the final form of the text rather than with the formational process. It is a fact that redaction-critical interpretation can easily become bogged down in minutiae, can posit an extreme degree of sophistication in the evangelists quite implausible for them, and can be notoriously subjective, witness the remarkable diversity of explanations of the purpose and message of Mark (see H. Anderson, *The Gospel of Mark,* New Century Bible [Grand Rapids: Wm. B. Eerdmans, 1981], 43–58). But this does not negate the continuing value of sober application of redaction-critical principles. Investigation of the views that developed in the early Christian communities as they are adumbrated in the final redaction of each Gospel is in its own right a genuine mode of historical criticism: we do need to glean as much information as the evidence will allow about the later post-Easter followers of Jesus.

9. E. G. Selwyn, "The Authority of Christ in the New Testament," *New Testament Studies 3* (1956–57): 86ff.

10. The reluctance or inability of many scholars to distinguish between the words and acts reported of the risen Christ in the Gospel's Easter witness and the words and acts of the precrucifixion Jesus is, to say the least, surprising. They seem to posit an identity of substance between the earthly Jesus and the risen Christ, as if what happened with Easter were *but another installment of Jesus' actual history.* No doubt this has to do with the desire to protect and preserve the historicophysical factuality of the resurrection. As nearly all Easter reports themselves eloquently suggest, it is not possible to think of an identity of *substance* between the historical Jesus and the resurrected Christ. The real continuity lies elsewhere: the disciples of Jesus before his death are exactly the same group (Judas, of course, excepted) who after his death bear testimony to his risen presence. In doing so, they are crossing the bridge between history and faith. It is quite natural therefore that the Easter traditions transmitted to us in their diversity by the evangelists should be indelibly stamped with the faith-theology perspective of early Christian communities and their leaders.

HUGH ANDERSON

11. See H. Anderson, "The Easter Witness of the Evangelists," in *The New Testament in Historical and Contemporary Perspective,* ed. H. Anderson and W. Barclay (Oxford: Basil Blackwell, 1965). Cf. P. Schubert, "The Structure and Significance of Luke 24," in *Neutestamentliche Studien für Rudolf Bultmann,* ed. W. Eltester (Berlin, 1954), 185ff.

12. Even a conservative critic like J. F. Collange (*De Jésus à Paul: L'éthique du Nouveau Testament* [Geneva: Labor et Fides, 1980], 37) is prepared to concede that most of the occurrences of the term ἐξουσία are redactional. He does add, however, that the reality they always express is undeniably characteristic of the Master of Nazareth—without really discussing the nature of that reality.

13. D. Daube, *The New Testament and Rabbinic Judaism* (London: University of London, Athlone Press, 1956), 206-7. The passage is from *b. Sukk.* 28a.

14. See, e.g., E. Käsemann, "The Problem of the Historical Jesus" (1953), in *Essays on New Testament Themes,* trans. W. J. Montague (Philadelphia: Fortress Press, 1982), 39; and G. Bornkamm, *Jesus of Nazareth,* trans. I. McLuskey and F. McLuskey (London: Hodder & Stoughton, 1963), 97.

15. See the examples cited by E. P. Sanders (*Jesus and Judaism* [Philadelphia: Fortress Press, 1985], 402 n. 14), G. Bornkamm (*Jesus,* 81), A. Harvey (*Jesus and the Constraints of History* [London: SCM Press, 1982], J. Jeremias (*New Testament Theology,* vol. 1, *The Proclamation of Jesus,* trans. J. Bowden [London: SCM Press, 1971], 118 n. 1), and E. Schweizer (*Jesus,* trans. D. E. Green [Richmond: John Knox Press, 1971], 14).

16. Sanders, *Jesus and Judaism,* 273.

17. See J. Neusner, *From Politics to Piety: The Emergence of Pharisaic Judaism* (Englewood Cliffs, N.J.: Prentice-Hall, 1973), 68ff. It is interesting to note that Neusner finds the Gospel evidence on Pharisaic outlook and practice in the time of Jesus to be historically sound as regards the Pharisees' great concern with Sabbath observance, dietary laws, ritual purity in eating, and ceremonial cleanness. These beliefs and practices come into view in those Gospel stories where they are specifically condemned (Mark 2:15-22; 7:1-13; Matt. 12:1-14; 23:1-36). But on the other hand the Gospels' portrayal of the Pharisees as the leading opponents of Jesus and of the bitter polemic against them reflects the situation of the church after 70 C.E. and is mere generalized invective. With the evangelists, the Pharisees frequently serve simply as a narrative convention (pp. 68-72).

18. See Sanders, *Jesus and Judaism,* 272.

19. See F. W. Beare, *The Gospel according to Matthew* (San Francisco: Harper & Row, 1981), 223-24.

20. E. Schweizer, *The Good News according to Matthew,* trans. D. E. Green (Richmond: John Knox Press, 1975), 193. Cf. Beare, *Gospel according to Matthew,* 200.

21. Beare, *Gospel according to Matthew,* 422-23.

22. Sanders, *Jesus and Judaism,* 21ff.

23. Luke's standpoint here contrasts notably with Matthew's. Matthew is concerned to show that particular events in the life of Jesus are precisely fulfilled in detail (see esp. Matt. 1:18—2:28).

24. See R. Schnackenburg, *The Gospel according to St. John,* vol. 1 (New York: Seabury Press, 1980), 510.

25. We must note, however, C. F. D. Moule's *The Origin of Christology* (Cambridge: Cambridge Univ. Press, 1977). Moule proposes that "development" is a more suitable term than "evolution" for the genesis of Christology. By that he means that the exalted Christology of the New Testament did not evolve out of the cultural environment of early Christianity but developed directly from the person and work of Jesus himself: it was all there in nuce in Jesus from the very first. The direct genetic continuity between the human Jesus and the exalted Christ is the resurrection, by which Jesus becomes an eternally living being, possibly like the "spiritual body" of 1 Corinthians 15, who can thus be described in terms appropriate to nothing less than God himself (pp. 53, 135ff.). But the notion of an identity of "substance," however conceived, between Jesus and the divine Christ is very hard to take. What we can speak meaningfully about is a certain continuity between the disciples of Jesus prior to the crucifixion and their life after Easter. Cf. H. Anderson, "Christology Is Unfinished Business," essay presented to the Edinburgh Theological Club, April 1982; and L. E. Keck, "Toward the Renewal of New Testament Christology," *New Testament Studies* 32 (1986): 3, 367–68. Contrast J. D. G. Dunn's *Unity and Diversity in the New Testament* (Philadelphia: Westminster Press, 1977) for a view closely akin to Moule's.

26. H. Anderson, *Jesus and Christian Origins* (New York: Oxford Univ. Press, 1964), 163–64. The quotation within the passage is from F. Gogarten's *Der Mensch zwischen Gott und Welt* (Stuttgart, 1956), 263ff.

27. Keck, "Toward the Renewal," 370.

28. Ibid.

29. Ibid., 372–73.

30. J. Jeremias, *New Testament Theology: The Proclamation of Jesus* (New York: Charles Scribner's Sons, 1971), passim.

31. Daube, *New Testament*, 206.

32. Ibid., 211.

33. Ibid., 207. Cf. Geza Vermes, *Jesus the Jew* (New York: Macmillan Co., 1974), 19: "The village scribes whom Jesus met regularly were men able to draw up contracts, marriage settlements, bills of divorce and to teach children in the schools, but are not to be confused with the luminaries of Jerusalem Pharisaism. Also there is no hint in the New Testament of Jesus having received any specialized training—not to mention the fact that rabbinic sources go out of their way to describe the Galileans as being in any case *shoteh*, 'stupid Galileans.'"

34. See J. Neusner, *The Rabbinic Traditions About the Pharisees before 70*, 3 vols. (Leiden: E. J. Brill, 1971).

35. See several Mishnaic texts, esp. in *'Abot*—e.g., 1.4 ("Let your house be a meeting-place for the sages; sit at the dust of their feet, and drink in their words with thirst") and 5.21 (where the regular course of training is described as "five years on scripture, ten on the Mishnah, thirteen of fulfilling the commandments and fifteen on teaching"). Cf. S. Westerholm, *Jesus and Scribal Authority*, Coniectanea biblica, New Testament 10 (Lund: C. W. K. Gleerup, 1978), 30–31; M. Hengel, *The Charismatic Leader and His Followers*, trans. J. C. G. Greig, ed. J. Riches (New York: Crossroad, 1981), 57; E. Lohse, *Die Ordination im Spätjudentum und im Neuen Testament* (Göttingen, 1951), 74–79; and J. Jeremias, *Jerusalem in the Time of Jesus: An Investigation into Economic and Social Conditions during the New*

HUGH ANDERSON

Testament Period, trans. F. H. and C. H. Cave (Philadelphia: Fortress Press, 1975), 235 n.9.

36. S. Westerholm (*Jesus,* 31ff.), to whose detailed arguments I am indebted at this point.

37. D. Daube, *New Testament,* 220ff. We suggested above (p. 291) that the New Testament regards all genuine authority as derived from a morally accredited source or person, and most characteristically from God himself. In Mark's account of the scribal colloquy with Jesus (11:27–33) there is an implied contrast between the scribes' notion of an authority passed on from one human being to another and the way in which Jesus seeks to turn attention toward another higher, heavenly authority. Cf. the distinction drawn between the authority Pilate assumes belongs to him as an official under the Roman *imperium* and Jesus' affirmation that the true source of all authority, including even Pilate's, is God alone (John: 18:10–11). Though it is quite conceivable that Jesus of Nazareth himself made that distinction, we are not supposing that either Mark 11:27–33 or John 18:10–11 is a straight historical report uninfluenced by the christological perspectives of the early Christian communities.

38. Weber, "Sociology of Charismatic Authority," 245–48. See Kee, *Understanding the New Testament,* 395.

39. J. Klausner, *Jesus of Nazareth,* ET from Hebrew (London: George Allen & Unwin, 1925), 173, 168. For a very different appraisal of the political temper of Galilee, see S. Freyne, *Galilee from Alexander the Great to Hadrian, 323 B.C.E. to 135 C.E.: A Study of Second Temple Judaism* (Notre Dame, Ind.: Univ. of Notre Dame Press, 1980).

40. Vermes, *Jesus the Jew,* 80–81.

41. C. G. Montefiore, *Rabbinic Literature and Gospel Teachings* (London: Macmillan & Co., 1930), 218. See Hengel, *Charismatic Leader,* 2.

42. A. Schlatter, *Der Evangelist Matthaeus,* 3d ed. (Stuttgart, 1948), 288. See Hengel, *Charismatic Leader,* 14.

43. Hengel, *Charismatic Leader,* 15.

44. Ibid., 16–37. Cf. Beare, *Gospel according to Matthew,* 214.

45. Sanders, *Jesus and Judaism,* 253.

46. Ibid., 252.

47. Beare, *Gospel according to Matthew,* 214.

48. R. Bultmann, *History of the Synoptic Tradition,* trans. John Marsh (New York: Harper & Row, 1963), 105, 119.

49. *Pace* Sanders, *Jesus and Judaism,* 214.

50. Hengel, *Charismatic Leader,* 5.

51. Ibid., 75.

52. J. A. Fitzmyer, *The Gospel according to Luke 1—9,* Anchor Bible (New York: Doubleday & Co., 1981), 836.

53. Beare, *Gospel according to Matthew,* 214.

54. Sanders lays great stress on the shocking impiety of the saying: Jesus negates what he knew full well was a specific and direct injunction of torah. Nevertheless, he rounds off his discussion of the passage as follows: "A modest conclusion about the pericope on burying the dead is in order. At least once Jesus was willing to say that following him superseded the requirements of piety and the Torah. This may

show that Jesus was prepared, if necessary, to challenge the inadequacy of the Mosaic dispensation" (*Jesus and Judaism*, 255).

55. Hengel, *Charismatic Leader*, 58, n. 76. How early and widespread crucifixion was may be gleaned from a reference in Plato's *Republic* in the course of a conversation between Adeimantus and Glaucon on injustice (2.361): "They will say that the just man . . . will be scourged, tortured and imprisoned, his eyes will be put out, and after enduring every humiliation he will be crucified, and learn at last that one should want not to be, but to seem just" (trans. Desmond Lee, Penguin ed.).

56. Hengel, *Charismatic Leader*, 59. Hengel himself is not insensitive to this: he is at pains to show how Jesus' own chosen way was threatened by political activists.

57. When Hengel (ibid., 59–60) acknowledges that the Pauline statements on "suffering with Christ" come closest to Jesus' saying about "carrying one's cross," he is in effect casting grave doubt on the authenticity of the saying. Of Matt. 10:34–39, Beare (*Gospel according to Matthew*, 250) writes, "It has become more and more clear that the discourse has moved far beyond the instruction for a mission to be carried on in the villages during the life time of Jesus. At Jewish hands, they might face flogging in the synagogue, or stoning by an angry mob, but not crucifixion; and there is nothing to indicate that sharp conflicts within the family were occasioned in those days."

58. Hengel, *Charismatic Leader*, 42ff., 63, 68.

59. Cf. W. Pannenberg, *Jesus—God and Man*, trans. L. L. Wilkins and D. A. Priebe (Philadelphia: Westminster Press, 1968), 73, 76. Pannenberg seems to think of *God's* confirmation of Jesus' claim in the resurrection as *a fact historically demonstrated* (p. 73). He is consequently able to regard the pre-Easter Jesus' claim to authority as standing from the beginning in relationship to the question of the future judgment of the Son of man according to the attitude taken by human beings toward Jesus (see Matt. 10:32–33). Jesus' claim to authority then is *proleptic* in structure. "Everything depends upon the connection between Jesus' claim and its confirmation by God" (p. 66). From the historian's standpoint, it is very hard indeed to see how an authority so heavily dependent on *future* verification could have impressed itself on those around Jesus then and there during his Galilean ministry. I have great sympathy with Sanders's strictures against the persistent tendency of Protestant scholars to retroject Christian theology into the mind of Jesus, and with his attempt in *Jesus and Judaism* at as scrupulously objective a historical reconstruction as possible of Jesus' own aim or intention and of the factors that culminated in his death. (I have tried in this paper to distinguish between redactional statements and historical fact.) I have even some measure of sympathy with Sanders's worry about the word "unique" as applied to Jesus, and with his assertion that what is unique is the result (he means the early Christian movement, p. 240). But whether the historian is justified in eschewing altogether (as does Sanders, p. 2) the question of whether and to what degree early Christian formulations are consonant with the words and acts of Jesus is doubtful. One is left wondering whether the philosophy of history from which he proceeds is too positivistic to leave room for the novel, the opaque, the mysterious which appears in the historical, whether the history of Jesus or the history of the early church.

60. Josephus, *War* 2.118, 258–60, 261, 263, 433. See Sanders, *Jesus and Judaism*, 240.

61. From this it will be clear that I do not share Sanders's very low estimate of the significance of Jesus as teacher (*Jesus and Judaism*, 7ff.). There is an intriguing irony in the fact that one who has assiduously sought to rescue Jesus research from the persistent denigration of Judaism that has so often accompanied it within the guild of New Testament scholars should drastically play down the very feature of Jesus' life that might link church and synagogue. Sanders has, of course, emphasized the direct continuity of Jesus with Judaism at levels other than teaching. Be that as it may, we do well to hearken to Jaroslav Pelikan's recent moving expression (*Jesus through the Centuries: His Place in the History of Culture* [New Haven: Yale Univ. Press, 1985], 20) of the very sad effects of "de-Rabbinizing" Jesus: "Would there have been such anti-Semitism, would there have been so many pogroms, would there have been an Auschwitz, if every Christian church and every Christian home had focused its devotion on icons of Mary not only as Mother of God and Queen of Heaven but as the Jewish maiden and the new Miriam, and on icons of Christ not only as Pantocrator but as *Rabbi Jeshua bar-Joseph*, Rabbi Jesus of Nazareth, the Son of David, in the context of the history of a suffering Israel and a suffering humanity?"

62. I have not taken up the question of how the miracles relate to the authority of Jesus. Perhaps he did think of his miracles as demonstrating his right to be a spokesperson for God. Perhaps he was regarded as a magician whose wonderful works commanded attention and caused a stir (see Morton Smith, *Jesus the Magician* (New York: Harper & Row, 1978). But neither his miracles nor, indeed, his exorcisms or healings would have stamped him as possessed of a uniquely authoritative messianic status (see Sanders, *Jesus and Judaism*, 156-73). The Gospel pericopes reporting miracles and exorcisms reflect, on the whole, the post-Easter church's belief in and witness to the divinely legitimated authority of the Christ. See H. C. Kee's significant contribution to the subject: *Miracle in the Early Christian World* (New Haven: Yale Univ. Press, 1983).

18

Shebna, Eliakim, and the Promise to Peter

BRUCE CHILTON
Bard College

A peculiar thing is promised Eliakim in the Isaiah Targum (22.22):

> And I will place the key *of the sanctuary and the authority* of the house of David *in his hand:* and he will open, and none shall shut, and he will shut, and none shall open.[1]

The peculiarity of this promise is to some extent superficial. Eliakim and Shebna are taken in the Targum as priestly figures, so that chapter 22 refers to a shift in cultic dispensations. Shebna is accused of self-seeking (v. 16) and is told that shame, the removal of the high-priestly turban, and mortal exile will be the result (vv. 17–19). In his place, Eliakim will be exalted, clothed in priestly garments, given full authority, and provided with a full spectrum of assistants (vv. 20–24). Within that context, the fact that Eliakim is promised the keys "of the sanctuary" in particular comes as no surprise.

What is surprising, however, is that v. 25c removes from Eliakim everything that has been promised to him:

> ... *he* will be cut down and fall, and the oracle *of prophecy* that was concerning him will *be void* ...

The perspective of the Targum generally helps, even here, to mollify our surprise. The encircling of the altar with the blood of the slain and the cessation of festal celebration are announced (29.1, 2) in view of high-priestly wickedness (28.1–4). An interpretive presupposition of the Targum is that it is plain for the world to see that Jerusalem is desolate while Rome prospers (54.1). High-priestly corruption has run its course, and the temple must pay the price until messianic restoration results in its rebuilding (53.5). That the present temple, and its priest, should pass is therefore axiomatic within the Targum.

Even when v. 25 is viewed from the perspective of the Targum overall, our surprise (however mollified) is not removed. No accusation of any sort is raised against Eliakim in the passage; he is (implicitly) a successor as worthy as his predecessor is unworthy. Until v. 25, permanency appears to be promised provided only that priesthood is properly conducted. Notably, *Lev. Rab.* 5.5 relates a discussion (between Rabbi Eleazar and Rabbi Judah) concerning the priestly office exercised by Shebna and Eliakim, not concerning the transition of authority from one to the other, and the same may be said of *Exod. Rab.* 37.1 in its citation of Isa. 22:23.[2] It must, of course, be observed that the Hebrew text to some extent controls the reading of the Targum, but it does not entirely explain the interpretation. The "peg" of the Hebrew text need not have been taken to refer to Eliakim, and—once it was so taken—the reversal of a negative statement is a targumic convention that might have been invoked here.[3] In addition, the reference to an "oracle *of prophecy*" is odd, since elsewhere (14:28; 22:1) that phrase refers to a promise that is kept, not broken.[4] Apparently, the meturgeman has not only reproduced the negative note of v. 25 (which any rendering of the Hebrew text might have caught) but has intensified it.

It is the purpose of this essay to consider attempts to explain the oddity of the promise to Eliakim, and on that basis to offer a fresh suggestion. In order to explain how Eliakim functions as a literary figure and at the same time expresses a distinctly social perspective attention will also be paid to the definition of the "exegetical framework" of the Isaiah Targum. The thesis that the promise was developed within the first century becomes more plausible when comparable usages from the period are also considered. At the close of the last section, our attention will focus on Matt. 16:18, 19. A quotation of Isaiah (in Targumic form or otherwise) within the saying attributed to Jesus cannot be proved, but its usage of language associated with the promise to Eliakim may offer a new prospect for construing Jesus' ministry.

THE IDENTITY OF ELIAKIM

Arie van der Kooij has offered a suggestion that would help to account for the surprising discontinuity between v. 25 and the preceding material in the Targum. He suggests that Shebna and Eliakim should be identified with Aristobulus II and Hyrkanus II.[5] Similarly, Leivy Smolar and Moses Aberbach refer the interpretation to Antigonus and Aristobolus III.[6] Of course, neither of these explanations, which involve merely the transfer of power to "Eliakim," can be accepted as interpreting the Targum as it stands at present, since they do not account for v. 25, which is the point at issue of the entire chapter, the climax of the transition that is described. The present form of the text, of course, *might* refer in retrospect to the foundation of what is soon to be annulled, by means of an earlier targumic paraphrase according to which Shebna was Aristobulus II (or Antigonus) and Eliakim was Hyrkanus II (or Aristobulus III).

It appears unwise, however, to insist on the particular identifications of Shebna and Eliakim that have been posited. Certainly, the contention made by Smolar and Aberbach that the passage can "only refer to" Antigonus and Aristobulus III is extreme.[7] Antigonus was exiled and killed (cf. *Tg. Isa.* 22.18 and Josephus *War* 1.18.2, 3 §§ 353–57), but the same fate befell Aristobulus II, albeit within a series of hectic developments (cf. *War* 1.6.6 §§ 138–41; 1.7.1 § 141; 1.8.6 §§ 171–74; 1.9.1 §§ 183, 184; van der Kooij, *Die alten Textzeugen,* 163.) The very fact that both sets of identifications are plausible when they are viewed from the perspective of how Shebna's fate is handled in the Targum vitiates any exclusive claim to credibility. Moreover, both identifications suffer from the lack of any reference in v. 18 to the violence of Shebna's death. To the extent that Pompey's entry into the treasury of the temple seems to be alluded to in v. 8 (cf. *War* 1.7.6 §§ 152–54; and van der Kooij, *Die alten Textzeugen,* 166, 167), van der Kooij's appeal for a reference nearer to that period than Smolar and Aberbach would allow does seem preferable, but no more than that.

Van der Kooij's identification is superior to that of Smolar and Aberbach only insofar as Shebna is concerned: both exegeses do far less justice to Eliakim. Even if we accept that before its present incorporation within the exegetical framework of the Targum, Shebna was used by the interpreter as a cipher of attack against Aristobulus II (or Antigonus), we must ask whether support for a faction of Hyrkanus II (or Aristobulus III) was actually expressed by the passage at any stage. Such support is precisely what both interpretations require, but none of the scholars involved asks whether it is in fact there.

The difficulty of van der Kooij, Smolar, and Aberbach is that they confuse the possibility of allusions to the last gasp of the Hasmonean period with a specifically Hasmonean perspective. The easy equation between Josephus's program and that of the meturgeman can distort our understanding of the Targum. The meturgeman could also allude to Pompey's entry into the treasury without providing anything like a specific identification of that general; the uncovering of treasure is itself emblematic of defeat (v. 8). If so, how much more might he have thought of Shebna as the image of priestly corruption without having a specific priest in mind? In that case, Eliakim is only a tragic emblem, a decent functionary who must pass with the decadent regime of which he is a part, not a precisely identifiable figure of history.

Moreover, if we approach the passage from a later Herodian, rather than a Hasmonean, perspective, we might think of Eleazar, the captain (*stra-tēgōn*) of the temple who led the refusal to sacrifice on behalf of the emperor

313

(see *War* 2.17.2 §§ 409, 410)[8] and who might well be described as an officer (*'mrkl*, cf. vv. 23–25) in Aramaic,[9] rather than as a priest (*khn'*). He was, moreover, the son of Ananias, so that his priestly pedigree is sound, and his fall was as evident as the burning of the temple. The purpose here, however, is not to trump a Hasmonean reading with a later Herodian reading but to suggest that, in the face of so many possible identifications of Shebna and Eliakim which the checkered history of the high priesthood might be used to augment (cf. Bruce, *New Testament History*, 53–64), it is unwise to suppose that any given set of them has an exclusive claim on the meaning of the text.

Some pair of identifications from the Hasmonean and/or late Herodian period might have been intended by the originating meturgeman, or meturgemanin, who looked forward to the replacement of a wicked priest with a faithful one. But by the time the Targum as we know it was transmitted, the end of that cultic dispensation which was in effect in the temple had become an inescapable reality (v. 25).

Who, precisely, in the minds of those who composed and transmitted the Targum, were Shebna and Eliakim? In order to answer that question, one must do more than choose two likely candidates from the general period during which the Targum took shape. One must ascertain the particular provenience of the passage as a traditional interpretation taken up into the Targum. The traditional pedigree of our passage is not in question, but to type the provenience of a traditional unit, as distinct from the document in which it is incorporated, is notoriously difficult. In the present case, whether we are dealing, for example, with a partisan of a Hasmonean group, who favored "Eliakim" over "Shebna," or with a sect altogether hostile to the contemporary administration of the temple, or with an anti-Roman phalanx that despised any tendency toward accommodation cannot be determined with any confidence. Each option seems plausible, and for precisely that reason none is entirely convincing.

The insistence on determining which, if any, of the above options is preferable derives from that form of historical curiosity which might be described as genetic.[10] History is commonly regarded as the explanation of past events on the basis of earlier events. As a result, the rhetoric of history, and even its assumptions about reality, tend to become causational. When and where that occurs, any historical statement will be found wanting which does not explain how any given event is the product of some group of antecedents. In the present case, any dissembling as to the identities of Shebna and Eliakim will frustrate the genetically curious historian.

However frustrated the historian might become, the fact remains that our uncertainty grows as more evidence is adduced, rather than the reverse. But that uncertainty only obtains at the level of history as a genetic account of past events. What becomes increasingly clear about our passage is that it celebrates the demise of Shebna, a figure of priestly corruption, and the ascendancy of Eliakim, a figure of corresponding rectitude. As social history, the text is far more eloquent than as genetic history.

The passage, both as an instance of literature and as a specimen of history, conveys a certain stance in respect of the temple. The attempt to understand its meaning cannot succeed if it is construed in purely literary or in purely historical terms. As has been suggested already, the passage is patient of historical curiosity only to a limited extent, and even then with the provision that curiosity of the appropriate sort is in effect. "Shebna" and "Eliakim" convey not information about specific persons and the programs of identifiable groups but an attitude of hostility toward priestly administration, and then the conviction that the temple will suffer, or already has suffered, as the result of that administration. That is, the text articulates its socially historical perspective when its literary affect is taken into account. If it is approached as if every image within it were a code to be deciphered, the result is that its meaning dissolves into a series of plausible but competing possibilities. On the other hand, there is no question here of dispensing with the understanding that the text is possessed of a historical dimension. A literary approach that allowed reference only to the "final form of the text," as if literature were incapable of retrospective or prospective reference, would yield an exegesis of the passage which is no more satisfactory than a genetically historical interpretation. Such a reading would simply leave us with the anomaly with which we began, that Eliakim is elevated only to fall. By allowing the text to speak within its socially historical idiom, in which traditional material has been taken up and revised, its literary integrity is not violated but confirmed: it speaks coherently of the concerns of varying times and circumstances.

THE FRAMEWORK OF THE
ISAIAH TARGUM

The consideration up to this point would suggest that our passage is susceptible of the technique of analysis developed and advocated in my *The Glory of Israel*. In that volume, the "exegetical framework" of the Isaiah Targum was isolated and described. The phrase "exegetical framework" was chosen in order to convey two crucial features that a critical reading of the Targum reveals. The first is that, however surprising the translation of a given pericope might be, at each point the Targum is to be understood as an instance of exegesis in which the meturgeman was proceeding on the basis of the (or a) Hebrew text, if not solely on that basis. To this extent, even if the constituents of the Targum are judged to be of varying provenience, as a whole it is an extended exegesis. The second feature is closely related to the first. The Targum in its assemblage of varying traditions is no disjointed farrago of exegeses: there is a demonstrably controlling framework of themes, manifested by a coordinated use of vocabulary, which articulates a coherent theology.

The development of this exegetical framework represents a considerable achievement in the evolution of early Judaism into rabbinic Judaism. At the same time, the framework itself manifests stages in its own growth:

> Before proceeding to distinguish between one framework and the other, one must have some grasp of the overall framework to which the framework inter-preters contributed, because the contribution of the individual meturgemanin becomes more distinctive when viewed within the context of the total edifice they built with their colleagues. The coherent usages of various terms in the overall framework centre on the restoration of the house of Israel. This res-toration involves a return from the dispersion to the land appointed by God, and therefore victory over the Gentile dominion. The entire earth will have to recognize that true glory which is uniquely God's. The Temple and Jerusalem, the designated geographical associates of the Shekinah itself, are very much at the heart of the restoration, and the sanctuary features particularly both as the locus of divine power and the focus of Israel's obedience. For obedience to the law is the *sine qua non* of divine favour, just as rebellion occasions God's wrath. But in the wrath or favour of his memra, God remains constant in his choice of Israel, to whom he issues the call to repent through the prophets, the agents of his holy spirit. Israel may accept or reject the divine work, but God's choice of Abraham is unchanging. Still, it is righteousness akin to Abraham's which the interpreters demand from their people in the prophet's name; a return to the law and correct Temple service were to them the content of repentance. Only such repentance could put Israel in a position to receive the vindication willed him by God. That is why the messiah's programme—of restoring law so as to occasion forgiveness—is so crucial in the Targum.

The principal and most striking feature of this overall Targumic framework is its perennial relevance to Israel. This is what permitted the Amoraic framework meturgeman to incorporate the contribution of his Tannaitic predecessors into his own work, what enabled the rabbis of Babylonia to authorize the transmission of the Targum itself, and what encouraged medieval scholars to make enough copies to ensure (substantively) the textual integrity of the Stenning and Sperber editions. Here is a message, in the name of the greatest literary prophet, which speaks to a dispersed and disoriented Israel living on the sufferance of Gentile officials, without a cult and yet expectant of a messiah who will restore the Temple and the autonomy of Israel. The Targum acknowledges these cir-cumstances—indeed it speaks (at one level) from an immediate experience of them—and it also articulates these hopes. But the Targum is no broadsheet whose purpose is to foment the uncritical expectation for vengeance among those who lived under various forms of oppression; hope is appropriate only for those who repent to the law; the promises of Abraham belong to those who behave as Abraham; the memra is always with Israel, but it might support or punish. The Targum has addressed all dispersed Israel in the time since the desolation of

Mount Zion seemed final, and it has done so—not as generality—but as comfort and challenge. To those to whom rabbinic literature is nothing more than academic legal discussion and speculative haggadah, the Isaiah Targum is a most eloquent answer, and the dearth of accessible modern language editions is unfortunate.

Yet the very success of the Targum in its extant form as a contribution to the spiritual life of dispersed Israel (that is, Israel as disoriented by the desolation of the cult, not only as geographically scattered) means that it is problematic to assign the overall framework to a single given period. Indeed, the usage by different framework meturgemanin of the same characteristic terms often makes it impossible with any certainty to decide when the work of one leaves off and that of another takes up, and the echoes between the Targum and the Shemoneh Esreh (for example) demonstrate that rabbis might responsibly have encouraged the use of such a paraphrase in almost any period between the dissolution of cultic practice and the medieval attestation of the document.

By itself, the Targum's understanding of the law as the central means of Israel's approach to God and the secret of his communal identity serves only to highlight the coherence of the interpreters' faith with the spiritual movement which found its voice in the Seleucid challenge and culminated with the rabbis. But the specific and emphatic association between the law and the cult in the Targum, and the expectation that a messianically restored Israel would attend to teaching which comes from the Temple, seemed especially (although not exclusively) similar to the fervent, literally expressed hope in Intertestamental literature. Such similarity was far more apparent in respect of "sanctuary" usage, because—while the concrete restoration of the Temple is a prominent expectation shared by the Targum, Intertestamental literature and early rabbis—the Amoraim appeared less eager to emphasize the building of the Temple as an immediate and central hope. At this point also, the internal evidence of the Targum suggested that two strata within the earlier framework should be distinguished, the first of which takes restoration to be a matter of regulating the cult properly, and the second of which assumes that physical rebuilding is necessary. The early framework meturgemanin hoped as passionately for Jerusalem's consolation as did one of their contemporaries, the author of the fifth Sibylline book, and their attitude was contrasted in our study with the tendency of rabbinic exegesis to see Jerusalem's vindication in ethical terms. Moreover, the Targumic descriptions of Jerusalem's oppression made it clear that the hope of the interpreters was articulated in critical circumstances: the Roman campaign against the city (stratum one) and its eventual success (stratum two) seem to have influenced the choice of language. A cognate differentiation between the attitude manifest in Intertestamental literature, the early Targumic framework and the Shemoneh Esreh on one hand, and rabbinic opinion from the second century onward on the other was made in respect of "exile" usage: a development from a literal hope for immediate, militarily triumphal return to the land to a more positive approach to exile as a condition endured by God with his people seemed apparent. At the same time, "exile" within the early framework is both a threat (at stratum one) and a reality (at stratum two). All usages of the term "Shekinah" in the Targum cohere with the primary type of idiom isolated by A. M. Goldberg ("Gegenwartsschekhinah") and suppose an identification with the Temple such

317

that the Shekinah is either sinned against by cultic abuse (stratum one) or removed because of such sin, but soon to return (stratum two). A more attenuated use of the term characterizes the Amoraic period. "Kingdom" in the Targum is associated with Zion, as is consistent with the viewpoint of the early meturgemanin. Their usage represents a development in the meaning of the term (which is evident in comparison with the usage of other Prophetic Targumim and the Mekhilta), in that the earlier understanding saw the kingdom in less restricted terms. But the connection of the kingdom with the sanctuary is also attested in the musaf prayer for pilgrimages, and is only a step in the direction of a nomistic understanding of the kingdom which was achieved at or near the end of the first century. The early framework interpreters' view of righteousness is, as in Intertestamental literature, communal and motivated by the hope of vindication; the Amoraim were no less emphatic in their call to be righteous, but they understand righteousness as a more individual duty and associate it more with obedience to the law (an association which is presupposed in their demand for right behaviour) and less with the teaching of the law (which was a crucial necessity in the days of the early meturgemanin).

For the Amoraic framework meturgeman(in), sin in general, rather than specifically cultic abuse, is the cause of exile to Babylon, and his hope for the eventual end of the Babylonian tyranny is linked more to individual than to ethnic repentance. In the sense that exile is the situation in which the individual is to cultivate righteous behavior, the Amoraic acceptance of exile as the *status quo* seems presupposed, and we found a near parallel to an "exile" reading from the later framework (Targum Is. 43.14) in the Pesiqta Rabbati (30.2), and many Amoraic parallels to a later and individualistic "repentance" reading (at Targum Is. 57.19). Moreover, Israel for this interpreter is more a "congregation" than a "house" (again, cf. Pesiqta Rabbati 37.3); a post-nationalistic perspective seems evident. On the other hand, it must be acknowledged and stressed that the Amoraic interpreter was an ardent traditionalist. He was willing, for example (at Targum Is. 48.15, 16), to let the work of his predecessors stand and transmit to his readers an imperative to follow Abraham in a vocation of cultic service rather than voice the call, fashionable in his day, for scholars to be heard with the respect due to Moses. Likewise, the Amoraic Isaian framework meturgeman (unlike his, or another's, practice in Targum Micah) effaced his own kingdom theology in favour of the viewpoint of a Tannaitic framework meturgeman. Interpreters at both the Tannaitic and Amoraic levels availed themselves of the introductory phrase, "The prophet said." The former typically employed it to articulate the demand for communal repentance and the hope for the renovation of prophecy thereafter; the latter used it to insist on right conduct in view of eschatological judgement (cf. Targum Is. 21.12 with Numbers Rabbah 16.23). The Amoraic meturgeman also developed the earlier picture of the messiah ben David who, with a priestly counterpart, gives the law from the Temple he restores into a figure who is proleptically active (Targum Is. 43.10, and not in name only) as a witness to God's sole efficacy as God.

What we have postulated to explain the growth of the Isaiah Targum is not a series of mechanical redactions, but the unfolding of an interpretative continuum. There is no way of determining the number of meturgemanin who were responsible for each of the individual readings contained in the extant manuscripts, and yet the evidence has substantiated our hypothesis, developed in the introduction, that the repetition of characteristic terms manifests an organizing framework. We have collated that evidence against selected data from Intertestamental literature, the Qumran finds, ancient Jewish prayers, Rabbinica and the New Testament, and we have been led by our exegeses to differentiate between the applications of these characteristic terms within the Targum itself. We have come to the conclusion—gradually, as the inquiry progressed, and term after term appeared to bear now one meaning, now a distinct (albeit related) meaning—that we must think of the framework as a developing, organizing principle which permitted more ancient readings to be transmitted even as their theological significance was adapted to the points of view of the meturgemanin and their readers. As rings on a tree, the two strata of the Tannaitic level and the single, although less substantial, Amoraic level stand out as witnesses to stages of growth. The shape of the tree was at each stage distinctive, but related to its shape at the next stage, and at every point it was recognizably the same tree that was growing.[11]

This passage has been quoted at length, in order to avoid giving any misimpression as to what is meant by "exegetical framework." The phrase designedly avoids the language of "source" and "redaction," at least as those terms have come to be employed. The perception of a framework of governing themes does not warrant the conclusion that all thematically similar exegeses in the Targum were taken up as a source into the framework, or that every exegesis was collated by a single "redactor" who thought these themes a good idea. One can only say, in literary terms, that the framework imputes coherence to the whole. Similarly, the historical information that can be gleaned from the framework is meager. My description of the provenience of the framework(s) is not out of keeping with the traditionally rabbinic understanding that both Jonathan ben Uzziel and Joseph bar Ḥiyya were involved in the formation of the Prophetic Targums, but it offers no particular support to that understanding. The fact remains, however, that the literary profiles of thematic frameworks can be collated with evolving patterns in other instances of Jewish literature. In other words, the exegetical framework of the Isaiah Targum is the plane of intersection between literary and socially historical approaches.[12]

Misunderstanding regarding the nature of the exegetical framework, as I have defined it, has resulted in an inaccurate assessment of my work, at least on the part of one reviewer.[13] Peter Nichels poses the question "What is an 'exegetical framework'?" He does not cite from the extensive passage quoted above, which would have answered the question in my own words, but attempts inductively to state my position:

One has the impression that he has done no more than relate (uncertainly in many cases) specific passages to specific historical and literary settings.

That impression is justifiable if one reads my book as a sequence of isolated paragraphs (much in the way critics of a certain generation have read the

Bible). But the passages treated were chosen, as any serious reader of my book will know, in view of their representative usage of terms and phrases that recur characteristically in the Targum. Lest there be any doubt, I should like to repeat what I said on p. 12:

> While historical and literary allusions might guide us to an understanding of the date and provenience of a given passage or motif, and language (if that were an established criterion) would help to establish the time and place of the final redaction of the whole, Targums as such are not farragos of tradition or *de novo* compositions, but specimens of extended exegesis. To discover the provenience and date of a Targum one must ask, first, what exegetical terms and phrases are so frequently used as to constitute characteristic conventions, and then, how do these conventions relate to historical circumstances, to the New Testament and early Jewish literature generally? Such conventions, when repeatedly used in a given work, would provide the ordering principle for traditional interpretations and for the inclusion of subsequent insights. This exegetical framework belongs to the *esse* of a Targum: without it, targumic readings are only a *pot pourri*, while with it even the addition of material does not constitute a recension, only an addendum.

The intention of the definition was to formulate an alternative to "source" or "redaction," as the italicized portion of the passage cited previously makes unmistakably (as I once hoped) plain.[14] The point, as I still think is evident, is to avoid the language of mechanical compilation.

A friend in the field of English literature warned that my simile of a tree, in the passage from the conclusion which was cited earlier, might seem too obvious to some; he felt it was already plain that my program did not involve anything that could be taken as a metaphor of the inorganic. He did not reckon with Nichels, who actually imputes to me the idea that my "exegetical framework" is to be identified with a "redaction." He rightly states, "'Redaction' would seem to indicate a more thorough editing than C. has claimed or demonstrated"; for precisely that reason, "C." never used the word "redaction." Because I said I had used a "modified form of redaction criticism" (p. 110), Nichels decided I thought all along that an "exegetical framework" was the same thing as a "redaction."[15]

It is, of course, annoying to have one's book reviewed on the basis of what it did *not* say, and I am happy to see that other reviewers have more clearly seen the point of my method.[16] But Nichels's confusion does betray the common assumption of genetic history within allegedly literary approaches. Despite my care in defining "exegetical framework," he concluded it must be a hypostatized entity, a "redaction" or a "source." He then compounded the confusion by suggesting that the term "trajectory" might serve better than "exegetical framework."

The notion of trajectory, as developed by Helmut Koester and James Robinson, was designed to describe the development of theologoumena used in various documents, with the aim of assessing early Christian ideology.[17] It has been criticized for creating its own hypostasis, a supposed entity out of the relationship among documents that happen to speak on similar subjects, and for being inherently teleological.[18] These criticisms must be met before the language of "trajectory" can be used precisely, and to refer to its usage in a review, as it if were an accepted part of critical usage, is most curious. Moreover, "trajectory," evocative though the term might be, is quite irrelevant to literary analysis. In assessing a Targum, the crucial issue is to appreciate the stance of the document generally in its presentation of disparate exegeses. The "trajectory" of any series of those exegeses might be traced, but that would not characterize the Targum as a whole.

The present purpose is not to claim inviolability for the phrase "exegetical framework" as a norm of targumic criticism. But before a replacement can be suggested, it is necessary to comprehend what the phrase does and does not seek to describe. In the absence of a method for locating the exegetical frameworks of Targums within Judaism, the way will be open to use selected readings to characterize entire compositions. Three recent studies of the Isaiah Targum manifest just this tendency. Smolar and Aberbach place the exegesis of the Targum in the Tannaitic period, and especially within the school of Aqiba.[19] Unfortunately, they do so without considering the body of evidence adduced by Churgin[20] and me for a substantive Amoraic phase in the development of the Targum. Even within their own terms of reference, the authors' attempt to limit the period of the Targum's development seems strained: they acknowledge allusions to the period after Aqiba (pp. 48, 80, 81, 82, 83, 88, 120).[21] Quite a different understanding of the Targum is assumed by Pierre Grelot in his study of the interpretation of the Servant Songs.[22] His starting point is the Amoraic phase of targumic development, and he claims that the understanding of the text is designed in part to counter Christian exegesis (pp. 220–23). He argues that the religious nationalism and the emphasis on the law in the Targum, as well as its picture of the Messiah in classically Davidic terms, betray an apologetic interest. In effect, he has seized on one possible strand in the tapestry of targumic development and used it to characterize the whole as an anti-Christian tract. Lastly, van der Kooij[23] takes the targumic emphasis on prophecy to betray a priestly interest and decides that the hero of the piece is Eleazar, the colleague of Bar Kokhba, whom van der Kooij identifies with Eleazar of Modiim (pp. 205–8). The argument is speculative in the extreme, and can be questioned at each point in its development; it scarcely bears the weight of the claim that the Targum did *not* grow out of the translational practice in synagogues and instead reflects specifically priestly interests.

When one keeps a view to the exegetical framework of the Isaiah Targum, varying stances are seen to be in tension, but the artificial program of forcing all of them into a single mold is avoided. That is the methodological point of *The Glory of Israel.* It may seem elementary, but previous, and even contemporary, practitioners of targumic investigation apparently have not grasped it. In the case of the present passage from the Targum, the first, Tannaitic, level of the framework, with its keen focus on the temple, is most in evidence. Indeed, it is precisely the sort of tension that is apparent between v. 25 and the foregoing material which makes it advisable to speak of strata within that initial level. Because we are dealing with exegetical frameworks, and not thoroughgoing redactions, the seams created by juxtaposing traditions of varying provenience sometimes remain visible.

THE PROMISE TO ELIAKIM IN
CHRISTIAN LITERATURE OF THE
FIRST CENTURY

Our finding in respect of the attitude conveyed in the targumic paraphrase of Isaiah 22 would be strengthened if a similarly voiced promise to Eliakim could be found elsewhere, but in the relevant period. As it happens, a generally recognized reference to Isa. 22:22 is to be found in Matt. 16:19, where Peter is promised that whatever he binds on earth will be bound in heaven and that whatever he looses on earth will be loosed in heaven.[24] Despite the distinction of the diction from the Masoretic text and the Targum, the syntactical similarity has been taken to be enough to warrant the judgment.[25] What is rather more significant for the present purpose, Isa. 22:22 is also cited in Rev. 3:7. There, one like a son of man (1:13) identifies himself as "the holy one, the true one, who has the key of David, who opens and none will shut, and shuts and none will open." That usage establishes quite clearly that the promise to Eliakim could be taken as a permanent one, as we posit for the earliest form of the targumic tradition within its framework.[26]

The Septuagint may also be said to have been influenced by such an understanding. It reads,

And I will give David's glory to him, and he will rule, and none will contradict.

As might be expected, that reading is supplemented or replaced elsewhere with a more literal rendering,[27] but as it stands it is a plainer, and therefore more emphatic, version of the promise to Eliakim than is found in the Masoretic text.

When the targumic interpretation of Isa. 22:22 is understood as we have suggested, a fresh approach to the promise to Peter in Matt. 16:18, 19 becomes possible. Those verses, of course, have been subjected to a great deal of discussion; for the present purpose, we are interested only in the degree of agreement between them and the Targum.[28]

Since the publication of Joachim Jeremias's classic study *Golgotha,*[29] the argument has been considered that the "rock" upon which Jesus promises to build his congregation is the cosmic foundation, Mount Zion. The suggestion of some allusion to Mount Zion is, in itself, not implausible, especially on the understanding that Isaian diction is used in the promise to Peter. Reference is frequently made to it in all the ancient versions of Isaiah, the nearest references in the Masoretic text being 18:7 and 24:23. The latter of those is of particular interest, since in the targumic interpretation a reference to the kingdom of God appears, a theologoumenon that also features in the promise to Peter.[30]

The difficulty with Jeremias's suggestion, however, is that it relies on taking *petra* in the promise as the cosmic rock, the antithesis to the "gates of Hades." That is, the saying is viewed as cultic only because and insofar as it is cosmological. Such a primary interest in cosmology is supported only by the reference to Hades; *petra,* in Greek *or* Aramaic, must be taken as a neutral term.[31] Generally, of course, the corpus of Jesus' sayings is not characterized by a cosmological interest, and it must be remembered that the "gates of Hades" might be understood as an immediately existential threat (cf. Isa. 38:10) and need not be taken cosmologically. For all of these reasons, Jeremias's suggestion has not won wide support.

The notion that a promise in respect of the temple is in effect here, however, is in some ways attractive. Elsewhere in Matthew, Jesus is presented as developing halakoth in respect of the temple. His teaching includes the taking of oaths (23:16–22) and instructions for the offering of sacrifice (5:23, 24), and a more elaborate story relates to the payment of the half shekel (17:24–27; cf. 23:23, 24//Luke 11:42). All of those passages are uniquely Matthean and yet are widely accepted as relating to the substance of Jesus' attitude toward the temple, as evidenced in the multiply attested accounts of his teaching about the widow's example of providing for the temple (Mark 12:41–44//Luke 21:1–4), of his occupation of the holy precincts (Matt. 21:12, 13//Mark 11:15–17//Luke 19:45, 46//John 2:13–17), of his discourse regarding the destruction of the temple (Matt. 24:1—25:46//Mark 13:1–37//Luke 21:5–36), and—most famously—of his prediction against the temple (John 2:19//Matt. 26:61//Mark 14:58). It would be quite coherent with this pattern of evidence if, as the similarity to the targumic interpretation would suggest, Jesus in Matt. 16:18, 19 were establishing the mechanism for articulating the cultic halakah. He would be doing so by assuming an attitude not unlike that of the meturgeman of Isa. 22:22 and by using the theological language of his time to stake out his position. That language appears to have focused on Eliakim and to have been influential in the formation of the Targum of Isaiah as it can be read today.[32]

NOTES

Versions of this essay were read at the yearly meetings of the Society of Biblical Literature (1985) and of the New Testament Colloquium of Harvard and Yale.

1. Renderings are based on my translation, *The Isaiah Targum. Translation, Introduction, Apparatus, and Notes:* The Aramaic Bible II (Wilmington: Michael Glazier, 1987).

2. Both of these passages are discussed at some length in "The Temple in the Targum of Isaiah," an essay that has appeared in the volume of my work *Targumic Approaches to the Gospels: Essays in the Mutual Definition of Judaism and Christianity,* Studies in Judaism (Lanham, Md.: Univ. Press of America), 1986.

3. The reversal of statements, from negative to positive and vice versa, is a well-known convention in *Targum Jonathan.* Instances of this and related phenomena are provided by J. F. Stenning in *The Targum of Isaiah* (Oxford: Clarendon Press, 1949), xvi.

4. For related usages, see Bruce D. Chilton, *The Glory of Israel: The Theology and Provenience of the Isaiah Targum,* Journal for the Study of the Old Testament—Supplement Series 23 (Sheffield: JSOT Press, 1982), 52–56.

5. Arie van der Kooij, *Die alten Textzeugen des Jesajabuches: Ein Beitrag zur Textgeschichte des Alten Testaments,* Orbis biblicus et orientalis (Göttingen: Vandenhoeck & Ruprecht, 1981), 161–64. Van der Kooij makes his claims on the basis of collations of targumic passages with Josephus's work; cf. H. St. J. Thackeray, *Josephus,* vol. 2, Loeb Classical Library (New York: G. P. Putnam's Sons, 1927).

6. Leivy Smolar and Moses Aberbach, *Studies in Targum Jonathan to the Prophets,* Library of Biblical Studies (New York: Ktav, 1983), 65, 66.

7. See van der Kooij, *Die alten Textzeugen,* 162, for the same claim in respect of his own, quite different, identification.

8. Cf. F. F. Bruce, *New Testament History* (London: Pickering & Inglis, 1980), 359, 360. Thackeray (*Josephus,* 482) relates the function to that of the *sgn;* but cf. n.9.

9. See Gustaf H. Dalman, *Aramäisch-neuhebräisches Handwörterbuch zu Targum, Talmud und Midrasch* (Hildesheim: Georg Olms Verlag, 1967), 24. Dalman refers both to *Oberster* and *Priesteroberster* as possible meanings. It is notable that in the *Targ. Jer.* 1.1, where the sense is evidently priestly, the *'mrkly'* are specifically located in Jerusalem. See also J. Levy, *Chaldäisches Wörterbuch über die Targumim* (Cologne: Melzer, 1959), 1:38, 39. In the Jeremiah Targum (52.24), the *mrkly* are mentioned after the high priest and the *sgn;* they correspond to the three keepers of the threshhold in the Masoretic text. A position in the priestly hierarchy, which is already implicit contextually in *Targ. Isa.* 22.22, does seem evident.

10. The critical stance taken in this section was developed in my *Beginning New Testament Study* (London: SPCK, 1986) and in my "Exorcism and History: Mark 1:21-28," in *Gospel Perspectives,* vol. 6, *The Miracles of Jesus,* ed. J. Wenham and C. Blomberg (Sheffield: JSOT Press, 1986), 253-71.

11. Chilton, *The Glory of Israel*, 97–102. A more precise allocation of material in the Targum according to the framework to which it belongs is available in the introduction of my commentary (see above, n. 1), xxiii–xxv.

12. By "social history" is meant the record and accounts of attitudes, beliefs, and practices in societies of the past. For recent, albeit varied, applications of the discipline, see Howard Clark Kee, *Miracle in the Early Christian World: A Study in Sociohistorical Method* (New Haven: Yale Univ. Press, 1983); Abraham J. Malherbe, *Social Aspects of Early Christianity* (Philadelphia: Fortress Press, 1983); and Wayne A. Meeks, *The First Urban Christians: The Social World of the Apostle Paul* (New Haven: Yale Univ. Press, 1983). In the study of Judaism, the literature itself is more directly susceptible of socially historical investigation since it is of a more communal nature than that of the Hellenistic world.

13. Peter Nichels, review of *The Glory of Israel*, by Chilton, *Catholic Biblical Quarterly* 47 (1985): 514, 515.

14. The earlier passage is taken from the conclusion of my *The Glory of Israel*. The italics have been added for the purpose of the present discussion. At the same time, I have taken the opportunity to make certain corrections that were introduced at the proof stage of producing the book but that unfortunately were not properly entered.

15. See ibid., 125 n. 49.

16. See the reviews by D. Bourget (*Etudes théologiques et religieuses* 59 [1984]: 255), R. Coggins (*Journal of Theological Studies* 36 [1985]: 275), R. P. Gordon (*Society of Old Testament Studies Book List* [1984]: 44), B. Grossfeld (*Journal of Biblical Literature* 104 [1985]: 138, 139), O. Kaiser (*Zeitschrift für die alttestamentliche Wissenschaft* 96 [1984]: 300), S. C. Reif (*Vetus Testamentum* 34 [1984]: 124), J. Ribera (*Estudios Bíblicos* 42 [1984]: 230–34), R. Tournay (*Biblical Research* 91 [1984]: 465–66), and R. White (*Journal of Jewish Studies* 35 [1984]: 106–8).

17. Helmut Koester and James Robinson, *Trajectories through Early Christianity* (Philadelphia: Fortress Press, 1971).

18. See Bruce Chilton, "'Not to Taste Death': A Jewish, Christian, and Gnostic Usage," *Studia Biblica 1978*, vol. 2, *Papers on the Gospels,* Journal for the Study of the New Testament—Supplement Series (Sheffield: JSOT Press, 1980), 29–36.

19. Smolar and Aberbach, *Studies,* 1, 29.

20. Pinkhos Churgin, *Targum Jonathan to the Prophets,* Yale Oriental Series (New York: Ktav, 1983).

21. Further criticism of their position, together with the criticisms of van der Kooij and Pierre Grelot, is available in "Three Views of the Isaiah Targum," *Journal for the Study of the Old Testament* 33 (1985): 127, 128.

22. Pierre Grelot, *Les poèmes du Serviteur: De la lecture critique à l'herméneutique,* Lectio divina 103 (Paris: Editions du Cerf, 1981).

23. Van der Kooij, *Die alten Textzeugen,* 198–203.

24. See, above all, John A. Emerton, "Binding and Loosing—Forgiving and Retaining," *Journal of Theological Studies* 13 (1962): 325–31. The observation of the allusion to Isa. 22:22 does not, however, rest on the particulars of Emerton's argument; cf. the ed. of F. H. A. Scrivener (Cambridge: Deighton, Bell, 1891) and of the Nestles, Kurt Aland, and others (Stuttgart: Deutsche Bibelstiftung, 1981).

25. Isaiah 22:22 is, quite correctly, not listed as quoted in Matt. 16:19 in the

editions of B. F. Westcott and F. J. A. Hort (London: Macmillan & Co., 1901) and the United Bible Societies (Stuttgart: Württemberg Bible Society, 1968).

26. The association of this passage with Matt. 16:18, 19 becomes even closer according to 2050 (dated 1170 in Nestle-Aland) and certain other minuscules. There, "of Hades" replaces "of David." But the association (even in the mind of the scribe of 2050) may only be apparent, since the son of man is already identified in Rev. 1:18 as holding the keys of death and Hades (cf. Job 38:17).

27. Cf. Alfred Rahlfs, *Septuaginta*, vol. 2 (Stuttgart: Württembergische Bibelanstalt, 1935); and Joseph Ziegler, *Isaias*, Septuaginta 14 (Göttingen: Vandenhoeck & Ruprecht, 1967).

28. I hope elsewhere to develop a fuller explication of the passage generally.

29. Joachim Jeremias, *Golgotha*, Angelos 1 (Leipzig: Pfeiffer, 1926), 68–77. Jeremias repeats and summarizes his arguments in the article on Hades in the *Theological Dictionary of the New Testament*, ed. G. Kittel and G. W. Bromiley (Grand Rapids: Wm. B. Eerdmans, 1978), 146–49.

30. Cf. my *The Glory of Israel*, 77–81; and my *A Galilean Rabbi and His Bible: Jesus' Use of the Interpreted Scripture of His Time*, Good News Studies 8 (Wilmington, Del.: Michael Glazier, 1984), published also with the subtitle *Jesus' Own Interpretation of Isaiah* (London: SPCK, 1984), 58–63. A more technical consideration of Jesus' use of the theologoumenon of the kingdom and its relation to targumic usage appears in my *God in Strength: Jesus' Announcement of the Kingdom*, Studien zum Neuen Testament und seiner Umwelt 1 (Freistadt: Plöchl, 1979).

31. It has become something of an axiom in modern interpretation that the term *kyp'* was used twice in the original form of the saying; cf. Max Wilcox, "Peter and the Rock: A Fresh Look at Matthew XVI.17–19," *New Testament Studies* 22 (1976): 74. *Pṭr'*, however, is a term (borrowed from Greek) which appears in Aramaic with the meaning "foundation"; cf. Dalman, *Aramäisch-neuhebräisches Handwörterbuch*, 332; and Charles Taylor, *Sayings of the Jewish Fathers* (Cambridge: Cambridge Univ. Press, 1897), 160.

32. The present case of dominical reliance on targumic tradition might be associated with those presented in my *A Galilean Rabbi*. It was not included in the original study because it does not present the more straightforward dictional or contextual connections between the Targums and Jesus' diction which are manifest in the other instances.

19

"Glory to Thy People, Israel":
Luke-Acts and the Jews

DAVID L. TIEDE
Luther Northwestern Seminary

CHRISTIAN HISTORY AND JUDAISM

Luke-Acts is a Jewish Christian story that fell into gentile hands. From at least as early as the second century, Luke's history of the beginnings of the Christian movement has been read as an account of the triumph of gentile Christianity at the expense of Judaism. In developing its myth of Christian beginnings,[1] normative Christianity has regularly interpreted this narrative as foundational to its claim of having displaced Israel as heir to God's promises. The apostolic speeches in Acts calling for repentance have become standing Christian indictments of Jewish complicity in Jesus' death and of the refusal of Jews to be converted by Christian proclamation of the gospel.[2]

The stakes are high in the current discussion of Luke's view of the Jewish people and their leaders, and it would be foolish to attempt even a historical study of the text without recognizing the pervasive influence that anti-Judaism has so long had in Christian theology and New Testament interpretation.[3] It would also be absurd to seek to disguise the uncompromising declarations Luke-Acts makes concerning Jesus, as if the divisions in Israel that the followers of this messiah further provoked were inconsequential. The stakes were high in the last third of the first century too.

Nevertheless, the sociology and identity of the first-century author and readers were significantly different from those of the communities of subsequent interpreters. Because recent critical scholarship has been able to challenge long-established traditions of reading Luke-Acts,[4] the questions at stake in Luke's context may again be pursued carefully and distinguished from the issues of the use that has been made of the text. Even the identification of the author simultaneously with Israel and with this messianist movement has become credible. Critical historical and literary studies have shed new light on the context and content of Luke's story as a tale told within the history of Israel rather than at the expense of "the Jews."

Recent historical research into first-century Jewish history has illumined this reading of Luke-Acts by successfully challenging the monolithic structures of "normative Judaism" and "apostolic Christianity." These edifices had been erected by interpreters of the first century and had long served the dogmatic interests of both subsequent traditions, but the cost was high to the historical complexity of the first-century sources. Now in place of idealized images of the origins of each heritage, which could always be used as a foil for the denigration of the other tradition, both the Pharisaic and messianist movements may be depicted as taking shape within a much more complex and diverse religious, cultural, political, and social context. The reconstructed past within which the Luke-Acts narrative may be read has changed.

In the decades surrounding the destruction of the second temple, several alternative traditions, subcultures, and methods of being "true Israel" were still actively competing.[5] In Luke-Acts, the Pharisees are depicted as the major contender with the messianist movement for the claim of being true Israel, and the charges of apostasy have become mutually acrimonious between these Jewish groups (see Acts 3:23; 21:21). The charges may reflect tensions within the messianist movement over the status of the law and the gentile mission,[6] so that the question of "true Israel" was being debated within the messianist movement itself as well as among the broader variety of Jewish groups. In turn, Luke's depiction of the Pharisees closing ranks with Paul against the Sadducees on the question of the resurrection (Acts 23:6–10) becomes more than a glimpse of the tensions among authorities, institutions, and groups over Israel's identity and role in God's design for the world. It is also a signal that the battleground between messianists and Pharisees over the interpretation of the faith of Israel was also their common ground against Jewish groups that they commonly rejected as heterodox. An investigation of the social, economic, and political realities that undergirded such surprising alliances would reveal that these various parties or sects were also identified and defined by factors beyond their competing orthodoxies.

At least it is clear that Luke-Acts manifests a struggle among the messianists as part of a complex of disputes among various Jewish groups over how to be "true Israel," over what the sins calling for repentance may be, and over what role the Gentiles have to play in God's judgment and salvation. It is no longer credible to disregard the complexity of late-first-century Jewish history by reading Luke-Acts simply as a story of "Christianity" versus "Judaism." Those terms acquire their traditional meaning only in the social and religious context of subsequent centuries, and they hide or even pervert more than they disclose the issues that were originally at stake in the story of Luke-Acts.

The narrative of Luke-Acts is not a straightforward account of the triumph of Christian history which provides an appropriate foundation for the myth of the ascendancy of gentile Christianity out of the ashes of Jewish history. Even the literary complexity of the narrative argues against such simplistic misuse. Thus the theme of the rejection of the Messiah and of the preaching of the apostles has been shown to be a major plot device of the whole story, filling the narrative with genuine pathos and tragic possibility and urgency.[7]

An adequate grasp of the unity of the narrative requires that Luke 1—2 be read in relation to Acts 28 so that the complementarity of these sections may not be suppressed by simple claims of either a gentile triumph or a Jewish tragedy. The ominous notes of Luke 1—2 must be carefully observed along with the promises, and the faith of some in Paul's proclamation in Acts 28 must not be overwhelmed by the note of rejection. Both the prophetic promises and the painful oracles of judgment alert the reader that the fundamental tension of the plot awaits a final resolution. The struggle of wills between a determined God and a willful Israel remains intense, invoking the repentance that must still precede the restoration of all in the kingdom of the exalted Messiah (see Acts 3:19; 1:8; 28:23–28).[8]

THE STORY OF THE FALL AND RISE
OF MANY IN ISRAEL

Before the literary complexity of Luke-Acts could be explored, the unity of the narrative had to be grasped anew. Henry J. Cadbury's monumental assessment *The Making of Luke-Acts*[9] still stands like a beacon on the far side of the tireless labors of the source and redaction critics of the 1930s to 1960s. Remarkably, many of the very materials the source critics had been so eager to assign to earlier "Jewish" stages of the tradition have emerged again as fundamental to Luke's literary project. The coherence and significance of the speeches of Acts and the infancy narratives are particularly telling cases. Through whatever traditions or sources these stories and their declarations may have been conveyed to the author, they are now Lukan compositions, and those who speak within these passages are reliable narrators.[10]

The oracles of Simeon are thus captured in a larger presentation of the circumcision of the Messiah and his portentous presentation in the temple in Luke 2. The thorough structuring of the annunciation, birth, and childhood stories of John and Jesus is so prominent as to invite close comparison of these wonder children throughout their ensuing careers[11] (see also Luke 7:16–19, 26–35; 16:16; Acts 10:37–38). The angels, faithful elders of Israel, and mother of the infant Messiah praise God in canticles and oracles concerning these children, and they are all to be implicitly trusted. This includes Zechariah, who is struck dumb for rather mild disbelief but later prophesies as one filled with the Holy Spirit (Luke 1:20, 67–79). The literary function of these episodes is, therefore, to sound the critical themes of the story in advance of the telling. They declare the promises and perils that God's rule will bring to bear on Israel and the nations through this messiah and his herald John. The speeches in Acts, in turn, serve to identify how this purpose and plan of God has unfolded (see esp. Acts 2:14–36; 3:12–26; 4:24–30; 10:34–43).

The general tone of these prophetic declarations in Luke 1—2 is joyful, full of hope and confidence, and extravagant in the vision of God's reign. John will precede Jesus "in the spirit and power of Elijah, to turn the hearts of the fathers to the children, and the disobedient to the wisdom of the just, to make ready for the Lord a people prepared" (1:17). This is the way in which God has "visited and redeemed his people," saving them from the fear of their enemies, guiding their feet in the way of peace (1:68–79). Jesus will be given the throne of his father David, "and of his kingdom there will be no end." This is how God has "put down the mighty from their thrones and exalted those of low degree" (1:51–55). The reader is thus alerted to the political connection that this birth took place within the census of Caesar Augustus during Quirinius's governance of Syria. When the heavenly messenger declares, "To you is born this day in the city of David a Savior, who is Christ the Lord," it is clear that Jesus' messiahship has everything to do with Israel's fate within the Roman order.

But as Robert Tannehill has shown so clearly,[12] all of this optimism and hopefulness is poignant and potentially tragic in Luke's narrative. First of all, the retrospective sermons, culminating in the last word of Acts 28, are not accounts of the gathering of all of faithful Israel, with the triumph of the Messiah over Israel's enemies. Grand displays of faith and of the Holy Spirit's restoring activity are especially prominent after the early speeches in Acts (see Acts 2:43; 4:4, 31; 11:21; 13:43–44; see also 21:20). But the latter portion of the narrative of Acts is marked by the recitation of Isaiah's indictment of Israel's deafness, blindness, and hardness of heart.

Second, the interpretation of the ominous ending of Acts has regularly been influenced by non- or anti-Jewish understandings of the historical circumstances in which Luke tells the tale. If Jerusalem and the temple had already been destroyed by the time Luke wrote this narrative, the promise that the Messiah first portended for Israel could now be merely a bitter reminder of failed hopes or recrimination for lack of repentance. Certainly the sense of an ending which has often been derived from Acts 28 is that the recitation of God's salvation history points only to the condemnation of Israel.

It must be granted that this view of the narrative as indictment has literary possibility and precedent. Stephen's speech in Acts 7 testifies that the salvation history that God intends may again be the damnation history of a "stiff-necked people, uncircumcised in heart and ears, always resisting the Holy Spirit" (7:51). Yet there is nothing anti-Jewish or foreign to Jewish tradition in such an indictment. The prophetic heritage long before taught how Israel's history could be recited against the nation. The Book of Deuteronomy is even constructed with just such a sense of an ending, in which Moses' speech, uttered before the fact, announces destruction verging on the utter annihilation of Israel (Deuteronomy 31—34). Jewish literature of the era surrounding the destruction of the second temple is replete with such strong prophetic diagnoses. Israel has always known how to confess sin, and Luke's narrative is a call to Israel to repent by accepting Jesus as Messiah and not "withstanding God" (see Acts 2:37–38; 3:19; 5:31; 17:30; 26:20).

It is also possible that Luke's narrative is fundamentally a tragic tale in which the hopeful promises that have been so joyfully announced are now only intensifications of their failure. Certainly, like many of his contemporary historians, Luke knew many of the conventions of tragic historiography. His version of the death of Jesus is particularly marked with such pathos and remorse and the haunting double vision of those who see what is happening and those who go blindly to their destruction.[13] The effect of such narratives must be assessed with extreme care, however, since tragic style may only be veiled self-justification, as when Josephus adopts the tragic mode to exonerate himself and the Romans or when Melito of Sardis stirs up hatred against the Jews while posturing deep sympathy.[14]

But these literary and historical possibilities are finally too improbable to the whole of Luke's story to be accepted. Instead, Luke's hopeful assurances in the infancy stories are to be taken at face value. They are not oracles doomed to fail. To be sure, the harsh prophetic words and the laments of the Messiah and his apostles stand in sharp contrast to the hopes of Israel's glory, indicating that the course of the fulfillment of these promises will not be easy or direct. The tragic proportions and potential of the story are such that the readers are profoundly aware that even God's saving will for Israel and the Gentiles is threatened. But tragic perils must not be confused with a story that is finally tragic. As Paul Minear has shown, even Luke's presentation of the boldness and confidence of the apostles is probably symptomatic of an "internal dialogue between credulity and skepticism" in a community where the possibility of failed hopes must be addressed.[15] Finally, Luke's narrative is a testimony to God's fulfillment of the scriptural promises and the transcending of the tragic possibilities of the story.

Furthermore, the hopes of the story are consistently stated in terms of God's promises to Israel. The persons who have the hopes and the content of their expectations are constantly identified in the language of the scriptural promises to Israel. Consider Luke's cardinal expressions of this yearning: Simeon, who was "looking for the consolation of Israel" (Luke 2:25); Anna, the prophetess, daughter of Phanuel, worshiping day and night and giving thanks to God and speaking of Jesus "to all who were looking for the redemption of Jerusalem" (2:38); Joseph, of the Jewish town of Arimathea, a "good and righteous man, who had not consented to their purpose and deed, and . . . was looking for the kingdom of God" (23:50–51); Cleopas and his companion who "had hoped that he was the one to redeem Israel" (24:21); Jesus' own disciples, who ask, "Lord will you at this time restore the kingdom to Israel?" (Acts 1:6; see also Luke 19:11); James, looking forward to the fulfillment of the prophetic promise of the rebuilding of the "dwelling of David which has fallen" (Acts 15:16); and Paul, who emphasized that it was for his "hope in the promise made by God to our fathers" that he was on trial (Acts 26:6; see also 24:15; 26:22). If Luke's stated purpose for his narrative is that the reader "may know the assurance of the things in which you have been instructed" (Luke 1:1–4), it is inconceivable that the hopes of these faithful in Israel will finally be disappointed.

Simeon's oracles, therefore, are crucial to the meaning of the narrative as a whole, because Simeon announces Israel's hope as God's will in no uncertain terms but he also alerts the reader that Jesus will provoke a crisis in Israel. His own credentials are above reproach, and the repeated mention of the Holy Spirit confirms all that he expects to see and sees. "This man was righteous and devout, looking for the consolation of Israel, and the Holy Spirit was upon him" (Luke 2:25; see also v. 26 ["And it had been revealed to him by the Holy Spirit"] and v. 27 ["And inspired by the Spirit he came into the temple"]). Jesus, Mary and Joseph, and Simeon are all fully obedient and observant of all dimensions of the law of Moses (vv. 21–23; so also Anna, v. 37).[16] His two oracles foreshadow the entire story, providing a portentous glimpse of what the Holy Spirit had long said through the prophets and would continue to say (see also Acts 28:25) concerning the purposes of God and the prospects of Israel.

The first oracle announces what the infant Messiah means to God. It is a testimony given in the form of Simeon's blessing of God, declaring God's faithfulness to the word given to Simeon and to the scriptural promises that it echoes. The parallelism of the passage indicates that the "salvation which thou has prepared in the face of all the peoples" is the same as the light which is given "for revelation to the Gentiles" and "for the glory of your people Israel." Even on a strictly literary level, the passage identifies God's salvation as a public disclosure in view of all the Gentiles but redounding to Israel's glory. The possibility that some of the Gentiles could see the light before all of Israel is gathered has already been broached, yet without any hint of rebuke of Israel. This first inspired oracle has disclosed that God's purposes and plans are wholly directed toward salvation. When seen in connection with Simeon's expectation of the "consolation of Israel," this "salvation" has the clear connotation of the "redemption," "restoration," "kingdom," and "hope" that all the other worthies in the story await.

But as Jesus' "father and mother" are amazed and filled with wonder at his first oracle, Simeon speaks a second oracle, which seems to confound the first or threaten it with tragedy. Uttered now as a "blessing" of Jesus' human parents and as a word to Mary, Simeon's oracle alerts the reader to the complexity of God's way of accomplishing the saving reign of this messiah. Certainly Simeon is still inspired and speaking for God, but now he is advising the reader, along with the faithful Mary and Joseph, that even God's salvation in Jesus will bring down many in Israel before it will have accomplished God's ultimate gracious purpose.[17] Humanity, and Israel and Mary in particular, are put on notice that God's reign or visitation of Israel is a divine confrontation with a willful people as well as a consolation to the faithful (see 1:68–69; 19:44). This salvation will be accomplished by God, but through human suffering (see also Acts 9:16).

The sequence of words is significant. This is not a prediction of the rise and fall of the Roman Empire, the Third Reich, or the kingdom of Herod. This is a prophetic oracle disclosing the fall that will come before the rising of many in Israel, and the passive voice alerts the reader once again that it is God who has set this child for such falling and rising and for being a controverted sign. This is the reader's advance warning of the way in which even unwilling human agents in the story will be found doing "whatever God's hand and will had predetermined would take place" (Acts 4:28). And God's initiative in this confrontation had the purpose ("in order that") of exposing the secret thoughts (*dialogismoi*) of the hearts of many (Luke 2:35). These are the veiled rejections (Luke 4:22; 5:22; 6:8; 13:31; 19:39), the misguided illusions (Luke 9:9, 46–47; 23:8), and doubts (Luke 24:38) that Jesus exposes in his adversaries and his disciples alike.

The "many in Israel" who will fall and rise in order that their rejection or resistance to God's reign be exposed will continue to be the focus of the narrative of Luke-Acts, with only a few episodes of similar rejections by Samaritans or Gentiles. This will be a story of a struggle of wills with a messiah who will confront the people in Nazareth (Luke 4:16–30), "some Pharisees" attempting to divert Jesus from his way to Jerusalem (Luke

DAVID L. TIEDE

13:31–34; 19:39–40), and those who send spies "pretending to be sincere" but in reality intent on trapping the Messiah (Luke 20—21).

So also the apostles who call Israel to repentance will constantly be encountering the resistance and rejection of many as well as repentance and faith of others throughout the entire story of Acts. Even the threefold turning to the Gentiles which punctuates Paul's mission in Acts (Acts 13:46; 18:6; 28:28) is always involved with the fall and rise of many in Israel. The last word is always about Israel, not only in Acts 28 but even in the Lord's word to Ananias concerning Paul: "He is a chosen instrument of mine to carry my name before the Gentiles and kings and the sons of Israel" (Acts 9:15). Far from concluding that God or the Messiah or the apostles are done with Israel, the whole of the narrative rather demonstrates that even the gentile mission is fundamental to God's determination to deal with a willful Israel. But the salvation that God intends, the restoration of all, and the kingdom of God itself are to be attested to Israel at the beginning and at the end. And in the midst of the rejection of many, others in Israel repent and believe and are restored to be the light to the Gentiles which was Israel's calling and glory all along (Luke 2:32; Acts 1:8; 13:47; 28:28).

The ending of the narrative in Acts 28 is, therefore, not the end of the story but a resumption of the themes sounded in Simeon's oracles. First Paul lays claim to his credentials as a faithful Israelite (Acts 28:17), while acknowledging that he remains in bonds because the "Judeans" had "spoken against" him.[18] Paul is asked to speak on behalf of "this sect which is everywhere spoken against" (Acts 28:22). Since Jesus has been identified as a "sign spoken against" (Luke 2:34), the reader ought not to be surprised to find that the messianist sect (*hairesis*) and its apostle would share that fate. Similarly the "great numbers" (Acts 28:23) of those who come and disagree with one another but largely reject Paul's testimony are at least reminiscent of the "many" in Israel who were predicted to "fall and rise" and the "many" whose "secret thoughts of the heart" were to be disclosed (Luke 2:34–35).

Now again Paul discerns, as Simeon did, that the Holy Spirit is speaking in the words of the prophet Isaiah to disclose the "heart of this people." Like Simeon, Paul speaks to the end about salvation by testifying to the kingdom of God and the Messiah and Lord Jesus (Acts 28:23, 31). Both of Simeon's oracles are still valid guides for grasping the scene, now as augmented by Paul's quotation of Isaiah. God is determined that this salvation and reign of Jesus be for light to the Gentiles and unto the glory of Israel, but for the present the hearts of many in Israel have been disclosed to be hardened against the understanding and healing that God intends for Israel.

334

THE GENTILE QUESTION

Within the literary structure of the narrative, a scriptural argument is also being pursued that provides another level of insight into what is at stake in the story. In fact, Luke-Acts provides a response to a cluster of related questions that persist from Luke 1—2 to Acts 28 and are anchored in the Christian claim that the Scriptures have been fulfilled in the Holy Spirit, the "promise of the Father," has been given. Have the promises God made to Israel failed? Have the prophetic oracles become mere indictments, with power only to condemn and not to save Israel? If the Messiah has come, why has not all of Israel been gathered, restored, forgiven, consoled, and redeemed? And how can the mission among the Gentiles be justified, especially the Pauline mission, which is vulnerable to criticism within and beyond the Christian movement for its aggressive initiatives beyond Israel and for the inclusion of Gentiles without their complete observance of the torah?

First-century Israel knew about the "light for revelation to the Gentiles." They had read and pondered the Isaiah passages: "I have given you as a covenant to the people, a light to the nations" (Isa. 42:6). The invocation of these passages in Luke's story at once indicts those who reject the Gentile mission and legitimates it as the proper glory of restored Israel. From beginning to end, Luke's narrative alludes to the critical passages from Isaiah and works within the peculiar logic of restoration and mission of Isa. 49:6: "It is too light a thing that you should be my servant to raise up the tribes of Jacob and to restore the preserved of Israel; I will give you as a light to the nations that my salvation may reach to the end of the earth." All Israel could agree that this was the vocation of the servant of God and of Israel. But how was this vocation to be exercised? How were these passages to be construed?

Israel also knew the peril of going the way of the Gentiles and their idols and abandoning faithfulness to the law of Moses. Deuteronomy and the prophets were full of such warnings, declaring that God would then use the Gentiles as the instrument of divine vengeance, and Jewish literature of Luke's era was alive with discussions of when and how restoration would take place, what kind of repentance was required, and where the Gentiles fit in the picture.

Thus the *Book of Jubilees* began its recitation of history as indictment and calling for repentance by stressing that Israel would abandon the law. "They will forget all my commandments that I give them and copy the Gentiles, their uncleanness and their shame, and worship their gods; and these will prove a stumbling-block to them, a source of distress and misery,

335

and a snare" (1.9). Then God will "hand them over to the Gentiles to be taken captive and to be preyed upon and to be devoured" (1.14). Only "after this they will turn to me from among the Gentiles with all their heart and with all their soul and with all their strength . . . and they shall be a blessing and not a curse" (1.16–17; see Gen. 22:18). "And I will circumcise the foreskin of their heart and the foreskin of the heart of their sons, and I will create in them a holy spirit, and I will cleanse them so that they shall not turn away from me again, from that day till eternity" (1.10–11).[19] Repentance is the theme, and Israel's relationship to the Gentiles is the focal issue. Restoration, and cleansing of the heart, and the presence of a holy spirit, are all at stake. But *Jubilees* is most concerned with the danger of those who would "teach all the Jews who are among the Gentiles to forsake Moses telling them not to circumcise their children or observe the customs" (to use the words of Acts 21:21; see also Acts 15:1). This rendition of the scriptural heritage stands in contrast to Luke's, and it may well have been the kind of argument used by those Jewish Christians who proposed that "unless you are circumcised according to the law of Moses you cannot be saved" (Acts 15:1). At least it is fascinating to see how these contrasting and perhaps competing traditions agree in their identification on the issues and texts while disagreeing on their interpretations.

Second Baruch and 4 Ezra, non-Christian documents contemporary with Acts, also ponder Israel's suffering after the Roman destruction of Jerusalem in terms of the place of the Gentiles in God's economy. Neither document could conceive of any salvation for the Gentiles apart from the observance of the torah. Nevertheless, 4 Ezra does envision the gathering of a people from among the Gentiles ahead of Israel as a reproach and a call for repentance: "When I came to them they rejected me and refused the Lord's commandment. Therefore I say to you, O nations that hear and understand, 'Await your shepherd: he will give you everlasting rest, because he who will come at the end of the age is close at hand. Be ready for the rewards of the kingdom, because the eternal light will shine upon you forevermore'" (4 Ezra 2:33–35; see also 2:10; 4:23 ["Israel has been given over to the Gentiles as a reproach"]).[20]

Second Baruch shares the conviction that the present is a time of divine judgment of Israel and that the Gentiles are God's instrument, but the last word will still be the fulfillment of God's promises: "Let us not now fix our attention upon the delights the Gentiles enjoy in the present age, but let us remember what has been promised to us in the end" (83.5). Furthermore, the present time may even be of some benefit to the Gentiles, and Israel's mission must not be neglected. *Second Baruch* has explored a more complex view than *Jubilees* of the place of the Gentiles in the divine economy, but the central question continues to be what all of this means for Israel in

God's plans. In the face of Israel's sin, God said, "I will scatter this people among the Gentiles, that they may do good to the Gentiles" (1.4), and "then after a short interval, Zion will be rebuilt, and its offerings will be restored again, and the priests will return to their ministry, and the Gentiles will come and acclaim it" (68.5).[21]

The Jewish Christian *Testaments of the Twelve Patriarchs* display how this discussion of Israel's relationship to the Gentiles continued into the second century. The scriptural traditions have been mediated to this author through a heritage of Jewish postbiblical interpretations.[22] But now the salvation of the Gentiles is fundamental to Israel's own fulfillment. Thus another Simeon testifies concerning Levi and Judah: "It is from them that God's salvation will come to you. For the Lord will raise up from Levi as it were a high priest, and from Judah as it were a king, God and man: he will save all the Gentiles and the race of Israel" (*Test. Simeon* 7.1–2). And Levi offers another paraphrase of Isaiah's verses concerning Israel as the "light to the nations": "A bright light of knowledge will make you to shine in Jacob, And like the sun will you be to the whole race of Israel. And a blessing shall be given to you and to all your sons, Until the Lord looks upon all the Gentiles with the affection of his son for ever" (*Test. Levi* 4.3–4).[23]

Luke's version of the oracles of Simeon clearly belongs within this larger Jewish discussion of Israel's glory among the nations within God's design and election. This was never a merely theoretical discussion, since Israel's identity and divine vocation were at stake, but the deliberation and debate became especially intense and difficult in the wake of the Roman destruction of Jerusalem and the temple. This was not only a national calamity. According to Israel's Scriptures, this was a reenactment of divine judgment on sinful Israel.

None of the literary testimonies cited above stated directly that Jerusalem had been ravaged by Rome. They were all composed as prophetic words after the fact, whether in the form of ancient utterances concerning the first destruction or as the oracles of an aged worthy seer who, having been blessed to "see the Lord's Messiah" (Luke 2:26), offered a prognosis of what the appearance of this "salvation" would mean to Israel and the Gentiles. None of them stated explicitly what their story proved about the pressing questions of their own day nor identified the intended audience of the work in any complete way. Perhaps these narratives survived in part because they did not foreclose the profound questions too quickly: Why have things turned out this way? What is the sin which requires repentance? What hope is there? Nevertheless, each narrative is a testimony of what it all means, a theodicy interpreting God's ways with Israel and the world, and a call for repentance leading to restoration.[24]

It would be helpful to the interpretation of Luke-Acts to know a great deal more about the occasion and context of its production. Both a literary analysis and an examination of the scriptural exposition of the narrative demonstrate the thoroughly Jewish (or Israelite) character of the story. Even the prominence of the justification of the gentile mission leaves many convictions about God and Israel's glory assumed, or only implied. This does not appear to be the work of a gentile author and community now reaching back to lay claim to Israel's heritage. It is more likely a Jewish Christian movement staking out the ground of "true Israel" or a mixed community of Jewish and gentile Christians responding to a persistently powerful minority of strictly observant Jewish Christians.[25] In any case, the oracles of Simeon demonstrate that the question of the status of the Gentiles is fundamental to Luke's view of God's Israel's divine calling and glory among the nations.

Luke has no romantic view of the Gentiles, no notion of a progressive history where the favor the gods once displayed toward the Greeks has now been transferred to the Romans, no concept of the displacement of Israel by the Gentiles in God's plan. The success of the gentile mission is both a reproach to obdurate Israel and a fulfillment of the vocation of true Israel, that is, of all those who have listened to Jesus, the prophet like Moses (Acts 3:23). Paul, God's "chosen instrument" of this mission, is thus still dealing with all Israel, with words of judgment for the unrepentant and of promise for the believers.

Deuteronomy and the prophets and the intertestamental traditions expressed all kinds of divine threats toward Israel and saw God's favor toward the Gentiles as a reproach to Israel, but they never entertained the idea that God would ever be faithless, even to a faithless people. Neither did Luke. Furthermore, the Gentiles are still understood by Luke to be the means of divine vengeance, but these Gentiles are Israel's enemies—probably the Roman armies, and certainly not the gentile Christians. When Luke speaks of Jerusalem being "trodden down by the Gentiles, until the times of the Gentiles are fulfilled" (21:24), the message is as clear as in 4 Ezra and 2 Baruch that the times of gentile domination of Israel will be limited by God's own righteousness. God's vengeance and vindication have their times of wrath and restoration, and the Messiah has already been exalted to God's right hand as "Leader and Savior in order to give repentance to Israel and forgiveness of sins" (Acts 5:31).

The mission of repentant Israel, of faithful Israel, is also to be a "light to the Gentiles." It is God who has given this repentance "even" to the Gentiles (Acts 11:18), and neither the apostles nor Israel can "withstand God" (Acts 11:17; see also Gamaliel's counsel in 5:39). This calling may become a reproach to those who reject the "word of God" (Acts 13:46–47), but it is Israel's vocation and blessing. The "glory of thy people Israel" is to be the "light for the revelation to the Gentiles." Just as *2 Baruch* suggested that even in the time of gentile triumph God wanted Israel to "do good to the Gentiles" (1.4), so Luke-Acts affirms the legitimacy of the gentile mission without ever suggesting that gentile supremacy is the final will of God.

God is never done with Israel in any of the scriptural, intertestamental, or New Testament documents, and Luke-Acts is no exception. God may be contending with Israel, even causing Israel to stumble, bringing "many in Israel" low in order that the salvation that God intends may be brought through repentance and restoration. Although in subsequent eras the narrative of Luke-Acts will be read only at Israel's expense or with a genuine or feigned sympathy for a failed history, it is a story that is confident of God's determined purpose to redeem Israel and even to restore Israel's glory of bringing the light of God's reign to the Gentiles. And at the center of the story, God's resurrection and exaltation of Jesus is God's way of finally transcending the tragic rejection of the Messiah and its real consequences for Jerusalem. Simeon's dire oracle concerning the falling of many in Israel and a sign spoken against has already been amply fulfilled within the narrative and at its end (Acts 28) and probably in Luke's world. But the restoration, the consolation, the redemption, the repentance, the forgiveness, and the reign of God which Simeon and all those other worthies in Israel expected has only begun to be inaugurated in the present time of Luke's story.

NOTES

1. See Robert L. Wilkin, *The Myth of Christian Beginnings* (Garden City, N.Y.: Doubleday & Co., 1971).

2. Popular Christian preaching has long been permeated with such claims, but scholarly interpretations have often supported these views on historical grounds with or without intention. See Ernst Haenchen, "The Book of Acts as Source Material for the History of Early Christianity," in *Studies of Luke-Acts,* ed. L. E. Keck and J. L. Martyn (Philadelphia: Fortress Press, 1966), 278: "Luke has written the Jews off."

3. See Charlotte Klein, *Anti-Judaism in Christian Theology,* trans. Edward Quinn (Philadelphia: Fortress Press, 1978).

4. A burgeoning scholarship on Luke-Acts is ample testimony to the wide diversity of approaches and contributions which could be mentioned. In the 1950s and 1960s, Hans Conzelmann's *The Theology of St. Luke,* trans. G. Buswell (London: Faber and Faber, 1960) actually intensified the traditional view of Luke on the Jews with its historical schematization, and the notion of gentile triumph at Jewish expense was explored further and criticized in the interpretations of Philipp Vielhauer, Ernst Käsemann, and Haenchen. Among the many challenges to this consensus, the most controversial and influential has been Jacob Jervell's "The Divided

People of God," in *Luke and the People of God* (Minneapolis: Augsburg Pub. House, 1972). See also Gerhard Lohfink, *Die Sammlung Israels,* Studien zum Alten und Neuen Testament (Munich: Kösel-Verlag, 1975); Augustin George, "Israel dans l'oeuvre de Luc." *Revue biblique* 75 (1968): 481–525; and Donald Juel, "Scriptural Interpretation in the Speeches in Acts," in the forthcoming Festschrift for Henry Fischel.

5. George Foot Moore's classic study *Judaism* (Cambridge: Harvard Univ. Press, 1927–30) established the concept of "normative Judaism," which was well received by both modern Christianity and Judaism as each sought to trace its tradition to some clear wellspring of the heritage. Now the tributary streams of both formative Christianity and formative Judaism appear much more complex, and interconnected with a broader range of Jewish traditions in the Greco-Roman era. See Jacob Neusner's clear discussion of these broad issues in *Judaism in the Beginning of Christianity* (Philadelphia: Fortress Press, 1984). See esp. p. 10: "The catalytic event in the formation of the kind of Judaism we now know as normative— that is, the Judaism that took shape in the documents produced by rabbis from the first through the seventh centuries—was the destruction of the Temple in 70 C.E. That same event proved decisive in the formation of Christianity as an autonomous and self-conscious community of Israelite faith." See also Jacob Jervell's assessment of the place of Luke-Acts within the intense Jewish-Christian discussion of the place of the gentile mission in the late 1st cent.: "The History of Early Christianity and the Acts of the Apostles," in *The Unknown Paul: Essays on Luke-Acts and Early Christian History* (Minneapolis: Augsburg Pub. House, 1984), 13–25.

6. E. J. Sanders has made the fascinating suggestion that "the Pharisees in the Gospel are the proto-types of the Christian Pharisees in Acts 15:5 who likewise advise that those desiring admission to the church should strictly follow the law of Moses and not rely on their 'belief' to get in" ("The Pharisees in Luke-Acts," in *The Living Text: Essays in Honor of Ernest W. Saunders,* ed. Dennis E. Groh and Robert Jewett [Lanham, Md.: Univ. Press of America, 1985], 181).

7. See Norman Peterson, *Literary Criticism for New Testament Critics,* Guides to Biblical Scholarship (Philadelphia: Fortress Press, 1978), 83; and David L. Tiede, *Prophecy and History in Luke-Acts* (Philadelphia: Fortress Press, 1980).

8. See David L. Tiede, "The Exaltation of Jesus and Restoration of Israel in Acts 1," in *Christians among Jews and Gentiles,* ed. George W. E. Nickelsburg and George W. MacRae (Philadelphia: Fortress Press, 1986), 278–86.

9. Henry J. Cadbury, *The Making of Luke-Acts* (London: SPCK, 1927). See also idem, *The Style and Literary Method of Luke,* Harvard Theological Studies 6 (Cambridge: Harvard Univ. Press, 1920).

10. See Martin Dibelius, "The Speeches in Acts and Ancient Historiography," in *Studies in the Acts of the Apostles* (London: SCM Press, 1956), 138–85; Ulrich Wilckens, *Die Missionsreden der Apostelgeschichte,* Wissenschaftliche Monographien zum Alten und Neuen Testament 5 (Neukirchen-Vluyn: Neukirchener Verlag, 1963); and Paul S. Minear, "Luke's Use of the Birth Stories," in *Studies in Luke-Acts,* ed. Keck and Martyn, 111–30.

11. See Joseph A. Fitzmyer, *The Gospel according to Luke 1—9,* Anchor Bible (New York: Doubleday & Co., 1981), 313–14.

12. Robert C. Tannehill, "Israel in Luke-Acts: A Tragic Story," *Journal of Biblical Literature* 104 (1985): 69–85.

13. See Tiede, *Prophecy and History*, 103-18.

14. See Josephus *War* 5.362-423 and Melito's "Homily on the Passion."

15. Paul S. Minear, "Dear Theo: The Kerygmatic Intention and Claim of the Book of Acts," *Interpretation* 27 (1973): 131-50.

16. See Jacob Jervell, "The Circumcised Messiah," in *The Unknown Paul: Essays on Luke-Acts and Early Christian History*, 138-45.

17. So in Acts 4:11-12, the rejection of Jesus is immediately connected with God's salvation, which is available to the "rulers of the people and the elders" only through the name of Jesus.

18. The use of the word "Jew" in Luke-Acts is a conundrum. Its usage in Acts by non-Israelites (18:14; 22:30; 23:27) or by Israelites speaking to non-Israelites (21:39; 23:20; 24:5) fits with the origins of the term in the administration of the region of Judea by the Hellenistic and Roman empires. In 14:1-2 there are believing and unbelieving Jews, that is, those who accept the preaching of Paul and Barnabas and those who do not. In 28:17, Paul addresses local Jews reporting that the Jews in Palestine spoke against him, and they report they have not heard any evil reports from Judea or from the "brothers" who have come. Certainly Ziesler has overstated the case in saying that after Acts 13:43-45 "*hoi ioudaioi* becomes a *terminus technicus* (as in the Fourth Gospel) for the opponents of Paul, the bringer of salvation" (Richard F. Zehnle, *Peter's Pentecost Discourse*, SBLMS 15 [Nashville: Abingdon Press, 1971], 65). Here again in 28:24-25 some are persuaded and others disbelieve, and there is division among these Jews.

19. *Book of Jubilees*, trans. R. H. Charles, rev. C. Rabin, in *The Apocryphal Old Testament*, ed. H. F. D. Sparks (Oxford: Clarendon Press, 1984), 11-13.

20. "The Fourth Book of Ezra," trans. B. M. Metzger, in *The Old Testament Pseudepigrapha*, ed. James H. Charlesworth (New York: Doubleday & Co., 1983), 527.

21. *2 Baruch*, trans. R. H. Charles, rev. L. H. Brockington, in *Apocryphal Old Testament*, ed. Sparks.

22. See Jean Daniélou, *The Theology of Jewish Christianity*, trans. John A. Baker (Chicago: Henry Regnery Co., 1964), 165 n.63: "This is indeed the very definition of Jewish Christian theology." See also John J. Collins, *Between Athens and Jerusalem* (New York: Crossroad, 1983), 154-74.

23. *Testaments of the Twelve Patriarchs*, trans. M. de Jonge, in *Apocryphal Old Testament*, ed. Sparks, 525, 528. See also *Epistle of Barnabas*, 14, where the Isaiah passages are cited but now in the context of Christian displacement of Israel (5.2) as heirs of the covenant.

24. See Tiede, "Exaltation of Jesus," 285-86.

25. See Jacob Jervell, "The Mighty Minority," in *The Unknown Paul*, 26-51.

20

Howard Clark Kee:
A Bibliography to September 1, 1986

MICHAEL R. GREENWALD, Swarthmore College
DOUGLAS R. EDWARDS, University of Puget Sound

The following structure has been used for each year:

1. Books
   Original editions
   Reprinted, revised, or new editions of previously published works
   Translations and non-American editions of previously published works

2. Articles
   Articles or chapters in books of essays
   Entries in reference works
   Articles in Festschriften
   Articles in published conference proceedings
   Articles in periodicals
   Republished articles (listed in same order as other articles)
   Translations of previously published articles

3. Librettos

4. Lectures that have been taped and stored in library files

5. Translations into English of the works of others

6. Reviews
   Titled reviews
   Other reviews

We would like to thank Mr. Hongki Kim, of Boston University, for transliterating into Roman characters the works of Professor Kee that have been translated into Korean.

1951

"The Paleography of Dated Greek New Testament Manuscripts before 1300." Ph.D. diss., Yale Univ., 1951, © 1976, pp. vi + 198. Microfilm, 1 reel, 35 mm.

"Christianity in the Near East Today." *Drew Gateway* 21 (1950–51): 10–15.

1952

"The Bible and the Work of [T. S.] Eliot and [Edith] Sitwell." *Friends Intelligencer* 109 (1952): 641–43.

"The Development of Eschatology in the New Testament." *Journal of Bible and Religion* 20 (1952): 187–93.

1954

"Biblical Authority: A New Authoritarianism." *Drew Gateway* 24 (1953–54): 201–7.

"Studies in the Primitive Church." Review of *Peter: Disciple, Apostle, Martyr,* by Oscar Cullmann, trans. Floyd V. Filson (Philadelphia: Westminster Press, 1953); and *The Birth of Christianity,* by Maurice Goguel, trans. H. C. Snape (New York: Macmillan Co., 1954). *Drew Gateway* 25 (1954–55): 45–47.

Review of *Christian Hope and the Second Coming,* by Paul S. Minear (Philadelphia: Westminster Press, 1954). *Drew Gateway* 25 (1954–55): 43–45.

Review of *The Interpreter's Bible,* ed. George A. Buttrick, vol. 9, *Acts and Romans,* by G. H. C. Macgregor and Theodore P. Ferris (Acts), John Knox and Gerald R. Cragg (Romans) (Nashville: Abingdon Press, 1954). *Drew Gateway* 25 (1954–55): 42–43.

Review of *Jewish Symbols in the Greco-Roman Period,* by Erwin R. Goodenough (New York: Pantheon Books, 1953). *Drew Gateway* 24 (1954–55): 224–25.

Review of *The Kingdom of God,* by John Bright (Nashville: Abingdon Press, 1953). *Drew Gateway* 24 (1953–54): 112–14.

1955

The Inescapable Question: Where Are You? New York: National Student Council of the YMCA and YWCA, pp. 32.

Review of *New Testament Studies,* by C. H. Dodd (New York: Charles Scribner's Sons, 1954). *Drew Gateway* 25 (1954–55): 171–72.

1956

"The Bible and Its Times." Review of *The Bible Today,* by G. R. Driver et al. (New York: Harper & Bros., 1955); *Everyday Life in New Testament Times,* by A. C. Bouquet (New York: Charles Scribner's Sons, 1954); and *How Our Bible Came to Us,* by H. G. G. Herklots (New York: Oxford Univ. Press, 1954). *Drew Gateway* 26 (1955–56): 141–42.

"Bultmann and His Critics." Review of *Kerygma and Myth: A Theological Debate,* trans. Reginald H. Fuller, ed. Hans Werner Bartsch (New York: Macmillan Co., 1954). *Drew Gateway* 26 (1955–56): 45–46.

"Lives of Jesus." Review of *The Life and Ministry of Jesus*, by Vincent Taylor (Nashville: Abingdon Press, 1955); and *The Life and Teachings of Jesus*, by Charles M. Laymon (Nashville: Abingdon Press, 1955). *Drew Gateway* 26 (1955–56): 45–46.

Review of Studies in Biblical Theology 12, *The Mission and Achievement of Jesus*, by Reginald H. Fuller; and 15, *Conscience in the New Testament*, by C. A. Pierce (Chicago: Alec R. Allenson, 1954–55). *Drew Gateway* 26 (1955–56): 56–58.

1957

Making Ethical Decisions. Layman's Theological Library. Philadelphia: Westminster Press, pp. 96.

Understanding the New Testament [in collaboration with Franklin W. Young]. Englewood Cliffs, N.J.: Prentice-Hall, pp. xx + 492.

"The Second Season of Excavation at Biblical Shechem. Part 1: What Goes On at a Dig?" *The Biblical Archaeologist* 20 (1957): 82–92. (Part 2 of this article is by Lawrence E. Toombs.)

"New Light on Old Words." Review of *The Eucharistic Words of Jesus*, by Joachim Jeremias (New York: Macmillan Company, 1955); and *The Parables of Jesus*, by Joachim Jeremias (New York: Charles Scribner's Sons, 1955). *Drew Gateway* 27 (1956–57): 93–94.

Review of *New Testament Faith for Today*, by Amos N. Wilder (New York: Harper & Bros., 1955). *Drew Gateway* 28 (1957–58): 62–63.

1958

"Christian Hope and the Mission of the Church." *Drew Gateway* 28 (1957–58): 168–77.

Review of *The Death of Christ*, by John Knox (Nashville: Abingdon Press, 1958). *Journal of Biblical Literature* 77 (1958): 165–67.

Review of *The Gospel of Matthew*, 2 vols., Harper's Annotated Bible Series (New York: Harper & Bros., 1957); and *The Gospels: Their Origins and Growth*, by Frederick C. Grant (New York: Harper & Bros., 1957). *Drew Gateway* 28 (1957–58): 133–34.

Review of *Resurrection and Historical Reason: A Study of Theological Method*, by Richard R. Niebuhr (New York: Charles Scribner's Sons, 1957). *Drew Gateway* 28 (1957–58): 217–18. (Incorrectly attributed to Howard Clark Kee. Review written by William R. Farmer. See *Drew Gateway* 29 [1958–59]: 54.)

Review of Studies in Biblical Theology 16, *Galilean Christianity*, by L. E. Elliott-Binns; 17, *An Approach to the Theology of the Sacraments*, by Neville Clark; and 20, *The Servant of God*, by Joachim Jeremias and W. Zimmerli (Naperville, Ill.: Alec R. Allenson, 1957). *Drew Gateway* 28 (1957–58): 134–36.

1959

Jesus and God's New People: The Four Gospels. Westminster Guides to the Bible. Philadelphia: Westminster Press, pp. 92.

The Renewal of Hope. New York: Association Press, pp. 190.

"The Nature and Necessity of the Resurrection according to the New Testament." *Drew Gateway* 29 (1958–59): 160–77.

1960

The Living World of the New Testament [in collaboration with Franklin W. Young]. London: Darton, Longman & Todd, pp. xx + 492. (British ed. of *Understanding the New Testament*, 1957.)

"Counter of Consensus." Review of *Paul and the Salvation of Mankind*, by Johannes Munck (Richmond: John Knox Press, 1959). *Christian Century* 77 (1960): 1154–56.

1961

"Historical Criticism and Theological Affirmation: The Broad, Ugly Ditch." *Drew Gateway* 32 (1961–62): 3–25. (Inaugural address upon appointment to full professorship.)

Review of *Zur Frage nach dem historischen Jesus*, by Ernst Fuchs (Tübingen: J. C. B. Mohr [Paul Siebeck], 1960). *Journal of Biblical Literature* 80 (1961): 276–78.

1962

The Bible and God's Call: A Study of the Biblical Foundation of Vocation [in collaboration with Montgomery J. Shroyer]. N.p.: Methodist Church Interboard Committee on Christian Vocations and Department of Ministerial Education, pp. 79.

In the Middle of the World: Word, World, and Sacrament. New York: National Student Christian Federation, pp. ix + 51.

Yoon Lee Gyuk Gyul Dan. Trans. Tong Whan Moon. N.p.: Christian Literature Soc. of Korea, pp. 148. (Korean trans. of *Making Ethical Decisions*, 1957.)

"Julius." In *Interpreter's Dictionary of the Bible* (*IDB*), ed. George Arthur Buttrick, 2:1026. Nashville: Abingdon Press.

"Mnason." In *IDB* 3:409.

"Nicodemus." In *IDB* 3:547.

"Nicolaus." In *IDB* 3:548.

"Niger." In *IDB* 3:549.

"Timothy." In *IDB* 4:650–51.

"Titus, Companion of Paul." In *IDB* 4:656–57.

"Defending Infant Baptism." Review of *Infant Baptism in the First Four Centuries*, by Joachim Jeremias (Philadelphia: Westminster Press, 1960). *Christian Century* 79 (1962): 272.

1963

"'Becoming a Child in the Gospel of Thomas.'" *Journal of Biblical Literature* 82 (1963): 307–14.

Review of *The Birth of the New Testament,* by C. F. D. Moule (New York: Harper & Row, 1962). *Drew Gateway* 34 (1963–64): 53–55.

Review of *Current Issues in New Testament Interpretation: Essays in Honor of Otto Piper,* ed. William Klassen and Grayden F. Snyder (New York: Harper & Row, 1962). *Journal of Biblical Literature* 82 (1963): 217–20.

Review of *A Greek Grammar of the New Testament and Other Early Christian Literature,* by F. Blass and A. Debrunner, trans. and rev. Robert V. Funk from the ninth-tenth German ed., incorporating supp. nn. of A. Debrunner (Chicago: Univ. of Chicago Press, 1961). *Drew Gateway* 34 (1963–64): 52–53.

1964

Review of *Christologische Hoheitstitel,* by Ferdinand Hahn (Göttingen: Vandenhoeck & Ruprecht, 1963). *Journal of Biblical Literature* 83 (1964): 191–93.

Review of *The Gospel according to St. Matthew,* by Floyd V. Filson, Harper's Commentary Series (New York: Harper & Bros., 1960); and *The Theology of St. Luke,* by Hans Conzelmann (New York: Harper & Bros., 1960). *Drew Gateway* 34 (1963–64): 169–71.

Review of *Jesus of Nazareth,* by Günther Bornkamm (New York: Harper & Row, 1961); and *The Prophet from Nazareth,* by Morton Scott Enslin (New York: McGraw-Hill, 1961). *Drew Gateway* 34 (1963–64): 179–80.

1965

Understanding the New Testament [in collaboration with Franklin W. Young and Karlfried Froehlich]. 2d ed. Englewood Cliffs, N.J.: Prentice-Hall, pp. xxii + 490.

"The Historical Jesus: A Survey of Literature (1959–1965)." *Drew Gateway* 36 (1965–66): 44–49.

1966

De wereld van het Nieuwe Testament [in collaboration with Franklin W. Young]. Baarn, Neth.: Bosch & Keuning, pp. 215, 148, 176. (Dutch trans. of *Understanding the New Testament.* Apparently translated from the 1957 ed. Vol. 1 may have been published in 1964. The publication date is not given but is deduced from the verso of the title page of the 2d Dutch ed., 1979. The translator's name is also not given.)

Trans. of "Reply," by Rudolf Bultmann. In *The Theology of Rudolf Bultmann,* ed. Charles W. Kegley. New York: Harper & Row, 267–87.

1967

Das Geschehen ohnegleichen: Panorama des Neuen Testaments [in collaboration with Franklin W. Young and Karlfried Froehlich]. Trans. Helmut Zechner from the 2d American ed. Stuttgart: Quell-Verlag, pp. 480. (German trans. of *Understanding the New Testament,* 1965.)

Hsinyüeh Shengching t'anyüan [in collaboration with Franklin W. Young and Karlfried Froehlich]. Trans. P. Y. Sie. Hong Kong: Chinese Christian Literature Council, pp. xvi + 555. (Chinese trans. of *Understanding the New Testament,* 1965.)

"Tel-er-Ras and the Samaritan Temple." *New Testament Studies* 13 (1967): 401–2.

Review of *Heilsgeschehen und Geschichte: Gesammelte Aufsätze 1933–1964,* by Werner Georg Kümmel, ed. Erich Grässer, Otto Merk, and Adolf Fritz (Marburg: N. G. Elwert Verlag, 1965). *Journal of Biblical Literature* 86 (1967): 108–10.

1968

"The Terminology of Mark's Exorcism Stories." *New Testament Studies* 14 (1968): 232–46.

Review of *The Meaning of "Fishers of Men,"* by Wilhelm H. Wuellner (Philadelphia: Westminster Press, 1967). *Journal of Biblical Literature* 87 (1968): 220–21.

1969

Review of *Sacramentum Mundi: An Encyclopedia of Theology,* 6 vols., vols. 1–3, ed. Karl Rahner, with Cornelius Ernst and Kevin Smyth (New York: Herder & Herder, 1968–69). *Journal of Biblical Literature* 88 (1969): 339–41.

1970

Jesus in History: An Approach to the Study of the Gospels. New York: Harcourt, Brace & World, pp. viii + 280.

Review of *Jesus and the Twelve,* by Robert P. Meye (Grand Rapids: Wm. B. Eerdmans, 1968). *Interpretation* 24 (1970): 116–17.

Review of *A New Catholic Commentary on Holy Scripture,* ed. Reginald C. Fuller (London and Camden, N.J.: Thomas Nelson & Sons, 1969). *Journal of Biblical Literature* 89 (1970): 222–26.

1971

"The Gospel according to Matthew." In *The Interpreter's One-Volume Commentary on the Bible,* ed. Charles M. Laymon, 609–22. Nashville: Abingdon Press.

"Scripture Quotations and Allusions in Mark 11—16." In *Society of Biblical Literature 1971 Seminar Papers* 2:475–502. N.p.: Soc. of Biblical Literature.

"Mark as Redactor and Theologian: A Survey of Some Recent Markan Studies." *Journal of Biblical Literature* 90 (1971): 333–36.

"The [Hellenistic] Pottery [from Ashdod]." *Ashdod II–III.* 'Atiquot, English ser. 9–10 (1971): 42–67 + pls. 14–19.

Review of *The New English Bible Companion to the New Testament,* by A. E. Harvey (New York: Oxford Univ. Press, 1970). *Theology Today* 28 (1971): 252–54.

Review of *The Office of Apostle in the Early Church,* by Walter Schmithals, trans. John E. Steely (Nashville: Abingdon Press, 1969). *Interpretation* 25 (1971): 224–26.

1972

"The Transfiguration in Mark: Epiphany or Apocalyptic Vision?" In *Understanding the Sacred Text: Essays in Honor of Morton S. Enslin on the Hebrew Bible and Christian Beginnings*, ed. John Reumann, 135–52. Valley Forge, Pa.: Judson Press.

Trans. of *The New Testament: A History of the Investigation of Its Problems*, by W. G. Kümmel [in collaboration with S. McLean Gilmour]. Nashville: Abingdon Press, pp. 510. (Trans. from the 2d German ed., 1970, translator's preface, 11–12.)

1973

The Origins of Christianity: Sources and Documents. Englewood Cliffs, N.J.: Prentice-Hall, pp. xi + 270.

Understanding the New Testament [in collaboration with Franklin W. Young and Karlfried Froehlich]. 3d ed. Englewood Cliffs, N.J.: Prentice-Hall, pp. xv + 446.

"Aretalogy and Gospel." *Journal of Biblical Literature* 92 (1973): 402–22.

Review of *Creation and Redemption: A Study in Pauline Theology*, by John G. Gibbs, Supplements to *Novum Testamentum* 26 (Leiden: E. J. Brill, 1971). *Interpretation* 27 (1973): 235–36.

Review of *Jesus*, by Eduard Schweizer, trans. David E. Green (Richmond: John Knox Press, 1971). *Journal of Biblical Literature* 92 (1973): 299–302.

Review of *The Sayings of Jesus in the Churches of Paul: The Use of the Synoptic Tradition in the Regulation of the Early Church Life*, by David L. Dungan (Philadelphia: Fortress Press, 1971). *Journal of the American Academy of Religion* 41 (1973): 652–53.

1974

Pentecost 3 [in collaboration with Gerard S. Sloyan]. Proclamation ser. C. Philadelphia: Fortress Press.

"The Linguistic Background of 'Shame' in the New Testament." In *On Language, Culture, and Religion: In Honor of Eugene Nida*, ed. Matthew Black and William A. Smalley, 133–47. The Hague and Paris: Mouton Press.

"Satan, Magic, and Salvation in the Testament of Job." In *Society of Biblical Literature 1974 Seminar Papers*, ed. George MacRae, 53–76. Cambridge, Mass.: Soc. of Biblical Literature.

1975

"Aretalogies, Hellenistic 'Lives,' and the Sources of Mark." In *Protocol of the Twelfth Colloquy, 8 December, 1974, The Center for Hermeneutical Studies in Hellenistic and Modern Culture*, ed. W. Wuellner, 1–21. Berkeley: Center for Hermeneutical Studies in Hellenistic and Modern Culture. (Responses by Donald Juel, Charles Kannengiessee, S.J., Anitra Bingham Kolenkow, David L. Tiede, and Morton Smith.)

"The Function of Scriptural Quotations and Allusions in Mark 11—16." In *Jesus und Paulus: Festschrift für Werner Georg Kümmel zum 70. Geburtstag,* ed. E. Earle Ellis and Erich Grässer, 165–88. Göttingen: Vandenhoeck & Ruprecht.

Trans. of *Introduction to the New Testament,* by W. G. Kümmel. Nashville: Abingdon Press, pp. 629. (Trans. from the 17th German ed., 1973.)

Review of Jacques Dupont, *Les Béatitudes,* vol. 2, *La bonne nouvelle,* Etudes bibliques (Paris: J. Gabalda, 1969); vol. 3, *Les Evangelistes,* completely reset (N.p., 1973). *Journal of Biblical Literature* 94 (1975): 132–34.

Review of *The Gospel according to Mark: The English Text with Introduction, Exposition, and Notes,* by William L. Lane, New International Commentary on the New Testament 2 (Grand Rapids: Wm. B. Eerdmans, 1974). *Journal of Biblical Literature* 94 (1975): 460–61.

Review of *The Secret Gospel: The Discovery and Interpretation of the Secret Gospel according to Mark,* by Morton Smith (New York: Harper & Row, 1973). *Journal of the American Academy of Religion* 43/2 supp. (1975): 326–29.

1976

"Aretalogy." In *Interpreter's Dictionary of the Bible,* supp. vol. (*IDB*Sup, ed. Keith Crim, 52–53. Nashville: Abingdon Press.

"Biblical Criticism, NT." In *IDB*Sup 102–4.

"Divine Man." In *IDB*Sup 243.

"Miracle Stories, NT." In *IDB*Sup 598.

"Miracle Workers." In *IDB*Sup 598–99.

"The Socio-Religious Setting and Aims of 'Joseph and Asenath.'" In *Society of Biblical Literature 1976 Seminar Papers,* ed. George MacRae, 183–92. Missoula, Mont.: Scholars Press.

Libretto for *New Land, New Covenant.* A bicentennial oratorio. Set to music by Howard Hanson. New York: Carl Fischer.

Review of *A History of the Criticism of Acts of the Apostles,* by W. Ward Gasque (Grand Rapids: Wm. B. Eerdmans, 1975). *Religious Studies Review* 2/4 (October 1976): 53–54.

Review of *The History of the Jewish People in the Age of Jesus Christ (175 B.C.–A.D. 135): A New English Version,* vol. 1, by Emil Schürer, rev. and ed. Geza Vermes and Fergus Millar, lit. ed. Pamela Vermes, org. ed. Matthew Black (Edinburgh: T. & T. Clark, 1973); and *Judaism and Hellenism: Studies in Their Encounter in Palestine during the Early Hellenistic Period,* by Martin Hengel, trans. John Bowden (Philadelphia: Fortress Press, 1974). *Religious Studies Review* 2/4 (October 1976): 4–7.

Review of *Kingdom and Community: The Social World of Early Christianity,* by John G. Gager, Prentice-Hall Studies in Religion Series (Englewood Cliffs, N.J.: Prentice-Hall, 1975). *Journal of Biblical Literature* 95 (1976): 506–8.

Review of ibid. *Religious Studies Review* 2/1 (January 1976): 44.

Review of *The Kingdom in Mark: A New Time and a New Place,* by Werner H. Kelber (Philadelphia: Fortress Press, 1973). *Journal of Religion* 56 (1976): 122–23.

Review of *The Origins of Christian Art,* by Michael Gough (New York: Frederick A. Praeger, 1973). *Archaeology* 29 (1976): 61.

Review of *The Post-Resurrection Appearance Stories of the Gospel Tradition: A History of Tradition Analysis, with Text Synopsis,* by John E. Alsup, Calwer theologische Monographien, ser. A, Bibelwissenschaft 5 (Stuttgart: Calwer Verlag, 1975). *Journal of Biblical Literature* 95 (1976): 672–73.

1977

Community of the New Age: Studies in Mark's Gospel. Philadelphia: Westminster Press, pp. xi + 225.

Jesus in History: An Approach to the Study of the Gospels. 2d ed. New York: Harcourt Brace Jovanovich, pp. vii + 312.

Review of *Kerygma and Comedy in the New Testament: A Structuralist Approach to Hermeneutic,* by Dan O. Via, Jr. (Philadelphia: Fortress Press, 1975). *Journal of the American Academy of Religion* 45 (1977): 371–72.

Review of *The New Testament Witness for Preaching: Mark,* by Paul J. Achtemeier; *The New Testament Witness for Preaching: Luke,* by Frederick W. Danker; and *The New Testament Witness for Preaching: John,* by D. Moody Smith (Philadelphia: Fortress Press, 1976). *Interpretation* 31 (1977): 296–99.

Review of *Redating the New Testament,* by John A. T. Robinson (Philadelphia: Westminster Press, 1976). *Religious Studies Review* 3/4 (October 1977): 256.

1978

"Ethical Dimensions of the Testament of the XII as a Clue to Provenance." *New Testament Studies* 24 (1978): 259–70. (Paper read at the Pseudepigrapha Seminar during the meeting of the Studiorum Novi Testamenti Societas at Duke University, August 1976.)

"Mark's Gospel in Recent Research." *Interpretation* 32 (1978): 353–68.

Review of *The Passion in Mark: Studies on Mark 14—16,* ed. Werner H. Kelber (Philadelphia: Fortress Press, 1976). *Journal of Biblical Literature* 97 (1978): 143–44.

Review of *The World History of the Jewish People,* vol. 7, *The Herodian Period,* ed. Michael Avi-Yonah. Jewish History Publications, 1st ser., Ancient Times (New Brunswick, N.J.: Rutgers Univ. Press, 1975). *Religious Studies Review* 4/2 (April 1978): 132–34.

1979

Christianity. Major World Religions Series. Niles, Ill.: Argus Communications, pp. ix + 117.

De wereld van het Nieuwe Testament [in collaboration with Franklin W. Young]. Trans. Lammert Leertouwer. 2d Dutch ed. Baarn, Neth.: Ten Have, pp. 535. (Dutch trans. of *Understanding the New Testament.* Verso of title page says that this is taken from the 3d American ed., although Karlfried Froehlich's name is not attached.)

"Community of the New Age," 1979 Lowell Lectures at Daniel E. Marsh Chapel, Boston Univ. Sound recordings. Lecture 1, "Expecting the New Age," delivered

October 10, 1979, Richard D. Nesmith presiding; Seminary Singers; Douglas R. Edwards and Joseph Williamson respondents (lecture followed by respondents and question-and-answer session [108 min. at 1 7/8 i.p.s.]). Lecture 2, "Evolving Structure and Discipline," delivered October 10, 1979, Harold H. Oliver presiding; Marsh Chapel Choir; Elisabeth Schüssler Fiorenza and Elizabeth Bettenhausen respondents (lecture followed by respondents and question-and-answer session [111 min. at 1 7/8 i.p.s.]). Lecture 3, "Engaging the World," delivered October 11, 1979, Nelle G. Slater presiding; Elaine Pagels and Justo González respondents (lecture followed by respondents and question-and-answer session [102 min. at 1 7/8 i.p.s.]).

Review of *Geschichte und Kritik der Markushypothese,* by Hans-Herbert Stoldt (Göttingen: Vandenhoeck & Ruprecht, 1977). *Journal of Biblical Literature* 98 (1979): 140–43.

Review of *Judaism and Christian Beginnings,* by Samuel Sandmel (New York: Oxford Univ. Press, 1978). *Religious Studies Review* 5/4 (October 1979): 298.

Review of *Paul: Apostle of the Heart Set Free,* by F. F. Bruce (Grand Rapids: Wm. B. Eerdmans, 1977). *Interpretation* 33 (1979): 316–20.

1980

Christian Origins in Sociological Perspective: Methods and Resources. Philadelphia: Westminster Press, pp. 204

Pentecost 1 [in collaboration with Peter J. Gomes]. Proclamation 2, ser. C. Philadelphia: Fortress Press, pp. 62.

Christian Origins in Sociological Perspective: Methods and Resources. London: SCM Press, pp. 204. (British ed. of the above work of the same title.)

The Origins of Christianity: Sources and Documents. London: SPCK, pp. xii + 270. (British ed. of the 1973 work of the same title.)

"Myth and Miracle: Isis, Wisdom, and the Logos of John." In *Myth, Symbol, and Reality,* ed. Alan M. Olson, 145–64. Boston Univ. Studies in Philosophy and Religion 1. Notre Dame, Ind.: Univ. of Notre Dame Press.

"Polyvalence and Parables: Anyone Can Play—A Response to J. D. Crossan's *Cliffs of Fall.*" In *Society of Biblical Literature 1980 Seminar Papers,* ed. Paul J. Achtemeier, 57–62. Chico, Calif.: Scholars Press.

"Paul the Apostle: Reaching Out in the Roman World." Lectures delivered at the Bible Workshop Series, Foundation for Biblical Research, Charlestown, N.H., October 2–3, 1980. 5 cassette recordings, 90 min. each.

Review of *The Catacombs: Rediscovered Monuments of Early Christianity,* by J. Stevenson (New York: Thames & Hudson, 1978). *Religious Studies Review* 6/2 (April 1980): 150.

Review of *Roman Society and Roman Law in the New Testament,* by A. N. Sherwin-White (Grand Rapids: Baker Book House, 1978). *Religious Studies Review* 6/3 (July 1980): 234.

Review of *Social Aspects of Early Christianity,* by Abraham J. Malherbe (Baton Rouge: Louisiana State Univ. Press, 1977). *Religious Studies Review* 6/1 (January 1980): 65.

Review of *The Sociology of Early Palestinian Christianity,* by Gerd Theissen, trans.

John Bowden (Philadelphia: Fortress Press, 1978). *Religious Studies Review* 6/1 (January 1980): 65.

Review of *The Testaments of the Twelve Patriarchs: A Critical Edition of the Greek Text,* by M. DeJonge, Pseudepigrapha Veteris Testamenti graece 1/2 (Leiden: E. J. Brill, 1978). *Catholic Biblical Quarterly* 42 (1980): 572–73.

1981

"The Conversion of Paul: Confrontation or Interiority?" In *The Other Side of God: A Polarity in World Religions,* ed. Peter L. Berger, 48–60. Garden City, N.Y.: Doubleday & Co.

"Mark's Gospel in Recent Research." In *Interpreting the Gospels,* ed. James Luther Mays, 130–47. Philadelphia: Fortress Press. (Reprint of 1978 article of the same title.)

"'The Man' in Fourth Ezra: Growth of a Tradition." In *Society of Biblical Literature 1981 Seminar Papers,* ed. Kent Harold Richards, 199–208. Chico, Calif.: Scholars Press.

Review of *Aelius Aristides and the New Testament,* by P. W. van der Horst, Studia ad Corpus Hellenisticum Novi Testamenti 6 (Leiden: E. J. Brill, 1980). *Religious Studies Review* 7/2 (April 1981): 164.

Review of *Mark's Treatment of the Jewish Leaders,* by Michael J. Cook (Leiden: E. J. Brill, 1978). *Journal of the American Academy of Religion* 49 (1981): 294–95.

Review of *New Testament Prophecy,* by David Hill, New Foundations Theological Library (Atlanta: John Knox Press, 1980). *Journal of the American Academy of Religion* 49 (1981): 677.

Review of *Paul and Power: The Structure of Authority in the Primitive Church as Reflected in the Pauline Epistles,* by Bengt Holmberg (Philadelphia: Fortress Press, 1980); *Pauline Partnership in Christ: Christian Community and Commitment in Light of Roman Law,* by J. Paul Sampley (Philadelphia: Fortress Press, 1980); and *Paul's Idea of Community: The Early House Churches in Their Historical Setting,* by Robert Banks (Grand Rapids: Wm. B. Eerdmans, 1980). *Theology Today* 38 (1981): 111–14.

1982

Das frühe Christentum in soziologischer Sicht: Methoden und Anstösse. Trans. Marianne Mühlenberg. Göttingen: Vandenhoeck & Ruprecht, pp. 190. (German trans. of *Christian Origins in Sociological Perspective: Methods and Resources,* 1980).

"Self-Definition in the Asclepius Cult." In *Jewish and Christian Self-Definition,* ed. Ben F. Meyer and E. P. Sanders, 3:118–36. London: SCM Press.

"Weber Revisited: Sociology of Knowledge and the Historical Reconstruction of Christianity." In *Meaning, Truth, and God,* ed. Leroy S. Rouner, 112–34. Boston Univ. Studies in Philosophy and Religion 3. Notre Dame, Ind.: Univ. of Notre Dame Press.

"Christology and Ecclesiology: Titles of Christ and Models of Community." In *Society of Biblical Literature 1982 Seminar Papers,* ed. Kent Harold Richards, 227–42. Chico, Calif.: Scholars Press.

"Maka Book Yum Yon Goo Yeo Choi Kun Dong Hyang." *Kidockkyo Sasang* (1982): 151–72. (Korean trans. of "Mark's Gospel in Recent Research," 1978.)

Review of *A Commentary on the Epistle of James*, by Sophie Laws (San Francisco: Harper & Row, 1981). *Horizons* 9 (1982): 133–34.

Review of *Die Entstehung des Christentums*, by Heinrich Kraft (Darmstadt: Wissenschaftliche Buchgesellschaft, 1981). *Religious Studies Review* 8/4 (October 1982): 377.

Review of *A Home for the Homeless: A Sociological Exegesis of 1 Peter, Its Situation and Strategy*, by John H. Elliott (Philadelphia: Fortress Press, 1981). *Religious Studies Review* 8/3 (July 1982): 285.

Review of *The Son of Man in the Teaching of Jesus*, by A. J. B. Higgins, Soc. for New Testament Studies Monograph Series 39 (Cambridge and New York: Cambridge Univ. Press, 1980). *Catholic Biblical Quarterly* 44 (1982): 678–79.

1983

Miracle in the Early Christian World: A Study in Sociohistorical Method. New Haven: Yale Univ. Press, pp. xi + 320.

Community of the New Age: Studies in Mark's Gospel. Reprints of Scholarly Excellence. Macon, Ga.: Mercer Univ. Press, pp. xiii + 225. (Reprinted and corrected ed. of the 1977 work of the same title.)

Understanding the New Testament. 4th ed. Englewood Cliffs, N.J.: Prentice-Hall, pp. viii + 408.

As origens cristãs em perspectiva sociológica. Trans. J. Rezende Costa. São Paulo: Edições Paulinas, pp. 153. (Brazilian ed. [Portuguese trans.] of *Christian Origins in Sociological Perspective: Methods and Resources*, 1980.)

Sae Shi Dae Yeo Gong Dong Chae: Maka Book Yum Yon Goo. Trans. Suh Joong-Suk. Shinyak Yon Goo Series 3. Seoul: Christian Literature Soc., pp. 302. (Korean trans. of *Community of the New Age: Studies in Mark's Gospel*, 1977.)

"'The Testaments of the Twelve Patriarchs' (Second Century B.C.): A New Translation and Introduction." In *The Old Testament Pseudepigrapha*, vol. 1, *Apocalyptic Literature and Testaments*, ed. J. H. Charlesworth, 775–823. Garden City, N.Y.: Doubleday & Co. (Trans. from the Greek text.)

"The Sociocultural Setting of Joseph and Aseneth." *New Testament Studies* 29 (1983): 394–413.

"Self-Definition in the Asclepius Cult." In *Jewish and Christian Self-Definition*, ed. Ben F. Meyer and E. P. Sanders, 3:118–36. Philadelphia: Fortress Press. (American ed. of the 1982 work of the same title.)

"The Gospel according to Matthew." In *The Interpreter's Concise Commentary*, ed. Charles M. Laymon, vol. 6, *The Gospels: A Commentary on Matthew, Mark, Luke, John*, 1–96. Nashville: Abingdon Press. (In reprinted ed. of *The Interpreter's One-Volume Commentary on the Bible*, 1971.)

"Four Perspectives II." Review of *The First Urban Christians: The Social World of the Apostle Paul*, by Wayne A. Meeks (New Haven: Yale Univ. Press, 1983). *Horizons* 10 (1983): 677–78.

Review of *The Messianic Secret in Markan Research, 1901–1976*, by James L. Blevins (Washington, D.C.: Univ. Press of America, 1981). *Catholic Biblical Quarterly* 45 (1983): 677–78.

MICHAEL R. GREENWALD AND DOUGLAS R. EDWARDS

Review of *The Archaeology of the New Testament: The Mediterranean World of the Early Christian Apostles,* by Jack Finegan (Boulder, Colo.: Westview Press, 1981). *Religious Studies Review* 9/2 (April 1983): 175.

1984

The New Testament in Context: Sources and Documents. Englewood Cliffs, N.J.: Prentice-Hall, pp. xi + 239. (Rev. ed. of *The Origins of Christianity: Sources and Documents,* 1973.)

Kristokyo Yeo Ki Won Ae Dae Han Sa Hoi Hack Gyuk Yon Goo. Trans. Suh Joong-Suk and Kim Myoung-Soo. Shinyak Yon Goo Series 4. Seoul: Christian Literature Soc., pp. 179. (Korean trans. of *Christian Origins in Sociological Perspective: Methods and Resources,* 1980.)

"The Social Setting of Mark: An Apocalyptic Community." In *Society of Biblical Literature 1984 Seminar Papers,* ed. Kent Harold Richards, 245–55. Chico, Calif.: Scholars Press.

"Ki Dook Lon Gae Gyo Hoi Lon: Krisdo Ching Ho Dul Gae Gong Dong Chae Yeo Model, 1982." *Kidockkyo Sasang* (1984): 239–61. (Korean trans. of "Christology and Ecclesiology: Titles of Christ and Models of Community," 1982.)

Review of *Between Jesus and Paul: Studies in the History of Earliest Christianity,* by Martin Hengel (Philadelphia: Fortress Press, 1983). *Religious Studies Review* 10/3 (July 1984): 289–90.

Review of *The First Urban Christians: The Social World of the Apostle Paul,* by Wayne A. Meeks (New Haven: Yale Univ. Press, 1983). *Second Century* 4 (1984): 52–54.

Review of *Jesus Walking on the Sea: Meaning and Gospel Functions of Matthew 14:22–23, Mark 6:45–52, and John 6:15b–21,* by John Paul Heil, Analecta biblica 87 (Rome: Pontifical Biblical Inst., 1981). *Journal of Biblical Literature* 103 (1984): 481–82.

Review of *The Lord's Table: Eucharist and Passover in Early Christianity,* by Gillian Feeley-Harnik, Symbol and Culture (Philadelphia: Univ. of Pennsylvania Press, 1981). *Journal of Biblical Literature* 103 (1984): 285–87.

1985

"Sociology of the New Testament." In *Harper's Bible Dictionary,* ed. Paul J. Achtemeier, 961–68. San Francisco: Harper & Row.

"Pauline Eschatology: Relationships with Apocalyptic and Stoic Thought." In *Glaube und Eschatologie: Festschrift für Werner Georg Kümmel zum 80. Geburtstag,* ed. Erich Grässer and Otto Mark, 135–58. Tübingen: J. C. B. Mohr (Paul Siebeck).

"Messiah and the People of God." In *Understanding the Word: Essays in Honor of Bernard W. Anderson,* ed. James T. Butler, Edgar W. Conrad, and Ben C. Ollenburger, 341–58. *Journal for the Study of the Old Testament* supp. ser. 37. Sheffield: JSOT Press.

"Christology and Ecclesiology: Titles of Christ and Models of Community." In *Christology and Exegesis: New Approaches,* ed. Robert Jewett, with Larry W.

354

Hurtado and Patrick R. Keifert as assoc. guest eds., 171–92. Semeia 30. Decatur, Ga.: Scholars Press.

"New Rule of God, New People of God." *Horizons in Biblical Theology* 7/2 (1985): 21–51.

"Medicine, Miracle, and Magic in the Roman World." Univ. Lecture, Boston Univ., April 8, 1985, pp. 26.

"The Social World of the New Testament." Lectures delivered at the Troy Conference Pastor's School, Foundation for Biblical Research, Charlestown, N.H. April 22–24, 1985. 9 cassette recordings, 90 min. each.

Review of *Harper's World of the New Testament,* by Edwin Yamauchi (San Francisco: Harper & Row, 1981). *Religious Studies Review* 11/2 (April 1985): 191.

Review of *Pagan-Christian Conflict over Miracle in the Second Century,* by Harold Remus, Patristic Monograph Series 10 (Cambridge, Mass.: Philadelphia Patristic Foundation, 1983). *Journal of Biblical Literature* 104 (1985): 371–73.

Review of ibid., *Second Century* (1985–86): 57–58.

Review of *Paul's Faith and the Power of the Gospel: A Structural Introduction to the Pauline Letters,* by Daniel Patte (Philadelphia: Fortress Press, 1983). *Horizons* 12 (1985): 166–68.

Review of *The Social Context of the New Testament: A Sociological Analysis,* by Derek Tidball (Grand Rapids: Zondervan, 1984). *Religious Studies Review* 11/2 (July 1985): 289.

1986

Medicine, Miracle, and Magic in New Testament Times. Soc. for New Testament Studies Monograph Series 55. Cambridge: Cambridge Univ. Press, pp. x + 170.

Foreword to *The Evidence for Jesus,* by James D. G. Dunn, ix–xi. Philadelphia: Westminster Press.

"Achaia." In *Dictionary of Bible and Religion (DBR),* ed. William H. Gentz, 19. Nashville: Abingdon Press.

"Acropolis." In *DBR,* 20.

"Acrostic." In *DBR,* 20–21.

"Aland, Kurt." In *DBR,* 32.

"Albright, William F. In *DBR,* 33.

"Annunciation." In *DBR,* 50.

"Antioch on-the-Orontes; Antioch of Pisidia." In *DBR,* 54.

"Antiochus III–VII." In *DBR,* 54–55.

"Apostle." In *DBR,* 60.

"Arimathea." In *DBR,* 68.

"Arndt, Johann." In *DBR,* 70.

"Arndt, William F." In *DBR,* 70.

"Beatitudes." In *DBR,* 112–13.

"Bible, Text of." In *DBR,* 127–31.

"Biblical Criticism." In *DBR,* 136–39.

"Bultmann, Rudolf." In *DBR,* 166–67.

"Corinth." In *DBR,* 225–26.

"1 and 2 Corinthians." In *DBR,* 226–27.

"Dead Sea Scrolls." In *DBR*, 254–58.

"Essenes." In *DBR*, 324–25.

"Exegesis." In *DBR*, 339–40.

"Gethsemane, Garden of." In *DBR*, 388.

"Gnosticism." In *DBR*, 396–97.

"Greek Religion, Philosophy, Language." In *DBR*, 411–14.

"Hands, Laying on of." In *DBR*, 424–25.

"Hasmoneans." In *DBR*, 428–29.

"Herodians." In *DBR*, 444.

"Herodium." In *DBR*, 444–45.

"James, Apostle." In *DBR*, 514.

"James, Brother of Jesus." In *DBR*, 514–15.

"James, Letter of." In *DBR*, 515.

"Jesus Christ." In *Academic American Encyclopedia* 11:403–6. Danbury, Conn.: Grolier.

"John, Epistles of." In *DBR*, 542–43.

"Judas Iscariot." In *DBR*, 562–63.

"Jude, Letter of." In *DBR*, 563.

"Keys of the Kingdom." In *DBR*, 577.

"Languages of the Ancient Near East and of the Bible." In *DBR*, 597–98.

"Laodicea." In *DBR*, 598–99.

"Lord's Prayer." In *DBR*, 626–27.

"Maccabean Revolt." In *DBR*, 640–42.

"Magi." In *DBR*, 644–45.

"Mary." In *DBR*, 661.

"Matthew, [Apostle]." In *DBR*, 668.

"Mediator." In *DBR*, 673.

"Messiah." In *DBR*, 683–84.

"Messianic Secret." In *DBR*, 684.

"Metaphor." In *DBR*, 684–85.

"Miracle." In *DBR*, 695–97.

"Moffatt, James." In *DBR*, 702.

"Mystery Religions." In *DBR*, 718–19.

"Pilate, Acts of." In *DBR*, 818–19.

"Pseudo-Matthew, Gospel of." In *DBR*, 854.

"Qumran." In *DBR*, 863.

"Resurrection of Jesus." In *DBR*, 886–87.

"Resurrection of the Dead." In *DBR*, 887–88.

"Sermon on the Mount." In *DBR*, 954–56.

"Sociology of Religion." In *DBR*, 989–91.

"Virgin Birth." In *DBR*, 1091–92.

Index of
Subjects

357

359

Index of
Ancient Sources

362